DATE DUE

DEC 0 2 1999			
APR 2 4 2000			
SEP 0 6 2005			
DEC 0 5 2012			

JUL 21 1989

Hitler's Undercover War

Also by William Breuer:

Bloody Clash at Sadzot
Captain Cool
They Jumped at Midnight
Drop Zone Sicily
Agony at Anzio
Hitler's Fortress Cherbourg
Death of a Nazi Army
Operation Torch
Storming Hitler's Rhine
Retaking the Philippines
Devil Boats
Operation Dragoon
The Secret War With Germany
Sea Wolf

Hitler's Undercover War

The Nazi Espionage Invasion of the U.S.A.

William Breuer

St. Martin's Press, New York

Design by Karin Batten

Library of Congress Cataloging-in-Publication Data
Breuer, William B.
  Hitler's undercover war.
  1. Espionage, German—United States—History—
20th century.   2. World War, 1939–1945–Secret
service—Germany.   3. World War, 1939–1945—
Secret service—United States.   I. Title.
D810.S7B67 1989   940.54'85   88–30807
ISBN 0–312–02620–X

First Edition

10 9 8 7 6 5 4 3 2 1

Dedicated to the
men and women of the
Federal Bureau of Investigation
(past and present) whose
courage, sacrifices, and devotion
have protected America from
subversive forces seeking
to destroy the nation
and her freedoms

Contents

Photo Section Follows Page 168

Hitler's Undercover
War

INTRODUCTION

On the beautiful summer day of June 28, 1919, German delegates signed the World War I treaty of peace in the Hall of Mirrors in the Palace of Versailles, outside Paris. It was one of Germany's blackest hours, for the victorious Allies had inflicted harsh terms upon the vanquished, including forced acknowledgment of German responsibility for starting the war.

But what created the greatest outrage in Germany was the fact that the nation, with hostile neighbors on all sides, had been virtually disarmed. Versailles restricted Germany to a *Reichswehr* (army) of only 100,000 "civilian volunteers," and this force was prohibited from having airplanes or tanks.

Almost before the ink had dried on the Versailles Treaty, the German army began to covertly circumvent its constraints. Under a cagey, monocled Old Prussian, General Hans von Seeckt, the Reichswehr became an elite formation. Instead of the civilian volunteers specified by Versailles, von Seeckt filled the ranks with the cream of the wartime army.

In 1926 the Reichswehr decided to clandestinely create an illegal "Black Luftwaffe." A special aviation branch, the *Fliegerzentrale*, was formed, and a few squadrons of antiquated airplanes were activated. But modern aviation devices and designs were sorely lacking; German industry, whose capacity had been

1

strictly limited by Versailles, could not provide the sophisticated technology.

So the Fliegerzentrale, under bull-necked Major Hugo Sperrle, a World War I flying ace, sent "scouts" abroad to purchase whatever aviation items were available on the open market. Efforts focused on the sleeping giant, the United States, whose industrial and technological capacity was booming. However, most of the wanted devices, such as aircraft designs, automatic bombsights, and retractable landing gear, were classified as U.S. military secrets and not available at any price.

Undaunted, Major Sperrle and his other Fliegerzentrale plotters decided that what they could not buy, they would steal. The task of pilfering United States defense secrets was handed to the *Abwehr*, Germany's secret service. Diminutive Colonel Fritz Gempp sent his nation's first post-World War I spy into the United States early in 1927.

At that time America was a spy's paradise; she would remain so for the next twelve years. Foreign agents and home-grown agitators roamed the country at will. No single federal agency was charged with countersubversive operations, and the United States was the only major world nation that had no secret service to ferret out the intentions of hostile powers. America had no Military Intelligence worthy of the name, and the State Department's Intelligence force consisted of one man.

Secure in the belief that two wide oceans protected the nation, Americans were obsessed with minding their own business. In 1929, when the U.S. Signal Corps was on the verge of cracking super-secret foreign codes, a horrified Secretary of State Henry L. Stimson fought its request for funds, exclaiming: "Gentlemen simply do not open other people's mail."

In 1924 a bright-eyed, energetic lawyer, twenty-nine-year-old J. Edgar Hoover, had been appointed director of the somnolent, politics-riddled Bureau of Investigation. Hoover rapidly booted out the hacks, replaced them with high-caliber, eager young attorneys and accountants, and infused the agency with professionalism. Unfortunately for national security, the FBI's primary function was to deal with the American underworld, not international intrigue.

Fearful of the threat of an oppressive national police force, many private citizens frowned on the FBI as snoopers, and Congress held the Bureau's funding, manpower, and authority to a minimum. Federal law denied the FBI the crime-busting tools it needed: wire-tapping under controlled conditions and the authority to intercept and open suspects' mail. These restrictions effectively handcuffed the FBI when a one-time German army corporal named Adolf Hitler and his National Socialist Party (Nazis) seized control of Germany in 1933, and began pouring spies and saboteurs into the United States.

During the next thirteen years, all the Nazis used what later became *de rigueur* in melodramatic spy novels and movies: spies, traitors, propagandists, thefts of secret plans, *femmes fatales*, bribes, traps, forgeries, codes, seduction of army and navy men, and devious plots to kidnap or murder persons holding military secrets.

Hitler's secret invasion of the United States would become the most massive espionage penetration of a major power that history had known and would result in the FBI and U.S. Military Intelligence fighting a high-stakes covert war thousands of miles from the battlefields across the seas. This is the story of how Hitler's minions swiped vital American secrets and influenced public opinion against the war. It is also the story of how innovative, dedicated, daring law enforcement officials awoke to the threat and countered the Nazi espionage invasion with knockout blows.

PART ONE

The
Early Years

1

A One-Man Espionage Vanguard

The man who walked down the gangplank of the SS *Berlin* in Hoboken, New Jersey, on the breezy afternoon of March 27, 1927, was thin, wore steel-rimmed spectacles, and lugged a battered suitcase. His German passport identified him as William Schneider, a piano tuner. Like thousands of other German nationals during this era, Schneider had come to the New World to seek a better life (or so he had told friends back in the Fatherland).

After passing through Customs, the immigrant hopped onto a ferry and crossed the Hudson River to the concrete canyons of New York City. There William Schneider disappeared forever. In his place emerged Wilhelm Lonkowski (his true name). He had been sent to the United States by Abwehr spymasters to steal military secrets and to organize an espionage network. Although the thirty-four-year-old Lonkowski had never been to America, spoke English only passably and with a thick accent, he had been selected to spearhead a German spy invasion because the Abwehr in Berlin had great confidence in his ability. Back in 1922 the Abwehr had sent Lonkowski into France on a spying mission, and the young man had produced outstanding results.

Before sailing from Bremerhaven, Germany, Lonkowski had been furnished a "shopping list" compiled by Major Hugo

Sperrle[1] and his officers at the Fliegerzentrale from American aviation magazines and trade journals. The scope of Lonkowski's mission would have staggered spies of a less robust spirit: One agent, somehow, on his own initiative, was expected to steal military secrets from such major corporations as Curtiss Aircraft, Westinghouse Electric, Seversky Aircraft, Federal Shipbuilders, Fairchild Aviation, Douglas Aircraft, as well as from the U.S. army's Mitchel and Roosevelt airfields, outside New York City. But Lonkowski was neither awed nor baffled by his assignment.

Back in Germany, Lonkowksi was carried on the Abwehr roster as Agent Sex (from one of his many aliases, William Sexton). Soft-spoken, unpretentious, clever, Lonkowski had been a mechanic in the Kaiser's air force in World War I and was a skilled aero-engineer. Born in the Selisia region of Germany, Lonkowski could not decide on a career after his discharge. Despite his talent as an aircraft designer, there were no job openings in the small German aviation industry shackled by Versailles. So he turned to spying.

Lonkowski was an uncomplicated man. He suffered from stomach ulcers and was a constant worrier. His face was undistinctive, plain with slightly oversized ears and an aquiline nose. Outwardly average in every respect, Agent Sex possessed the traits that are crucial to a successful spy: a quick wit, a devious nature, an innovative bent, and a deep dedication to a cause—even if that cause was greed for money.

By February 1928, nearly a year after stepping off the *Berlin* at Hoboken, Lonkowski had melted into the American scene. Now he felt secure enough to cease lugging around his "cover," a piano-tuner's kit (he had yet to tune his first piano). He began probing the region for a legitimate job that would both bring in some money and provide a plausible base for his espionage operation. He found what he was searching for at the Ireland Aircraft Corporation on Long Island, outside New York City, and acquired a position there as a mechanic.

Due to hard work, a keen mind, and an extensive knowledge of aviation, Agent Sex rapidly was promoted to a job involving the hiring of employees. Soon that post began to pay dividends when, in October 1928, two German men who had just arrived in the United States applied for jobs at the firm. Twenty-eight-year-old Werner Georg Gudenberg had served in the German navy, doing electrical work on torpedo boats during the war, and now was an engineering draftsman. Otto Herman Voss, who was in his early twenties, was an aircraft mechanic. Lonkowski put the two men on Ireland's payroll, after making a mental note that they would be ideal recruits for his Nazi spy ring.

Within days Agent Sex began subtly seducing the two new employees, playing one against the other. First he invited Voss for a few beers at a local tavern, and after an hour of waxing sentimental over the Fatherland, Lonkowski dropped a hint that he was an Abwehr spy, then studied Voss's face for a reaction. Voss never changed expression. Encouraged, Agent Sex revealed (falsely) that Voss's pal Gudenberg was slipping him blueprints stolen from Ireland Aircraft. Didn't Voss think that he should be equally loyal to the Fatherland?

A few days later Voss began sneaking to Lonkowski confidential or secret data. Lonkowski quickly copied the material, then it would be returned to its official resting place. Next Agent Sex hosted Gudenberg at the same beer joint and repeated the scenario, telling the spy prospect that Voss was helping the Fatherland. Gudenberg was impressed and began pilfering the blueprints he had been working on, and Lonkowski copied them.

By early 1932 the glib and persuasive Agent Sex had recruited several other spies who worked in various aircraft plants along the eastern seaboard. Not only did he receive stolen plans and blueprints from his subagents, but he had been running the entire gamut as a superspy, often stealing aviation secrets himself. Getting stolen military secrets to Germany was no problem. On the fast German luxury liners crisscrossing the Atlantic—the *Hamburg*, the *Bremen*, the *New York*, and the *Europa*—were Abwehr couriers known as *Forschers*. These agents were carried on the ships' lists as stewards and engineers. Agent Sex used prearranged passwords to make certain that he was turning over espionage materials to a legitimate courier.

At the other end of the line, the Abwehr had planted *Umleitungsstelle* (transfer agents, or U-men) in nearly all major European ports. When a German liner docked, a U-man would meet the Abwehr courier, preassigned passwords would be exchanged, and a package of information collected in the United States would be handed to the relay man and rushed to Hamburg or Berlin.[2]

Even though Lonkowski's spy ring was pouring a stream of American aviation information into Germany, Major Sperrle at the Fliegerzentrale kept pressing for more. By now Lonkowski had quit his job at Ireland and was working full time at masterminding his mushrooming espionage network, so he hit on a novel approach for picking the brains of top U.S. aircraft executives, engineers, and designers. He arranged to become the accredited American correspondent for *Luftreise*, a popular German aviation magazine.

Wearing his journalist hat and flashing *Luftreise* credentials, Lonkowski entered several aircraft plants in the East to conduct interviews with key personnel. As he had anticipated, the persons Lonkowski approached were willing—even eager—to be written up in a prestigious aviation publication with worldwide readership.

Most of those interviewed were quite expansive and often could not resist boasting of their secret technological advancements, after which they would hastily caution the "reporter": "Of course, that's strictly off the record."

"Of course, of course," Lonkowski would reply with an understanding nod. "If that were printed, it might get into the wrong hands."

Following each interview, Lonkowski would rush a detailed report to Abwehr headquarters in Berlin. A "ghost" would write Lonkowski's article and submit it to *Luftreise* for publication. The off-the-record aviation secrets that the spy reporter had extracted from the unknowing American interviewee were shuttled on to Major Sperrle.

Unknown to Agent Sex, another German spy in New York City, pudgy, bespectacled Dr. Ignatz Theodor Griebl, was making impressive progress in spreading Nazi propaganda and organizing his own spy ring. Dr. Griebl was a well-known surgeon and obstetrician who enjoyed a lucrative practice, especially in Yorkville, Manhattan's German community. But to the Abwehr in Germany, Griebl was referred to by the code name Ilberg. In the Abwehr's thick registry of worldwide undercover agents, he was number A.2339 (the "A" indicating that he was a producing spy).[3]

Griebl had served as an officer in the German army in World War I and studied medicine at the University of Munich before coming to the United States in 1925. He completed his medical training at Long Island University and perfected his English at Fordham. A brother, Karl, was a close friend of Dr. Paul Josef Goebbels, chief of Adolf Hitler's Ministry of Propaganda. In the late 1920s Griebl and his wife, Maria, who had been a World War I Austrian army nurse, took out American citizenship.

Since reaching his adopted homeland, Dr. Griebl had been highly active in community and political activities in Yorkville, also known as Little Berlin. In his numerous public speaking engagements, he insisted that the American and German flags (and later the Nazi swastika) be displayed with equal prominence. Griebl's commission as a first lieutenant in the United States Army Medical Corps hung in a conspicuous place in his office, and he proudly told patients that he was expecting to be promoted to captain.

When Ignatz Griebl began organizing his spy ring, one of the first names that popped into his mind was that of Christian F. Danielson, a one-armed, German-born engineer who designed destroyers for the U.S. Navy. Griebl had met the fifty-one-year-old Danielson several years earlier. He invited the engineer, who was employed at the Bath Iron Works in Maine, to visit him in New York and sent along seventy-five dollars to cover expenses.

Danielson had come to the United States as a boy of twelve and later became a naturalized citizen. However, he was deeply attached to the Fatherland and had three daughters living there. So hardly had Danielson greeted Griebl in New York City than he expressed an eagerness to spy for Germany.

Griebl drove Danielson back to Bath, checked in at a hotel, and gave his new spy a "shopping list." While Griebl lounged in his room, Danielson hurried to the works and copied the blueprints of a destroyer he was helping to design. Early the following morning the engineer turned over his pilfered documents to the beaming physician. Two weeks later German admirals in Berlin were poring over the warship drawings.

Another close associate of Griebl's was Heinz Spanknoebel, the chief Nazi propagandist in the United States. Spanknoebel, who was invariably labeled "notorious" when mentioned in New York newspapers, was a foul-mouthed man with such an abrasive personality that even many of his Nazi contacts despised him. As loyal American groups of German-born citizens publicly denounced him, he became both a hindrance and an embarrassment to the Nazi bigwigs in the Third Reich.[4]

In October 1933 Spanknoebel found himself in hot water: A federal warrant charged him with violating a United States law by failing to register as an agent of a foreign country. Law enforcement officers searched for the propagandist but could not find him. Spanknoebel was hiding in a safe place—the Yorkville home of Dr. Ignatz Griebl.

Berlin sent word that Spanknoebel was to sneak back to the Fatherland at once. It was feared that the adverse publicity of a public trial might focus a spotlight on the expanding Nazi espionage network in the United States. Whatever Spanknoebel's reasons were—perhaps he liked the spotlight, even a dubious one—the propagandist refused to depart.

On the night of October 27, Griebl, his wife, and Spanknoebel were having dinner. There was a sharp rap on the door. Griebl, like most physicians, thought nothing of being bothered at any time of the day or night. He opened the door, and a stone-faced man pushed past him. Griebl did not recognize him. Spanknoebel did—and paled. The frowning intruder was Hellmuth von Feldman, an agent of Josef Goebbels.

"You have your orders!" Feldman barked, glaring at the nervous Spanknoebel. "Why haven't you followed them?"

A loud argument erupted between the two antagonists, with threats hurled back and forth. "Get up, you *Schweinehund!*" Feldman bellowed, whipping out a Luger and pointing it at the now-quaking Spanknoebel.

Mrs. Griebl broke into tears. Griebl pleaded, "Now, now, no shooting here; it will ruin me." The doctor was clearly more concerned with his own reputation than he was over the fact that an intruder was threatening to ventilate his good friend and dinner guest.

White-faced, Spanknoebel rose from the table. Feldman

poked the pistol muzzle into the propagandist's ribs and ordered, "*March!*"

Less than an hour later Heinz Spanknoebel, his customary swagger gone, was aboard the *Europa* at Pier 86. Guarding him were two armed, brown-shirted storm troopers. Shortly after dawn the ship sailed, and ten days later Spanknoebel, still under guard, arrived in Berlin. There he must have articulated a powerful defense before Nazi authorities, because all was forgiven. Foul-mouthed, crude Heinz Spanknoebel was given a cushy job in Goebbels's Ministry of Propaganda.[5]

2

"The U.S.A. Is the Decisive Factor"

One morning early in November 1933, not long after Dr. Griebl's dinner party had been interrupted by a wild-eyed Nazi brandishing a pistol, a pale, slender man appeared at the physician's Yorkville office for treatment of stomach ulcers. A first-time patient, he gave his name as William Sexton. The waiting room was packed with patients, so Sexton took a seat and waited. An hour later he was stretched out on an examination table, and while Dr. Griebl probed about the patient's abdomen, the two men engaged in idle conversation.

Suddenly the patient blurted: "Dr. Griebl, don't you remember me? I met you in France briefly in 1922. I'm Wilhelm Lonkowski."

Griebl looked startled, removed his stethoscope from his ears, and stared hard at the patient. Was this some sort of police trick? Indeed Griebl had been in France back in 1922—on a secret mission for Colonel Fritz Gempp of the Abwehr. Gempp had sent Lonkowski to France at the same time on an independent covert mission, and the two spies' paths had crossed in Paris.

Slowly a look of recognition spread over Griebl's face. "Mein Gott, I remember you, Herr Lonkowski!"[1]

Since Griebl had once been a spy for the Fatherland, Lonkow-

14

ski knew that he could speak freely. So while the physician continued with his examination, Lonkowski related his experience as a spy during the past six years. Griebl listened without comment. Then, his eyes twinkling from behind tortoiseshell glasses, Griebl disclosed that for more than a year he, too, had been building a spy ring and sending American secrets back to the Fatherland.

"Mein Gott!" Lonkowski exclaimed. He had not been aware that there were other German agents in New York who were not members of his own network. Out of this bizarre encounter, Lonkowski and Griebl agreed to merge their rings, and sealed the wedding with a handshake and toast of *schnapps*.

A few days later Lonkowski returned for a medical appointment, and the two men took inventory of their pooled networks. They had in their bag and making regular "deliveries" an engineer in the Federal Shipbuilding Company in Kearny, New Jersey; a captain in the United States Army; two agents in the Seversky Aircraft plant at Farmingdale, Long Island; a few spies at Roosevelt and Mitchel airfields; a designer in the Curtiss Aircraft plant at Buffalo, New York; a draftsman in a firm of naval designers in New York City and one in a Baltimore corporation developing a new four-blade propeller; agents in the U.S. Navy yards at Newport News, Virginia, Boston, Massachusetts, and in other defense installations.[2]

The Lonkowski-Griebl espionage apparatus functioned like a well-oiled machine. When the Black Luftwaffe placed an urgent "order" for the specifications of a pontoon that Seversky had developed for an experimental seaplane, Lonkowski passed along the request to his subagent at the plant. The employee required only twenty-four hours to steal the information, and a few days later copies were on the way to the Third Reich.

As the months passed, the Lonkowski-Griebl combine harvested a bountiful crop of secret or restricted U.S. military information: army maps and troop strength tables; blueprints for three modernized navy destroyers; drawings of devices that the Lear Radio Corporation was building for the army and navy; detailed reports of experiments with chromium; an army critique on tactical air exercises at Mitchel Field; and specifications of every airplane being built at Seversky.[3]

*   *   *

Meanwhile, across the Atlantic, monumental events were erupting behind the scenes in Germany. Hardly had *Der Fuehrer* and his Nazi storm troopers seized control of the strife-ridden nation than they began scheming to rearm. Hitler cautioned Josef Goebbels never to allow the words "general staff" to appear in the press. The annual official rank list of the German army ceased publication in 1933, so that its swollen list of officers would not give away Hitler's plot.[4]

Stone-faced General Wilhelm Keitel, chairman of the Working Committee of the Reich Defense Council, warned his staff on May 22: "No document must be lost, since otherwise enemy propaganda will make use of it. Matters communicated orally cannot be proven; they can be denied."[5]

In mid-December 1933 Hitler summoned Rear Admiral Wilhelm Franz Canaris to the *Reichskanzlei* (Reich Chancellory) in Berlin. The post of Abwehr chief had fallen vacant, and Canaris had been selected for the job. There was an urgency to the conference. Versailles had ripped into shreds Germany's secret service, and the fuehrer's covert rearmament plans needed eyes and ears around the globe.

"What I want," Hitler said to Canaris, "is something like the British Secret Service—an Order, doing its work with passion."[6]

On New Year's Day, 1934, his forty-seventh birthday, the five-foot-four, gray-haired Canaris became Nazi Germany's supreme spymaster. He was an unlikely choice to fill that sensitive position. Of Greek parentage, Canaris was not a Nazi Party member, nor would he ever become one. In fact, he loathed what he considered to be the unprincipled brutes with whom the fuehrer had surrounded himself, people like Hermann Goering, Heinrich Himmler, Julius Stryker, and Reinhard Heydrich.

Canaris plunged into the task of rejuvenating and expanding the Abwehr with a dynamism that belied his frail physique and low-key personality. He reorganized the agency into three primary sections responsible for espionage, counterespionage, and sabotage. *Abwehrabteilung* I (Section I), headed by Colonel Hans Piekenbrock, Canaris's longtime personal friend, was charged with espionage operations in foreign countries.

Wilhelm Canaris was born in the coal-mining city of Dortmund and graduated from the Naval Academy at Kiel. When World War I erupted, he was the flag and Intelligence officer on the cruiser *Dresden*, which was coaling in the Danish West Indies. She slipped out of the harbor and for 214 days was a marauding terror in the southern oceans, sinking a string of British merchant ships.

For more than three months British men-of-war hunted for the elusive *Dresden*, and finally she was trapped and sunk by three cruisers off the east coast of Chile. Most of the *Dresden's* crew, including Canaris, made it ashore and were interned by the Chilean government. But Canaris escaped and, in a series of hair-raising escapades, reached Berlin on September 17, 1917. Ill and exhausted, the young officer was a skeleton of a man. But his adventures earned him the Iron Cross, presented by Kaiser Wilhelm II himself.

Once his health was recovered, Canaris was promoted to captain and received his first real taste of the sinister world of cloak-and-dagger machinations: He was assigned to Captain Kurt von Krohm, the Kaiser's spy chief in Spain. Canaris's "cover" was that of military attaché, but his true function was to survey possible bases for U-boats along the coast of neutral Spain and to carry out sabotage operations against Allied shipping in Spanish harbors.

At the conclusion of the war Canaris, who spoke seven languages, became a shadowy figure of intrigue within the German navy, dabbling extensively in covert missions through Europe and in the volatile Balkans. Now, in 1934, with Germany secretly rearming, Wilhelm Canaris would draw on his wealth of clandestine experience to mastermind Adolf Hitler's secret invasion of the United States.

One of Canaris's outposts was the *Nebenstellen* (nest) at Wilhelmshaven, an ancient port city of some 95,000 people on the North Sea. Wilhelmshaven was a subbranch of the *Abwehrstellen* (branch), also known as Ast X, at Hamburg, one hundred miles to the east. Ast X was directly responsible for espionage in North and South America and in England.

Headed by *Kapitaen-leutnant* Erich Pfeiffer, Wilhelmshaven had emerged as the most productive Abwehr outpost in the world. For into that city was pouring the flood of intelligence being collected in the United States by the Lonkowski-Griebl spy network.

Pfeiffer was a shadowy figure, a man of mystery with many aliases. He was known variously to his agents in the field as "N. Speilman," "Herr Dokter," or "Dr. Endhoff." Pfeiffer was the Abwehr's control officer for Lonkowski and Griebl.

Early in June 1934 Pfeiffer ordered his pair of ace spies to go to Montreal for a *Treff* (as the Abwehr called secret meetings of its agents) with the most important Nazi agent in Canada, a designer employed by a corporation that was doing work for the U.S. Navy. Almost monthly the Canadian shipped three to five rolls of film to Germany, each roll containing thirty-six negatives of classified and secret airplane designs.

Griebl and Lonkowski were astonished by the Canadian's latest coup: He had gotten his hands on the blueprints of a new type of U.S. antiaircraft gun that utilized an electromagnetic device that increased the number of shells the gun was capable of firing per minute. These top-secret drawings and specifications were in Berlin before the War Department in Washington had studied and approved them.

On February 2, 1935, the supreme spymaster Admiral Canaris strolled into Dr. Pfeiffer's Wilhelmshaven nest. Canaris had come to see for himself the outpost that had been producing such a bountiful harvest of intelligence. Customarily a placid man, the little admiral was excited by what he found, and delivered a short address to the staff. As was his habit while speaking informally, Canaris paced back and forth, hands clasped behind his back, and slightly stooped.

With a trace of a lisp, the big chief described the United States as being "one of the key targets" in the Abwehr's worldwide operations. "The U.S.A. must be regarded as the decisive factor in any future war," he declared. "The capacity of its industrial power is such as to assure victory, not merely for the U.S.A. itself, but for any country with which it may be associated." [7]

Six weeks after Admiral Canaris's Wilhelmshaven visit, on March 16, 1935, widespread rejoicing erupted in Germany:

Adolf Hitler officially repudiated the restrictions imposed by the Versailles Treaty, symbol of Germany's war defeat and humiliation. The fuehrer decreed universal military service (a draft) and the formation of thirty-six army divisions, roughly a half-million men.

Now the Abwehr put the heat on Ignatz Griebl and Wilhelm Lonkowski for even more American military secrets. So the two spies hatched a devious plot to obtain information at minimal risk. German-born engineers and scientists working on American defense projects would be lured back to the Fatherland by dangling big money before their eyes. Once in Germany, the dupes would be coerced into disclosing U.S. military secrets learned while in trusted and sensitive jobs in their adopted homeland.

An early target in the intricate scheme was Irwin Backhaus, a Long Island, New York, resident with a good reputation. Backhaus was an employee of the Sperry Gyroscope Company and an expert in the design and construction of automatic pilots for airplanes. He was widely known and highly regarded in his field.

In April 1935 a letter came asking Backhaus to meet with a civilian engineer at the St. George Hotel in Brooklyn to hear a highly lucrative job proposal. Like most others, Backhaus was willing to consider a legitimate offer that promised a high salary. On the appointed day, Backhaus went to the rendezvous and was greeted by a man who identified himself as a German engineer (actually, he was an Abwehr agent).

The American listened silently as the "engineer" recited details of a high-paying two-year contract, plus healthy bonuses, if Backhaus would go to Germany to work. No dummy, Backhaus knew the current pay scales in Germany. There was something fishy here. What would he have to do to earn this big money? Soon it dawned on him: He was expected to steal every Sperry blueprint that he could lay his hands on, then, once in Germany, spill Sperry technology secrets.

Backhaus, a loyal American of German birth, was outraged. Without another word, he clamped on his hat and stomped out of the St. George.[8]

*　*　*

Not far from the concrete canyons of Manhattan, a tall, attractive young woman named Senta de Wanger was operating the Clinton Wine Shop, a large liquor store at 330 Clinton Street, Hempstead, Long Island. She had a keen business brain and was a hard worker, so the wine shop prospered. Behind her back, acquaintances called her *Die Wilde Senta* (the Wild Senta).

Born in Ulm, Germany, in 1907, the dark-haired beauty had set off for the United States at twenty-one years of age, and in a short time she opened an interior-decorating firm at 7 Park Avenue, New York City. Her real family name had been Dirlewanger, but before leaving her home in Stuttgart for America she had changed it to Dirwa. She spoke with a guttural accent, a trait her numerous suitors considered to be a point of charm. When she became a naturalized American, Senta took the name de Wanger.

In early 1935 the drab and frowsy wife of Nazi spy Wilhelm Lonkowski began paying almost daily visits to the Clinton Wine Shop. Her husband was gone from home for long periods of time, and Mrs. Lonkowski had begun to drink heavily. Her favorite was gin. Bound by bonds of language and the Fatherland, Mrs. Lonkowski and Senta de Wanger became close friends and confided in each other.[9]

One day Mrs. Lonkowski brought her husband to the wine shop, and after a friendly conversation the couple invited dark-eyed de Wanger to their flat for dinner. Later, de Wanger returned the courtesy with a dinner for the Lonkowskis at her large, rambling old house at 83 Lincoln Boulevard, in Hempstead. Soon she invited the couple to move in with her, explaining that she had grown depressed from living alone with so many empty rooms. They accepted and were given two rooms of their own and "the run of the house."

De Wanger thought that Lonkowski was jobless, so she took only $20 per month rental from the couple. It was but a few days until Lonkowski, despite his presumed lack of finances, insisted on installing his own telephone. Why didn't he simply use her house phone? de Wanger pondered fleetingly. And the tall beauty was only mildly curious when Lonkowski set up a photographic darkroom, spent long hours there, but, contrary to the conduct of most photography buffs, he never displayed his pictures.

It was not long before Lonkowski began throwing wild parties for army officers and men stationed at nearby Roosevelt and Mitchel airfields. That suited Die Wilde Senta just fine: She was invariably the object of attention of a house full of eligible young men. The wine flowed, the guests grew tipsy, and the merrymaking roared on into the wee hours of the morning.

Lonkowski told the American airmen that he had been a flying ace during the Big War (actually he had been a mechanic). So the wide-eyed youths would crowd around him while he spun hair-raising tales of his aerial combat with famed American ace Captain Eddie Rickenbacker. Awed by their host's deeds of derring-do and with tongues loosened by liquor, the airmen fell all over each other trying to impress Lonkowski by revealing everything they knew about the airfields.

As the weeks passed, de Wanger grew suspicious of Lonkowski. A private telephone. A secret darkroom. No apparent job. Where was he getting the money to buy liquor for the wild parties? It was strange, she reflected, that Lonkowski would be gone for several days, then return home without a word concerning where he had been.

On occasion de Wanger would subtly question Mrs. Lonkowski about Wilhelm's actions, but the wife was evasive. One day, in her husband's absence, Mrs. Lonkowski drained a quart bottle of gin and began jabbering boastfully. "My husband is very smart," she told her hostess in a slurred voice. "He is no mere piano tuner. He gets lots of money from Germany. Lots of money. He knows all about airplanes and the army. Wilhelm is a *big* man! He knows all the big shots back in the Fatherland."

Indeed Wilhelm Lonkowski did get "lots of money" from Germany—from Adolf Hitler's treasury. His Abwehr salary was $500 per month (a considerable sum at the time), along with a healthy bonus for each U.S. military secret that reached Germany and a sizable allowance for travel, lodging, bribes, and liquor.

Two days after the drunken Mrs. Lonkowski blabbed about her husband, Agent Sex cornered his landlady. Furious, he barked: "Why have you been asking my wife all those damned questions?" De Wanger stammered and stuttered, but he cut her off. "You know too goddamned much already!" he shouted. "Now you must be told more, so you'll know enough to keep your mouth shut. I am what you have guessed. And you, Senta, are going to help me!" [10]

Bewildered and indignant, de Wanger ordered Lonkowski to get out of her house by sundown. He laughed sarcastically and reminded her that she had parents in Stuttgart. If she did not help, Lonkowski snapped harshly, they would be arrested, put in concentration camps, or even executed. De Wanger paled— she had heard that such things were being done in Hitler's New Germany.

Die Wilde Senta was trapped. She was afraid. Clearly, this snarling man had powerful contacts in Germany. Reluctantly the young woman agreed to become a cut-out (part-time courier) for the Lonkowski-Griebl spy network. Whatever her motivation—fear of Lonkowski's brutal threats or a secret desire to serve the Fatherland—de Wanger began shuttling packages of stolen secrets to Forschers on the *Europa* and the *Deutschland* and carrying envelopes (presumably containing Abwehr instructions) from the ship's couriers to Nazi agents in the New York City region.

3

Confrontation at Pier 86

In August 1935 Wilhelm Lonkowski and his wife drove to Buffalo, New York, to hold a Treff with Werner Gudenberg, one of his early recruits at Ireland Aircraft. Lonkowski later had used his connections to plant Gudenberg in the Curtiss Airplane and Motor Company in Buffalo, but he had become annoyed with his subagent in recent months. Gudenberg had been contacting Lonkowski infrequently and had been sending only marginal material clipped from newspapers and aviation magazines. Was he trying to ease out of Nazi espionage?

Gudenberg had been doing well for himself in the American free enterprise system. He was now a foreman over thirty-five men and was bringing home a substantial paycheck each week. Along with his attractive wife and infant daughter, Gudenberg was living the good life of any other middle-class American family.

In Buffalo, Lonkowski had hardly begun talking with his subagent than he felt there was basis for his suspicions. Gudenberg avoided discussing espionage matters, especially when they related to Curtiss Aircraft. But Lonkowski was at his persuasive best. He reminded Gudenberg of the loyalty that all "good Germans" owed to the New Germany, and he reminisced about the old days in the Fatherland. Clearly Gudenberg was agonizing over the priority of his loyalties to the Third Reich and to his adopted homeland. But the next day he brought home several Curtiss blueprints for Lonkowski to trace.

A week later, back in Hempstead, Senta de Wanger received a package postmarked Buffalo. With it were instructions for her to take the package to Pier 86, in New York harbor, and turn it over to a Karl Schlueter, a steward on the SS *Europa*, when she docked in a few days. De Wanger had no way of knowing that Schlueter was the ship's *Orstgruppenfuehrer*, the Nazi Party functionary who had total control of the *Europa* under the guise of a lowly steward. An Orstgruppenfuehrer could even issue orders to a ship's captain—and they had better be obeyed.

At the appointed time, de Wanger boarded the *Europa* and searched diligently for Karl Schlueter. She asked several ship's officers and crewmen where he could be found, but all were evasive. Finally the woman abandoned her search. A babe in the woods in the espionage business, she blithely handed the package of military secrets from the Curtiss plant to a purser and asked that the bundle be turned over to Schlueter.

A few days later Lonkowski returned home from Buffalo and promptly asked de Wanger about the package. When told that she had handed it to a purser, Lonkowski flew into a rage.

"I'll kill you!" he roared. "I'll kill you myself if it falls into the wrong hands!" [1]

De Wanger was petrified.

For many days Lonkowski stayed inside the house and fretted. His ulcers were paining him severely. He paced back and forth like a tiger in a cage, cursing and threatening to murder Senta. Each time the phone or doorbell rang the spy jumped. He was suspicious of a new postman and an electric-meter reader. Every few minutes he peered from behind the curtains to see if anyone was outside.

Then one day Lonkowski received a letter from Germany, signed with a phony name, but he knew that it was from Karl Schlueter. The message said merely "Order received." Only then did Lonkowski relax, and a degree of harmony returned to the three-person ménage at 83 Lincoln Boulevard.

Pier 86 on the Hudson River in New York was teeming with passengers and their friends on the late afternoon of September

25, 1935, as the luxury liner *Europa*, pride of the North German Lloyd Line, was about ready to sail for Bremerhaven, Germany. The fast ship had already made a run to her home port and back since Senta de Wanger's *faux pas* with the package of aircraft secrets. Morris Josephs, a Customs agent, was mingling with the crowd near the vessel when he spotted a thin, bespectacled man carrying a violin case. A *Europa* steward who had been talking to the man drifted away as the uniformed Josephs approached.

"What kind of violin have you in that case?" Josephs asked pleasantly.

"Oh, just an ordinary fiddle," Wilhelm Lonkowski replied evenly. He shot a quick glance upward just in time to see the "steward" to whom he had been talking, the ship's Orstgruppenfuehrer, scramble up the gangplank and disappear from view.

"Is that so," said the Customs agent. "Mind letting me look at it?" [2]

Josephs's request was due to a personal interest in violins, not to a suspicion that this man might be trying to smuggle out goods without paying duty on them. As the Customs agent lifted the instrument from its velvet-lined case, his eyes widened. Under the violin was a collection of papers that looked like photocopies of airplane blueprints.

Josephs replaced the musical instrument, closed the lid, and said, "Will you come with me?"

In the Customs office at the pier, Josephs and John W. Roberts, supervising Customs agent for the New York area, searched the spy and found in his pockets film negatives and several letters written in German and addressed to various persons in the Third Reich. The film appeared to show drawings of airplanes, and the letters contained wording that seemed to refer to aircraft specifications.

Roberts questioned Lonkowski, who said he was a piano tuner and lived on Long Island. But what was he doing with all those letters and films with the curious drawings? They were simply material to illustrate an article he was doing for the German aviation magazine *Luftreise*, for which he worked part time as United States correspondent.

Not knowing what action, if any, to take, Roberts telephoned

Major Stanley Grogan at the Intelligence office for the army's Second Corps Area at Governor's Island in New York Harbor. Grogan was out, so a young private was sent to investigate. He didn't know what to do either, but he managed to locate Major Grogan by telephone and gave him a rundown on the situation at Pier 86.

An hour later Grogan arrived at the Customs office, glanced at the detainee, who was seated calmly in a corner, and thumbed through the materials that had been found in the violin case and upon Lonkowski. Part of one letter stated:

> Enclosed you will find an enlargement of the cover for automatic sights of machine guns. With reference to the (unintelligible word) ammunition which I am to obtain from the captain, I have as yet received no information. I understand the captain has already contacted von Papen. The captain is a Swiss, although he is in the American infantry.[3]

Major Grogan asked Lonkowski to explain this passage, which seemed like curious wording for an article in an aviation magazine. Lonkowski remained unruffled and gave confusing answers. Von Papen, he explained, was an infantry captain at Monticello, New Jersey. (A later records check would show that there was no "von Papen" who was an infantry captain in the United States Army.) At another point the spy said that von Papen "is now in Austria."

The name "von Papen" apparently did not ring a bell with either Grogan or the Customs agents. Lonkowski was not asked if his "von Papen" was Colonel Franz von Papen, a Nazi bigwig and confidant of Adolf Hitler who had gained wide notoriety while German military attaché in Washington prior to the U.S. entry into World War I. At that time von Papen had been charged by federal authorities with flagrant and widespread espionage and sabotage activities in America.

Nor did the authorities at Pier 86 seem to know that Colonel von Papen was indeed in Austria—as Hitler's ambassador—where he was spreading Nazi propaganda and creating unrest.

Another letter found on Lonkowski indicated that secret military information was being pilfered from Langley Field, an army air base in Virginia. Part of the letter read:

> As regard your query reference to construction of bulkheads, etc. of Seversky [Aircraft Corporation] airplane floats. I expect sketches shortly . . . It will require some time to get the desired information about the water tank at Langley Field.[4]

Other portions of the letters gave evidence that defense secrets were being stolen at other plants or from within the U.S. military establishment:

> I have just been informed that FLFZ airplanes, which for more than a year were used in the Army and Marine Corps, were authorized for foreign delivery . . . please inform me at once if you are still interested in Curtiss X-2 [the navy's supersecret new experimental light bomber].[5]

There were photographs of a new Curtiss fighter plane and of the Voight scout bomber, for use on aircraft carriers. Attached to the photographs were highly technical reports on each airplane's design and capabilities. A sheaf of memoranda told of three new Boeing bombers being inspected by the army and a four-motored bomber, to be known as a B17, or Flying Fortress, that was being designed and built by the Glenn Martin Company in Baltimore. Another new bomber, a memo stated, was being designed by the Douglas Aircraft Company of Santa Monica, California.

After an all-night session, Major Grogan and the Customs agents huddled to discuss what to do next. They realized that they didn't know the detainee's name. One called across the room, "Hey, fellow, what's your name?"[6]

Lonkowski paused and licked his lips, apparently pondering if he should give an alias. Finally he replied, "William Lonkowski."

"Well, Mr. Lonkowski," Customs agent Roberts said evenly,

"you can go now. But be back in three days. We might have a few more questions to ask you." [7]

Casually, Lonkowski put on his hat and with a pleasant "Good morning, gentlemen" strolled out of the office and onto the pier. His heart was thumping madly, and he fought off an overpowering urge to glance back over his shoulder, to run. Flagging down a Yellow Cab, Lonkowski leaped inside and sped along streets not yet heavy with rush-hour traffic toward his home on Long Island.

Lonkowski could not believe his good fortune. He had been caught red-handed while loaded down with stolen U.S. military secrets. But these incredibly naive Americans had turned loose one of Nazi Germany's most dangerous and productive spies—without even bothering to take down his address.

Haggard and exhausted, Lonkowski reached home, drew out all the money in his bank account, burned his codes, pitched a few clothes into a suitcase, and rushed to Dr. Griebl's office in Manhattan. Griebl hid him until late at night, then drove the spy to the physician's summer home outside Peekskill, in suburban Westchester County, New York.

Two mornings later a pair of operatives from the Office of Naval Intelligence (ONI) were making their routine rounds of the New York waterfront. They ran into Customs agent Morris Josephs and were told about the curious event centering around a violin case that had occurred on the previous Saturday. The ONI men were curious and went to the Customs office on Pier 86 where Lonkowski's pictures, negatives, and letters had been tossed into a drawer.

"Holy smoke!" one navy man exclaimed. "These are naval experimental planes! What happened to the guy who had them?"

The Customs agent shrugged. "G-2 let him go," he replied. [8]

Nearly apoplectic, the naval investigator telephoned his New York office, which in turn quickly reported the episode to ONI headquarters in Washington. There Lieutenant Commander Ellis M. Zacharias was ordered to grab a plane to New York and "find out what this mess is all about." Two hours later Zacharias was sitting in the office of the ONI's district director in New York and listening to a tale that he found almost impossible to believe.

Commander Zacharias rushed to Governor's Island to get more details from Major Joseph Dalton, the G-2 (Intelligence). "Major," the naval sleuth said, "to me this is a pure case of espionage, and I feel that your people should have communicated immediately with ONI." Dalton was still not convinced. In an offhand manner he replied, "Well, it did not seem like much to us!"[9]

Lonkowski hid for four days at Griebl's place outside Peekskill while the physician arranged for continuation of his flight. Then Griebl sent his own late-model luxury automobile and a driver to fetch Lonkowski and take him to Canada. The chauffeur was Ulrich Haussmann, a member of Griebl's ring who had been a pilot in the German air force in World War I and was now in the United States under the guise of a reporter for a German magazine.[10]

Haussmann drove his passenger to the Canadian border at Rock Island, Vermont. This was the crucial test. No doubt word had been flashed to be on the lookout for the escapee. Both men breathed sighs of relief as a bored U.S. border guard waved them on.

The two spies raced on to Montreal, where they contacted the German consul, who had already been alerted by Commander Erich Pfeiffer in Germany that Lonkowski was coming. Pfeiffer had been notified by Ignatz Griebl. The consul sent Lonkowski to Rivière-de-Loup, a port city on the broad St. Lawrence River, where a German freighter had just finished unloading. The escapee was smuggled aboard. Already instructed by Pfeiffer to head for the open sea the minute Lonkowski arrived, the skipper hoisted anchor and sailed for Germany.[11]

In the Fatherland, Wilhelm Lonkowski was hailed by the Abwehr as a conquering hero. His seven-year undercover mission in the United States had been a productive one, both for the flood of U.S. military secrets obtained for the Third Reich and for his own pocketbook. As an additional reward for his services to the fuehrer, Lonkowski was given a top job in the Air Ministry.

Agent Sex, one of history's greatest spies, would never know that there had been no real need for his precipitate flight from the United States. Almost before Lonkowski had reached Canada, the incriminating espionage materials found on him at Pier

86 were pigeonholed at Governor's Island and the episode largely forgotten.

Not long after Lonkowski had returned to Germany, in the fall of 1935, naval sleuth Lieutenant Commander Zacharias and his wife were attending a gala party given by the Japanese naval attaché, Captain Tamon Yamaguchi, in the Chinese Room of the Mayflower Hotel in Washington. Suave and big for a Japanese, the courteous, friendly Yamaguchi had been under cursory surveillance by the ONI for several months after it had become apparent that the Japanese were intensifying their espionage activities in the United States.

Zacharias and his immediate superior at ONI, Captain William D. Puleston, shared the view that Yamaguchi, who spoke English fluently and had an extensive knowledge of the United States, was the Nipponese espionage ringleader in America. So Zacharias had made it a point to see the Japanese naval officer, both socially and officially, as often as possible. He became a fixture at all of Yamaguchi's parties.

Now in the Mayflower, Zacharias casually sipped a cocktail and gazed around the room. Among the guests were the two German military attachés, Lieutenant General Friedrich von Boetticher, a smooth operative, and Vice Admiral Robert Witthoft-Emden. As the afternoon wore on, Zacharias was struck by a curious fact: The Japanese and German attachés had become quite friendly. In earlier months their relationship had been reserved, even cool.

Based on the German/Japanese love-fest in the Mayflower, Zacharias was convinced that some dramatic new development between the two nations had taken place behind the scenes. But the ONI sleuth had no way of knowing that what he was witnessing had evolved from a lethal espionage power struggle that had been raging in Nazi Germany.

When Adolf Hitler had seized power in 1933, a military secret service was functioning within a camouflaged general staff; both had been banned by the Versailles Treaty. Called the Section of Foreign Armies and Statistical Bureau, the secret service was headed by Colonel Fritz Bredlow, an officer of high ethics who refused to conduct aggressive espionage activities.

Bredlow's reluctance to send agents into the United States, France, and Great Britain infuriated the fuehrer, who was determined to create a foreign spy network of unprecedented scope. Hitler's frustration over Bredlow's stubbornness was resolved on the night of June 30, 1934. A squad of storm troopers broke into Bredlow's office in the War Ministry on the Bendlerstrasse, dragged the colonel from his desk, and riddled him with bullets in the courtyard.

Hitler promptly appointed Bredlow's successor, Colonel Walter Nicolai, a ruthless and unscrupulous officer who had been in dictatorial charge of the Kaiser's spy apparatus during World War I. Shrewd and tireless, Nicolai soon presented Hitler with a unique proposal: creating a German/Japanese spy alliance to accelerate the buildup of a Nazi spy network in the United States. The fuehrer gave the proposal his enthusiastic endorsement.

At a series of secret meetings in 1935, Colonel Nicolai made a formal offer to the Japanese to pool their espionage resources. He pointed out that only Caucasians could do effective spying in the United States, since Oriental agents would be more easily detected. The Japanese bought the proposal, and Hitler appointed Eugen Ott, who would later become German ambassador to Japan, to coordinate activities between the two nations' secret services.

Neither Hitler nor Colonel Nicolai realized how eager the Nipponese had been to enter into this pact. For eight years the generals and admirals who had an iron grip on the Japanese government had held that an armed conflict with the United States was inevitable. In 1927 the Nipponese warlords had drawn up a secret plan called the Tanaka Memorial, a blueprint for military conquest of vast expanses of Asia and war with America.

Now in the Mayflower Hotel, Commander Zacharias sought out his wife and told her that something was afoot, that the German and Japanese military attachés were fawning on one another, and that the couple must remain until the end of the party to see what would happen. Across the huge room, now thinning of guests, von Boetticher and Witthoff-Emden were again clinging to old pal Captain Yamaguchi.

The pair of Germans glanced at Zacharias. Plainly they were irritated that he had not left the party. It developed into a cat-

and-mouse game: Who would outwait whom? In numerous parties given by the Japanese in the past, the German attachés had always left early. Finally, when Yamaguchi noticed that nearly everyone had gone and waiters were clearing up the debris, he headed for the door. Commander Zacharias took satisfaction from the fact that the annoyed von Boetticher and Witthoff-Emden, Hitler's eyes and ears, walked from the Chinese Room just ahead of Zacharias and his wife, who departed with the genial host, the spymaster Captain Yamaguchi.

The next morning Zacharias discussed with Captain Puleston the curious scenario at the Mayflower. Both agreed that German Intelligence was now working in close alliance with the Japanese. So within forty-eight hours ONI began a surveillance of the Alban Towers, an imposing apartment building at the intersection of Wisconsin and Massachusetts avenues. In an upper-level suite, Captain Yamaguchi maintained a combination living quarters and offices from where he conducted cloak-and-dagger activities.

Naval Intelligence electronic eavesdropping soon picked up mysterious clicking noises that seemed to be coming from the building. On the assumption that these sounds were being produced by a Japanese electric coding machine, an elaborate break-in was conceived to covertly inspect the device. So while Commander and Mrs. Zacharias entertained Captain Yamaguchi at dinner one night, a cryptanalyst, navy Lieutenant Jack S. Holtwick, and a chief radioman named McGregor, donned civilian electrician's outfits and bluffed their way past the Alban Towers doorman. They took an elevator to Yamaguchi's suite, found that it was not being guarded, and used a special instrument to open the door without leaving a telltale mark. The two sleuths conducted a thorough search but did not find an electric coding device. The source of the clicking noises would remain a mystery.

However, ONI continued its surveillance of what, unknown to scores of other Alban Towers tenants, had become the command post for the Japanese/German espionage alliance in the United States.

* * *

Across the Atlantic, Adolf Hitler had been continuing to pump iron into the German *Wehrmacht* (armed forces) and by 1936 he felt it had sufficient muscles for him to defy the Allied powers that had inflicted the Versailles Treaty on the Reich. The fuehrer ordered his War Minister, Field Marshal Werner von Blomberg, to prepare to occupy the Rhineland, a large territory west of the Rhine River that had been demilitarized by Versailles. Blomberg and Hitler's generals were aghast. France was reputed to have the most powerful army in the world, and when the Wehrmacht moved into the Rhineland, no doubt Great Britain would join France and once again crush Germany.

Without notifying Hitler, Blomberg issued orders that if the French contested the Wehrmacht occupation, the invading force was to pull back across the Rhine. On March 7, 1936, a few battalions of troops went in, to be greeted by delirious enthusiasm of the Rhineland's largely German civilian population.

Not a shot was fired. Hitler had gained a valuable military advantage but also an enormous psychological victory, for France and England did not move a finger, and the United States hardly uttered a protest, her leaders and her people determined to "keep out of other nations' quarrels."

4

Interlude with the Abwehr Bigwigs

A bright-blue sky hovered over New York City on the afternoon of June 1, 1937, as the SS *Europa* sailed majestically out of the harbor, bound for Bremerhaven. Among those on board were Dr. Ignatz Griebl and his "traveling companion," a tall, statuesque blond beauty in her late twenties who was identified on the passenger list as Mrs. Katherine Moog Busch of New York. However, she preferred the name Kate Moog, by which she was known to her friends.

Inhibited not one iota by the fact that he was married, and despite a back-breaking schedule of espionage and medical duties, Dr. Griebl for years had found time to engage in a long chain of amorous adventures. His reputation in Yorkville's German colony was that of an ardent womanizer. "Ignatz," said a friend, reflecting the view of many, "regards himself as God's gift to women!"

Hardly had the ship hoisted anchor than Griebl, now thirty-six years of age, held a Treff in spacious cabin F-21 with the *Europa's* Orstruppenfuehrer, the shadowy Karl Schlueter. They had much to discuss and conferred periodically throughout the voyage.

When the *Europa* docked at Bremerhaven, Griebl and Kate Moog were greeted by a beaming reception committee headed by Dr. Erich Pfeiffer, chief of the Abwehr's Bremen outpost.

(Pfeiffer had moved his operation from Wilhelmshaven to the Federal Building in downtown Bremen.) Griebl had come to Germany for a vacation, but the Abwehr rolled out the red carpet for him, as befitting the triumphant return of a conquering hero. The wide-eyed Kate Moog was dazzled by the VIP reception; her boyfriend clearly was an even more important man than she had thought him to be.[1]

Griebl and Moog were whisked to Berlin on an express train, in a specially reserved compartment, and they were ensconced in a huge suite in the Adlon, one of Europe's most famous and luxurious hotels.

Less than an hour after they entered the Adlon suite, there was a sharp knock on the door. Two solemn-faced uniformed men entered. One was short, bald, and pudgy, the other tall and blond. They introduced themselves as Commander Udo von Bonin and navy Captain Herman Menzel. Griebl had known who they were the moment he saw them: high-ranking Abwehr officers from Berlin. During the Atlantic crossing, Karl Schlueter had spoken often of the two. With a mixture of awe and pride, the Europa "steward" had related details about the time that he had been interviewed by the two Abwehr bigwigs.

Menzel and von Bonin wasted little time in small talk, and within minutes of their arrival they were escorting Dr. Griebl across Berlin to 76-78 Tirpitzufer, the closely guarded headquarters of the Abwehr's worldwide espionage apparatus. Overlooking the famed Tiergarten and its spreading chestnut trees, the headquarters occupied two former townhouses. Griebl and his escorts took a creaking old elevator to the fourth floor, where they entered the office of the Big Chief, Admiral Wilhelm Canaris. In keeping with Canaris's simple lifestyle, the office was far from pretentious. Behind his chair was an inscribed photograph of Adolf Hitler. On his desk was a symbol that could have represented the secret service of any nation; three brass monkeys, one looking over its shoulder, one cupping its ear and listening, and the third with its hand over its mouth.

Griebl felt a surge of awe in the presence of Canaris, the inscrutable supreme spymaster, one whose very name conjured visions of mystery and intrigue. Not only was the admiral one of Germany's most powerful figures, answerable only to Adolf Hitler, but top Nazi Party officials and military leaders feared this unimpressive little man with the slight speech impediment. Rumor had it that Canaris had used his far-flung spying apparatus to compile damaging dossiers on each of the Nazi bigwigs, dossiers that were said to be in Canaris's private safe—and only he had the key.

"I have summoned you here, Dr. Griebl, because I wish to thank you personally for your work in the United States," the Abwehr chief said. "You have served the fuehrer and the Fatherland well. I am sure that you will continue, and even increase, your efforts." [2]

Canaris paused briefly, staring directly at Griebl. Resuming, the admiral said that the fuehrer did not expect him to continue his risky duties in the United States due solely to loyalty to the Fatherland. Griebl would be given a beautiful home in Bavaria, and the rank and pay of a captain in the German Air Defense (soon to be known as the *Luftwaffe*). Beginning immediately, the pay would be accumulated until the time Dr. Griebl came back to live in the Third Reich—presumably through desire or to escape the clutches of the United States authorities. [3]

Peering through his tortoiseshell eyeglasses, Dr. Griebl replied that he was flattered by the profusion of praise from one of the Third Reich's towering leaders and that he would gladly accept from the fuehrer the financial rewards and rank of captain. Consequently, Griebl became possibly the only person to hold simultaneously a commission as a lieutenant in the United States Army Reserve and the rank of captain in the German Luftwaffe.

Concerning the generous offer of a house in Bavaria, the physician said that he had had his eye on a home in the city of Giessen, so could that property be substituted? Griebl quickly added that the Giessen home belonged to a Jew named Berliner. "Could a little pressure . . ." Griebl's voice trailed away. Menzel and von Bonin blanched over the American's audacity.

Canaris nodded. "Several aspects of the matter would be a trifle . . . well, bluntly, illegal," the spymaster replied. "But in view of your services to the [Nazi] Party, I am sure they can be overlooked." [4] (A few weeks later in New York, an Abwehr courier would deliver to Griebl the title to the confiscated Giessen estate.)

The next day Dr. Griebl and Kate Moog lunched on the Hotel

Eden's roof garden as guests of Commander von Bonin and Captain Menzel. It was supposed to be a social affair, but the Abwehr officers had other motives. Von Bonin and Menzel promptly focused their attention and whatever charm they could muster on the curvaceous Miss Moog.

"You have been in Washington, Fräulein?" von Bonin asked in a casual tone.

"Oh, yes, quite often," she replied, flattered by the high-ranking German's interest.

"Some of the highest officials and most powerful leaders of your country are your friends, no?" he asked pleasantly.

Moog was befuddled. Her eyes widened in wonderment. What was von Bonin suggesting? She stammered out a denial.

Von Bonin's pleasant demeanor vanished. He leaned forward and snapped, "Fräulein, there is nothing we do not know about you. We know about your connections in Washington . . . certain senators and important officers of the army and navy. You can be useful to us," he added. "As useful, in your way, as Dr. Griebl." His eyebrows raised suggestively.

Kate Moog glanced at her lover. He avoided her gaze and continued to spoon up his soup.

Revealing a trace of exasperation in his tone, von Bonin said that the United States paid its army and navy officers poorly and that many of them were deeply in debt. The Abwehr, he declared, knew who these debt-ridden officers were through a spy planted in a loan office in Washington. This agent had access to loan reports from a rating bureau, reports intended to make certain that there would be no excessive borrowing by desperate military men.

Moog's amazement grew. "But I still don't see how—"

Commander von Bonin cut her off. "Fräulein, you are a beautiful young woman," he snapped harshly. "If you opened a fine house or apartment in Washington and surrounded yourself with pretty *Madchen* and much good food and wine . . ."

Moog still looked bewildered. "Don't you see?" the Nazi spymaster explained in an impatient tone. "You invite these officials and the debt-racked army and navy officers to your establishment, and our agents can tell them how they can make some extra money by only providing a little information, and . . ."

"Oh!" The blonde gasped. "Oh!" She had seen the light. The Abwehr wanted her to be the working madam of a deluxe Washington brothel in order to extract U.S. military secrets.

Aware that his target was now enlightened, von Bonin told her that the German government would pay for the "house" and the expense of operating it. "Unfortunately," he added apologetically, "we will not be able to pay you or your *Madchen* salaries at first. Besides, they would be getting money from their customers, he intimated.

Von Bonin shrugged his shoulders when Moog gave no specific reply and said that the "proposition" was in the hands of Dr. Pfeiffer, who would take it up with her again at a later date.[5]

Back at the Hotel Columbus in Bremen on June 23, on the eve of Griebl's and Kate Moog's departure for the United States, the physician and Pfeiffer were having 7:00 P.M. cocktails. Moog was to join them for dinner an hour later. Normally a secretive man, Pfeiffer's tongue was loosened by the liquor, and he could not resist the temptation to boast about the Nazi spy operations he was helping direct in the United States.

"There are a lot of things I could tell you, *Herr Doktor,* which would amaze you," Pfeiffer said. "For after all, Griebl, though you are the trusted head of our espionage base in New York, we are not foolish enough to allow any one man to know too much. Even you might be apprehended and forced to talk."

"That is possible," Griebl conceded, "but highly improbable. They are fools in the United States. They do not think of espionage. Besides, I am above suspicion. I am not only a reputable, prominent physician, you remember, but also an officer in the United States Army Reserve."

Pfeiffer ordered another martini. "You are a clever man, all right, Griebl," he continued. "But you must realize this is a far more elaborate, far vaster matter than anyone besides the leaders here in Germany comprehend." The Abwehr officer emptied his glass, then added, "I'll wager that you don't know even one-tenth of our agents in the United States."

Suddenly the two men rose as Kate Moog, exquisitely groomed and clad in a silver, low-cut evening gown, joined them. The dinner was lengthy and enhanced by copious amounts of wines and liqueurs. Customarily stiff and formal, Pfeiffer unbent and insisted on showing the town to his two guests. He took them to the Astoria Cafe, Bremen's most pretentious nightclub.

While the orchestra played lilting melodies of love, Pfeiffer, Griebl, and Moog sat at a table in a corner and drank and talked. His voice now slurred, Pfeiffer told of his agent who had credentials to enter all United States Army installations in the East, and how this spy had recently sent the Abwehr valuable data after visiting the U.S. Army chemical warfare center at Edgewood Arsenal, Maryland. Pfeiffer boasted that he had "a couple of real good boys" in the Panama Canal Zone (controlled by the United States). In Washington, he said, the Abwehr had an informant on the staff of a prominent senator and another in what he called "President Roosevelt's inner circle." He bragged about how the "inner circle" agent had pilfered reports of a secret conference in which gaping deficiencies in U.S. warships were discussed.

The German drained yet another martini glass. "I tell you, Herr Griebl, at every strategic point in the United States we have at least one of our operatives," he said. "The United States cannot plan a warship, design an airplane, develop a new device that we do not know of it at once."[6]

Pfeiffer paused briefly and studied the effect of his startling disclosures on the two Americans. "You do not know how far we have gone in your country," the Abwehr officer declared. "Our destiny under Adolf Hitler is boundless! Do you hear, *Herr Doktor,* boundless!"

Pfeiffer's booming voice was masked by the blare of music and the buzzing din of conversations among the swarm of well-heeled and tipsy revelers. "But that is not enough!" he exclaimed, banging his hamlike fist on the table. "We must have more information. We want blueprints of the aircraft carriers *Yorktown* and *Enterprise!* We want the United States mobilization plans and the plans for the defenses of your eastern seaboard! We want the plans for the fortifications of New York harbor!"

Again the German's fist struck the table. "Do you understand me, Griebl?" he roared. "Do you understand me?"

"*Ja,* Herr Commander, I understand you," the American replied.

At three o'clock in the morning the celebration broke up and

Pfeiffer staggered out of the nightclub, followed by his two guests. A few hours later, on June 24, the pudgy Dr. Griebl and his five-foot-ten girlfriend sailed for New York.

Shortly after Griebl returned to his medical practice in York-ville, he held a Treff with thirty-four-year-old Gustav Guellich. Guellich had been recruited by the physician in April 1935 and had replaced Wilhelm Lonkowski as the spy ring's star per-former. A native of Munich, Guellich had come to the United States in 1932 and was a metallurgist in the laboratories of the Federal Shipbuilding Company, a division of U.S. Steel, in Kearny, New Jersey. An emaciated bachelor who suffered pe-riodic spells of depression, Guellich kept to himself and carried out his shipyard duties quietly and efficiently. His follow work-ers at Kearny considered him to be an odd duck.

Gaining access to secret or classified materials from his van-tage point in the sensitive shipyard laboratories, Guellich sent to the Abwehr in Germany a flood of high-grade data about the United States navy. Often this intelligence was collected merely by photocopying restricted materials that crossed his desk.

Among Guellich's "deliveries" were specifications of an un-derwater sound device; assorted warship deck guns and their shells; much metallurgical research information; description of a new teargas shell; blueprints of several destroyers under con-struction; drawings of a new Smith & Wesson handgun; and actual samples of cables being installed on navy vessels.

On January 7, 1936, unobtrusive Gustav Guellich scored his greatest coup: a four-page report entitled *Experiments with High-Altitude Rockets* in the United States. It contained details of work that had been done by Professor Robert H. Goddard, who was on the staff of a university in Worcester, Massachu-setts. Goddard, Guellich wrote, had made "a substantial break-through in the development of rocket-propelled missiles." [7]

Guellich's espionage bonanza created a flap in Berlin, and the spy was besieged for more information. Unbeknownst to Guellich, German scientists were also conducting rocket ex-periments, and Professor Goddard's findings would be an enor-mous boon to the Nazi project. Taking a bus on a trek of nearly 2,500 miles to a barren locale in New Mexico, Guellich watched, without interference from anyone, what may have been the first launchings in history of rockets. For the next two years Guellich would send Berlin a stream of reports on U.S. missile developments.[8]

One afternoon in September 1937 there was a knock on Guellich's door at the Hotel Martinique, on New York's West 32nd Street, where he lived. It was Karl Eitel, one of Erich Pfeiffer's principal couriers on a cross-Atlantic liner. Eitel brought exciting news—belated recognition. Pfeiffer had elevated Guellich one notch up the Abwehr totem pole, from number F.2307 (a subagent), to Agent 2336, a full-fledged spy.

5

The Man Who Stole
the Secret Bombsight

New York's cavernous Madison Square Garden was packed to the rafters on the night of October 3, 1937, for a rally of the German-American Bund. Twenty thousand persons rocked the building with frenzied cheers when 1,500 men of the *Ordnung Dienst* (the Bund version of Hitler's Nazi storm troopers) goose-stepped in. At their head was a burly bruiser named Wilhelm Böning, a machinist and father of four children. Marching in precise military formation, Böning and the others were clad in grayish-blue tunics, with black cuffs and neckbands, black forage caps with silver braid, and black trousers and boots.

Showered with thunderous applause, the storm troopers strutted about the floor of the Garden, saluted a huge swastika-emblazoned Nazi flag with outthrust arms, and shouted, *"Heil, Hitler!"* The crowd went wild. Outside, New York police stood watch to prevent the intrusion of protesting groups bent on clashing with the storm troopers.

The most deafening cheers erupted when Fritz Kuhn, the *Bundesfuehrer,* waddled to the podium to speak. Born in Bavaria, Kuhn had served in the Kaiser's army in World War I and had come to the United States in 1923. For a decade he had worked as a chemist in Henry Ford's automobile plant in Detroit, but in his spare time he had been a hyperactive leader of the local Bund. In December 1935 Kuhn had been appointed as the supreme fuehrer in the United States and promptly launched a national campaign to spread the Nazi gospel.

Highly energetic, Kuhn was short, squat with a fat rump. His accent was thick, and when excited, his English often became unrecognizable.

He spoke in English but sprinkled his talk liberally with German words and phrases. Although he started slowly, Kuhn soon flew into a rage. Shaking his hamlike fist he blared into the microphone that there was a plot afoot to prevent greater German (that is, Nazi) representation in the United States. He quoted the slogan of the People's League for Germanism (a Josef Goebbels creation): "In admiration and deep faith, our racial comrades in foreign states look up to the Reich and its Fuehrer!" Time and again Kuhn heaped abuse on the Jews—a sure-fire crowd pleaser. His brief but fiery speech was interrupted repeatedly by heavy applause and rousing cheers.

His pudgy frame shaking with emotion, the Bundesfuehrer closed by shouting: "Opfer! Opfer!" (Sacrifice! Sacrifice!) The throng roared back: "Heil, Hitler! Heil, Amerika!" There was yet another barrage of Nazi salutes, a rash of heiling, and a loud singing by twenty thousand voices of the Nazi marching song, Horst Wessel Lied, and of Deutschland Uber Alles (Germany Over All).[1]

Since Kuhn had taken over as Bundesfuehrer, Bund membership had been climbing steadily. Precise figures were a closely guarded secret, but the FBI estimated that in 1937 there were some 75,000 members nationally. New York City alone had six Bund branches, and there were others in twelve surrounding communities. There were branches in Chicago, St. Louis, Los Angeles, Philadelphia, Salt Lake City, Boston, Portland (Oregon), Detroit, Seattle, Minneapolis, Kansas City, Milwaukee, Cleveland, and in Georgia and Texas.

Directed from Berlin by the Deutsches Ausland Institut (German Overseas Institute, the Foreign Section of the Nazi Party, under Dr. Ernst Wilhelm Böhle) and backed by money from Hitler's treasury, the German-American Bund flourished during the 1930s. Its structure was the same as that of the Nazi Party in Germany. The United States had three gaue (districts), each with its own fuehrer or gauleiter.

There were four groups in the German-American Bund:

Jugenschaft and *Mädchenschaft* (male and female Hitler Youth corps); *Ordung Dienst* (storm troopers); *Frauenschaft* (women's auxiliary) and *Deutscher Konsum Verband* (league of business-men). One of the principal functions of the latter group was to mail hate literature urging the boycott of American firms that did not subscribe to Nazi ideals. Trained Abwehr agents, dis-guised as staff members of various German consulates in the United States, furnished Bund leaders with advice on espio-nage and sabotage operations.

On the overcast morning of October 17, 1937, two weeks after Kuhn and his Nazi storm troopers were goose-stepping around Madison Square Garden, Dr. Hans Rankin strolled down the gangplank of the liner *Bremen* at Pier 86 in New York harbor. The forty-year-old Rankin, a stout, blond man of average height, was the managing director of an export-import firm in Ham-burg, and he had come to the United States on a business trip.[2]

The Customs inspector gave Rankin's suitcases the normal cursory scrutiny but was intrigued by his walking-cane um-brella. "How does it work?" the official asked curiously. The amiable Dr. Rankin gave a brief demonstration. "A pretty slick trick for a spy," the inspector quipped. Rankin joined the man in laughter over the joke.[3]

But Rankin knew it was no joke. He was indeed a Hitler spy who had come to America to organize an espionage ring. Dr. Rankin and his position at the Hamburg export-import firm were but "covers." Actually he was a major in the Abwehr, and his real name was Nickolaus Ritter.

Son of a university president, Ritter was an unlikely candi-date for his job: chief of Hamburg's Ast X air intelligence sec-tion, or IL (*I* for Abwehr I, the espionage branch, *L* for *Luft*, or air). He had had no experience either as a pilot or as an intelli-gence officer. So Ritter had been as astonished as anyone when the big chief himself, Admiral Wilhelm Canaris, selected him for the Hamburg post.

Since the Hamburg branch was charged with culling intelli-gence from the United States, Major Ritter did possess two sig-nificant qualifications: He had spent ten years in the United States as a textile manufacturer and spoke "American" English fluently.

In early 1937 Ritter's textile business had collapsed (as did

countless other American firms during the Great Depression).
Broke and desperate, he was approached by General Friedrich
von Boetticher, the German military attaché in Washington,
who suggested that Ritter return to Germany and join Adolf
Hitler's rapidly expanding army. So the bankrupt businessman
sailed to the Fatherland, received a major's commission, and
was assigned to the Abwehr.

Shortly afterward, in July of that year, Canaris directed Ritter
to "expand intelligence work immediately to cover the air force
and aviation industry in the United States." The major was shattered by the order. It was difficult to reconcile himself to the
idea of working against the country he loved best next to his
own native land.[4]

Espionage greenhorn that he was, when he reported to Hamburg Major Ritter had been jolted to learn that Ast X, under
navy Captain Joachim Burghardt, had become infected with a
serious case of chronic lethargy. Burghardt had been perfectly
satisfied to let his eager beaver at the Bremen subbranch, Dr.
Erich Pfeiffer, direct the networks in and reap the bountiful harvest of intelligence from the United States.

Ritter had been shocked again to learn that the air intelligence section of Ast X existed in name only—it did not have a
single spy in the United States. In fact, Ast X had but one
"sleeper" in America, an agent named Everett Minster Roeder,
who worked at the Sperry plant on Long Island.

Almost at once Luftwaffe bigwigs began bombarding Major
Ritter with demands that his nonexistent agents produce data
on one of America's most closely guarded secrets, a revolutionary and highly accurate bombsight. By mid-1937 it had become
common knowledge in global aviation circles that such a device
had been developed separately by three American scientists,
Elmer Sperry and Carl T. Norden in association with Theodore
H. Barth.

Meanwhile, Ritter had come to terms with himself over spying on his adopted country, so he made a crucial decision: He
himself would go to organize an aviation spy ring in the United
States. Who in Ast X knew the country more intimately or
spoke American English better than he did?

Now, after clearing Customs in New York, Ritter lugged his
two suitcases and a briefcase to the Taft Hotel, north of Times

Square, and checked in. He stashed his novel walking-cane umbrella in a corner. Only Ritter and a few Abwehr men at Hamburg knew that the umbrella had a hollow center for carrying messages.[5]

Late on the afternoon of October 19, two days after his arrival in New York, Ritter took a Yellow Cab to a drab flat at 245 Monitor Street, in the New York borough of Brooklyn. He alighted from the taxi, glanced around to see if he was being followed, then walked rapidly up the street to number 262. A heavyset, middle-aged man in a soiled blue shirt responded to Ritter's knock. "Herr Soehn?" the spy inquired. "*Ja,* I am Soehn," the other replied cautiously.

"Well, I'm pleased to meet you, Pops. I bring greetings from Roland."

"Pops" was the Abwehr's code name for Heinrich Soehn, and "Roland" was the prearranged cover name for this Treff.[6]

Soehn was a low-level operative in the Nazi spy network in the New York area, a bumbling individual whose home served as a letter box. Productive spies would take their "deliveries" to the shabby flat and Pops would forward the materials by mail to Germany.

So Ritter was not especially interested in Soehn. Within minutes he asked the Nazi stooge if he could arrange a meeting for him with "Paul." Of course, of course, Pops replied.

Two days later Major Ritter returned to Pops's dwelling for the Treff with Paul. A few minutes later a husky, blond man with pleasant features arrived. "*Herr Doktor,*" Pops said importantly, "*hier ist der Hermann.*" "Paul" was thirty-five-year-old Hermann W. Lang, who worked in the Norden factory (at 80 Lafayette Street in Manhattan) that was producing the Norden bombsight, reputed to be the world's best.

Lang had come to the United States from Germany in 1927, and at the time of the Treff with Ritter his naturalization had not been completed. For the past several weeks he had been sending to Germany drawings of a few components of the bombsight, but without the remaining parts they were of little use to Nazi scientists.

In a memorandum, Lang had told the Abwehr: "The target results obtained with it [the bombsight] in the USA are extraordinarily good."[7]

Outwardly Lang had been leading the routine life of a middle-class citizen, living with a doting wife and a pretty young daughter on 64th Place in suburban Glendale. He told Ritter that his wife was unaware of his double life. When the couple retired for the night, Lang waited until she was asleep, then slipped downstairs to the kitchen and traced blueprints that he had sneaked out of the Norden plant under his clothing.

Seated in Soehn's living room, Major Ritter casually sized up Lang and found him to be quiet and reserved, a laboring man who, through hard work and dedication, had been promoted to inspector at the Norden plant. Lang explained to the Abwehr officer that, while the United States had been good to him, he wanted the New Germany to have the bombsight too. "I can never forget the Fatherland," he declared emotionally. Time and again Lang stressed that he had no interest in money for his espionage activities.[8]

Overwhelmed by the patriotism of this seemingly unsophisticated man, the Abwehr spymaster got to his feet, shook hands warmly with the Norden inspector, and in a voice choked with emotion said, "Herr Lang, you are a fine German. On behalf of Adolf Hitler and the Third Reich, I congratulate you, and I thank you! Now how many more blueprints can you get us?"[9]

Perhaps Major Ritter would not have been so emotional over Lang's "patriotism" had he known that a few months later Lang would deposit three thousand dollars into his depleted New York bank account—courtesy of the treasury of the Third Reich.

Lang explained that he had a batch of other drawings secreted in his home, tracings he had laboriously created on the table in the cold kitchen in the wee hours of the morning as his unknowing wife slept peacefully upstairs. Ritter rubbed his hands in glee.

On the following night Lang handed Ritter all the blueprint copies of portions of the Norden bombsight that he had completed. The Abwehr officer arranged to get these to a courier on the *Bremen*, which was to sail for Germany the next day. In the meantime, Lang got his hands on every blueprint he could. Two weeks later, on the eve of Ritter's departure for home, Lang, Soehn, and the major met for a farewell drink, and at its conclusion the Norden inspector handed over the remainder of his blueprints.

Ten days later in Berlin, Admiral Canaris himself was agog at what Major Ritter's ace spy in the United States had produced. A technical expert told the Abwehr chief, "This is what we have been looking for, for months . . . This will revolutionize our whole bombing strategy." [10]

Using Hermann Lang's stolen blueprints and specifications, Luftwaffe technicians built a model of the *Nordensches Zielgeraet* (Norden bombsight). However, the Norden did not replace the German bombsight (called the *Lothfe*) but greatly influenced its development. Hitler was preparing for war and the Lothfe was already in production and installed in many Luftwaffe aircraft.

A few weeks after Major Ritter returned to the Third Reich, the Abwehr invited "Paul" (Hermann Lang) to Berlin—all expenses paid—in order to thank him personally for his enormous contribution to the fuehrer. Lang spent a mind-spinning week being fêted by high-ranking Abwehr officials, including an audience with a beaming General Hermann Goering, chief of the German air force.

Lang's personal escort through the festivities was Major Hans Jochin Groskopf of Canaris's headquarters in Berlin. Conspicuous by his absence was Major Ritter, who had engineered the espionage coup at the risk of a prison term in the United States. The conniving Groskopf, Ritter would learn, had schemed to receive full credit for the Norden bombsight theft.

6

The Gestapo Sets Up in America

Twenty-two-year-old Eleanor Böhme was a classic Nordic beauty—blonde, blue-eyed, fair-skinned. Born in the United States, her parents were German immigrants who maintained a deep love for the Fatherland. When Eleanor was a freshman at Elmhurst (Long Island) High School, outside New York City, her parents took her on a trip to Germany. After a year at New York's Hunter College, Eleanor spent two years in the Third Reich, studying at the University of Berlin. In mid-1937 she returned to Hunter and was graduated with a bachelor of arts degree.

Miss Böhme's social life centered on the German organizations that were rife in Manhattan's Yorkville. She loved to visit the German luxury liners berthed in New York harbor and dance the night away with ships' officers and crew members. Eleanor's striking good looks and vivacious charm made her the belle of the ball. On one of her visits to the *Europa* she met the "steward" Karl Schlueter.

On October 18, 1937, the day after the Abwehr spymaster Major Nickolaus Ritter, alias Dr. Rankin, had arrived in New York, the telephone jangled in the Böhme home in Elmhurst. Eleanor answered the summons and heard the caller identify himself as "Karl . . . Karl Schlueter." Böhme winced. Schlueter had been pestering her on and off for many weeks, apparently with romance in mind. He asked her to meet with him at a Walgreen's drugstore in Manhattan's Times Square, and spoke of helping her get a job "worthy of your talents." Reluctantly Böhme agreed to the rendezvous; in the Great Depression, she was desperate for work.

Over ice-cream sodas at Walgreen's, Schlueter probed constantly into Eleanor's background, education, friends, and "willingness to work for the New Germany." Böhme was bewildered: What kind of work? Schlueter was evasive. At no time did he intimate what may have been the true purpose of the rendezvous: to allow him to size Böhme up for employment as a spy.

A month later Eleanor received a typewritten letter on North German Line stationery. It was unsigned, but she presumed that it came from Schlueter. Enclosed was a card that read: Kate Moog, 276 Riverside Drive, New York City. The letter suggested that Böhme contact Miss Moog about "an interesting job offer."

Böhme had never heard of Kate Moog. And she was suspicious of Schlueter's repeated hazy references to a job for her. But in January 1938 Eleanor telephoned Moog, told her of Schlueter's letter, and made an appointment for a job interview.

It was a bitterly cold and snowy day, with an icy wind whipping through the concrete canyons of Manhattan, when Böhme pushed the buzzer at 276 Riverside Drive, in a stylish neighborhood, and was greeted by the long-limbed (six foot one in high heels) Kate Moog, chicly dressed in an ensemble from a smart Fifth Avenue boutique. Dr. Ignatz Griebl's girlfriend was at her charming best and reached out to shake hands warmly with her caller. As she did, Kate pressed a packet of matches into Eleanor's hand, a curious action, the interviewee reflected fleetingly.

Eleanor, from a middle-class family, was dazzled by Moog's luxurious, exquisitely furnished, fourteen-room apartment and by her stable of six servants. Kate had been born in Germany of wealthy parents, who brought her to the United States as a young girl: prior to her relationship with Griebl, Moog, a shrewd businesswoman behind a façade of constant gaiety, had opened a nursing home for the aged in New York, and prospered.

Gracious and friendly, Moog served coffee and subtly probed into Eleanor's background and views. Böhme noticed that

Moog, as had Schlueter at the Walgreen's rendezvous, came back time and again to her "willingness to work for the New Germany."

An hour after arriving, Böhme departed. Trudging through the snowy streets to a bus stop, she reflected on the strange interview. At no time had Kate Moog given any indication of the nature of her business enterprise, nor of what kind of work she had in mind for the applicant. Now Eleanor removed Moog's packet of matches from a pocket and examined it. Her suspicions heightened. Written on the inside cover in red ink were jottings that looked like those used in spy codes, the kind she had seen in the movies. Puzzled and upset, Böhme returned home. She would never again see Kate Moog or Karl Schlueter—mainly because the FBI had gained inklings of Griebl's spy ring and was closing in on some of the principal agents.[1]

Manhattan was blanketed with snow on the night of December 12, 1937, when Wilhelm Böning, the burly Nazi storm trooper chief who had led his 1,500 men as they goose-stepped around Madison Square Garden during Fritz Kuhn's huge rally, spoke at a meeting of the German-American Bund in the Grand Central Palace in Yorkville. Afterward, the rough-hewn Böning and a handful of Bundsmen gathered at a corner tavern to hoist a few beers and to boast of their war escapades while fighting with the Kaiser's army. Listening to the tales was John Baptiste Unkel, an officer in the Bund branch at New Rochelle, a New York City suburb.

Unkel, fifty-one years of age, was born at Linz, on the Rhine. He came to the United States in 1910 and in 1913 enlisted in the United States Army. He was stationed in the Panama Canal Zone, deserted, was caught and served eighteen months in prison. Somehow, despite his jail term, he reenlisted in the U.S. Army in 1917 and spent two years during the war at Fort Slocum, New York.

Not to be outdone, Unkel now began bragging to Böning and the others about his own experiences in the United States Army. He spun a tale about how he had helped to build fortifications in the Panama Canal Zone. Finding himself the focus of attention, Unkel bragged that he had a complete set of plans of the fortifications. Böning's ears pricked up. Here was a chance to strike a telling blow for the Fatherland; the Panama Canal, he knew, was one of the United States' most crucial—and vulnerable—overseas military outposts.[2]

Early the next morning Böning contacted Fritz Ewald Rossberg, who was reputed to be the assistant Gestapo chief in New York City, and a Treff was held that night at the Franz Siegel Tavern, on East 8th Street. Böning was bursting with excitement about Panama Canal plans.

Then Rossberg grew excited. "Arrange to see those plans," he ordered. "If they are real, we must have them!"

Böning caught up with Unkel at the headquarters of the German-American Bund, at 178 East 85th Street. "Those plans you spoke of the other night, they are of great value," the storm trooper chief declared. "You must produce them."

Unkel grew suspicious. Was Böning an FBI plant? He demanded to know who wanted the plans. Böning refused to tell him. Unkel replied that he had to know whom he was dealing with.

Böning looked up Rossberg again and told him of Unkel's refusal to turn over the plans. Rossberg exploded: "We must get them—by force if necessary!"

Rossberg informed Dr. Griebl of Unkel's Panama Canal plans. Griebl ordered Rossberg to go all out in pursuit of the documents. Meanwhile, Böning had told Unkel that he would put him in touch with the man who wanted the plans. A few nights later, at a Bund meeting in New Rochelle, a mystery man (he gave a phony name) approached Unkel and asked, "Are you a loyal German?"

Unkel was on guard, and told the stranger that he was an American citizen. The man kept asking if Unkel was a loyal German, and finally he demanded that the Panama Canal fortification plans be turned over to him.

Now Unkel's boasting had turned sour. Was this stranger a German secret agent? An FBI agent? Unkel said he didn't have the plans any longer. Suddenly the stranger's tone turned menacing, even threatening. Then where in the hell were the plans? Unkel shrugged.

Whoever the mystery man was (investigators would never identify him for certain), he promptly went to Böning and told him Unkel refused to turn over the plans. Böning contacted Rossberg. "Unkel's lying!" Rossberg snapped. "If we can't get them any other way, we'll break into his house and get them. If Unkel tries to stop us . . ." [3]

In the Third Reich, the Gestapo chief was Heinrich Himmler, an owl-faced, one-time chicken farmer, who was also leader of the *Schutzstaffel* (SS), the fuehrer's elite, black-uniformed body-guard. The very name Gestapo struck fear into the hearts of most German citizens. In early 1937 Hitler decreed that actions of his secret police could no longer be challenged by any court or individual but were subject to review only by Heinrich Himmler. The Gestapo chief would be, in effect, reviewing his own actions.

Against this backdrop of awesome Gestapo power in the Third Reich, in August 1937 a hard-eyed German thug named Rudolf Bittenberg arrived in New York City to organize a Gestapo network, as though the United States were a Nazi province. Bittenberg's gang was to spy on anti-Nazis and harass them, browbeat loyal American citizens of German birth who were not pro-Hitler, trail Nazi spies suspected of betrayal and "deal" with them, and commit mayhem on Americans of whatever ancestry who incurred the wrath of honchos in the Third Reich. [4]

Bittenberg came to America disguised as an assistant purser on the SS *New York*—but his word was law aboard ship. Even the *New York's* captain, Commodore Fritz Kruse, had to kowtow to and take orders from this Nazi oaf and strongarm man. (Bittenberg had gained his Gestapo rank as a result of laurels earned in the Nazi Party's head-beating purges during its struggle to seize power in Germany.)

A day after debarking, Bittenberg and two other men barged into the office of Captain Wilhelm Drechsel, New York port superintendent of the German lines. Drechsel, who came from the traditional seafaring mold of the Old Germany, was not involved in Nazi spy rings, but he had received orders from Berlin to "show every courtesy and aid" to Bittenberg. The Gestapo chief in the United States demanded that Captain Drechsel furnish his two hooligans with passes that would permit them to roam the piers at any time and to board any German ship, with-

out interference by Drechsel or his staff. The captain had no
choice but to obey.

One of the men with Bittenberg was Karl Friedrich Herrmann, who would become Gestapo head for New York City. The
slick-haired, lean, dark-eyed Herrmann was born in Coblenz in
1905. His life's ambition had been to be a waiter, and he served
an apprenticeship at the Cornelius Hotel in Dusseldorf and later
became a full-fledged waiter in a hotel at Elberfeld. For the next
four years he bounced around as a waiter in ten places in Germany. When Adolf Hitler gained power, Herrmann became an
ardent Nazi, and the waiter was proud that the Party had asked
him to be of covert service to the Reich—by spying on his fellow workers.

By 1934 the ambitious Herrmann had proved himself to be a
consummate stool pigeon. He came to the attention of a Nazi
bigwig in Hamburg, Gustav Lanhans, who placed Herrmann in
a series of jobs, ostensibly as a steward on German ocean liners.
But his true function was to squeal on crew members and German citizens who might drop indiscreet remarks about Adolf
Hitler and the Nazi regime. Again, Herrmann came through
with flying colors.

In June 1937 Herrmann was summoned to Hamburg and was
awed to find himself in the presence of Herr Schleckenbag, the
Gestapo chief in that city.[5] Schleckenbag grilled Herrmann for
nearly two hours, probing for a chink in the stool pigeon's Nazi
armor. He found none: Herrmann was undoubtedly a Hitler
zealot, ruthless and dedicated. So Schleckenbag appointed him
Gestapo chief in New York City.

Elated, Herrmann listened avidly as Schleckenbag outlined
his duties, explaining that his principal courier between the
Reich and New York would be Heinrich Bischoff, a steward on
the *Europa*. (Actually, Bischoff was a Gestapo agent.) Bischoff
would bring Herrmann's reports back across the Atlantic and
directly to Schleckenbag.

Herrmann had entered the United States by fraud. He secured
a visa from the American consulate in Hamburg on the basis of
an affidavit signed by Herman Umbreidt, then the owner of the
Café Hindenburg in Manhattan, who identified himself as a
close relative of Herrmann's. But Umbreidt had never heard of

Karl Herrmann—the glowing letter and its signature were forgeries, crafted by Gestapo technicians in Hamburg.

Herrmann easily melted into the American scene. Despite the
Great Depression and widespread unemployment, he obtained
jobs as a waiter, first at the Longchamps Restaurant in Manhattan and then at the Brooklyn Club in Brooklyn. Not only did
these jobs provide him with plausible "cover," but the twenty to
thirty dollars he received in tips each week augmented his mea-
ger Gestapo pay.

Not long after Karl Herrmann settled down in New York, Gestapo courier Heinrich Bischoff brought him his first major investigative mission. His bosses back in Germany had gotten it
into their heads that a dangerous, anti-Nazi counterespionage
ring, operating under the auspices of an unknown nation, was
spying on Nazi spies in the United States and seeking to disrupt
their work. Herrmann was told by Hamburg that the masterminds behind the anti-Nazi network were two New York
women, Mrs. Thomas Manville and Antonie "Astra" Strassmann.[6]

Herrmann plunged into his investigative task with all the zeal
he had displayed in squealing on cooks and bottle washers back
in the old days. Within two weeks he notified Hamburg that he
had uncovered four other members of the insidious anti-Nazi
ring, all of them German citizens: a man named Hassfurter, another named Aichner, a Fräulein Drachau, and a Fräulein
Fichtner. Herrmann's reports hinted darkly of clandestine meetings that had been held by these four suspects at Cherbourg and
Southampton and other European ports of call of German ocean
liners.

Mrs. Thomas Manville, the reputed brains of the anti-Nazi
operation, was an unlikely candidate to be a sinister cloak-and-
dagger mastermind, a fact that apparently did not sink into
Herrmann's brain. She was a kindly, frail, elderly (charitably, in
her late seventies) lady who lived in a spacious suite in the
stylish Savoy-Plaza Hotel in Manhattan. Publicly, she was noted
for being the extremely wealthy mother of middle-aged Tommy
Manville, a big-spending playboy who was featured regularly
on the society pages for his zany escapades and his twelve mar-
riages, give or take a couple.

Mrs. Manville traveled extensively, liked to take German ships, made friends easily, and on debarking gave gifts to those who had been especially nice to her—chefs, hairdressers, stewards, and waiters. Gracious almost to a fault, Mrs. Manville invariably invited these passing acquaintances to visit her at the Savoy-Plaza whenever they were in New York.

Invariably, the German ships' employees accepted the offer, for Mrs. Manville entertained royally. Word of a stream of German visitors traipsing in and out of the Savoy-Plaza suite had reached Gestapo or Abwehr ears, so the frail but extroverted matriarch had been pinpointed as the mastermind of an anti-Nazi counterespionage ring. For what other reason would she be entertaining and lavishing gifts on persons of modest stations whom she barely knew?

The matriarch's co-conspirator, according to the Gestapo in the Third Reich, Astra Strassmann, had to be deeply involved in the operation. Not only was she a close friend of Mrs. Manville's, but Astra had been forced to flee Germany because she was said to have had Jewish blood in her family tree. Vengeance against the Nazis was her motive, the Gestapo had concluded.

Born in Berlin in 1901, Astra was a world figure. She had been a stage and radio star in Germany, became interested in flying, and, after becoming a famed international pilot, gained her greatest recognition, in May 1932, when she flew in the giant German airplane, the Dorner DO-X, from the United States to Berlin, with refueling halts at Newfoundland and the Azores. The German *herrenvolk* (people) went wild and showered adulation on the beautiful aviatrix.

Then the Hitler regime came into power. Tainted by a trace of Jewish blood, Astra, her prominent physician father, and her mother, both Christians, were expelled from their clubs and professional associations. No longer was Astra the darling of the Fatherland. She left Germany to make her home in the United States. Astra brought with her the assets—brains, beauty, charm, and wit—that would launch her into a highly successful career buying and selling patents worldwide.

Astra became even more suspect in the eyes of the Gestapo when it was learned that her influential Washington friends included high-ranking army and navy officers, members of Congress, and Roosevelt administration leaders. These contacts were for business and social reasons, but to Herrmann and the Gestapo they meant only that Astra was plotting against the Nazi regime.

Suddenly the investigation of the anti-Hitler counterespionage ring in the United States collapsed like a house of cards in a hurricane. There had never been such an organization. Even the buffoon Herrmann finally realized that the elderly, frail Mrs. Manville could hardly be capable of masterminding devious plots, and neither could Astra Strassmann, who spent much of her time globe-hopping on her patent business.

Of the "accomplices" uncovered by the bumbling Herrmann, Aichner was merely a minor official in a tour agency, Hassfurter was a steward on the *Europa*, Drachau was a maid and Fichtner a stewardess on that same ship. Their only involvement with Mrs. Manville was they had served her in her travels and had visited her at the Savoy-Plaza.

Not all the Gestapo actions in the United States were buffoonery. In 1938 the FBI received secret information that the Gestapo bigwigs in the Third Reich were planning to have Astra Strassmann lured back to the Fatherland, or kidnapped, if need be, so that she could be tried for unspecified "crimes" against the Hitler regime. A police guard was placed at her New York home.

Comic-opera figures as they were during their early years in the United States, these Gestapo agents would get bolder, cagier, and more dangerous. The FBI was concerned. Whatever devious plots the Gestapo might hatch, the Feds knew that large numbers of men on the German ocean liners calling at New York would help perpetrate the deeds.

7

A Blind Contact in *The New York Times*

On the bitterly cold night that ushered in the year 1938, raucous celebrations were raging in Yorkville, just as they were in countless locales across the nation. Every rathskeller, café, and beerhall along East 86th Street was crammed with noisy revelers. As the night wore on and copious quantities of schnapps, beer, and wine were consumed, the din grew deafening—joyous shouts, toy-horn blowing, the vigorous shaking of rattlers.

Adolf Hitler's spies were mixed in with the merrymakers. Spies, too, have to let down their hair on occasion. At the Café Hindenburg, Dr. Ignatz Griebl was hoisting glass after glass of *Mosel Bluemchen* with one arm, while clinging to the other arm and giggling endlessly was the blond beauty, Kate Moog.[1]

Nearby, at the popular Maxi's, Karl Schlueter was host to a tableful of guests and vying for the honor of being the drunkest and the loudest. Between hefty belts of schnapps, the SS *Europa* Orstgruppenfuehrer pawed amorously at his companion, twenty-seven-year-old Johanna "Jenni" Hofmann, a hairdresser on the ship. Jenni considered herself to be Schlueter's girlfriend—and she was a courier in his spy ring.

Jenni was attractive, poised, and self-assured. Her wealth of wavy, auburn hair framed a delicate, fair skin and set off her light-blue eyes. Schlueter's girlfriend or not, crew members on the *Europa* gossiped about the provocative way she carried her trim figure and the coy glances that indicated she was quite sensitive to, and aware of, other men.

Miss Hofmann had been born and grew up in Dresden, and attended a trade school to learn the hairdressing trade. In 1936 she went to work as a hairdresser on the North German Lloyd Line's *Gneisenau*, where she met Karl Schlueter. The wily Abwehr agent paid court to her, and when he transferred to the *Europa* to launch his espionage operations against the United States, Jenni went with him.[2]

One day on the high seas, Schlueter confided to her that he was an agent of the German secret service and regaled the awed and unsophisticated young woman with tales of the glamorous life of a spy. He spoke of the glories of patriotism and Adolf Hitler and Nazi Germany. Jenni was thrilled. When he offered to make her a secret service agent too, she accepted eagerly.[3]

Schlueter explained that she was to be his assistant—her eyes glowed in anticipation—in carrying messages and instructions from the Abwehr in Germany to Nazi spies in the United States, and to bring back to the Fatherland the military secrets they had stolen.

Now, in the boisterous New Year's Eve celebration at the Café Hindenburg, Schlueter, from time to time, vigorously slapped on the back a guest at his table whom he called Theo. A medium-sized man in his late twenties with black hair brushed straight back, Theo was actually Guenther Gustav Rumrich, one of the slickest and most productive Nazi spies in the United States.

Amid the café's hubbub, Schlueter took Theo into a corner and slipped him the latest "shopping list" from the Abwehr in Bremen. Even the customarily cocksure Rumrich was startled by the audacity of the items on the list: copies of construction drawings of the aircraft carriers *Enterprise* and *Yorktown* and information about experiments the army Signal Corps was carrying out at Fort Monmouth, New Jersey, involving the detection of approaching aircraft. (Later this development would be known as radar.)

Hardly had Rumrich digested the written requests than

Schlueter sprung another demand, couching his request in casual terms: "By the way, Theo, we need about fifty blank American passports for agents we're sending into Russia. Think you can get them?"

Rumrich swallowed hard. Then Schlueter added, "Bremen's willing to pay one thousand dollars for the batch of passports." Theo beamed. "And Bremen is also prepared to pay another thousand for the U.S. Army's mobilization plans for the eastern seaboard. Can you get them?"

Rumrich was elated. Two thousand dollars! This was a hundred times more than the twenty dollars per week he had gotten not long before for washing dishes in a Manhattan greasy-spoon restaurant.

Rumrich was born on December 8, 1911, in Chicago, Illinois, where his father, Alphonse, a graduate of the *Kadetten Schule* (military school) in Vienna, was secretary of the Austria-Hungarian consulate. When Guenther was two years old, his father was transferred to a post in Bremen, and the boy grew up in war-torn Europe. In 1929, at the age of eighteen, Guenther could not find a job. But he learned that, due to his birth in Chicago, he was an American citizen, so he decided to seek his fortune in the United States.

On September 28, 1929, Rumrich arrived in New York, with one hundred dollars in his pocket and only a few words of English in his vocabulary. For nearly two weeks he posed in Yorkville as the son of a rich man in Germany. Soon he was penniless and had to drop the masquerade.

Rumrich went to work as an office boy at George Borgfeld, Importers, at fifteen dollars per week. He proved to be a misfit and was fired. Desperate, he applied to join the U.S. Army and was accepted on January 25, 1930. It took six months for Rumrich to get his fill of army life—he was too arrogant to take orders. With thirty dollars in his billfold, he deserted, hitchhiked to Pittsburgh, and was soon broke. He turned himself in as a deserter, was court-martialed and sentenced to six months. In four months Rumrich was released and resumed his army duties.

A curious mixture of shiftlessness, arrogance, and brains, Rumrich began a self-study of medicine, and shortly after leaving the guardhouse, the U.S. Army promoted him to surgical technician and assigned him to the station hospital at Fort Hamilton, New York. A year later he took the examination for promotion, passed it at the top of the list, and was appointed sergeant.

For the next three years Sergeant Rumrich apparently carried out his duties satisfactorily while serving in the Panama Canal Zone, and in July 1935 he was transferred to Fort Missoula, Montana. There he engaged in a liaison with a pretty, sixteen-year-old farm girl who lived near the post (he soon married her) and reverted to playing the big shot, no doubt to impress his sweetheart. While on leave, he pitched wild parties, drank in swanky watering holes, and feasted in fine restaurants.

To support his high living, Rumrich began stealing money from the Fort Missoula hospital fund. Near discovery, Rumrich deserted again. He fled by bus to Minneapolis, reaching there on January 3, 1936, and took another bus to Chicago, to throw possible pursuers off his trail. Then it was on to Pittsburgh and finally to New York, where he arrived haggard, exhausted, and broke—a deserter and fugitive. Rumrich began washing dishes at Meyer's Restaurant, at ten dollars per week. Soon he quit and found a similar job at the Spic and Span restaurant, at 42nd Street and Eighth Avenue, at two dollars more per week.

While browsing in the New York Public Library, Rumrich read a book written by Colonel Walter Nicolai, the clever German spymaster in World War I, and was fascinated. So in early January he wrote to the colonel, in care of the *Voelkischer Beobachter* (Public Observer), the official Nazi daily newspaper in Berlin. Rumrich identified himself as "a high official in the United States Army" and said that if "the proper authorities" were interested in his services they should place an advertisement to "Theodor Koerner" in the Public Notices column of the *New York Times*. (Koerner was a noted nineteenth-century German poet.)[4]

Colonel Nicolai was no longer in the espionage business, but he turned over Rumrich's letter to the Abwehr, and it eventually wound up on the desk of *Kapitaen* Ernst Mueller, naval intelligence chief at Ast X in Hamburg, together with a recommendation to hire Rumrich if he looked "safe." Mueller conducted an extensive investigation through spies and two Gestapo agents in the United States and became convinced that it would be prudent to make the blind newspaper contact. Mueller had the *New York Times* ad prepared, and took it to an Abwehr courier, First Officer Franz Friske, on the liner *Hamburg*, which was about ready to sail for New York.

Kapitaen Mueller gave Friske the sheet of paper with an ad on it and an American ten-dollar bill. When the *Hamburg* docked in New York on April 3, 1936, Friske turned the ad and the ten-dollar bill over to Captain Emil Maurer, at the Hapag-Lloyd office at the harbor. (Hapag-Lloyd was the operating merger of the North German Lloyd Line and the Hamburg-American Lines.) Maurer in turn sent to the *Times* by messenger the ad and the ten dollars, together with a letter ordering insertions to be made on April 6 and April 10.

At the *Times* the advertisement was read by classified advertising manager Charles W. Hoyt. He grew suspicious. The ad looked to him like some sort of a spy code (he had seen spy movies). So Hoyt telephoned Captain Maurer and naively asked if there was a code being used in the ad, did the ad have some ulterior motive? Maurer chuckled and replied, no, no, certainly not. What on earth would he be doing inserting a message containing a hidden code? It was just some sort of personal matter between First Officer Friske and an old friend, Theodor Koerner. (Indeed Koerner was *old*—he had been dead for more than a hundred years.)[5]

Satisfied that no one would be using the staid *New York Times* for espionage contacts, Hoyt accepted the ad. Since the cost was six dollars, he mailed a refund of four dollars. Maurer then shuttled the refund on back to the anemic Abwehr treasury.

Months had slipped past since Rumrich had mailed the letter to Nicolai. He had scanned *The Times* Public Notices column daily and had always been disappointed. Now, on the afternoon of April 6, he was thumbing through *The Times* once more. Suddenly he felt a surge of exultation. Leaping out at him from the page were the words:

Theodor Koerner. Letter received. Please send reply and address to Sanders, Hamburg 1, Postbox 629, Germany.[6]

Sanders was *Kapitaen* Ernst Mueller at Ast X.

Rumrich immediately fired off to "Sanders" a long letter in which he outlined his qualifications. He said that he was eager to serve the fuehrer and the Third Reich, that he was close to an officer at Mitchel Field who handled secret codes, and that money was no object in his services—although, he confessed, it would be helpful if his expenses could be covered, for he was down on his luck at the present time.

The new spy signed his real name, but gave his address at the Denver Chemical Manufacturing Company on Varick Street, New York, where he worked as a translator and which was near to his home in the Bronx. (When he had deserted from Fort Missoula, Montana, he left behind his pregnant teenage bride and was now living in a dingy rooming house.)[7]

Kapitaen Mueller sent Rumrich's second letter to Dr. Erich Pfeiffer at the Bremen Abwehr nest, and the peripatetic Karl Schlueter was given the task of contacting Rumrich and sizing him up. A short time later Schlueter arranged a Treff at the Café Hindenburg.

The Orstgruppenfuehrer was impressed by the glib Rumrich, who launched a long spiel extolling the virtues of *Der Fuehrer*, Nazi Germany, and the ideals that Hitler stood for. Schlueter quaffed down large steins of beer and listened silently. When Rumrich concluded his eulogy, Schlueter wiped the froth from his mouth and said, "*Ja, ja*, Herr Rumrich, for the Fatherland— and for money!"

Despite his cynicism, Schlueter returned to Germany and gave a glowing report on the man who was an army deserter, a fugitive, a thief, a liar, a braggart, a failure in the workplace, and a borderline alcoholic. Cunning beneath a façade of brutishness, Schlueter had—accurately—discerned hidden traits in Rumrich that would make him a devious and productive masterspy.

Four weeks after the Café Hindenburg Treff, Rumrich was handed his first "job": reporting on the units (and their strengths) guarding the Panama Canal, together with the names of the commanding officers. Child's play, Rumrich gloated. He already knew most of the data through memory—he had served in the Panama Canal Zone. The rest of the information he obtained rapidly at the New York Public Library merely by consulting a military publication, the *Army and Navy Register*.

Bremen was delighted with Rumrich's work. A short time later it was Rumrich's turn to be jubilant. The mail brought a letter of thanks from "Sanders," his Abwehr boss in Bremen—along with two twenty-dollar bills.[8]

Guenther Rumrich (code-named Crown by the Abwehr) now plunged into his task with vigor, creating his own spy network. Pfeiffer in Bremen bombarded Crown with requests for information on the United States defenses on the eastern seaboard, and Rumrich promptly began producing accurate data.

Pfeiffer next wanted the venereal disease rate in the U.S. Army. So Rumrich telephoned the hospital at Fort Hamilton, a post guarding the entrance to New York harbor, and in an authoritative tone told the corporal on duty: "This is Major Milton of the Medical Corps, and I'm calling from the corner of Fourth Avenue and 86th Street in Brooklyn. I'm in New York to deliver a classified lecture on VD in the army, but I left my notes in Washington. I want you to quickly get me the figures on the total number of men stationed at Hamilton, and how many of them have contracted VD and what kind."

Duly impressed by the order, the corporal had a clerk rapidly pull together the data, handed it to a private, and told him to take the file folder by taxi to a "Major Milton" who would be waiting in civilian clothes at a specified Brooklyn streetcorner phone booth.

Feigning an urgency to get to his meeting, Rumrich took the folder from the young private and handed him a dollar bill to pay the thirty-cent taxi fare. "Keep the change!" Rumrich told the soldier.

By computing the venereal disease ratio at Fort Hamilton with the personnel strength of the U.S. Army as a whole (a figure well known to the world's intelligence agencies), Rumrich was able to provide Bremen with an almost precise figure.

Steadily, Pfeiffer's demands became more ambitious and complex. In 1937 he asked Crown for a closely guarded secret: the signal code between the U.S. fleet and shore batteries. Rumrich promptly telephoned an old friend from his Panama Canal days, Leipzig-born Private Erich Glaser, who was now with the Army Air Corps at Mitchel Field. Cautiously, Crown advised the twenty-seven-year-old Glaser what he needed, and a Treff was set up at the Café Hindenburg. The airman brought with him the army's top-secret Z-code, and while a band blared out German tunes, Rumrich slipped into a back room and calmly copied the document.

Glaser was rewarded by a payment of thirty dollars.

Gustav Rumrich continued to pull off dazzling espionage coups. But he never knew precisely for whom he was working. If caught, he had been instructed to say that his boss was Major Christopher Draper, c/o Plane Advertising Ltd., Bretterham House Strand—London, W.C. 2. The British army reserve officer whose name and address those actually were had no knowledge of any spy operation.[9]

The Abwehr deliberately kept Crown confused. He knew that "Sanders" was no doubt an alias, but letters to him from Sanders, who gave a post office box in Hamburg for an address, were postmarked New York. Without explanation, in October 1936 the "Sanders" letters were brought to him by couriers. A month later Rumrich was told to write to a new address: "Fräulein Gisela School, Gneisenaustrasse 26, Hamburg."

In November 1937 "Sanders" disappeared. In his place on letters sent to Crown was a new signature, "N. Spielman," who, unknown to the spy, was Dr. Pfeiffer, leader of the Bremen Abwehr nest. At the same time "N. Spielman" surfaced, Rumrich was instructed to address future letters to Jennie Wallace Jordan, No. 1 Kinloch Street, Dundee, Scotland.

Rumrich had no way of knowing that this unpretentious Scot widow of a German soldier killed in World War I would unwittingly bring about the downfall of a large portion of the Nazi spy apparatus in the United States.

8

A Bizarre
Kidnapping Plot

Just past midnight on January 28, 1938, Washington, D.C., was sleeping peacefully under a blanket of snow when the trans-Atlantic teletype in the gloomy War Department building began furiously clicking out a lengthy, coded message from London. It was late that afternoon before the transmittal was completed, decoded, and brought to the desk of Lieutenant Colonel C. M. Busbee, an intelligence officer.

Busbee was shocked by the cable. If it was true, it would mean that the United States had been penetrated by a massive Nazi espionage apparatus. The cable had been sent by the U.S. military attaché, who had seen a mass of startling evidence collected by MI-5, England's venerable secret service.

The curiosity of a postal carrier in Dundee, Scotland, had pried off the lid of the German spy apparatus in the United States. One of the mailman's patrons on Kinloch Street, fifty-one-year-old Mrs. Jennie Jordan, had relatives only in Great Britain and Germany, he knew. Yet the hairdresser received a flood of mail from all over the world—France, Holland, Canada, the United States, and countries in South America. Almost daily the Scotswoman loaded down the postal carrier with outgoing envelopes addressed to many overseas locales.

In late 1937 the mailman told superiors of his suspicions, and they reported his misgivings to postal officials in London. The information was shuttled on to the War Office in Whitehall, where MI-5 was headquartered, and wound up in the hands of Major W. E. Hinchley Cooke. Cooke launched an investigation and learned that Mrs. Jordan had made several unexplained trips to Germany in 1937.

Under a rarely invoked law in cases involving national security, British Intelligence officers were permitted to secretly open and examine citizens' mail.[1] Mrs. Jordan's mail was opened, and its contents stunned even the MI-5 operatives long steeped in cloak-and-dagger machinations. There was no doubt about it: The petite hairdresser's home was a mail-relay station for an international Nazi spy network. Incoming envelopes were addressed to Mrs. Jordan at No. 1 Kinloch, Dundee, but smaller, sealed envelopes inside were written to an N. Spielman.

Mrs. Jordan would remove the sealed envelopes for N. Spielman, insert them in other envelopes, and, using her own return address, mail them to an assortment of places and post office boxes in Germany, from where the letters would be shuttled to Dr. Pfeiffer in Bremen.

It was also clear to MI-5 that the United States was the principal overseas target of the German espionage apparatus. Many letters to N. Spielman were postmarked in New York City and bore the signature Crown.[2]

Now at the War Department in Washington, Colonel Busbee rushed the ominous message from London to his superiors, who began burning the Atlantic cable to verify its authenticity. Shortly after dawn the next morning, Busbee flew to New York and huddled with Major Joseph Dalton, G-2 of the Second Corps Area at Governor's Island. One of Dalton's functions was counterespionage, but his entire force for chasing spies in a multistate region consisted of himself and three assistants, all of whom were bogged down in routine paperwork. Dalton, a dedicated officer, was shaken by London's disclosures.

Dalton called a cab and, along with Busbee, rushed to the New York office of the FBI in Foley Square, where they conferred with G-men for long hours. A week later the FBI agents were intensely studying the intercepted letters written to N. Spielman by the Nazi agent Crown. Captain Guy Liddell of MI-5 had flown the letters and other incriminating evidence to Washington.

Crown's letters were especially alarming: He and his ring were preparing to carry out at least three devious plots. The most dangerous of these was a scheme to steal secret plans for the defense of the eastern seaboard of the United States by kidnapping—and killing, if need be—a high-ranking army officer who had access to this information.

The Nazi target at Fort Totten, New York, was Colonel Henry W. T. Eglin, commander of the 62nd Coast Artillery, an antiaircraft outfit helping to guard the nation's largest city. FBI agents quickly warned Eglin to be on guard. But only later would the G-men learn the full details of the bizarre kidnapping plot.

Rumrich's first stratagem had been to have a *femme fatale* lure the fifty-year-old Eglin to a guest room in the old McAlpin Hotel, at Broadway and 34th Street in midtown Manhattan. Once in the room with coast defense maps, charts, and plans in his possession, Eglin would be overpowered and rendered unconscious by chloroform administered by Karl Schlueter and another gang member, who would be on hand disguised as window washers. Then the *femme fatale* would grab the colonel's briefcase of secret data and rush it to Rumrich, who would be waiting in the lobby.

That scenario was abandoned when none of the conspirators could come up with a ploy for getting Colonel Eglin to bring along the wanted data, and by the fact that inquiry had shown Eglin was not the type of man who could be enticed to a rendezvous with a woman in a hotel room.

Undaunted, Rumrich and his spies concocted another scheme. A former corporal in the U.S. Army who was familiar with military terminology would write bogus orders over the signature of Major General Malin Craig, the army's chief of staff. The phony orders would direct Colonel Eglin to gather all the eastern seaboard defense information and bring it to a secret meeting at the McAlpin. Another Crown spy with a military background was to telephone Craig's orders directly to Eglin at Fort Totten.

Colonel Eglin would be instructed not to divulge the nature of the secret conference to anyone, to arrive alone promptly at 12:20 P.M. on a specified day, and to wear civilian clothes. On arrival at the hotel, Eglin was to take a seat in the main lobby and await being paged as Thomas W. Conway, after which he would identify himself by that name to an army officer (a Crown spy) in civilian clothes. The "officer" would lead Eglin into the trap, a guest room where Schlueter and the other agent would overpower the colonel and grab his secret papers.

"You are not to kill Eglin," Rumrich instructed the two accomplices, "unless absolutely necessary."

As an added devious touch to convince police that the mugging—or murder—had been pulled off by Communist agents, the strongarm men would leave their window washers' garb behind, together with a copy of the *Daily Worker*, the New York–based Communist newspaper.

When informed of the Nazi plot by the FBI, Colonel Eglin laughed it off, insisting that he would never have been taken in by the phony orders. But he agreed to play the key role of "pigeon" in a countertrap that the FBI, working with Army Intelligence, planned to spring. The G-men's counterplot called for Eglin to follow the Nazis' orders and identify himself as Thomas W. Conway to Crown's confederate in the hotel lobby, at which point FBI agents, disguised as hotel employees and as guests idling in the lobby, would nab the spies. All was in readiness for the counterplot, which would be triggered when Colonel Eglin received the phony "General Craig" telephone call from the spy ring.

But the bogus call never came. It developed that Karl Schlueter had gotten nervous over Rumrich's brazen strongarm plot, to be perpetrated in broad daylight in the center of bustling Manhattan. Schlueter had insisted that Crown write to N. Spielman in Bremen and outline the plans for the McAlpin Hotel caper. Begrudgingly, Rumrich had agreed. This had been one of the letters intercepted by MI-5 in Dundee, Scotland.

MI-5 had carefully steamed open the incriminating letters, then had resealed them and permitted them to continue on to Dr. Pfeiffer in Bremen. (MI-5 had no idea of the identity of N. Spielman, other than the obvious fact that he was a high-ranking Nazi spymaster.)

Pfeiffer exploded on learning of Rumrich's kidnap scheme. What was Crown trying to do, unmask the entire Nazi espionage apparatus in the United States? The Abwehr officer promptly fired off a cable to Schlueter in New York, ordering him to instruct Crown to abandon his grotesque melodrama.

Rumrich was depressed by the order: The badly needed thousand-dollar bonus he had been promised for delivering plans for the defense of the eastern seaboard had slipped through his fingers.

These were nerve-racking days at the FBI office in Foley Square. Suddenly the Bureau had learned that a dangerous and far-reaching Nazi espionage network was entrenched in the United States and apparently centered in New York City. And the FBI did not know the identity of a single spy. Each time the telephone rang in the New York office agents expected to get word of a spectacular Nazi espionage coup.

From the MI-5 intercepts in Scotland and by educated deduction, the G-men were able to piece together a profile of the mysterious Crown: He lived in New York City; was a man of some education; had served in the United States Army as an officer or worked for an officer; was familiar with photography; and used the hunt-and-peck system on a typewriter. Clearly, he was a man of daring and innovation. His German was fluent and he spoke American English like a native; he was married and probably had a small child. Financially, Crown was living over his head and owed a lot of money—even to the point of desperation, the FBI profile concluded.

But what was Crown's real name, and how could he be picked out from the nine million people in Greater New York?

While the FBI hoped for a break that would lead them to Crown, agents in New York pondered means for breaking up another of his plots revealed in the MI-5 intercepts. Intervention in the plot would be difficult, if not impossible, for Crown's letters to N. Spielman did not reveal full details. But it appeared that Crown was working on a scheme to obtain secret information about the huge new aircraft carriers *Yorktown* and *Enterprise* by forging President Franklin D. Roosevelt's signature onto counterfeit White House stationery.

Crown had given N. Spielman precise specifications for fifty bogus White House letterheads and envelopes. He enclosed a newspaper clipping of Roosevelt's White House letterhead that had appeared in *The New York Times* in 1937.

The forgery "order" had been mailed on January 19, 1938, and was postmarked at the Bronx Central Annex, New York. By whatever means Crown planned to carry out this White House stationery stratagem, there was a clear urgency to the request, for the masterspy had asked that his printing "order" be rushed to him by courier.

While FBI agents in Foley Square were pondering the Crown enigma, an excited G-man, waving a letter, burst into the office. "Look at this!" he called out. A bewildered young ensign, stationed on the aircraft carrier *Saratoga* at San Pedro, California, had received the strange letter and turned it over to Naval Intelligence. It read:

> You need money? You can get it easily. Put an ad in the Public Notices column of the *New York Times,* as follows: "Brownie. OK for contact. W.B."
>
> Do not inform Intelligence Service, at your peril. We are powerful and strike hard. We must see you before your transfer to the *Enterprise.*"
>
> —BROWNIE

Brownie, the FBI theorized, was Crown, and he had cooked up this latest scheme to get secret information on the *Enterprise.* Brownie's letter had been mailed at the Bronx Central Annex, New York, the same post office that Crown used to post letters to N. Spielman. FBI lab technicians went to work on the Brownie letter, but the paper was ordinary and impossible to trace. The typing was magnified a hundred times to bring out peculiarities, but that was of no value without the typewriter.

Still at a dead end in their efforts to unmask Crown, FBI agents turned to the files of Military Intelligence. Perhaps under a heading of "Spies" or "Espionage" they might detect an item that had seemed of no significance at the time but now might lead them to the elusive Nazi masterspy. Tedious digging turned up a brief entry:

> "Wilhelm Lonkowski. Suspected spy. Reported 9/25/35 by U.S. Customs and Military Intelligence."

Hopes soared. This grain of information could be the key to unlocking the German spy network. These bright expectations were quickly dashed: Lonkowski had disappeared two and half years earlier. The G-men had no way of knowing then that they had gained their first inkling about the espionage adventures of Wilhelm Lonkowski (Abwehr code name Agent Sex), who had been one of history's most prolific spies until caught red-handed—and then released—by Customs agents at New York's Pier 86, back in September 1935.

Meanwhile, the man the FBI was searching for, Guenther Rumrich, had become acutely pinched for money. About a year earlier, after accumulating a small nest egg from his Abwehr pay, Crown had brought his blond eighteen-year-old wife Guri and their small son from Montana and ensconced the family in a comfortable five-room flat in the Bronx. Now he was having a difficult time in paying the rent. So Rumrich concocted another scheme to haul in the thousand-dollar bonus that the Abwehr had promised him for pulling off another caper.

Rumrich was under the impression that Dr. Pfeiffer would pay that big bonus for fifty passport blanks, but what Pfeiffer actually wanted were *blank* passports. Passports required a personal appearance by applicants and were difficult to obtain. Passport blanks were merely forms to be used in applying for the documents and were handed out to anyone asking for them.

On February 14, 1938, Rumrich took the subway from the Bronx all the way downtown to Grand Central Station. There he entered a phone booth and placed a call to Ira F. Hoyt, chief of the New York branch of the State Department's Passport Division, located in the Sub-Treasury Building, at Wall and Pine Streets. "This is Edward Weston," Crown told Hoyt.

"Who?"

"Edward Weston, the Undersecretary of State."

"Oh, yes, Mr. Weston. I didn't know you were in New York. What can I do for you?"

Rumrich felt a twinge of uneasiness. Hoyt was pleasant and businesslike, but Crown thought he detected a trace of suspicion in the passport chief's tone. Abwehr's thousand dollars flashed before his eyes, so Crown decided to brazen it through.

In an authoritative tone Rumrich replied, "I require fifty passport blanks. Please have them delivered immediately to the Taft
Hotel. Address the package to Edward Weston. I'll be waiting in
the lobby for your messenger."[3]

Indeed Hoyt's suspicions had been aroused. He knew of no
one in the State Department named Edward Weston. And with
passport blanks available merely by walking up to a counter,
why had the caller gone to such elaborate lengths to try to obtain them? Hoyt promptly contacted the Alien Squad of the
New York Police Department and notified T. C. Fitch, a security
officer with the State Department. A dummy package for Edward Weston was prepared for delivery to the Taft Hotel.

Meanwhile, the customarily cocksure Crown had been af-
flicted by a severe case of cold feet. A sixth sense warned him
that he was about to trip himself up. So instead of going to the
Taft to pick up the passport blanks, he waited forty minutes,
then telephoned the hotel. Any package there for Edward
Weston? No, replied the Taft clerk.

Two hours after Rumrich had placed the call to the Passport
Office, he was still gripped with anxiety. No doubt the package
had arrived at the Taft by now, so he telephoned the Grand Central Station Western Union and directed that a messenger be
sent to the hotel to bring back the package to its office and hold
it for him. Then Crown took the subway to 167th Street, near
his home in the Bronx, telephoned the Western Union Office
from a corner booth, and asked if the package had been picked
up. A boy had been sent, the woman explained, but no package
had been there.

Exhausted, depressed, sick to his stomach, Crown returned
home and went to bed. He tossed and turned. Should he forget
about the passport blanks before he walked into a trap? Time
and again through a sleepless night the Abwehr's money
danced before his eyes.

During his lunch hour the next day, Crown left the Denver
Chemical firm and telephoned the Grand Central Station Western Union once more. He felt a surge of elation when a young
woman replied, "Yes, Mr. Weston, we have your package and
are holding it for you." At the same time she signaled a pair of
detectives who had been shadowing the Weston dummy package, first to the Taft, then to the Western Union office.

Again Rumrich was gripped by the strange sensation that a trap was being laid for him. So he told the woman to forward the package to the Varick Street Western Union, which was near to Denver Chemical. Then he took up a position a short distance from Varick Station Western Union to watch for the arriving messenger. But at 12:55 P.M. his lunch hour was over and he returned to work.

That afternoon Rumrich found it difficult to concentrate on his translation duties. Why hadn't the messenger brought the package to the Varick Street Western Union? He decided that the distance had been too great for the boy to have arrived by 1:00 P.M. So at 3:00 P.M. Rumrich telephoned the nearby King's Castle Tavern, where he often ate lunch, and asked the proprietress to accept a package from Edward Weston. She agreed. Then he called the Varick Street Western Union and was told that the Weston package had arrived. Rumrich ordered the package to be taken by messenger to the King's Castle Tavern.

Rumrich hurried to a drugstore directly across the street from the Western Union office and sat at the soda fountain, from where he could get a clear view outside. A few minutes later he saw a Western Union messenger leave the office with a package under his arm and head toward the King's Castle Tavern. Crown followed the boy at a discreet distance.

Rumrich saw the messenger enter the tavern, and waited. Two minutes . . . five minutes . . . ten minutes. Why didn't the boy come out? The spy glanced around nervously and felt like fleeing. But with his bonus so close at hand, Rumrich entered the dimly lit tavern, took a stool at the bar, ordered a beer, and peered casually around the crowded room. The Western Union boy was nowhere to be seen.

Beads of perspiration broke out on Crown's forehead. He sensed hostile eyes staring at him. Slowly he got to his feet and, without asking for the package, strolled out the front door. His knees felt like jelly. After walking for a short distance, he regained his composure. *He had to get that package!*

Coming upon a neighborhood boy at play, Crown said, "Son, there's a package for me at King's Castle Tavern. My name is Edward Weston. I owe the bartender money, so I can't go in there. If you pick up the package for me, I'll give you these two dollars."

The boy snatched the pair of greenbacks and trotted toward the tavern. A short time later he was back and handed the package to Rumrich. Just then two New York Alien Squad detectives rushed up, grabbed Crown, and clamped handcuffs on him. Driving downtown with their prisoner, the detectives thought that they had nabbed some two-bit con artist. They had no way of knowing that this mild-mannered young man was one of the slickest Nazi spies in the United States.[4]

9

A Nazi Canary Sings

By any yardstick, Guenther Rumrich was a cool customer. While detectives grilled him at Alien Squad headquarters, he puffed calmly on cigarettes and protested repeatedly that he knew nothing about a scheme to steal passport blanks nor had he ever heard of Edward Weston. Well, the detectives asked, if Rumrich never heard of Edward Weston, why had he taken the package for him from the neighborhood boy?

Rumrich feigned embarrassment, grinned sheepishly, and said that he was ready to "confess." He explained that he had taken the day off from Denver Chemical to "do some drinking" and in Steuben's Bar, in Times Square, had struck up a conversation with a stranger who identified himself as Edward Weston. His drinking buddy had asked him to pick up a package for him at King's Castle Tavern, Rumrich continued, and while he was accepting the bundle the detectives pounced on him.

Rumrich stuck to his story. Then Special Agents Fitch and L. Clifford Tubbs of State Department security were called in. They questioned the suspect periodically over three days. The officers didn't quite know how to treat the suspect, a pleasant, clean-cut young family man, for they had nothing significant against him. So at night Rumrich was lodged in the comfort of the Hotel New Yorker.

On February 18, the third day of the suspect's captivity, two detectives escorted him home to see his wife and child. Nothing to worry about, Rumrich assured tearful Guri. There had been a mixup and he would be released soon. While Rumrich was consoling Guri, the detectives noticed a letter addressed to Rumrich and written in German on SS *Europa* stationery. At their request, the suspect agreed to read the letter aloud in English. The letter seemed to be routine, but the detectives took it with them.

Meanwhile, a party unknown to the officers probing the case leaked to the press the fact that one Guenther Gustav Rumrich, age twenty-seven, of the Bronx, had been arrested and suspected of implication in a plot to steal passport blanks. When *The New York Times* hit the streets on the morning of February 17, the world knew that Rumrich was in police custody. However, the story was badly garbled, and the prisoner came across as some kind of nut who had hatched a half-baked plot to steal passport blanks when he could have had them by merely walking up to a counter and asking for them.[1]

Word that Crown had been grabbed by police spread like wildfire in the shadowy ranks of the Nazi spy apparatus. Untold numbers in the United States crept out of their holes and scurried off in panic. Secret papers were burned, codes destroyed, clues obscured, tracks covered. Abwehr posts in Berlin, Bremen, and Hamburg received coded radio flashes of Crown's arrest. German ships on the high seas, headed routinely for the United States, received urgent orders to fake manifests, alter courses, and drop off spies and couriers at ports where American authorities would be least likely to get to them.

Among those who heard of Guenther Rumrich for the first time when they read the *Times* account were G-men in Foley Square. Probably a small-time hood, they conjectured, but in light of the fact that they were up against a blank wall in their Nazi spy-ring probe, why not question him?

Saturday morning, February 19, two New York Alien Squad sleuths brought Rumrich to the FBI office. Handed over with the prisoner was the letter on *Europa* stationery that the detectives had found in his flat. After the city police officers departed, Rumrich was left alone in a room with FBI Agent Leon

G. Turrou, a veteran with a keen insight into criminal behavior. Turrou sat silently at his desk, staring intently into Rumrich's eyes. The prisoner had deliberately been left standing. Minutes ticked past. Still not a word from either adversary. Then the G-man saw that Rumrich's facial muscles had started to twitch. He had been standing erect, soldierly, but now he began to shift slightly from foot to foot.

Suddenly the prisoner, now visibly agitated, blurted, "Why am I here? What has the FBI got to do with passports?"

Turrou's interest in the suspect heightened. If Rumrich was afraid of the FBI, he must have some major illegal activity to conceal.

"Sit down, Guenther," the agent said evenly, nodding toward an armchair. Turrou pushed a buzzer and ordered food and coffee. While Rumrich relaxed in the comfortable seat, the two adversaries munched on sandwiches, sipped hot coffee, smoked, and engaged in seemingly idle banter. Actually, the FBI agent was subtly coercing Rumrich into telling the story of his life.

As the suspect rambled on at length, Turrou's nimble mind grew increasingly suspicious. Rumrich's background matched almost identically the profile of Nazi agent Crown that the FBI had earlier pieced together.

Now Turrou picked up the letter written in German that had been found in Rumrich's home and began reading it aloud. (Turrou spoke seven languages.) It seemed to be an innocent letter, but the sleuth noticed that the writer referred in several places to "furs," a word spies all over the globe used to denote secret plans. Turrou flipped over to a second page, and his eye dropped to the bottom. His pulse quickened. Leaping out at him was the typed signature: "*N. Spielman.*"

The G-man's mind spun. Had he stumbled onto the break of breaks in the FBI's effort to crack open the Nazi spy network? Could this mild-mannered young man seated before him be the dangerous and elusive Crown?

Turrou paused for a few minutes to collect his thoughts. Then he rose slowly from his chair, walked over to the suspect, leaned forward, and said matter-of-factly, "Guenther, you aren't the fool that you've painted yourself. I'll tell you who you are: you're a damned important Nazi spy—Crown!"[2]

It had been but a shot in the dark, but Turrou's arrow struck the target—dead center. Rumrich jumped as though he had been shocked by an electrical bolt. His eyes widened, his face turned ashen. Then he slumped down in his chair, defeated, a portrait of dejection. "All right, I'm ready to talk," he said softly.

For three nights and two days the questioning of Guenther Rumrich continued. When his formal statement was completed, it ran to some ten thousand words. At night Crown was kept in the guardhouse at Governor's Island, a secret prisoner known only as "Number 13." The FBI was taking no chances of another damaging leak to the press.

Although it had his confession, the FBI again reached a dead end. Rumrich insisted that he had been acting as a lone agent, that he knew of no other German spies or couriers operating in the United States. On February 22 Agent Turrou had him brought in. Crown, he discerned, had become worried. Apparently the spy expected a lawyer with bail to show up, somebody to arrive with money for his wife and child.

Turrou took a psychological gamble. "Well, Guenther," he said in a cynical tone, "it looks as though your fine-feathered Nazi pals have deserted you."[3]

Rumrich's eyes flashed with anger. "Yes, it does!" he replied bitterly. "That's why I want to help you smash the bastards!"[4]

Rumrich cursed for nearly a minute. Then, jaws clenched, he told about Karl Schlueter and his courier/girlfriend Jenni Hofmann, and said that they would arrive in New York aboard the *Europa* on February 24, two days away. FBI agents met the liner and checked the crew list. Out leaped the words "Karl Schlueter—steward." But hopes were dashed. Next to the name was scrawled: "Did not sail."

Indeed the Orstgruppenfuehrer had not sailed. Just as the *Europa* had been ready to depart Bremerhaven, the Abwehr received the flash about Crown's arrest. Schlueter had been yanked off the ship.[5]

Agent Turrou continued to run down the list. His pulse quickened. There were the words: "Johanna Hofmann—hairdresser." That night FBI agents concealed themselves near the *Europa* gangplank and watched. Earlier that day, through a ruse, two of them had gotten a good look at the red-haired woman, so when Hofmann came strolling down the gangplank they recognized her immediately. Despite the cold, she was wearing only her white uniform. Arms folded across her chest for warmth, Jenni paced back and forth on the pier, glancing one way and then the other. Clearly, she had a prearranged rendezvous with someone. The courier was now on United States soil, so the G-men slipped from the shadows and took Jenni into custody.

She was indignant. *"Was ist das alles?"* (What is this all about?) she demanded.

"Government officers," one replied, flashing his badge. Jenni reeled slightly and looked for a moment as though she was about to faint.

The hairdresser was taken to FBI headquarters in Foley Square. By now she had recovered her composure. In response to questions, no, she had never heard of Karl Schlueter; no, she had never heard of Guenther Rumrich. She laughed aloud at a suggestion that she was deeply involved in a Nazi espionage ring.

As the grilling wore on, Jenni Hofmann became less sure of herself. She took on a hunted look. Her face sagged and her hands trembled slightly. Had she not been the FBI's most significant clue to cracking open the German spy network, the agents would almost have felt sorry for her.

Eventually Hofmann began to reveal chinks in her protective armor. Yes, on second thought, she did know Karl Schlueter— but only as her lover. "Rumrich," her voice raised angrily, "there is no Rumrich. It is a lie, a fake. There never was such a man as Rumrich . . ."

Suddenly the door opened and in walked a solemn-faced man. Hofmann gave an audible gasp. "Hello, Jenni," Guenther Rumrich said.

The hairdresser turned pale. She slumped deeper into her chair, eyes downcast. Suddenly she looked up at the FBI agents and said, "You win. What do you want to know?"

Hofmann was not easy to break. When questioning resumed the next morning her memory had become faulty. She could not recall the names of anyone in New York with whom she had been in contact other than Rumrich.

The Feds tried a new tack. Would Hofmann tell them in detail the story of her life? Flattered, indeed she would. The woman began with her birth, and two hours later reached the point where she had met Karl Schlueter. Carried away with her own story, Jenni regaled the agents about how the Orstgruppen-fuehrer had recruited her as a courier and how important she was. Why, only a day before *Europa* had sailed on her current voyage Schlueter had given her a packet of letters to be delivered to specified New York contacts.

Jenni's recital halted abruptly. She had blundered into a damaging admission. A trace of a cynical smile bore grudging recognition of her latest defeat in this duel of wits. Jenni told the FBI men that the letters were aboard ship, under a bunk in her cabin, in a leather bag.

Asked to write a note to someone in authority on the *Europa* so the bag could be retrieved by the FBI, Hofmann shrugged her shoulders and agreed. Two hours later the leather bag was back in the Bureau's office, and the hairdresser unlocked it. She wore a smug look, even a hint of a smile. This time *she* had outwitted her adversaries, for most of the letters were written in code. No doubt Jenni rejoiced inwardly over the looks of consternation on the faces of her "tormentors."

The agents demanded that she furnish them with the key to the code. She had no key. The FBI men pleaded, begged, and cajoled. Hofmann stood her ground. Now an agent began reading one of the letters that was not in code. It was addressed to a certain Dr. Ignatz T. Griebl, 56 East 87th Street, New York City. Nothing significant there. Just a note regretting the writer's inability to see the physician. The agent laid the Griebl letter aside; it would be investigated later.

Meanwhile, an FBI man continued to poke around inside the leather bag. "Look at this!" he called out, waving a sheet of paper. It was covered with curious symbols—the key to the code. Jenni's brief triumph had turned sour. "I'll read the letters for you," she said resignedly. Without as much as glancing at the key, she rapidly translated the letters into German, which Agent Turrou spoke like a native.

All the letters were from Karl Schlueter. One was to Jenni herself, another to a Miss Kate Moog, 276 Riverside Drive, New York City. That was the first time the FBI had come across Moog's name. Schlueter's letter to her seemed innocent; it gave no hint that the Abwehr in Germany hoped to make her the Mata Hari of the spy ring and madam of an ornate espionage brothel in Washington, D.C.

A letter—with seventy U.S. dollars attached—to Guenther Rumrich was far more revealing. Schlueter prodded Crown to get the plans for the aircraft carriers *Yorktown* and *Enterprise* and reminded him of the thousand dollars the Abwehr would pay. Ironically, Schlueter told Crown to "turn over the [stolen] U.S. passports to Jenni." This misfired passport caper had caused Crown's downfall.

Confronted with the flood of incriminating evidence, Jenni Hofmann dictated and signed a German-language confession. FBI agents then put the heat on Guenther Rumrich to explain the points that Karl Schlueter had made in his letters. The now thoroughly subdued Crown implicated his Nazi stooge, Erich Glaser, the Mitchel Field private who had stolen a top-secret military code for Rumrich in return for thirty dollars.

FBI agents brought in Glaser. He had made no protest and came along quietly. A tall, rather handsome man, now twenty-nine years of age, he denied any involvement with or knowledge of a Nazi spy ring. Thirty minutes after Glaser's questioning had begun, Guenther Rumrich was brought into the room. Glaser's eyes bulged, his jaw dropped. Crown, eyes downcast, muttered softly, "I'm sorry, Erich."

In the meantime, the G-men had been intensely probing the background and activities of Dr. Griebl. Hofmann was asked about him. Her face glowed as she gushed, "Oh, Herr Doktor Griebl is a *big* man in America!"

Suspicious, Leon Turrou and two other G-men drove to Griebl's home in a block of old-fashioned but ornate flats in the heart of Yorkville. A uniformed doorman admitted the agents into the building, but a nurse in the physician's office looked at the strangers disapprovingly. The Herr Doktor was a busy man, and he had no time to see them, she declared haughtily. "Oh, he'll see us all right," Turrou replied, flashing his badge. The woman showed a trace of alarm, then disappeared into the back. A few moments later Griebl walked into the room. Behind thick glasses, his eyes looked frightened. He was pale and his jaw muscles quivered.

After identifying themselves, the G-men merely invited

Griebl to come to headquarters, explaining that they had some questions for him. The doctor did not even ask why. This curious reaction deepened FBI suspicions. Griebl was supposed to be a respectable, prominent physician, yet he offered no protest when three G-men suddenly appeared to haul him away.

At Foley Square, Dr. Griebl fended off questions with the dexterity of a hockey goalie deflecting pucks. He was composed, polite—and denied everything. He knew nothing about Nazi spies in America and doubted if there were any. He had never heard of Karl Schlueter or Guenther Rumrich or Jenni Hofmann or Erich Glaser.

"Surely you would remember Jenni," an FBI man ventured. "She's red-haired and a well-built young woman, a real looker, and she's been in your office several times." Griebl smiled and agreed that he would not have forgotten a woman with those attributes, but said that "I swear to you that no such girl ever came to my office."

An agent nodded and the door opened. In walked Jenni Hofmann. Griebl turned ashen. Facial muscles twitched. Shoulders sagged. He was totally deflated. Asked if she had ever seen this man before, the hairdresser replied softly, "Yes, that's Dr. Ignatz Griebl."

Speaking in German, Leon Turrou asked, "Jenni, is this the man from who you picked up packages of spy material for delivery to [Nazi] spy headquarters in Bremen?" She said that Griebl was the man.

Griebl grew livid. "That's a goddamned lie!" he shouted.

Jenni left the room. Griebl was still shaking with rage. Yes, he admitted, he now recalled seeing her; she had come to his office once or twice to pick up some material about Jews to take back to Germany. But he continued to deny any knowledge of a Nazi spy ring.

Since he claimed to be innocent, the FBI men stated, Griebl would surely have no objection to their searching his office. No, none at all, he replied. For an hour and a half, the Feds searched and found nothing remotely connected to spy activities. Dr. Griebl, his composure recovered, stood by calmly. The agents were about to call off the search when, in the corner of the doctor's desk, a small paper packet of matches was noticed. An agent held up the innocent-appearing packet. Griebl stiffened.

Again the color drained from his face. There were no matches in the packet, but written in red ink on the inside cover was a set of strange symbols. Agent Turrou recognized the scrawl immediately—it was the same key to the Nazi code that had been found in Jenni Hofmann's bag.

Caught red-handed, Griebl appeared to be ripe for a confession. But the quick-witted physician had rapid recuperative powers. All right, he had been lying, Griebl admitted. He did know a Karl Schlueter, a steward on the *Europa*. Schlueter, the doctor explained, had been to his office a few times to collect information on Jews in the United States. But that was all. The steward must have left behind this packet of matches inadvertently.

Griebl no doubt felt secure in implicating Schlueter, for he must have known that the Orstgruppenfuehrer had been yanked off ship after Rumrich had been arrested.

Suddenly a door was thrown open and Kate Moog raced across the room and flung herself into the arms of Dr. Griebl. Apparently she had learned that he'd been confronted by the FBI. Ignoring the federal agents, she smothered the doctor with passionate kisses, murmured endearments, and began hurling frantic questions at her pudgy boyfriend.

Griebl comforted the distraught woman. It's all a mistake, he assured her. Laughing, he explained that some stupid girl, a hairdresser on the *Europa*, had become hysterical and told the FBI that he, a prominent physician, was actually the leader of a German spy ring.

Curvaceous Kate, clad in expensive furs, whirled on the FBI men. "He's innocent, you ignorant bastards!" she shouted. "How dare you treat this great man this way!"

The hour was late. Griebl and the furious Kate Moog were ordered to be at the FBI office in Foley Square at 9:00 A.M. An agent was posted at Griebl's front door (his office was in the same building as his flat), and two other agents drove Moog home. A third FBI man kept watch at her front door.

At Foley Square the next morning Kate was turned over to a matron and FBI agents began boring in on Dr. Griebl. Calm and polite at first, Griebl wilted steadily under a barrage of charges that he could not explain plausibly. As the morning wore on, he trapped himself in a tangled web of contradictions. He became angry and confused. Perspiration popped out on his forehead. He stammered and stuttered. Finally, when he learned that the FBI knew the precise dates on which he and Moog had registered at the Taft Hotel for trysts, the Nazi masterspy broke. "All right," he said softly. "I'll talk."

And talk he did. For three hours he told the amazed FBI men about the massive Nazi spy conspiracy in the United States, going back to the arrival in Hoboken of Wilhelm Lonkowski (Agent Sex), clear back in 1927. Mesmerized, the G-men listened as Griebl related how the Nazis had penetrated nearly every major military installation in the United States, scores of defense plants, and even high-level government agencies in Washington.

Griebl, in the words of the G-men, "sang like a canary." He put the finger on two Gestapo leaders in America, Karl Herrmann and Fritz Rossberg, and on spies Otto Voss and Werner Gudenberg and a dozen others. The doctor told how the Nazis had stolen blueprints and specifications of U.S. warships, airplanes, and weapons. For the first time the FBI learned all about the Abwehr workings in the Third Reich, about Canaris and Pfeiffer and von Bonin and Menzel, and clues that led right into Adolf Hitler's inner circle.

After Griebl had talked for six days, with time off for meals, sleep, and breathing spells, large portions of the German espionage operation in the United States had been unmasked. The G-men rubbed their hands in glee. Now they had scores of clues—and all of them were hot.

10

Some "Big Fish"
Escape

Now that the Federal Bureau of Investigation had its hands on one of Adolf Hitler's masterspies in the United States, the agency had to handle him adroitly. Shrewd, egotistical Ignatz Griebl was the key to smashing the Nazi espionage network. When the doctor was treated as though he were a witness (not as a prisoner), as long as discussions were held without guards, if questions were not asked harshly, Griebl told all he knew. If these standards were violated, he would clam up and suffer an acute loss of memory.

So the FBI and the U.S. Attorney's office decided to take a calculated risk: Dr. Griebl would not be taken into custody. He was far more valuable as an all-knowing and talkative stool pigeon than he would be as a sullen—and silent—jailbird.

Griebl held no illusions: He knew that he was caught between a rock and a hard place. During one interrogation the physician suddenly halted, buried his face in his hands, and moaned, "Ach, Gott! What I am doing is signing my own death warrant in Germany!" [1]

With Griebl pointing the finger, the FBI began to round up the suspects. Karl Herrmann, the reputed Gestapo chief in New York, was one of the first targets. He lived in the flat of Margaret Simpson (not her real name), who billed herself as an actress, at 75 West 89th Street. The sleuths expected to tussle with a burly, hard-eyed bruiser, one whose image was consistent with that of the stereotyped Gestapo agent. But when collared by a G-man and told that he was being taken to headquarters for questioning, the thin, dapper Herrmann replied meekly, "Yes, sir." [2]

At Foley Square, when given a lie-detector test (results of which were not admissible as court evidence), the needle reacted violently when Herrmann swore that he was not a Gestapo agent nor involved with an espionage gang.

In the meantime, the FBI picked up Wilhelm Böning, the New York storm trooper leader, and John Baptiste Unkel, the German-American Bund officer, in New Rochelle, New York. Badly frightened, both men told all they knew about Fritz Rossberg's efforts to secure the Panama Canal fortifications plans that Unkel had boasted he possessed. Unkel denied that he had ever had such plans, although he said that Rossberg had tried to get them from him. Böning refused to admit that he had been involved in Rossberg's plot to break into Unkel's house and steal the Panama Canal materials.

On the morning of March 29, 1938, the FBI took Rossberg into custody and confronted him with Unkel's and Böning's statements implicating him in spy activities. "They're liars!" he snapped. Questioned for many hours, Rossberg repeated time and again that he was just a simple laboring man, that he knew nothing about Gestapo or Abwehr espionage in the United States. [3]

With no firm evidence on which to hold Rossberg, the FBI gave him a strict warning not to leave the city and released him for the time being.

Early the next morning, the FBI office in Foley Square received a telephone call from Rossberg's nearly hysterical wife. She demanded to know how long her husband was going to be held. That was the FBI's first inkling that the Gestapo leader had vanished. An agent promptly checked with North German Lloyd Line at Pier 86 and was told that the German liner *St. Louis* had sailed during the night. The Feds demanded that the steamship-line office radio the ship to ask if Rossberg was aboard. The inquiry was dispatched, but no reply was received. It was clear to the FBI: The Gestapo agent had fled, abandoning his young wife and child to fend for themselves as best they could.

For two weeks the U.S. Department of Justice angrily protested the German government's failure to reply. Then came a cable from the North German Lloyd Line headquarters in Bremen. It stated that one Fritz Rossberg, a German national, had been discovered as a stowaway when the *St. Louis* was halfway to Europe. But, the cable explained, he had paid for a third-class passage, so was permitted to debark at Bremerhaven, just like any other passenger.

Apparently the FBI would never know for certain if Rossberg had taken with him the fortifications plans for the Panama Canal, nor even if such plans had been in the hands of John Unkel. However, in April the FBI intercepted a letter that Rossberg had written to a friend, Ernst Ramm, who lived in Manhattan. Rossberg gloated that he had received a hero's welcome in Germany (presumably from the Gestapo) and that he was extremely proud of what he had achieved for the Nazi Party in the United States. The letter closed with: "Heil, Hitler!"

Meanwhile, Ignatz Griebl had squealed on Otto Voss, the Seversky Aircraft employee whom Wilhelm Lonkowski had recruited as a spy a decade earlier. FBI agents asked Griebl, in the words of the American underworld, to put Voss "on the spot" for them, so they could shadow Voss and probe his activities before closing in on him. Griebl agreed readily.

Griebl telephoned Voss and, on a pretext, asked him to come to his office. Two Feds were concealed in the doctor's suite when Voss arrived at 8:00 P.M. the next night. Griebl, playing his stool-pigeon role to the hilt, greeted old friend Voss with a warm handshake and called him by name for the benefit of the hidden G-men. They got a good look at their quarry: Voss was about forty years of age, gaunt, about six foot two and a bean-pole-thin 160 pounds.[4]

FBI agents trailed Voss around the clock for ten days. They looked into his bank account and discovered that, on a Seversky salary of forty-five dollars per week, he had stashed away eight thousand dollars. Moreover, Voss had bought a new car of late, paying in cash. He and his wife had taken two trips to Germany, traveling first class, during the past year, and Voss had paid heavy freight charges in order to bring along his spiffy new automobile.

On March 9 two FBI agents arrested Voss at the Seversky

plant. Taken to Foley Square, he was grilled for many hours and, squinting through silver-rimmed spectacles, denied vehemently any connection with German espionage. Spy ring? What spy ring?

That afternoon the suspect asked to drop by his home on Jericho Turnpike, Floral Park, Long Island, to explain to his wife and child why he was being held by the FBI. The Feds knew, through prior investigation, that his wife was not home during the day. So what was Voss's motive? Probably to destroy evidence, the agents concluded.

Two G-men drove the suspect home, and Voss looked concerned when the agents indicated that they would go inside with him. An innocent man would have nothing to hide, they pointed out. Voss shrugged his shoulders.

Poking around the house, the agents discovered that Voss was scrupulously methodical: hundreds of letters and bills that he had received during the past decade were neatly cataloged. A thick diary, which the Feds pocketed, contained lengthy and detailed passages going back many years.

Back at Foley Square, Voss's questioning resumed. So adamant were his denials of any knowledge of Nazi spying that the FBI men began to ponder if a mistake had been made. All they had to link Voss to espionage was Ignatz Griebl's word—and the conniving doctor was clearly dedicated to saving his own skin. Then Agent Leon Turrou picked up Voss's diary and began thumbing through it. Almost at once his pulse quickened. Folded inside the pages was a note to Voss dated three years earlier and signed by . . . *Wilhelm Lonkowski!*

Turrou, masking his elation, walked slowly across the room and confronted the suspect with the note. "All right, Voss, you've got a lot of explaining to do," the agent snapped. "We know all about Wilhelm Lonkowski, so make it easy on yourself!" Turrou had fired a shot in the dark; actually, at this point the FBI knew little about masterspy Lonkowski, other than what Griebl had told them about him.[5]

For perhaps two minutes, a pall of silence hovered over the room. Wordless, Turrou and Voss stared into each other's eyes. Finally the suspect emitted a soft sigh and said, "What is it you want to know?"

During the next few days the high-living, big-spending Otto

Voss reeled off a lengthy spiel on his life and his ten years as a German spy against his adopted homeland. He had stolen every military airplane blueprint that Seversky had. Time and again he stressed that his actions had been motivated not for money but for his love of the Fatherland. Bail for the confessed spy was set at $10,000, a sizable amount at the time. Voss's wife appeared in court with a cashier's check for the sum and gained his release.

FBI eyebrows were raised. Who had put up the $10,000? The Gestapo? The Abwehr? Home-grown Nazi sympathizers? Or had Otto Voss been raking in from his treachery even larger amounts than the Feds had surmised? Now an intense search was launched for several witnesses to testify against the Seversky employee. Mysteriously, all of them had vanished. The FBI felt that Voss would also flee, so a federal judge raised his bail to $25,000, a figure that Voss's wife could not meet, and the spy was jailed.

In the meantime, the Feds had been searching for Werner Georg Gudenberg, another spy fingered by Dr. Griebl. The doctor swore (apparently truthfully) that he had lost track of Gudenberg. Through tedious gum-shoeing, the FBI traced him to the Curtiss Aircraft plant at Buffalo. Hopes were dashed. Gudenberg had quit his foreman's job some months earlier, and Curtiss officials did not know where he had gone.

Finally Gudenberg was located at the Hall Aluminum Aircraft Company, at Bristol, Pennsylvania, and two FBI agents interviewed him from noon until 7:00 P.M. in an upstairs bedroom of his modest frame home. Gudenberg admitted that, as far back as 1928 and continuing over a period of years, he had given information and blueprints taken from various aviation plants to Wilhelm Lonkowski. But he strongly denied stealing U.S. military secrets.

Back in New York, the FBI and the U.S. Attorney's office were impressed with Werner Gudenberg's apparent frankness, cooperation, and deep remorse over what he had done. Despite having been burned badly in the Fritz Rossberg affair, the law officers decided to take another calculated risk: Gudenberg would remain free in the hope that he would lead the FBI to other Nazi agents.

Gudenberg was shadowed night and day, but he made no move toward contacting sources known to be Nazis, nor did those parties try to reach him. There seemed to be little danger that Gudenberg would flee. He had a good-paying job, clearly loved his pretty wife and young child, and made no effort to withdraw his $700 balance from the bank. Gradually surveillance of the suspect was diminished, then dropped. FBI manpower was limited, and the agency had bigger fish to fry.

One of these "fish" was a mysterious figure named Karl Weigand, who had been fingered by Guenther Rumrich. All Rumrich knew was that Weigand was a big shot in the sinister world of Nazi espionage and that he made regular trips from Germany to New York. Evidence was uncovered that Weigand had even posed for photographs with Hans Dieckhoff, who had been Hitler's ambassador to the United States.[6]

Rumrich did not know which ships Weigand traveled on, so FBI men searched passenger lists and manifests of each arriving German vessel. No Karl Weigand was listed. Then the Feds turned to their prize stool pigeon, Ignatz Griebl, who seemed sincerely puzzled. Even he had never heard of Weigand. Then find out who he is, Griebl was ordered.

Two days later Griebl contacted the FBI, presumably after making inquiries around Yorkville. Karl Weigand was a phony name, Griebl reported. His real name was Theodor Schütz, and he was the Orstgruppenfuehrer on the *New York* and one of the most trusted operatives in Ast X at Hamburg. The physician even provided a description of Schütz: middle-aged, medium height, with sharp, lined facial features.

Late in April 1938 the *New York* arrived at Pier 86. FBI agents waiting at the dock boarded the liner and inspected her manifest. They found the words "Theodor Schütz, steward," and alongside was the notation: "Signed off at Havana, Cuba."

Havana, Cuba? Why would a passenger vessel sailing between New York and Germany alter its course to Cuba? Clearly, the Nazi espionage grapevine had been functioning, and the Abwehr in Germany had gotten word that Karl Weigand, alias Theodor Schütz, was going to be met in New York by agents of the FBI.

The Feds were furious over the leak. One by one the big Nazi fish were wiggling off the FBI's hook. First the Gestapo kingpin Fritz Rossberg had fled, then Karl Schlueter had eluded the FBI dragnet, as had several smaller minnows. Now Schütz.

Commodore Fritz Kruse, the *New York's* skipper, was confronted in his richly appointed cabin by the angry G-men, who demanded to know why the ship had made the side trip to Havana. A heated squabble erupted. Kruse bellowed that where his vessel went was none of the FBI's business.

"Well, we're making it our business!" a Fed snapped. Kruse was reminded that he was now in the United States, and, since a criminal action was being investigated, he could be hauled off the ship and taken to FBI headquarters for questioning. That threat did the trick. Kruse showed the Feds a copy of his order: "Steward Schütz to be signed off at Havana, and to return immediately to Germany without touching the United States . . ."

Investigation revealed that Schütz had been put up in Havana's most luxurious hotel—courtesy of Hitler's treasury—and that he would take the ship *Memel* to Germany in a few days. The FBI prepared to fly an agent to Havana to bring Schütz back but was overruled by high levels in Washington who didn't want to create an international incident.

In the meantime, the Abwehr chiefs in Germany had apparently become nervous. Schütz did not wait for the *Memel*, but instead grabbed a tramp steamer bound for Vera Cruz, Mexico, and from there took another ship to Germany.

For a month after the G-men had clashed with Commodore Kruse aboard the *New York*, they had been prodding Captain Drechsel at the Hudson River German Lines' port office to produce from the Third Reich an explanation of why Schütz had been dumped in Havana. Finally Drechsel received a letter from his home office: Karl Weigand had been taken to Cuba because the German government suspected him of smuggling currency out of the Third Reich, so he was brought home for prosecution. One fact was conveniently overlooked: Schütz could have been more easily put on a liner for Germany from New York City, without the added cost of sidetracking the SS *New York* to Havana.

At 6:00 A.M. on May 11, 1938, FBI Agent Leon Turrou was deeply asleep in his New York hotel room. His telephone jangled impatiently. Picking up the receiver, Turrou heard a hysterical, high-pitched voice: "Oh, Mr. Turrou, something terrible has happened. Ignatz—Dr. Griebl—has disappeared!"

It was a tearful Kate Moog. "Do something, do something!" she pleaded. "He's been kidnapped! They're taking him to Germany! He'll be killed!"

Now fully awake, Turrou leaped from bed, and in less than an hour FBI agents were checking into the activities of their ace stool pigeon. Dr. Griebl's schedule for that day listed fifteen patients and two surgeries. He had not withdrawn funds from his hefty bank account and had given no signs of fleeing. These factors caused the Feds to lean toward the initial theory that a Nazi hit squad may have abducted—or murdered—Griebl.

Later that morning FBI men interviewed the doctor's tearful wife, Mitzi. Disheveled, bleached-blond hair in tangles, she related events of the previous night.

Just prior to 9:00 P.M., Dr. Griebl invited her to ride along with him to see a patient in Greenwich Village. She was thrilled over his unexpected attentiveness. Outside the patient's flat, Mrs. Griebl waited in the late-model luxury car. When her husband came out, he drove toward Pier 86 on the Hudson River.

A full moon was splashing iridescence on the waterfront, and two German liners, the *Hansa* and the *Bremen*, could be seen tied up at the dock. The *Bremen* was aglow with lights, for she was to sail in two hours. Griebl parked near the pier, told his wife that he had an appointment on the *Bremen* and would be back "real soon." It was then 10:30 P.M.

Mrs. Griebl waited. And she waited some more. Midnight came, and still no husband. Cries of "All visitors ashore!" rang out. Now the huge vessel drifted away from the pier. Ignatz Griebl was nowhere to be seen. Panic-stricken and distraught, Mitzi leaped from the car and dashed around the dock. She inquired at the *Hansa*, but no one had seen her husband.

Mitzi could not drive, so she telephoned the New Niagara Garage, 1832 Second Avenue, and asked that a man be sent to drive her home. When she reached her ornate apartment, her mood changed from fear to one of suspicion. She grew furious. Ignatz, the philanderer, had slipped out of another *Bremen* exit and at that very moment was holding a tryst with Kate Moog, she concluded.

Just past 3:00 A.M. Mrs. Griebl telephoned her romantic rival, bitterly accusing Kate of harboring Ignatz in her bedroom. Moog denied the charge so vigorously and sobbed so hysterically over her boyfriend's plight that Mitzi felt she was telling the truth. Each woman was now convinced that Griebl had been lured aboard the *Bremen* on some pretext, had been overpowered, and was bound for Germany to face Nazi vengeance for "singing" so loudly to the FBI.

Either through hysteria or due to some sinister design, Mitzi Griebl had spun a tale that was full of holes, the Feds concluded. Those discrepancies could be probed later.

In the meantime, the FBI men at Foley Square went into action to try to get Dr. Griebl back. An inquiry revealed that the *Bremen* was now two hundred miles at sea, so Captain Drechsel at Pier 86 was asked to radiotelephone the ship to find out if the doctor was aboard. Two hours later Captain Adolf Ahrens, the *Bremen's* skipper, replied: A man who identified himself as Dr. Ignatz Theodor Griebl was aboard—as a stowaway.

Assistant U.S. Attorney Lester C. Dunigan quickly contacted the Coast Guard, and a seaplane was warmed up. Dunigan and an FBI agent were preparing to fly out to sea, overhaul the *Bremen*, arrest Griebl, and bring him back to New York. But first the Feds fired off a radio dispatch to the ship, asking if Captain Ahrens would surrender the fugitive.

Ahrens did not answer for over an hour. Apparently he was awaiting instructions from the *Bremen's* Orstgruppenfuehrer, who would have to contact Ast X in Hamburg. Finally, an evasive reply came from the *Bremen:* The weather was foul, visibility was poor, and a seaplane trip would be exceedingly hazardous. In New York, the federal men were deeply touched by Ahrens's concern for their well-being, but they radioed back that they were coming after Griebl anyhow.

An hour later Captain Ahrens replied that he would have to halt the *Bremen* and lower a boat to put Griebl off, that the 1,300 passengers would panic, and he refused to take responsibility for any disaster that might ensue. Ast X won that round. Washington canceled the seaplane flight.

But the FBI was not giving up the fight. It dispatched another signal to the *Bremen* "ordering" Ahrens to surrender Griebl to "the proper authorities" at Cherbourg, France, the ship's first stop. The FBI then contacted the State Department, which fired off a cable to Paris, requesting U.S. Ambassador William Bullitt to arrange with the French officials to arrest Griebl at Cherbourg.

The French agreed, and the *Bremen* was notified. However, a few hours later Captain Ahrens received a message from his Hamburg office: The German government had issued strict orders that Griebl was not to be put off at Cherbourg, nor would he be permitted to leave the ship until she had reached a German port.

Another big Nazi fish had wiggled off the FBI's hook. But others would not be so lucky.

11

A Dramatic Gesture to Awaken America

Early in May 1938 banner headlines across the United States told the story: U.S. Attorney Lamar Hardy in New York had impaneled a grand jury to hear secret testimony about a Nazi spy conspiracy. An early witness would be Werner Gudenberg, the Hall Aluminum Aircraft employee who had admitted passing along aircraft information to Wilhelm Lonkowski for many years.

On the afternoon of May 25, Gudenberg bid good-bye to his wife and child at their home in Bristol, Pennsylvania, told them that he would return in a few days, and left for New York City. Testifying the next day at the Federal Building, Gudenberg was frank and cooperative. In the words of the American underworld, he "spilled the beans."

Early the following morning Captain William Drechsel, superintendent of the German Lines office in New York, arrived in a breathless state at a grand jury anteroom. Waving a cablegram, Drechsel reminded FBI agents that they had requested him to provide prompt notice of stowaways. "Well, look at this message I just received from Captain Koch on the *Hamburg*, which sailed last midnight," Drechsel exclaimed.

A G-man grabbed the cable. It said that a stowaway had been found aboard the *Hamburg*, and his name was—*Werner Georg Gudenberg!*

The FBI men were stunned and angry. So was U.S. Attorney Hardy. They huddled and concluded that Gudenberg had met with foul play. If he had planned to flee, thereby deserting the wife and child he loved so dearly, why would he have testified voluntarily before the grand jury? The Feds theorized that Abwehr or Gestapo agents had been watching the Federal Building, and when Gudenberg emerged they accosted him and forced him to admit that he had testified. Then the accosters, through force or threats of violence to his wife and child, had strongarmed Gudenberg aboard the *Hamburg*—whose skipper conveniently looked the other way.

Both Hardy and the FBI had grown frustrated over the flight of key figures and witnesses in the Nazi spy apparatus. They were furious that Adolf Hitler's hatchet men had grown so bold and defiant that they had actually kidnapped a star U.S. government witness almost from the very steps of a courthouse in broad daylight.

Hardy grabbed a telephone and put in a call to the Justice Department in Washington. Justice in turn contacted the State Department with Hardy's dire warning: Hitler's regime was conniving in the disappearance of witnesses and suspects. Consequently, State gave Hardy the green light to take whatever steps were deemed to be prudent to get Werner Gudenberg off the SS *Hamburg*.

By trans-Atlantic telephone, Hardy explained the Gudenberg kidnapping to Ambassador Bullitt in Paris. Bullitt contacted French officials and received assurance that Gudenberg would be taken off the *Hamburg* at Cherbourg. A call to Ambassador Joseph P. Kennedy, Sr., in London, resulted in the same arrangement with British authorities if the *Hamburg* were to reach Southampton first.

However, the Hitler regime had other ideas. When the *Hamburg* arrived at Cherbourg, waiting French police were told that Gudenberg was too sick to talk or even to be carried from the ship on a stretcher. At Southampton, the next port of call, he was still too ill to be moved, the vessel's skipper declared. So Werner Gudenberg sailed on to Germany to face an unknown fate.

Meanwhile, FBI agents had been investigating Mrs. Mitzi Griebl's tale of the mysterious circumstances surrounding her husband's disappearance. They became convinced that she had been lying, that Mrs. Griebl, despite her bitter hatred of Kate Moog, had connived with her husband's girlfriend to cover up the fact that Ignatz Griebl had not been kidnapped but fled on his own volition.

A few weeks after Griebl vanished, FBI suspicions heightened when the two love rivals independently contacted Foley Square to tell of a letter that each woman had received from Griebl. The letters, one to "My Dearest Mitzi" and the other to "My Dearest Kate," were almost identical. Poor Ignatz wailed about the "indignities and hardships" that were being inflicted upon him in Germany. The Nazis had forbidden him to communicate with anyone and had taken away his Medical Association card, pistol permit, and driving license, he moaned.

What was behind this ploy? the FBI wondered. Clearly, Griebl, with the probable connivance of the Abwehr, had intended for the Feds to see these two letters. If the Nazis were preventing him from communicating with anyone, as Griebl claimed, how had he managed to mail letters from Germany to his wife and girlfriend?

Only much later would the Feds learn that the glib and cagey Ignatz Griebl had talked his way back into the good graces of the Hitler regime, apparently by convincing his Abwehr masters that he had outwitted the FBI, and demonstrated his loyalty to the fuehrer by fleeing when the federal sleuths were ready to arrest him. A few weeks after Griebl's arrival in the Third Reich, he was practicing medicine and prospering.

Meanwhile the FBI put a tail on Mrs. Griebl. In early June 1938 it was learned that she had shipped a trunk to her husband, and a few days later the tail caught her and her friends red-handed trying to ship Griebl's new luxury automobile to him. And finally Mitzi was detected buying a ticket on the *Bremen* to sail to Germany on June 14.

Before she could flee, Mrs. Griebl was taken into custody as a material witness. But hardly was she behind bars than Nazi adherents in the United States, along with self-appointed civil liberties groups, began shrieking to the high heavens that this poor, unfortunate housewife was being persecuted. Outpourings of sympathy for her plight grew more strident when Mrs. Griebl announced to the press that she was ill. Later she was released on $5,000 bail and permitted to take the *Bremen* to Germany.

The Feds were being thwarted at every turn. Adolf Hitler appeared to be winning this covert duel of wits in the United States. FBI morale hit bottom. But Lamar Hardy, a hard-hitting prosecutor, pumped new life into the Nazi spy conspiracy investigation. He hurried to Washington, huddled with Administration and Justice Department officials, and pleaded for more action against the Nazi spy apparatus.

"The important point is that the American public must be made aware of the existence of this [Nazi] spy plot, and impressed with its dangers," Hardy stressed. "Our government and citizens must be awakened!" [1]

On June 20, 1938, the Justice Department dropped a bombshell. The federal grand jury in New York indicted eighteen persons on charges of conspiring to steal United States military secrets. The mass indictment was a largely a dramatic gesture to show the world how outraged the United States was over the Nazi espionage invasion. Only four of those charged were in FBI custody: Jenni Hofmann, Erich Glaser, Otto Voss, and Guenther Rumrich. All but one of the others were either espionage bigwigs in the Third Reich or spies who had fled from the United States. Named in the indictment were: Commander Udo von Bonin; Commander Dr. Erich Pfeiffer; Commander Hermann Menzel; *Kapitaen* Ernst Mueller; "Sanders," first name unknown (who was actually Mueller); all of the Marine Nachrichten Stelle, in Hamburg; "Schmidt," first name and headquarters unknown; Karl Eitel, Germany; Herbert Jänichen, Germany; Theodor Schütz (alias Karl Weigand), Germany; Karl Schlueter, Germany; Wilhelm Lonkowski (seven aliases), Air Ministry, Berlin; Dr. Ignatz Griebl, fugitive in Germany; Werner Gudenberg, escapee to Germany; and Mrs. Jennie Jordan, Scotland, serving four years in a British prison.

Meanwhile, across the Atlantic, on March 13, 1938, Adolf Hitler had sent his booted legions plunging into Austria, and that tiny nation was gobbled up without a shot being fired. The fuehrer called it an *Anschluss* (annexation). Austrian Nazi leader Dr. Arthur Seyss-Inquart was appointed by the fuehrer to be the puppet chancellor, and Austria became a part of *Grossdeutschland* (Greater Germany).[2]

Later that same month eighteen journalists, who worked for legitimate United States newspapers and magazines, were invited to the Austrian Embassy in Washington—all expenses paid. All were American citizens of German ancestry; none knew that he had been selected after a careful study of his background. None had been told in advance of the reason for the invitation: an offer of a high-paying job on a chain of Nazi newspapers that would be published in eleven cities in the United States.

The journalists were incensed. They guessed rightly that the Third Reich's treasury would be behind this project, which was designed to generate Nazi propaganda across America. Not a single newsman accepted the offer.[3]

The grandiose Nazi newspaper-chain scheme was the brainchild of Dr. Ernst Böhle, the young, widely traveled intellectual who was head of the Deutsches Ausland Institut (German Overseas Institute) in Berlin. Böhle's function was to "Nazify" all persons of German descent who lived outside the Third Reich —primarily the 30 million Americans who had German blood in their veins. At Stuttgart in the summer of 1937, the mild-mannered, bespectacled Böhle had told the Nazi-created Congress of Germans Living Abroad: "The complete German who is a citizen [of another country] is always a German and nothing but a German."

Under Böhle's guidance were two official Third Reich organizations, *Welt-Dienst* (World Service), located at 4 Daberstedterstrasse, Erfurt, and *Deutscher Fichte-Bund* (German Fighters Society), whose headquarters was in Hamburg. Their purpose was to supply American propaganda saboteurs with tons of anti-Jewish and other disruptive materials designed to incite racial clashes and open rebellion. Shipped to the New World in unmarked crates, the pamphlets, tracts, and flyers were distributed by hundreds of Nazi adherents.

A typical eager Nazi propaganda spear-carrier in the United States was Swedish-born Olov E. Tietzow, whose passion was to promote his brand of "Americanism" through the credo: "Unite Under the Swastika—Symbol of Loyalty to American

Ideals." Tietzow was fuehrer of The American Guard, a "White Man's Party." He had written that "as far as the Fathers of the Republic are concerned, they are nothing but Masonic monkeys." Presumably, President Franklin Roosevelt was considered to be the chief monkey.[4]

Pro-American

THE AMERICAN GUARD

Freedom   Justice

"THE WHITE MAN'S PARTY"

UNITE UNDER THE SWASTIKA
SYMBOL OF LOYALTY TO AMERICAN IDEALS

A naturalized American, Tietzow was sort of a traveling medicine-show huckster, dispensing Nazi snake oil. A tireless missionary, he deluged the country with Nazi pamphlets, each headed with a design showing an American eagle clutching a swastika. At one time he had written: "The coming struggle here in America will be fought, not with ballots, but with bullets . . ."[5]

Within two years Tietzow had operated out of bases in Minneapolis, Chicago, Boston, Buffalo, New York, Charleston (West Virginia), and most recently in Pittsburgh. Not all of his pamphlets came from the printing mills of the Third Reich: He confided to associates that Fritz Kuhn's German-American Bund had provided him with "pretty good money" to pay for printing his own materials.[6]

Across the Atlantic in early September 1938, the German warlord was again rattling his saber. This time Hitler made known his intention to take over the Sudetenland, a portion of Czechoslovakia peopled by two million ethnic Germans. With war clouds hanging over Europe, Prime Ministers Neville Chamberlain of England and Edouard Daladier of France pleaded with the fuehrer to meet with them in Munich on September 28 to negotiate his proposed takeover.

In the United States H. V. Kaltenborn, perhaps the nation's most popular radio commentator, conducted a marathon newscast over CBS while the crucial Munich pow-wow was in progress. Speaking in his nasal twang, Kaltenborn assured his millions of anxious listeners: "I am convinced that Neville Chamberlain will not come away from Munich empty-handed."[7]

Indeed the mild-mannered, umbrella-toting Chamberlain did not return to London empty-handed: He came waving a worthless scrap of paper that Hitler had signed. In what came to be known as the Munich Pact, the fuehrer swore that he had no further territorial claims in Europe, so the French and British sold out Czechoslovakia by pledging to stand by idly while Hitler grabbed off the Sudetenland.

Grinning broadly at the London airport, the angular Chamberlain told reporters, "This guarantees peace in our time!"

Meanwhile, tensions had increased between the governments of the United States and Germany. In late 1938, in a gesture of mutual distrust and thinly veiled hostility, President Franklin Roosevelt and Fuehrer Adolf Hitler both recalled their ambassadors, leaving the embassies in Washington and Berlin in care of *chargé d'affaires*.

That exchange of diplomatic slaps would prove to be a boon to German espionage in the United States. The recalled ambassador, Dr. Hans Dieckhoff, had been at his post in Washington for a year but had never been able to make up his mind if he wanted to become a dyed-in-the-wool Nazi. So espionage machinations had been minimal at the ugly brick building on Massachusetts Avenue that housed Hitler's embassy.

With Dieckhoff's departure, chargé d'affaires Dr. Hans Thomsen, an ambitious, gung-ho Nazi, converted the German Embassy into a hotbed of intrigue, a base for extracting United States secrets from the high and the mighty in Washington, New York, and elsewhere.

At the United States Courthouse in New York City on October 14, 1938, security was intense as the trial opened for the eighteen persons (fourteen of them *in absentia*) charged with a con-

spiracy to steal U.S. military secrets. Presiding was Federal
Judge John C. Knox, a tall, graying jurist with a reputation for
scrupulous fairness.

Guenther Rumrich (Agent Crown) pleaded guilty, then took
the witness stand and for three days reeled off the intricate tale
of the Nazi spy apparatus in America as he knew it. Henry C.
Dix, the attorney representing Jenni Hofmann, tore into Rumrich, charging that he was a Communist and that he had conspired with the FBI to concoct the false story he had told from
the stand.

Next Dix introduced a lengthy deposition (more than seventeen thousand words) that he had taken from Dr. Ignatz Griebl
in Germany several weeks earlier. In his written testimony,
Griebl blasted FBI agent Leon Turrou, who had played a key
role in unmasking the Nazy spy operation in the United States.
Turrou, Griebl declared, was a radical and a crook, an unprincipled scoundrel who had tipped off Griebl that it was time to
flee and had accepted a $5,000 bribe from the physician to aid
in his escape. Griebl swore that the flood of incriminating statements he had made to the FBI were lies, designed to mislead
the investigators.

The trial droned on for weeks. Scores of U.S. government witnesses took the stand, mainly FBI agents, stenographers, and
others who had heard and observed various confessions made
by the defendants. Finally the trial concluded. In his charge
to the jury, Judge Knox leaned over backward to be fair. He ordered the panel, at least two of whom were German-born, to
disregard the nationality of the accused and to give them consideration equal to that of American citizens. On November 29
the jury retired to deliberate.

All through the trial, a melodrama with comic-opera over-
tones had been unfolding. Each day the courtroom was packed
with spectators, and among them were eight or nine Nazi spies.
FBI agents were also in the audience, and they knew who the
spies were. So did Judge Knox (as he would later tell the media). Two of the Nazi agents sat at the press table, masquerading
as foreign correspondents. All of the spies scribbled notes
furiously.

There were always far more spectators shoving and pushing
to get into the courtroom each morning than there was space for

them. It was a case of first come, first served. So the Nazi spies got in line each day two hours before the courtroom doors opened. All day the poor devils did not get a chance to eat or to heed the call of nature, for fear that they would have to report to their masters that they had lost their seats. Each time a recess was called, the Nazi agents would leave the courtroom with the rest of the spectators so as not to focus attention upon themselves, then immediately took up places at the head of the line so they would be the first to get in again.

The four defendants were found guilty, and, on December 2, they stood before a solemn Judge Knox for sentencing. Jenni Hofmann was sobbing softly into a handkerchief. A pall of silence flooded the chamber.

"Had these defendants been apprehended [spying] in Germany, their fate would have been much more fearful," Judge Knox said in handing down the sentences: Jenni Hofmann, four years in prison; Otto Voss, six years; Erich Glaser, two years; and Guenther Rumrich, whose cooperation with the government was taken into consideration, two years.[8]

Each spy could have received twenty years. However, U.S. Attorney Lamar Hardy was satisfied, telling the press: "The convictions are a condemnation of the German espionage system, directed by high officials in Germany. They serve as a warning to any nation engaged in or contemplating such activities in the United States."[9]

Despite the lofty phraseology, Hardy and the FBI knew that they had only scratched the surface. The prosecutor's remarks were intended to awaken the nation to the perils it faced from the ominous Nazi spy penetration.[10]

America yawned.

In Berlin, Abwehr chief Wilhelm Canaris shrugged off the spy-trial hullabaloo. He merely tightened security and continued to infiltrate agents into the United States. However, a scapegoat was required for the worldwide flood of negative publicity for the New Germany. That scapegoat was Dr. Erich Pfeiffer, chief of the Bremen nest of Ast X.

For more than three years Pfeiffer had been showered with

praise by Canaris and other Nazi bigwigs for the intelligence bonanza his spy rings had been reaping in the United States. Now he was booted out of his job and given only menial tasks in which he would, Canaris said, "be unlikely to do any more harm." [11]

PART TWO

A Floodtide
of Espionage

12

Fritz and Her Serene Highness

On the gray morning of March 4, 1939, a horde of American newspaper reporters and photographers swarmed aboard the SS *Hamburg*, just berthed in New York harbor, and jostled for position around a husky, lantern-jawed German diplomat, Captain Fritz Wiedemann. Debonair and articulate, Wiedemann was a widely known figure in the Third Reich and in embassies of the world. He had been infantry corporal Adolf Hitler's company commander in World War I (hence the captain title), and since the Nazis had come to power the forty-six-year-old Wiedemann had been a confidant of and troubleshooter for the fuehrer.

Wiedemann would replace Baron Manfred von Killinger, who had been in the United States since 1937. Killinger had been one of Hitler's storm trooper chiefs during the Nazis' long struggle to seize national power, but that close tie did not prevent authorities in the Third Reich from putting him on trial for the murder of a Catholic clergyman, Matthias Erzberger. Killinger was sentenced to eight months, for the record, but never served a day of the term.[1]

From his San Francisco base, Killinger had been so flagrant in organizing units of the German-American Bund and engaging in other machinations on the West Coast that his subversive actions had been unmasked by the media. Headlines splashed across the United States were so embarrassing to the Hitler regime that Killinger was called home hastily.

Now, on an open-air deck of the *Hamburg*, Captain Wiedemann was bombarded with questions, most of them concerning the reason why Hitler had sent him to the United States. Aware of the hostile climate toward Nazism in America and the black eye given the New Germany as the result of the recent conviction of the four German spies in New York, the new consul general replied evenly, "My only intention and wish is to act as an intermediary in creating goodwill between our two countries."[2]

The Federal Bureau of Investigation doubted that Fritz Wiedemann had come as a goodwill emissary. Earlier, J. Edgar Hoover, in Washington, had received a warning relayed from Brussels by way of the U.S. State Department, quoting a "source close to the fuehrer." The source said that Wiedemann's mission was to organize pro-Nazi and anti-Jewish propaganda operations in the United States and to convert the San Francisco consulate into a hotbed of espionage.

The ample ground for FBI suspicions resulted in a handful of Hoover's men in disguise being on the *Hamburg* to greet Wiedemann. It seemed odd indeed that Hitler would appoint one of his principal confidants to so modest a post as consul general in San Francisco. FBI misgivings were heightened when the Justice Department received another report from a secret source that declared Wiedemann's true role would be that of another Franz von Papen, the Kaiser's notorious (to the Americans) spy who masterminded an extensive German espionage and sabotage network in the United States just prior to America's entry into World War I.

Since late 1938 rumors had been rampant in European centers of international intrigue that the suave Fritz Wiedemann had played a key behind-the-scenes role in helping the fuehrer secure the Munich Pact, one of Hitler's greatest diplomatic triumphs. Wiedemann had indeed contributed handsomely to that coup, teaming with a clever, scheming socialite whose original name had been Stefanie Richter—Steffi to her friends.

Daughter of a Viennese lawyer, red-haired Steffi had married Prince Friedrich Francois Augustin Marie Hohenlohe-Waldenburg, an officer in the Austrian army at the time. Although Stefanie and the prince were divorced in 1920 (she charged adultery), she retained her royal title and encouraged people to address her as Her Serene Highness.

Over the years, Stefanie became a familiar figure flitting about the capitals of Europe, entertaining lavishly and living the high life. Her Nazi sympathies had become well known, and she was enthralled on being introduced to Adolf Hitler, a bachelor with a gift for charming women. Through the fuehrer, the princess met the dashing Captain Fritz Wiedemann.

A recurring topic of gossip in the social whirl of Europe had been conjecture over where Steffi obtained the money to support her extravagant lifestyle. Early in 1939 that mystery was solved. Stefanie filed suit in London against the prominent Lord Rothermere, claiming that the wealthy British publisher had reneged on a 1932 contract in which he agreed to pay her twenty thousand dollars a year for life. Her duties were vague. She claimed that her role was that of Lord Rothermere's personal "ambassadress" to Adolf Hitler and to other heads of state in Europe.

On the stand, Rothermere admitted that he had actually paid Her Serene Highness an even higher figure. But his lawyer argued that Stefanie was engaging in blackmail by filing the suit, and the presiding judge appeared to agree. He ruled that there was no legal evidence that Rothermere had signed a lifetime contract.

Exhibits submitted by the defense attorney during the trial included a letter written by Fritz Wiedemann to Lord Rothermere on behalf of Adolf Hitler. Wiedemann said that he was expressing the fuehrer's delight for Her Serene Highness's kindness in introducing Lord Rothermere to him (Hitler). Wiedemann added that (in Hitler's opinion) "it was her groundwork which made possible the Munich agreement." [3]

Princess Stefanie's role in the Munich coup had originated in June 1938, when she had been invited by General Hermann Goering to his medieval castle, Karin Hall. During a lengthy conversation the corpulent Luftwaffe chief told the socialite of his pet scheme for easing mounting tensions in Europe: He himself would work secretly to gain British concessions advantageous to the Third Reich.

Goering outlined his plot. He would slip covertly into London and confer with the British foreign secretary, Lord Halifax.

The meeting would have to be arranged with a great deal of finesse, for Hitler's foreign minister, Joachim von Ribbentrop, would have to be kept in the dark. He could not learn that the Luftwaffe commander was injecting himself into the realm of foreign policy.

Ribbentrop was an archrival of Goering's and had clawed his way up the Nazi totem pole to his present lofty post through ruthless double dealings. Abrasive and outspoken, Ribbentrop was hated by almost all the other bigwigs around the fuehrer.

What was needed, Goering explained to Princess Stefanie, was someone to make discreet contact with Lord Halifax and arrange for Goering's visit. Numerous names were discussed before the two connivers settled on the ideal candidate—Fritz Wiedemann.

When approached by Her Serene Highness, Wiedemann was horrified. Go to London behind Ribbentrop's back—behind *Der Fuehrer's* back? Stefanie was persistent. Finally Wiedemann agreed to ask Hitler for approval, and, surprisingly—to Wiedemann at least—the fuehrer gave him the green light.

An enthusiastic Princess Stefanie promptly hopped the English Channel and, through her high-level social connections, obtained an audience with Lord Halifax. The foreign secretary agreed to meet secretly with Goering's emissary Wiedemann, and a few days later the two men held a long private discussion. Her Serene Highness was not present, but Hitler's old company commander told her later that the conference was "quite successful."

Then, before Hermann Goering could sneak incognito into England to see Lord Halifax and wring concessions from him to avoid war in Europe, all hell broke loose in Berlin. A furious Ribbentrop had gotten wind of Goering's plot, and he rushed to the Reich Chancellory and got Hitler to squash any future negotiations with Lord Halifax by Wiedemann or Goering.

Discussions over war and peace would be held with the British (and the French) a few weeks later at Munich, and it would be the ambitious Joachim von Ribbentrop who would be at Hitler's elbow, helping to obtain the "peace pact" that was destined to alter the course of history. But it had been Fritz Wiedemann and Her Serene Highness who had paved the way for the fuehrer's resounding diplomatic triumph by deducing from the Halifax talks that England was dealing from weakness and prepared to concede almost anything for peace in Europe.[4]

Now, in March 1939, Captain Wiedemann left New York by train for his new post in San Francisco. From the time that the diplomat had met with reporters on the *Hamburg*, FBI agents would shadow him around the clock.

Wiedemann's train had hardly pulled out of Grand Central Station than J. Edgar Hoover was handed another secret report from a clandestine source: Fritz Wiedemann's teammate, Princess Stefanie, would soon rejoin him in the United States. As predicted, Her Serene Highness arrived in New York in mid-May, and was tailed by the Feds from the moment she set foot on American soil.

Stefanie, garbed in expensive furs, took a train westward, and on May 29 FBI agents watched her stroll into a restaurant in Fresno, California. Minutes later she was greeted affectionately by a handsome, graying man whom the sleuths recognized as Captain Fritz Wiedemann.

Early the next morning Wiedemann and the princess climbed into an automobile and, along with their shadows, drove to Sequoia National Park. After an overnight stop, the two Germans motored on to Hillsborough, a San Francisco suburb, where Stefanie became the house guest of Consul General and Mrs. Wiedemann.

It was soon possible to drop the shadows, for the FBI developed "other sources" that gave a play-by-play account of Wiedemann's and Stefanie's daily activities.[5]

Meanwhile, on March 16, 1939, a group of New York business and professional men met at the Lexington Hotel and founded the American Fellowship Forum. Its stated purpose was to focus public attention on solutions to domestic social and economic problems. Appointed to be national director of the forum was a tall, well-groomed former professor of German literature at Columbia University, Dr. Friedrich Ernest Auhagen.

Dr. Auhagen was a paid Nazi agent. A former lieutenant in the Kaiser's army, he had come to America in 1923 and, after Hitler gained power, became employed by the German secret service. Auhagen's advanced degrees in economics and engineering allowed him to secure teaching jobs at prominent American universities—an ideal "cover" for his covert work.

Auhagen may have loved the Fatherland, but he was infatuated with Uncle Sam's greenbacks as well. He raked in regular sums of money from Dr. G. Kurt Johannsen, a Nazi paymaster in Hamburg, and substantial payments came from a wealthy American industrialist, Dr. Ferdinand A. Kertess, president of the Chemical Marketing Company of New York City.[6]

Headquarters of the American Fellowship Forum were established in New York City, and in June the group began publishing a slick magazine called *Today's Challenge*. Dr. Auhagen was its editor, and the first issue contained an article by him entitled "A New Europe." Auhagen praised the outcome of the Munich Pact as "the most hopeful beginning of the New Europe." Contributing articles to the first issue of *Today's Challenge* were two members of Congress, Senator Ernest Lundeen of Minnesota and Representative Hamilton Fish of Buffalo, New York.

Billed as associate editor of *Today's Challenge* was George Sylvester Viereck, whose pro-Nazi sympathies were well known to the FBI. Born in Munich in 1884, Viereck had come to the United States in 1901 and liked to boast that he was a descendant of the Hohenzollerns (a claim that no doubt would have been a surprise to that German ruling dynasty).

Glib, shrewd, and energetic, George Viereck may well have been the world's highest-paid propaganda saboteur. In 1934 he had admitted before a congressional committee that he had been pocketing $500 per month from Dr. Otto Kiep, the Nazi consul general in New York. But that was peanuts compared to an additional $1,750 per month that he was paid by an American "publicity firm" under contract to the German Tourist Bureau. As United States correspondent for a Munich newspaper, the *Munchner Nauests Nachrichten*, whose editor was Dr. Giselher Wirsing, an aide to Josef Goebbels, Viereck received $500 each month. And the official Nazi propaganda agency in the United States, the German Library of Information, located at 17 Battery Place, New York, slipped Viereck yet another $500 monthly.

For his part, Dr. Kertess, the Chemical Marketing Company

head, did far more than merely stuff greenbacks into Viereck's grasping hands; he himself was deeply engaged in espionage work for the Third Reich. Drawing on his extensive business connections, Kertess shuttled information on ship movements in New York harbor to the German consulate in New York, from where it was relayed to the Nazi naval attaché in Washington.[7]

Across the Atlantic, a German named Heinrich Sorau, an international businessman with contacts high in Nazi officialdom, was constantly crisscrossing Europe on a covert pursuit—recruiting spies for the Abwehr. Sorau was actually Captain Hermann Sandel, deputy to Major Nickolaus Ritter (alias Dr. Rankin), air intelligence chief at Ast X in Hamburg. Captain Sandel and the nature of his work were known to the FBI, but he appeared in Bureau files under a flock of aliases—Kurz, Sebold, Sandell, Sorau, and others.

Sandel had been a pilot in the German air force in World War I and later spent ten years in the United States before returning to the Fatherland in 1938 to join the growing Abwehr. Most of his time in America had been spent in a series of dishwashing jobs. Curiously, he spoke German, his native tongue, with an American accent.

Sandel was the stereotypical German army officer, from his blond pompadour to his polished boots: ruddy complexion, Iron Cross, thick neck, and all. In his Abwehr post he had come a long way since his days scrubbing pots and pans in Depression-gripped America. A connoisseur of fine wines and a gourmet, Captain Sandel was at ease in upper social circles, or, if his mission demanded, he could curse like a mule skinner and drink beer and eat sauerkraut in the lowliest restaurants.

During one of his recruiting jaunts into Austria, Heinrich Sorau met up with Lilly Barbara Stein, who claimed to be a "hosiery model" in Vienna at the time. Sorau, the business high-roller, and the dark-haired, hazel-eyed Lilly established a relationship that resulted in her traveling with the Abwehr officer to the capitals of Europe.

Suddenly Adolf Hitler sent his army plunging into Austria, and Lilly, who was not pure Aryan, found herself in trouble.

Frightened, she took a train to Hamburg and appealed to Sorau for help. Yes, he told her, he could get her out of Germany safely—to the United States, in fact—provided that she did as he asked. And what was that? Still in the guise of an influential business wheeler-and-dealer, Sorau said, "Well, I am interested in a huge firm [Nazi Germany] with important deals all over the world. I need reports on our interests abroad, especially in America."[8]

Lilly Stein was bewildered and hesitated. Now Sorau identified himself as an Abwehr officer and demanded that she go to work as a spy for the Third Reich. She would serve the Fatherland faithfully, without question. And what if she did not? Sorau's face turned hard and he snarled, "If not, my dear Lilly, we have enough evidence against you to result in your imprisonment—or death!"[9]

The woman was petrified. She felt faint. How had she ever managed to get herself trapped in this nightmare? Trapped or not, Stein was soon taking training at Klopstock Pension, the Abwehr's secret espionage school in a multistory building near Hamburg police headquarters. Stein had no way of knowing that *Der Fuehrer* always called this place the Academy. Indeed it was operated much like an academy. The room to which Lilly was sent to learn the tricks of the espionage trade was much like a college classroom. The instructor (who used an alias) sat at a desk on a raised platform, and there were blackboards behind him.

Stein glanced around and saw that there were about thirty recruits in her class, mostly males over thirty years of age with a sprinkling of women. The students were taught the use of the Leica camera and how to make microfilm. A microfilm, they learned, was a piece of celluloid about half the size of a postage stamp and was used in a camera equipped with a special lens. When a sheet of ordinary paper measuring eight by ten inches was photographed on microfilm, the tiny piece of such film could easily be concealed, even under the tongue or in the hair. In emergencies the film could even be swallowed and, with luck, retrieved several hours later. At its destination, enlargement devices would restore the document to its original size.

Stein and her classmates were taught the time-honored use of invisible inks for sending reports home. The most common of these secret liquids was made by dissolving a headache-remedy tablet called Pyramidon in alcohol. Each ingredient could be purchased routinely over the counter in drugstores.

The Academy students learned how to use codes (simple ones, in most cases, for many of the recruits were not overly burdened with intelligence) and about the various divisions of the Nazi spy system: the collectors, the transmitters, the couriers, the drops, and the specialists (a euphemism for saboteurs). Many were taught sophisticated techniques for using explosives and deadly poisons.

Instructors explained how to operate a special radio transmitter-receiver, the *Agenten-Funk* (*Afu*, for short), developed by the electronics firm Telefunken. Compact and lightweight (thirty pounds), the Afu fitted easily in a small suitcase, and spies could readily carry it about without arousing suspicion.

Radio communication was the heart of the Abwehr's worldwide espionage network. The guiding genius behind the wireless communication between Germany and the United States was lean, scholarly Lieutenant Colonel Werner Trautmann, who set up a nerve center in a rambling old frame house in a sparsely populated section of Hamburg. On the second floor was a battery of forty-three receiving sets, while the transmitters had been erected about a thousand yards away in an open field.[10]

By mid-1939 Abwehr chief Wilhelm Canaris had spun a tangled web of global intrigue, surpassing by far anything of its kind that history had known. The espionage organization had some ten thousand permanent employees in addition to thousands of full- or part-time spies, saboteurs, informers, and couriers, operatives who were the backbone of the Abwehr.

"Without agents on the ground, we are reduced to collecting bits and pieces, looking through the press [of other countries], and waiting at our desks for intelligence to be handed to us on a silver platter," Canaris often reminded subordinates.[11]

Admiral Canaris made no bones of the fact that he played a ruthless game of numbers. Every agent was expendable. His theory was to flood a targeted country with agents, even if they were not highly trained or motivated, because it would be impossible for all of them to be caught. Even the most dull-witted spy could send back some useful information before blundering into capture.

One of those unmotivated German agents was Lilly Stein, who arrived in New York in early spring 1939, a few weeks after Captain Wiedemann had landed there. In her pocketbook were a few hundred dollars, a secret code designed just for her, and a microfilm of instructions concealed in the bottom of a box of face powder. Lilly was awed by New York, its bustle, towering buildings, and innate hostility.

To establish a legitimate "cover," the spy newcomer opened a small shop, dealing in beach accessories, in lower Manhattan, but the enterprise failed quickly. In Hamburg, Ast X refused to pump any more money into the "front." Meanwhile, Stein dipped her toe gingerly into the espionage pool, clipping bits and pieces of military information from newspapers, picking up military gossip from newfound friends, and strolling along the New York docks to cull information on ship sailings.

Lilly mailed her reports to an innocent-sounding address in Germany, one that had been provided by her controller in Hamburg. Unknown to her, only information harmless to the United States ever reached its destination. Not long after she had arrived, the FBI put Stein under surveillance and arranged to have her mail intercepted and inspected.

Her woes multiplied. She was nearly broke and in constant fear of being evicted by her landlord and arrested by police. She grew thin and haggard looking, and her appeal to Ast X for funds brought only a bitter scolding from her mentor, Captain Sandel. So to make ends meet, Stein had to return to occasional "modeling."

To the cold-blooded spymasters in the Third Reich, Lilly Stein was expendable.[12]

13

Roosevelt Meets Abwehr Agent C-80

On a bright Sunday morning in April 1939, Berlin was a city waking up late, recovering from a sixty-hour work week. Half-empty streetcars, infrequent passersby in their Sunday best, an occasional group of *Hitlerjugend* (Hitler youth) striding along briskly, their Nazi marching song, the *Horst Wessel*, echoed through the deserted streets.

Only in the government quarter, in the vicinity of the empty banks and fashionable shops, was there activity. A row of automobiles of all colors and sizes was parked before the handsome white palace at 8/9 Wilhelmplatz, where, day and night, beat the heart of the Nazi propaganda world.[1] Since March 1933 the Ministry of Propaganda had been operating in that structure, under the guiding genius of Dr. Paul Josef Goebbels, an indefatigable, diminutive official known behind his back as the Propaganda Dwarf.

Since early on this serene sabbath, Goebbels had been poring over a stack of material about President Roosevelt. Culled over the past several years, the information was stored in the Abwehr's "morgue," along with a vast collection of personality analyses of hundreds of other world leaders. These analyses had been painstakingly prepared by a platoon of Ph.D.'s of the Berlin Psychological Laboratory, under the direction of Colonel Albrecht Blau, and contained nearly all there was to know about the makeup of Roosevelt and other global figures who might aid or menace the Nazi cause.

President Roosevelt had been kept under close scrutiny since the fall of 1936 when one of Dr. Blau's ace "observers," a shadowy figure named F. Schoenemann, glibly talked his way past Secret Service men and onto the President's election-campaign train bound for Lincoln, Nebraska. It had been the kind of situation, had the Secret Service known of Schoenemann's true identity, that causes those charged with protecting America's chief executive to wake up at night in cold sweats—a hostile agent at arm's length from his target.

Schoenemann's mission, however, had not been one of violence. Colonel Blau had told him to merely "get as close as you can to Roosevelt and observe his character." [2]

In the guise of a foreign reporter (his credentials had been forged by the Abwehr), Schoenemann, as ordered, studied Roosevelt's every psychological characteristic, every habit, and every opinion. At the conclusion of the campaign swing, during which the beaming "foreign correspondent" shook hands with the President, Schoenemann filed an exhaustive report with the Berlin Psychological Laboratory. His observation included the wording: "War [from Roosevelt's point of view] is identical with militarism which Americans abhor, but a war for peace, a war to end war, is not only permissible but even necessary . . . Under President Roosevelt, [war] represents a danger of the first magnitude, threatening our [the Nazis] security and our future." [3]

As a result of Schoenemann's report, Roosevelt would be a marked man with the Hitler regime, one who could become a menace to the Third Reich. Now, in 1939, Goebbels was preparing a worldwide campaign of psychological sabotage against the American President, with the goal of undermining his credibility with his own people and with uncommitted nations— and to keep Roosevelt from interfering with the fuehrer's grandiose plans for One Europe.

Goebbels planned to plaster the label "War Monger" onto Roosevelt, so that any action the President might take against Nazi Germany would be met with global howls of protest. The propaganda chief kicked off his anti-Roosevelt offensive by unleashing a blistering series of attacks in the *Voelkischer Beobachter*, the Nazi Party's official daily newspaper. Under a blaring headline ROOSEVELT'S SHAMEFUL TREASON, Goebbels shrieked that the President was conniving to betray the American people into an "unjust war" with Germany and her allies. Roosevelt, he declared, was inspired by "Jews and Communists." Goebbels called for the President's impeachment.

A conveyor-belt stream of provocative rumors and poisonous slander aimed at Roosevelt's character and political philosophy poured out of 8/9 Wilhelmplatz. No lie was too grandiose, no vilification too obscene for the Nazi psychological saboteurs.

Faithfully, Nazi adherents in the United States leaped aboard Goebbels's "Impeach Roosevelt" bandwagon. In Milwaukee tens of thousands of leaflets charged Roosevelt with treason and urged Americans to: "Get Out the Rope and on to Washington!" A pro-Nazi rag printed in Wichita, Kansas, headlined: "Save America by Impeachment Now!" A Detroit-based sheet shouted "Impeach Roosevelt!" and a strident propaganda saboteur in Omaha, Nebraska, screamed in his newsletter: "America Is in Danger: Impeach FDR!"

The anti-Roosevelt propaganda barrage was not fired only by wild-eyed Nazi adherents and hangers-on. The "Impeach Roosevelt" slogan penetrated deep into all sections of American society, and it was picked up and reechoed by patriotic isolationists, most of whom, no doubt, were unaware that the battle cry had originated in Herr Goebbels's fertile mind at 8/9 Wilhelmplatz, Berlin.

In the late spring of 1939, just as the impeach-Roosevelt offensive was gaining momentum on both sides of the Atlantic, an attractive woman of about thirty years of age drove up to the gate of a major U.S. Army post in the South. She alighted and, with a portfolio under one arm, pranced provocatively up to the military police sergeant on duty. The impeccably groomed woman explained that she was conducting a survey for the U.S. Civil Service Commission. The government wanted only a few simple facts, she pointed out, failing to mention that it was the German government that wanted those facts.

An army captain was summoned, and the woman smiled and handed him her business card. It identified her as Susan Wadsworth, a survey specialist with the Civil Service Commission. She began plying the officer with questions. How many men were in the post? What were their units? How long were the units expected to remain there? The captain's suspicions were aroused immediately, for he knew that the Civil Service Commission would go to the War Department for information and that the commission did not conduct military surveys, anyhow. But the officer was cordial and fended off the questions.

The woman apparently sensed the captain's misgivings, for she mumbled something about being late for an appointment, climbed into her car, and drove off. Military authorities at the post promptly notified the FBI, but that agency already knew about the woman and had, in fact, shadowed her at random in recent months.[4]

Far from being a hard-working federal employee, Susan Wadsworth was actually Merry Fahrney, playgirl heiress to a fortune that her father amassed in the United States, the nation the daughter was now trying to subvert as a spy for Adolf Hitler.

Fahrney was well known in Washington, as were her pro-Nazi foibles. But she ran in intellectual circles where it was considered chic to be eccentric and to espouse a far-out cause, so her outspoken adulation of the fuehrer and Nazism was dismissed by her friends as merely the whim of a poor little, jaded rich girl.

But to Fahrney, her beliefs were no whim. Early in 1938, at a Washington cocktail party, she had engineered an introduction to Dr. Herbert Scholz, counselor at the German Embassy in the capital. Tall and handsome, married to the wealthy daughter of a top executive in I. G. Farben, the huge German chemical trust, Scholz was on the "must-invite" list of every society lioness in Washington.

Scholz was cloaked in mystery. It was whispered in the capital's social whirl that he was actually a Gestapo agent, masquerading behind the façade of a cosmopolitan playboy of impeccable manners and style. His image as a cloak-and-dagger operative, in the United States on some sinister mission, only added to his desirability as a guest at upper-crust cocktail parties and dinners.

The evaluation of the German diplomat almost hit the mark. Scholz was the resident director in the United States of the *Sicherheitsdienst* (or SD), the secret service of the SS, Hitler's private army and a military order that combined the rites of romantic Teutonism with cold-blooded power politics.

Leader of the SD—and Dr. Scholz's boss—was SS Brigade-fuehrer (Brigadier General) Reinhard Heydrich, cold-eyed, ruthless, yet an outstanding athlete and a violin virtuoso. Tall, blond, and hawk-nosed, Heydrich (who would later become known as the Butcher of Prague) was only thirty-four years of age in 1939. But due to his cruel nature and the exhaustive investigative apparatus he commanded, he was feared and hated by other Nazi bigwigs around Hitler.

Reinhard Heydrich was extremely ambitious, and envisioned the day when all German espionage services would be united under one leader—with himself as that leader. He maintained a curious relationship with Wilhelm Canaris, who was old enough to be his father. The two spymasters rode horses together in Berlin's Tiergarten (a pristine park), dined together in elegant restaurants, and entertained in each other's home. Yet the SD and Abwehr were bitter rivals—as were Heydrich and Canaris, personally.[5]

Vivacious Merry Fahrney had always believed in the direct approach, so minutes after having been introduced to Dr. Scholz, she invited him to a luncheon date to hear "an interesting proposition." Dashing and debonair, the SD spy had become accustomed to being accosted by beautiful young women, so he agreed to the rendezvous. Hardly had the couple finished ordering at Pierre's, a posh restaurant on Connecticut Avenue, than Fahrney launched a lengthy spiel about her admiration for Nazism. She concluded the oration by offering her services as a spy.

Scholz was well acquainted with Merry Fahrney's background, for she had been in the society pages regularly for her offbeat antics and a highly publicized marriage or two. Recognizing the espionage potential of one who circulated in the best circles in Washington, Scholz promptly accepted her offer.

Fahrney was delighted. Routine social gatherings had become such bores. Now there was a purpose in her life. She plunged eagerly into her covert mission and would prove to be a dedicated and productive spy for Reinhard Heydrich's SD. But hardly a discreet one. She insisted on periodic visits to the German Embassy on Massachusetts Avenue, and her persistent badgering of important U.S. figures eventually reached the ear of the FBI. Merry was placed under surveillance but was not arrested, for the Feds hoped that the wealthy adventuress would lead them to other Nazi agents. [6]

All through the stifling hot days of summer 1939, disquieting rumors that Adolf Hitler was preparing for war had been flooding official Washington. At dawn on September 1, 1939, the fuehrer struck. Five German armies, paced by swarms of shrieking Stuka dive bombers and hundreds of tanks, poured over the Polish frontier and began converging on Warsaw from three sides. Unleashed had been a mechanized juggernaut, bristling with guns, the like of which an awed world had never known. Its speed and power and finesse would create a new word in the languages of many nations: *Blitzkrieg* (lightning war).

When Hitler curtly rejected a British ultimatum to withdraw from Poland, England and France, on September 3, declared war on Nazi Germany.

In the musty, cramped old War Department building in Washington, the generals were stunned, not by Hitler's invasion of Poland but by the sophisticated technological advancements with which the fuehrer's war machine was equipped. No one in America would ever know for certain how the German armed forces, emasculated by the Versailles Treaty twenty years earlier, could suddenly emerge with these modern devices. Only much later would compelling evidence surface that the massive theft of American military secrets by German spies during the previous twelve years had played a crucial role in helping Hitler to create this seemingly invincible juggernaut.

Less than a week after the Wehrmacht launched its assault, two United States Coast Guard men were patrolling the shores of the Atlantic on Long Island. Through their binoculars they spotted a yawl called the *Lekala* riding at anchor about a mile offshore. Seven men were sprawled about the deck, apparently doing nothing. Suspicious, the Coast Guard men rode out to the *Lekala* and confronted the skipper, Edward Kerling. The young man was surly and defiant, snapping that it was nobody's business what he was doing on the yawl, where he was bound, or how he had come into possession of the craft.

The Coast Guard men promptly made the affair their business and took Kerling ashore for questioning. He disclosed that he was a butler working for a wealthy family in Short Hills, New Jersey. Coast Guard officers were curious over how a man on a butler's salary could purchase a yawl worth many thousands of dollars. Kerling shrugged and made no reply.

Notified of the *Lekala* affair, the FBI preferred no charges against Kerling. J. Edgar Hoover believed in letting a fish out on the line to see where he would lead. (In the case of Edward Kerling, it would lead him to execution as a spy, in Washington, D.C., in mid-1942.) Tails were put on Kerling and his six cronies. Not surprisingly, the *Lekala* men made frequent visits across the Hudson River and into northern New Jersey and became involved in activities of the German-American Bund, which was thriving in that area.

G-men inspected the *Lekala* and found that she was carrying enough concentrated food to last the seven-man crew for a few years. That led them to conclude that Kerling and his crew had a rendezvous scheduled with a German submarine, to which the provisions would be transferred. This theory was reinforced when geodetic surveys revealed that the waters where the *Lekala* had been riding at anchor were ideal for a submarine to lie on the bottom until it was time to surface.

Just two weeks after the big guns of Hitler's Wehrmacht began to roar in Poland, William Rhodes Davis, a wealthy American businessman, was ushered into the Oval Office in the White House for a secret meeting with President Roosevelt. A day earlier, on September 14, an influential public figure had telephoned Roosevelt and asked the chief executive to meet with Davis "on a matter that might be of the highest importance to the country and to humanity."[7]

Roosevelt knew that Davis, a free-wheeling private international oil speculator, had long been playing footsie with Nazi Germany, for the State Department had been building a dossier on the fifty-year-old Montgomery, Alabama, native since 1927. So the President asked Assistant Secretary of State Adolf A.

Berle, Jr., his most trusted advisor on espionage and security matters, to be present for the meeting. At the time, neither Roosevelt nor Berle knew that William Davis was carried on the Abwehr roster in Berlin as Agent No. C-80.[8]

Davis had a rags-to-riches background. As a youth he had been a hobo of sorts, and in 1913, at age twenty-three, he had started his own oil company in Muskogee, Oklahoma. By 1938 he controlled the Crusader Oil Company, with extensive holdings in Texas, Louisiana, and Mexico. Overseas, Davis owned terminals and distribution facilities throughout Sweden and Norway. He lived the high life of the *nouveaux riches:* palatial mansions in Houston and in fashionable Scarsdale, New York. His vast oil empire was directed from a plush suite of offices on the thirty-fourth floor of a building in New York's Rockefeller Center.

Now, in the White House, William Davis received a cool reception from solemn-faced Franklin Roosevelt and Adolf Berle, who listened without comment as the oil baron reeled off his plan for "world peace." Three days earlier, Davis explained, he had received an urgent cable from General Hermann Goering, with whom he had been "doing business in Germany" for seven years. Goering suggested that Davis try to determine if President Roosevelt would either act as a peace arbitrator himself or assist in securing the leader of another neutral nation to perform in that role.

"The Germans desire to make peace," Davis said, "providing that certain of their conditions are met."[9]

No doubt Roosevelt was galled to find himself holding court for an American citizen who had furnished huge quantities of precious oil for Adolf Hitler's war machine, which at that precise moment was brutalizing a nearly defenseless Poland. Back in 1936 Davis, aware that Nazi Germany was desperate for oil, had concocted a scheme that would both relieve the acute fuel pinch in the Third Reich and line his own pockets. Davis proposed building his own refinery in Germany, but the facility would be paid for with assets from Boston's First National Bank that the Nazis had confiscated under a trumped-up pretext.

Davis collared Dr. Hjalmar Schacht, president of the Reichsbank, to sell his scheme. Schacht, an elderly, dignified financier from the mold of Old Germany, was shocked. Davis was proposing to "legally" steal the Boston bank's funds. Schacht virtually kicked the American out of his office.

Davis had not soared from hobo to wealthy international wheeler-dealer by accepting defeat meekly, so he wrote down his proposal and mailed it to Adolf Hitler himself. A few days later Davis was seated in a board room, explaining his oil plan to the disgruntled Dr. Schacht and twenty other high-level German financiers.

Davis could sense by the stone faces that his proposal to steal the Boston bank's money was falling on deaf ears. Just then a door opened and the fuehrer strode into the room. "Gentlemen," Hitler said evenly, "I have reviewed Mr. Davis' proposition and find it feasible. I want the Reichsbank to finance it." [10]

The fuehrer had spoken. There was not a dissenting vote. Soon work began on Davis's huge refinery, called Eurotank, at Hamburg. Now what Hitler needed was oil to refine.

For the second act of his scheme, Davis negotiated a complex barter deal with Mexican President Lazaro Cardenas in which Mexico agreed to furnish oil to the Third Reich in return for German industrial products. Between September 1938, when the first tanker left Vera Cruz for Germany, and until war broke out in Europe a year later, more than 400,000 tons of Mexican oil flowed into storage tanks of the German Wehrmacht. In the process, William Davis was getting even richer. His Hamburg refinery was operating around the clock in three shifts.

Suddenly Davis's oil bonanza was cut off. The British navy had thrown a blockade around the Third Reich and was intercepting any shipment that might aid the fuehrer's war effort. Davis tried to circumvent the blockade by sending oil to Italy for transshipment to Germany, but the British blocked this ruse, also. Davis was desperate: His goose that had been laying gold eggs for a year had ceased producing.

So the oil tycoon's fertile brain hatched a bizarre plot: Now that Poland was clearly doomed, if the shooting could be halted in Europe, his oil shipments from Mexico to the Third Reich could be resumed. The goose would begin cackling once more. But the entire scheme hinged on peace breaking out. By cable from Mexico, Davis outlined his proposal for restoring peace to Hermann Goering in Berlin: The oil baron would induce President Roosevelt to arbitrate a cease-fire in Europe.

Like most world leaders, Goering had a devious bent that liked to dabble in machinations. So he gave Davis's "peace plan" the green light and asked the Abwehr to coordinate arrangements. For the clandestine operation aimed at President Roosevelt, Davis was assigned Abwehr code number C-80; Goering's "cover" name was "Harold."

Now, seated in the Oval Office Davis waited for Roosevelt's response. Despite his loathing of the man, the President remained noncommittal and did not reject the plan outright. Like any shrewd politician, Roosevelt was keeping his options open.

Before departing, Davis said that the German government had asked him to meet secretly with unidentified Nazi bigwigs in Rome on September 26. Would the President like Davis to report back on what took place at the Italian pow-wow? Roosevelt cautiously replied that he was always interested in information that would shed light on the European situation.

There was ample reason for the President's eagerness to be enlightened. As the United States lacked a secret service, Roosevelt had to rely on newspaper and radio reports, along with sketchy rumors passed along by U.S. military attachés overseas, for information on what was taking place in Europe. In this time of peril for the free world, the President of the United States was blind.

When Davis had left, Adolf Berle told the President that he considered the oil baron to be "almost a Nazi agent." Roosevelt agreed, but said he didn't see how he could do anything about it. Davis had broken no American laws, as far as the President knew.

A few days later Davis flew to Rome, where a Nazi contact told him that Hermann Goering was eager to hear firsthand about the conference with Roosevelt and wanted Davis to fly to Berlin. Even though his passport specified that he was restricted to visiting Italy, the oil speculator rushed to Berlin.

Goering glad-handed Davis on his arrival and took him to his baronial Karin Hall estate, where the two men held lengthy discussions on the Mexican oil situation and the Roosevelt peace plot. Goering urged Davis to follow up on the White House peace initiative, so on October 9 the Nazi emissary landed by Pan-American Clipper at Port Washington, Long Island. Early the next day Davis, through an American intermediary, tried to make an appointment with the President.

In the meantime, Roosevelt had had a change of heart about William Davis's "peace plan." The closest the insistent caller could get to the President was Brigadier General Edwin M. "Pa" Watson, the chief executive's genial appointments secretary. Roosevelt was far too busy to see the oil tycoon, Watson said over the telephone.

President Roosevelt had indeed been busy. He was confronted daily not only with major decisions growing out of the war in Europe, but there was another haunting specter: the danger from the accelerated invasion of the United States by Nazi spies, propagandists, and saboteurs. This clandestine threat would require major counteraction.

14

"We Have a Distinct Spy Menace"

Shortly after the German military juggernaut had plunged into Poland, J. Edgar Hoover rose to speak at a convention of police chiefs in San Francisco. Hardly had the applause died than the FBI chief rocked the audience by declaring that the major domestic threat to the nation was no longer marauding American gangsters such as John Dillinger and "Pretty Boy" Floyd and "Machine Gun" Kelly. Rather the new peril was the deep penetration of the United States by the Nazi espionage apparatus.

Speaking in his rapid-fire, straight-from-the-shoulder style, Hoover exclaimed: "We have a distinct spy menace." [1]

Consequently, the top G-man added, "President Roosevelt has instructed the Federal Bureau of Investigation to take charge of all investigative work in matters involving espionage, sabotage, and subversive activities."

For the first time in her 163-year history, the United States would have a single federal agency designed to combat insidious forces seeking to subvert the nation. The FBI, Roosevelt had directed, would work in close cooperation with army and navy Intelligence.

Hoover's dire warning was echoed in Congress by FBI supporters. Senator Styles Bridges of New Hampshire gave the Senate a "list of explosions, fires and other acts which may have been caused by sabotage in this country during the past few months."

"It is about time we buckle up our belts and start to deal with these things with a firm hand," Bridges thundered on the floor of the Senate. "It is time for action . . . this is no time to twaddle!"[2]

John Edgar Hoover, a robust, iron-jawed supersleuth, had emerged in just a few years as a living folk hero of law enforcement. Although the FBI had been in existence in one form or another since 1908, few Americans had ever heard of it until the G-men began rounding up or gunning down bloodthirsty gangsters in the early 1930s. Nearly six feet tall, with coal-black eyes and wavy black hair, Hoover walked briskly, and, when he spoke, his words emerged in crisp, staccato bursts.

Hoover, a bachelor, lived with his elderly mother and a pet dog in the same modest frame house in Washington where he had been born. He had never been known to take a woman on a date. His few close friends would say that he feared a romantic entanglement might give the FBI a bad name if it were to go sour. Besides, he had no time for romance and was wedded to his work, aides Clyde Tolson and Frank Baughman were quick to point out.

Hoover fought crime and subversion with a vitality that bordered on passion. He would tackle a dozen fast-breaking cases at once, shooting out a barrage of teletyped instructions and inquiries to a few core field offices sprinkled about the nation or barking out orders over the telephone. Associates of "The Director," as he preferred being called, professed awe over his energy. When a big case was breaking, Hoover remained in his office for seventy-two hours at a stretch.

No Boy Scout or Trappist monk ever had fewer vices than the FBI chief. He drank moderately and then only on special occasions, hardly ever smoked, and was never known to tell an off-color joke. His lone "vice," associates would quip, was his diversion of reading crime-busting comic strips, such as "Secret Agent X-9" and "Dick Tracy," on those rare nights at home when he was not working late at the Bureau.

Edgar (as President Roosevelt called him) was nearly as demanding about the conduct of his G-men and staffers as he was about his own demeanor. All agents had to have a degree in law or accounting (this stringent requirement would be waived a few years later when the FBI expanded) and had to pass a competitive entrance examination. A character check then scratched a large number of otherwise qualified applicants. "We can't afford to merely *be* right," Hoover would often state. "We must give every *appearance* of doing right."

Before an applicant became a full-fledged G-man, he had to endure an exhaustive, three-month course in crime-busting techniques—designed by Hoover—and demonstrate a proficiency with several weapons. FBI agents were on call twenty-four hours a day, and Hoover sent out inspectors who dropped in unannounced to check on his men in the field.

The Director was showered with honorary college degrees and other honors. In the late 1930s he took to the speaker's platform to make ringing pronouncements on anything that struck him. In Chicago he scolded an audience of mothers for contributing to juvenile delinquency by playing bridge when they should be home tending to their children. Hoover launched highly publicized broadsides aimed not only at crooks and subversives, but at anyone whom he felt sympathized with them. He lambasted "sob-sister judges, shyster lawyers and other legal vermin," and "political liberals and other sentimental moocows" who believed in lightening the sentences of "criminal jackals and subversives."

Hoover's verbal salvos drew heavy counterfire. For the first time he began to hear indignant voices from other than the American underworld and Nazi adherents. Some liberals in Congress thought he was "getting too big for his britches." Senator Kenneth McKeller of Tennessee moved to slash the FBI budget and at a hearing on the matter told Hoover, "It seems to me your department is running wild." Senator George Norris of Nebraska expressed the fear that Hoover was shaping the FBI into "a homegrown Gestapo."[3]

Undaunted, Hoover told the press that his detractors were suffering from "mental halitosis."[4]

The Director counterattacked his critics from strength. He knew that the big boss (President Roosevelt) was firmly in his corner, and, in an era when there was still a clear line between the good guys and the bad guys, the overwhelming majority of Americans were Hoover boosters.

In the looming all-out war on Hitler's secret invasion of the United States, J. Edgar Hoover would be the American field marshal directing tactical operations and the FBI building would be the frontline command post. Hoover would have to charge onto the battlefield with one arm tied behind his back, confronting such major roadblocks as public indifference and the continuing refusal of Congress to grant the FBI limited wire-tapping rights.

There was no doubt in Hoover's mind about the scope of the foe's operation. For by late 1939 Hitler's masters of skulduggery had fielded in the United States a formidable army of spies, saboteurs, propagandists, couriers, go-betweens, cut-outs, go-fors, stringers, sleepers, straphangers, and Peeping Toms.

Most of the supporting cast for the horde of hard-core Nazi agents was homegrown, a motley crowd of small-time operators who were motivated by love for Hitler's Germany or for American greenbacks. Spying often brought drama into their otherwise humdrum lives. Many were satisfied to get an occasional tiny handout and/or a pat on the back. Most were willing stockholders in the fuehrer's espionage corporation, others were dopes or dupes, blissfully unaware that the information they were providing would wind up in Berlin and be used to subvert the United States.

Not far from Hoover's command post in Washington was the nerve center for Nazi espionage operations in America—the German Embassy on Massachusetts Avenue. Inside that dreary old brick building, Dr. Hans Thomsen, the zealous Nazi and chargé d'affaires, had concentrated the most conspiratorial den of spies to be found in any Third Reich embassy in the world. A hotbed of intrigue.[5]

When armed violence had erupted in Europe, Thomsen became convinced that America would eventually declare war on Germany, or at least break off diplomatic relations, actions that would expel Hitler's diplomatic corps and leave Joachim von Ribbentrop's Foreign Ministry without its own eyes and ears in the United States. So Thomsen, a shrewd practitioner of devious machinations, began to spin a coast-to-coast web of forty-seven full-time V-men (agents) who would furnish crucial intelligence that the closed German Embassy and consulates could no longer obtain. He divided the United States into four districts and organized an undercover network in each one.

At the same time, Thomsen sought out the services of correspondents from neutral nations and promised each a monthly salary of $350 (a tidy sum at the time). If the United States entered the war, they would act as Germany's eyes and ears, mostly in Washington and New York, and provide Thomsen with information that would "protect German interests." The chargé d'affaires assumed that the reporters would be astute enough, and eager enough to get their $350 monthly, to provide him with the "right kind" of information.

Dr. Thomsen was skilled in developing key contacts. One stringer, the diplomat cabled Berlin, was a "close friend" of Attorney General Homer S. Cummings. Through this covert source, Thomsen was able to send to Berlin a steady stream of reports on what was transpiring at President Roosevelt's cabinet meetings and elsewhere in Washington's corridor of power.[6]

Thomsen was unaware that the SD chief in Berlin, the ambitious SS Brigadefuehrer Reinhard Heydrich, who trusted no one, had planted a high-grade agent in the Washington embassy. One of his functions was to spy on masterspy Thomsen. Known in Gestapo circles as "The Baron," Ulrich von Gienanth was listed as Second Secretary of the embassy, a modest post. Actually Gienanth, a one-time SS storm trooper, was Gestapo chief in the United States.

Scion of an old, aristocratic Prussian family, Gienanth mingled easily in top Washington diplomatic and society circles. The social graces and elegance acquired from his affluent upbringing served as ideal "cover" for his Gestapo role in America.

Baron von Gienanth had been ordered to concentrate on subverting prominent Americans whose backgrounds or actions reflected sympathies to the cause of Adolf Hitler and Nazism. So he promptly zeroed in on thirty-eight-year-old Laura Ingalls, a renowned aviatrix, socialite, dancer, and actress. Many Americans regarded her as eccentric. She had first come to the attention of Nazi bigwigs in Germany when, on September 26, 1939, she made headlines by flying over and "bombing" the White

House with keep-out-of-the-war leaflets. Subsequently she became a tireless speaker, traveling from one end of the country to another, exhorting large rallies to fight the Roosevelt administration's "war program."

Soon Ingalls became a paid agent in the secret employ of the Third Reich. She worked cheaply—three hundred dollars per month—considering her renown. Her money and instructions came from Baron von Gienanth, although she was in secret contact with Hans Thomsen, also. "The Baron" was delighted with Ingalls's work, and wrote one of his agents concerning the fiery, rabble-rousing speeches the aviatrix was giving to cheering crowds: "It's just what the King and Mamma did in the early days [in Germany]." In the code used in the letter, "King" meant Hitler, "Mamma" was von Gienanth, and the "early days" referred to the Nazis' bitter struggle to seize power.[7]

Meanwhile, on a gray morning late in January 1940, a man was fidgeting nervously at the rail of the liner *Bremen* as she sailed into New York harbor. Coat collar turned up against the icy winds, hat brim pulled low across the eyes, the furtive figure watched the approach of a small boat carrying the port pilot (who would guide the ship to her pier) and the customary port officers and saw them climb aboard. Minutes later a member of the boarding party slipped up to the man at the rail and whispered: "You are to be S. T. Jenkins. As soon as we dock, go to the Belvoir Hotel. Wait in your room!"

That night, "Jenkins" waited anxiously. Just before 10:00 P.M. he heard a key turn softly in a lock; two men slipped into the adjoining room. Cautiously "Jenkins" opened the connecting door and shook hands with the pair of G-men. "Jenkins" was a double agent, on the payroll of the FBI.

For more than two hours the German related a story that would send shockwaves of concern through the ranks of the FBI. "Jenkins" said that he had been recruited as a spy by the Abwehr and that his espionage class had graduated at Klopstock Pension in Hamburg. In a farewell address, the school's "principal" told the class: "The greatest problem of the fuehrer's agents in America is keeping in touch with us. The Americans have given us a great deal of trouble. But before long we shall be communicating back and forth with impunity. I cannot explain the method now, but watch out for the dots— *lots and lots of little dots!"* [8]

Until this point, the FBI had been regularly uncovering enemy communications techniques; the Bureau had solved secret inks, had broken codes, and, on one occasion, had successfully probed the riddle of an innocent-looking box of safety matches taken from a Nazi spy's pocket. Four of the matches, which looked to the casual eye just like the others, were ingenious little pencils that wrote invisibly. (A chemical would expose the writing.) The FBI had detected microfilm letters rolled around spools and covered with thread and others stitched into the spines of magazines. And one negative had been secreted inside the barrel of a common fountain pen, which had to be broken to uncover the incriminating note.

But what was this "lots of little dots" technique?

J. Edgar Hoover convened a crash conference, and guesses flew concerning the meaning and significance of the Abwehr officer's boast. An FBI physicist who had attained significant results in microphotography was called in, and he began conducting experiments based largely on agents' guesses. FBI men in the field searched frantically for some telltale clue that might solve this perplexing riddle. But a solution eluded the sleuths, and the mystery of the "lots of little dots" would haunt Hoover and the Bureau for many months to come.

The FBI had good reason to be concerned, for the Germans had created a masterpiece of espionage communication, an ingenious technological breakthrough called the *Mikropunkt* (microdot). Developed by the Institute of Technology in Dresden, the process permitted the Germans to photograph a large sheet of paper and reduce it to the size of a postage stamp. Then, using a new type of microscope, it would be photographed again and shrunk to the size of a dot (such as one at the end of a typed sentence). Hiding places for the espionage dot were infinite—in any kind of letter or document, or even on the outside of an envelope.

On a windy morning in late March 1940, at the same time that the FBI was trying desperately to solve the "lots of little dots" enigma, fifty-seven-year-old Simon Emil Koedel was eagerly opening a hand-written letter in his drab flat at 660 Riverside Drive, New York City. Koedel, a motion-picture projectionist, was one of the world's colorless men, an unpretentious individual who had been born in Bavaria but came to the New World in time to serve three years in the United States Army in World War I.

Koedel seldom engaged in small talk with friends. But they had often heard him say, "I love Germany with all my heart and am willing to give my life for her." Now, as Koedel scanned the letter, postmarked in Germany, he felt his heart begin to pound: The Fatherland needed his help. Soft-spoken Simon Koedel was a paid agent of the Abwehr, No. A-2011. Written in code and signed with the name of a fictitious friend in Cologne, the letter puzzled Koedel. He was being asked to find out if the French ports of La Rochelle, Nantes, and St. Nazaire could handle vessels larger than tankers.

Koedel had no way of knowing that the request had originated in the Berlin headquarters of the *Oberkommando der Wehrmacht* (armed forces high command), where feverish preparations were underway for launching Adolf Hitler's next operation: a powerful Blitzkrieg into France and the Low Countries.

In 1935 Koedel had returned to the Old Country and, excited over the bright promise of Nazism, had offered his services as a spy to the Abwehr. He was trained at the Academy in the art of espionage, then told to return to New York as a "sleeper" and wait for a call to go into action. Back home, Koedel waited anxiously for that summons to duty, but the months slipped by into years, and it never came.

On September 5, 1939, he opened a cablegram from Germany; his eyes went to the signature—"Hartmann." The contents were meaningless except for one word: "alloy." That was the code word informing the lean, gaunt, humorless "sleeper" that he was being activated as an agent. Koedel was euphoric.

Simon Koedel had not been inactive through the years, despite his despair over not being given specific assignments by his Abwehr masters in Hamburg. He had used his $200 monthly pay from the Germans to establish a fake identity and to cultivate sources, some of them in high places. He applied for membership in the American Ordnance Association, a lobby for a strong national defense, and sent along his old U.S. Army discharge papers as proof of his interest in the field. He gave his occupation as chemical engineer and said that he had large stock holdings in major defense corporations. The association accepted him as a member.

Soon Koedel was writing letters on stationery of the American Ordnance Association to members of the military affairs committees in both houses of Congress. Senator Robert Reynolds of North Carolina responded with praise for Koedel's interest in national defense matters and invited the "chemical engineer" to call on him in Washington.

Meanwhile, Koedel had been attending meetings of the ordnance association, where speakers briefed members on armament developments in the United States. At his request, the War Department placed him on its press-release mailing list. He strolled up brazenly to the gates of defense plants and facilities, flashed his ordnance association card, and usually was admitted. Sometimes officials would escort Koedel on a tour of the plant.

Late in November he tried this ploy at the army's top-secret Chemical Warfare Center at Edgewood Arsenal, Maryland. Guards would not permit him to enter. Undaunted, Koedel quickly contacted the ordnance association office in Washington, and an official there telephoned the War Department. Why was this distinguished chemical engineer and loyal booster of a strong national defense being barred from Edgewood Arsenal as though he were a spy? The War Department read the riot act to the Edgewood Arsenal commander, and a few days later Koedel entered the facility and received a guided tour.

That same night, while details were still fresh in his mind, Abwehr Agent A-2011 wrote a detailed report on what he had observed and been told that day. Two weeks later Abwehr officers in Berlin were poring over the document.

Now, four months after the Edgewood Arsenal bonanza, Simon Koedel pondered how he could obtain the wanted data on the French ports. An idea struck his fertile mind. He contacted his acquaintance in Congress, Senator Reynolds, and asked for the information, explaining that one of his "holdings" wanted to make shipments to France. Reynolds looked into the request, responded, and on April 9 Koedel sent a message to Hamburg: "According to the United States Maritime Commission, those [French] ports are not limited in their facilities but are capable of handling ships loading oil and coal as well as general cargo." [9]

While Simon Koedel and swarms of other Nazi spies in the United States were busily snooping out military secrets, Dr. Hans Thomsen was keeping his finger on the pulse of American popular opinion. On January 12, 1940, he wrote to Ribbentrop: "The sympathies of the overwhelming majority of [American] people are with our enemies, and America is convinced of Germany's war guilt." [10]

Thomsen was deeply involved in a keep-America-neutral campaign because his boss, Ribbentrop, had been appointed by Adolf Hitler to mastermind the pacification operation. The foreign minister's grand strategy was to pound the United States with a deluge of keep-out-of-war propaganda and for saboteurs to refrain from committing acts of violence that might arouse the sleeping giant and draw her into the shooting war.

Thomsen became highly agitated when he picked up rumblings over the Nazi grapevine that professional saboteurs were being infiltrated into the United States. On January 17 the diplomat warned Ribbentrop that "dire consequences [to Nazi plans] could result if any attempt is made to carry out sabotage operations in the United States at this time." [11]

Despite Thomsen's urgent warning, the saboteurs rumor persisted. On January 25 he fired off a cable to Berlin: "I have learned that a German-American, von Hausberger, and a German citizen, both of New York City, are planning acts of sabotage against the American arms industry by direction of the Abwehr. I gravely call attention to the danger which such activities, if discovered, would represent to German-American relations, especially during the current period of tension." [12]

Thomsen anxiously awaited a reply. None came.

Four weeks later, on February 20, a husky man walked into the German Embassy, identified himself as Walter von Hausberger, and said that he had been sent to the United States to carry out sabotage on a massive scale. Hausberger said that he had contacted the embassy because of a slight personal problem: He was out of funds and the Abwehr would send him no money.

A week later a self-styled master saboteur who called himself Julius Georg Bergmann also appeared at the embassy with the same problem: He was flat broke.

Dr. Thomsen was horrified to be sheltering a pair of boom-and-bang desperadoes, who might well blow to smithereens the Nazi grand design for keeping the United States officially neutral. He cabled Berlin, protesting the appearance in Washington of the two saboteurs. Came a reply from the Foreign Ministry: It had checked the matter with Admiral Canaris—Hausberger and Bergmann were unknown to the Abwehr.

Thomsen fired back another cable: If the saboteurs were not Abwehr agents, then why had they been trained in sabotage at Klopstock Pension in Hamburg? A week later a "clarification" arrived from Colonel Erwin von Lahousen, a covert operations officer in Canaris's Berlin headquarters. Lahousen had suddenly recovered his memory. He had indeed dispatched Hausberger and Bergmann to the United States—but only as "observers." The two agents had strict orders not to conduct any action remotely resembling sabotage, Colonel Lahousen swore.

In actual fact, the Abwehr, for more than a year, had been implementing a master plan for launching a series of sabotage plots in the United States. Through spies in America a long list of key sabotage targets had been drawn up, a detailed compilation that included power plants, factories, railroads, water works, and telephone exchanges. Nazi agents in the United States also obtained descriptions and maps of all major cities. One eager spy mailed to Berlin the blueprints of New York City's water supply system, and another supplied details and maps of strategic spots in the U.S. railroad system, such as the Horseshoe Curve of the Pennsylvania Railroad near Altoona and the Hell Gate Bridge over the East River in New York City. Yet another agent furnished maps and blueprints of water-filtration plants and reservoirs for Los Angeles.

Reports for sabotage purposes were diversified. An enterprising Nazi spy suggested to Hamburg that German saboteurs sneak into the United States by aircraft, and he provided a map showing the locations of more than fifty Long Island golf courses that could be used for landing fields. However, most of the sabotage operations, according to the Abwehr's master plan, would be carried out by German-born American citizens. They would be recruited in the United States, brought to the Third Reich for training at the Academy, then returned to their adopted homeland and planted in locales near key targets.

Far from being a benign "observer," Walter Hausberger was an ardent boom-and-bang operative. Since arriving in America early in 1939, he had planted saboteurs at the Packard, Ford, Chrysler, and Hudson automobile factories in Detroit; at the Harrison Gas Works in New Jersey; in the New York Liquidometer Factory; and at the four Brewster aviation plants, as well as recruiting a sizable number of sympathizers whose job it was to slow down manufacturing operations.[13]

Julius Bergmann, the other spy the nervous Dr. Thomsen had been forced to harbor, was a hardened old pro in the espionage and sabotage fields. Bergmann was an alias; his true name was Georg Busch, a fanatical Nazi and one-time music publisher. He had reached the United States in January 1939, posing as a "part-Jewish" refugee escaping from the Nazis. He promptly purchased a modest frame home in a New York City suburb (with Abwehr funds deposited for him in a Manhattan bank) and began collecting a large cache of explosives, caps, and fuses.

Bergmann planned to blow up ships in New York harbor. Taking along a pair of stevedores he had recruited, the old pro made several reconnaissance missions to vessels tied up on the waterfront and was astonished over the total lack of security. Looking for places to hide bombs, the three saboteurs boarded the *Effingham* and the *Independence Hall* and wandered around the big freighters for more than thirty minutes without being challenged.

Bergmann excitedly told Hamburg that he could easily blow several vessels "sky high" and that all he needed was funds to begin active operations. But no money was forthcoming. Fearful that ships being blown up in New York harbor might tilt America toward involvement in the shooting war, Joachim von Ribbentrop had squashed sending money to saboteurs in America —at least for the present time.

15

Counterspy
Ace-in-the-Hole

Wilhelm Georg Debowski had fought in the Kaiser's army as a corporal in a machine-gun outfit on the Western Front during World War I and was badly wounded in the bloodbath on the Somme. Soon after hostilities ceased he came to the United States, changed his name to William Sebold, and obtained a job as a machinist, a trade at which he was skilled. Sebold married an American girl, loved America, decided to become a citizen, and was determined to be loyal to his new *Vaterland*. Like many other Americans of German ancestry, Sebold retained many traits from the Old Country. He loved beer and sauerkraut and pickled pig's knuckles, and belonged to a German glee club.

Early in 1939 Sebold grew nostalgic to see Germany again. So he saved his money and took a leave of absence from his good-paying job as a draftsman at Consolidated Aircraft Company in San Diego. In June he said good-bye to his wife and crossed the Atlantic on the SS *Deutschland*, landing in Hamburg. While waiting to clear Customs, Sebold was approached by two Gestapo men, both of whom were polite yet seemed ominous. They told Sebold to come with them. The draftsman was concerned; he had heard tales of strange things that had been going on in Hitler's New Order.

"So you plan to return to America?" the short, stout Gestapo agent said to Sebold after they had climbed into an automobile. "That corresponds exactly with our plans. We can use men like you in America."[1]

That remark created a new surge of anxiety in Sebold. Did the Gestapo man mean that he was expected to spy against his beloved America? He was reflecting on that possibility when the automobile pulled up to a large, brownstone building, where he was ushered into a cavernous office to be greeted by a smiling, black-uniformed SS officer. "Welcome to Germany!" the other said graciously, shaking hands with the new arrival. "My name is Colonel Paul Kraus, chief of the Hamburg Gestapo."[2]

Noting that Sebold was perspiring and licking his lips nervously, Colonel Kraus said, "Don't be concerned, Herr Sebold. You're among friends in the New Germany. Here, have a cigarette."

As the American puffed on the cigarette, Colonel Kraus reeled off a lengthy recital of Sebold's background, going back to his boyhood days at his birthplace of Mülheim-on-Ruhr—the Gestapo officer knew more about Sebold than Sebold knew about himself. And the German was aware that Sebold's aging mother, two brothers, and a sister lived in Mülheim.

Finally Kraus pulled out a folder from his desk, and the American could see the wording on it: Consolidated Aircraft Company, San Diego, California, USA. Reading from a document, the German ticked off production figures at Consolidated Aircraft, then asked Sebold pleasantly if the report was accurate. The draftsman was stunned: Those figures were precisely correct. How had the Gestapo obtained these secret figures from an American aircraft plant some seven thousand miles away? Sebold pondered. That nagging question was cleared up quickly.

"We have a Gestapo agent in the Consolidated Aircraft plant, right where you work," Colonel Kraus pointed out with a trace of pride. "This agent not only furnished all the background information on you, but the production figures as well."[3]

There were moments of thick silence. Then Kraus said, "Well, Herr Sebold, are those Consolidated Aircraft figures accurate?" Sebold pointed out that he was an American citizen, owed his allegiance to that country, and refused to cooperate with the Nazis. Kraus laughed bitterly. "I would remind you, Herr

Sebold, that you were born in Mülheim," he declared. "Once a German, always a German."

Now the kid gloves were removed. "Your kin live in Mülheim, Sebold, not in the United States. If you refuse to cooperate, we cannot guarantee their safety . . ." Kraus's voice trailed away, casting an even more sinister connotation to the threat. "You will spy in the United States for the Fatherland!"[4]

Bill Sebold, American as apple pie, baseball, and the hot dog, felt trapped. Loyalty to his adopted land or to his mother, brothers, and sister—which would it be? Before he could reply, Colonel Kraus, pleasant once again and blowing cigarette smoke rings, told Sebold to think over his proposal for a few days.

As the American started to leave the room, Kraus remarked evenly, "Herr Sebold, I understand that your relatives in Germany are wonderful people."

Bill Sebold promptly caught a train for Mülheim, and since the family home was crowded, he checked in at the Hotel Handelshof. Hardly had he finished unpacking than he set off by foot for his mother's home. A Gestapo agent tailed him, another went into the Handelshof and confiscated a letter and a postcard that Sebold had mailed to his wife in San Diego.

The reunion between the one-time Wilhelm Debowski and his kin was warm and joyous—at the beginning. Almost within minutes the American noted that a drastic change had come over his two brothers and sister since he had last been in Germany, fifteen years ago. All three of them worked in arms factories, and they stressed to their brother from across the Atlantic that the Third Reich was merely preparing to defend itself against the United States.

President Roosevelt, one brother told Sebold, had been conniving to conquer Germany since he had entered the White House in 1933. Sebold was astonished by such a nonsensical charge. "Where did you learn that?" the American asked. A sister proudly exclaimed in a conclusive tone, "Why, *Der Fuehrer* said so in a speech!"[5]

Sebold, a perceptive man, knew that his loved ones had been infected with the Nazi virus. So, as pleasantly as possible, he set out a true picture of the United States alongside the distorted one painted by the clever propaganda minister, Dr. Josef

Goebbels. This resulted in a loud fuss, with Sebold and one brother almost coming to blows.

When Sebold, drained emotionally, returned to the Handelshof that night, he found that someone had entered his room and rifled through his luggage and belongings. Apparently theft had not been the motive—nothing was missing. Rage gripped the traveler. No doubt the Gestapo had paid him a call in his absence.

For three days Bill Sebold wandered around the ancient city of his birth, mulling over the nightmare into which he had been trapped. He had no choice: Either he spied for the Nazis in the United States or his mother, brothers, and sister were doomed, and it would be unlikely that he himself would get out of the Third Reich alive. Colonel Kraus was delighted to hear Sebold's decision and told the spy recruit that he would live in Hamburg for three months while taking espionage training at the Academy.

In late June a letter for Sebold came to the Hotel Handelshof, postmarked Berlin. It was signed by a Dr. Gassner, of whom the American had never heard. The message read:

> My dear friend:
> I would like to see you on July 8 in the Hotel Duisburgerhoff in Berlin at noon. I got your address from a mutual friend. If you realize what is best for you, you will by all means keep this appointment. I will recognize you.[6]

Bill Sebold knew he had to comply with the threatening orders of this mysterious writer. So at the appointed time on July 8, the American was greeted in the Duisburgerhoff lobby by a stout, middle-aged man who identified himself as Dr. Gassner. (Only months later would Sebold learn his true identity—Abwehr Major Nickolaus Ritter, alias Dr. Rankin, air intelligence chief at Ast X, the agent who had engineered the theft of America's supersecret Norden bombsight.)

Gassner ushered Sebold into the dining room where a waiter seated the two men at a reserved table in a quiet corner. "Well, how's things in America?" Gassner asked. Not waiting for a reply, he said, "America has great possibilities. We plan to take full advantage of its great natural resources."[7]

Sebold was stunned. What did the man mean by that puzzling remark? Noting the other's bewilderment, Dr. Gassner added, "The Third Reich will be acting in self-defense when it takes over the United States. We have no choice. We are being forced into the position of having to crush America before it crushes us."

Sebold ventured a mild protest. "But, *Herr Doktor*, I haven't seen any evidence of such plans in the United States," he said.

"Of course not," Gassner agreed. "Roosevelt is a very clever man, and a cunning one. His people do not know what he is doing."

Gassner then explained in considerable detail the espionage and sabotage apparatus at work in the United States, of agents planted in the armed forces, government agencies in Washington, defense plants and shipyards. Sebold pretended to be impressed, but asked if the Federal Bureau of Investigation didn't know that such things were going on. Gassner conceded that the FBI may have known about them in a general way.

"That man Hoover and the Federal Police over there are not quite clever enough," the Abwehr officer declared smugly.[8]

Bill Sebold returned to Mülheim to await Abwehr orders, and a month later he crossed the majestic Rhine River into Cologne. Years earlier he had been to Cologne, the Pearl of the Rhine, many times and knew the city well. Taking a circuitous route to shake off Gestapo tails, the draftsman slipped into the American consulate, where he told his story to Vice Consul Dale W. Maher and handed over the copious notes he had made of his discussion with "Dr. Gassner."

Consulate officials told Sebold that if the Gestapo had detected his visit here, he was to explain that his American passport was about to expire and he had gone to the consulate to get it renewed (it had indeed nearly expired). Sebold was instructed to return in two days to pick up his extended passport.

When he called back at the Cologne consulate, the American officials informed Sebold that they had gotten in touch with the U.S. State Department in Washington, and State in turn had contacted the Justice Department. Both agencies were in favor of Sebold's continuing to play along with the Abwehr and Gestapo. What they did not tell Sebold was that the FBI had quickly conducted an investigation into his background before the green light had been given.

Early in September Sebold began taking the espionage course at the Academy. Emphasis was given to radio operations. The Abwehr told the American that they would provide him with money and when he returned to the United States he was to buy radio parts and establish his own clandestine station for communicating directly with Ast X in Hamburg.

On December 19 supreme spymaster Admiral Wilhelm Canaris visited the Academy. Sebold's instructors explained to the Abwehr chief how delighted they were with the student spy; Sebold had mechanical skills and was adaptive and dedicated. Equally important, they pointed out, the American's loyalty was assured for his mother and other close kin in Mülheim were unknowingly being held hostage.

Before departing Hamburg, Canaris telephoned his office in Berlin to inquire about the state of health of his two beloved dachshunds. No matter if he was traveling in Germany or abroad, it had long been his habit to telephone daily and, from an aide at Tirpitz Ufer, receive a detailed rundown on the dachshunds' eating habits and bodily functions. When his dogs were ill, Canaris plunged into deep depression. At Abwehr headquarters, an ambitious officer's chances for promotion would be squashed if the admiral only heard that he had talked disparagingly about dogs. Consequently, 72-76 Tirpitz Ufer was crammed with outspoken dog lovers.

Finally, in late December, Sebold was ready to "graduate" from the Academy, and the Abwehr gave him the alias William G. Sawyer to be used in the United States. Major Ritter congratulated the American and handed him a small slip of onion-skin paper on which was typed four names:

Frederick Joubert Duquesne, in care of Air Terminal Associates, Wall Street, New York City; Lilly Barbara Stein, 127 East 54th Street, New York City; Hermann Lang, 59-36 20th Street, Woodbridge, Long Island; and Else Weustenfeld, 312 West 81st Street, New York City.

Sebold was given four microfilms, which were to be concealed in the back of his watchcase. The films were identical, and he was to give one each to the four persons on the slip of paper. Sebold realized that the Abwehr did not trust him; he was not told the contents of the messages.

On January 30, 1940, Sebold was aboard the SS *Washington* when she sailed out of Genoa, Italy, bound for New York. Before leaving Hamburg he had used a secret contact to tip off the U.S. consulate in Cologne that he would be on the ship. One suit pocket bulged with the thousand dollars the Abwehr had given him. All through the stormy crossing Sebold agonized: Was he doing the right thing? He grew fearful and saw Nazi spies all over the ship.

When the *Washington* steamed into New York harbor on February 8, Sebold stood at the railing and watched a tugboat, carrying the usual immigration and Customs officials, edge up to the big ship. Then he turned and walked rapidly along the deck, opened the unlocked door of a cabin, and entered. Anxiously he waited as the seconds ticked past. One minute . . . two minutes . . . three. He was beset with countless worries. Beads of perspiration broke out on his forehead.

For weeks Sebold had lived in fear that the Nazis in the Third Reich would unmask his double dealing. During the past ten days he had been haunted by the thought that the American consulate in Cologne had somehow failed to notify the FBI in Washington that he was coming. If the Cologne office had dispatched the message, what if Nazi moles in the FBI intercepted it? Sebold knew that German spies had penetrated deeply into the U.S. government.

Suddenly the cabin door opened and three grim-faced men slipped inside. For long seconds Sebold and the strangers stared wordlessly at each other. A frightening specter struck Sebold: Could this be a Nazi hit squad? Then one of the newcomers flashed a badge, called out "FBI," and gave a prearranged password. Sebold issued a sigh of relief and handed over the microfilms from his watchcase.

The G-men felt that the Gestapo may have sent spies to the pier to see who got off the ship with Sebold and where they went. So they told Uncle Sam's counterspy ace-in-the-hole to go alone directly to a certain hotel in Yorkville, where Hoover's men would contact him after dark.

While "William G. Sawyer" was holed up in the hotel, technicians at the FBI office in Foley Square enlarged the four microfilms. All were identical and written in German. A translator disclosed the Abwehr's "shopping list" for its New York-based network:

1. Find out if International Telegraph and Telephone have offered the French and English governments a new procedure of bombing which works as follows: The airplane is directed by some sort of a ray against the target and crosses a second ray shortly before reaching the target by which the bombs will be released.
2. There is said to be a branch factory of the French plant of Potez at Montreal. Find out the exact location, type of aircraft, how many they are turning out each week, number of employees.
3. Find out all you can about Professor Alden (not real name), an expert for chemical warfare. He is supposed to have developed a new means of protection against mustard gas . . . by which cloth uniforms are impregnated.
4. Find out everything possible about new developments in the line of antiaircraft guns. Weight, caliber, weight of shell, muzzle, velocity, highest elevation, range, firing speed. Manufactured by who? Where? How many employees?
5. Is there anywhere in the States an antiaircraft shell with a so-called Electric Eye being manufactured? If so, find out everything you can.
6. Get copy of United States Senator Barbour's Espionage Law.
7. Keep us up-to-date in all developments in the aircraft industry. Always keep an eye on all that is going on at the leading plants, especially Curtiss, North American Aircraft, Glenn Martin, Douglas, Boeing, United, Lockheed, and the leading motor plants, especially Wright and Pratt and Whitney.
8. The Bell Corporation is said to have developed a cable of high frequency service. Find out if it has been introduced into the Army . . . Get hold of a sample.
9. What is new about anti-fog devices?
10. What is new about bacteriological warfare from airplanes? All details.

11. Find out all about new gas mask developments. All details. Get a mask.
12. Pertaining to Sperry Range Finders, find out if latest range finder is equipped to register changes in altitude and how it is being done.
13. Find out if there are going to Europe whole units or single aircraft with personnel of the U.S. Army and Navy as camouflaged Volunteer Corps.
14. Report immediately when there are any signs of mobilization, like calling up volunteers, establishment of Drafting Offices, and calling in reserve officers and reservists on a large scale . . . Also shipment or take-off of U.S.A. units and shipping of large amounts of war materials out of U.S. Army and Navy stores in Europe. Use code for cable reports.[9]

Now that Bill Sebold had established contact with the FBI, he let no grass grow under his feet in his role as America's ace counterespionage operative. He contacted the four undercover agents on the list given to him by Abwehr Major Ritter back in Hamburg.

16

Hitler Finances an FBI Coup

Sixty-two-year-old Frederick Joubert Duquesne was the brains of Abwehr Major Nickolaus Ritter's New York-based spy ring. At various times in his forty years as a spy, he had posed as a magazine writer, lecturer, newspaper correspondent, botanist, and scientist. Now, in early 1940, he had opened an office in a Wall Street high-rise building, masquerading behind a meaningless company name, Air Terminal Associates.

Two days after William Sebold arrived in New York, he called on Duquesne at the Air Terminal Associates office. "I'm William Sawyer," the visitor said, adding the password he had been given by the Abwehr in Hamburg: "I bring you greetings from Rantzau, Berlin, and Hamburg." The two men shook hands, and Sebold felt a curious sensation: He was face-to-face with the insidious operative against whom he would conduct a relentless, subtle duel of wits in the months ahead.

Both conspirators settled into chairs and began idle chitchat. Then Duquesne arose and whispered in Sebold's ear, "We can't talk here. You never know where the damned FBI has planted a bug."[1]

Fritz Duquesne, a wise old owl, was taking no chances, so the pair held their Treff at the Little Casino, a small *beertube* at 206 East 85th Street in Yorkville. There the two conspirators could talk safely, for the genial owner and bartender, Richard Eichen-

151

laub, was "one of our boys," Duquesne explained, pointing to the middle-aged, potbellied figure drawing beer behind the counter.

An animated man with wavy, reddish-gray hair, Duquesne was never one to hide his light under a basket, so he wanted to make sure that Bill Sebold fully appreciated that he was doing business with a towering espionage mastermind. While the jukebox blared out German tunes, the two men quaffed beer, and Duquesne regaled the other with a litany of his lifetime as a professional spy.

Born in South Africa, Duquesne trumpeted that he had joined the German secret service during the Boer War, forty years earlier. He had been motivated, the Old Boer told Sebold, by his "insatiable hatred of the British." Punctuated by curses, Duquesne told how he had allegedly seen his mother tortured and killed by British soldiers in South Africa and how he had sworn revenge for that "dastardly deed." In World War I Duquesne had spied for the Kaiser in both England and South America, and he crowed that he had personally sabotaged a large amount of British shipping. "Yes, Herr Sawyer," he confessed, "my wartime feats were fabulous!"

Sebold hardly got in a word. Duquesne bragged that he was an expert saboteur and the inventor of several new types of bombs currently being used by Nazi spies in the United States. Fritz had even greater plans of destruction for the coming war between the United States and Germany. And such a war was coming, and soon, Duquesne assured his audience of one. Among other sabotage jobs, he was working out details for firing the monstrous French luxury liner *Normandie*, then berthed indefinitely at a Hudson River pier in Manhattan.[2]

Duquesne, who had come to the United States after World War I and later was naturalized, arranged with Sebold for another Treff, this one to be held at the Old Boer's fashionable apartment at 24 West 76th Street. A few days later, when the two men were seated in Duquesne's living room, Sebold handed over one of the four microfilms that he had brought from Hamburg. Using special equipment concealed in a storeroom, Duquesne enlarged the film and spent twenty minutes reading its contents. Even he was astonished by the magnitude of the Abwehr's list.

How on earth was all that information supposed to be sent to Hamburg? Duquesne reflected aloud. No problem, Sebold assured him. He explained that Major Ritter had instructed him to set up a shortwave radio station near New York City for that specific purpose. Ritter had deposited "a large sum of money" into Sebold's account with the Chase National Bank to pay for the radio parts and a small house for the station.

Duquesne beamed with delight. There had long been a crucial need for a rapid and direct method for getting stolen military secrets to Germany.

Next the counterspy went to see Hermann Lang, but found that the Nazi agent had moved to 74-36 64th Place, Glendale, Long Island. On March 23 Sebold called on him. When Lang, a self-assured man with bushy eyebrows, responded to the knock, Sebold promptly spoke the password: "I bring you greetings from Rantzau, Berlin, and Hamburg." Not long into the ensuing conversation, Sebold was shocked to learn that Lang, who had stolen many of the supersecret Norden bombsight blueprints in 1938, was still employed as an inspector at the Norden plant.

A newcomer to the shadowy world of intrigue, Bill Sebold was learning that spies, who live in the lonely realm of anonymity, seize every opportunity to boast of their accomplishments to fellow conspirators. Lang was no exception. Puffing on a cigarette, Lang claimed to be a personal friend of General Hermann Goering. "You know," Lang declared in a conspiratorial tone, "Goering considers the Norden bombsight the most important thing in the world!"

Next Sebold sought out Else Weustenfeld, a stockily built, middle-aged divorcée who worked as a secretary in a law office in the building that housed the German consulate, at 17 Battery Place. Born in Essen, Germany, she had been a naturalized citizen for nearly fifteen years. Weustenfeld, like Lang, was extremely talkative in private. Adolf Hitler, she gushed . . . a great man. She spoke frequently about "our Nazi boys" in referring to the Wehrmacht.

Bill Sebold may have been disappointed in seeing Lilly Stein for the first time. Based on rumors circulating back at the Academy in Hamburg, Lilly was a modern-day Mata Hari, who moved about in high circles and was the lover of numerous prominent American men. Beautiful and exquisitely sculptured, Sebold had heard. Instead he found that Lilly was a haggard-looking, fearful woman who expected to be arrested at any minute. But she was well versed in codes and secret inks, and her new address, an apartment at 232 East 79th Street, served as a letter drop for Nazi spies.

Clearly, the black-haired, buxom "model" was desperate for money. She assured "Mr. Sawyer" that "we are doing great things here," that she knew of practically every new development in the Detroit manufacturing plants, and that she hoped "Sawyer" would send good reports to Hamburg on her work. Stein put the microfilm Sebold had given her under a magnifying glass and told him that she already knew the answers to some of the questions (a true statement).

Fritz Duquesne was not the only one to be delighted that Bill Sebold had been ordered to build a shortwave radio station. So was J. Edgar Hoover, who had taken a personal interest in the project. Hoover's men picked out and bought, using Major Ritter's Abwehr funds, a small frame house in a sparsely populated area at Centerport, Long Island, a short drive from Manhattan, as the location of the station. It would be operated by FBI agents M. H. Price and J. C. Ellsworth. One of them had been a "ham" (licensed amateur radio operator) for several years and could send thirty words per minute in code, while the other had once lived in Germany and spoke the language like a native Berliner.

The final step was to register the Centerport operation as an approved amateur station, just in case any radio hams around the United States would happen to become suspicious.

Now the FBI would have a direct pipeline into the Abwehr hierarchy in the Third Reich—if all went well. And Director Hoover took impish glee from knowing that Adolf Hitler was financing the FBI coup. However, the entire stratagem would be a ticklish affair. Duquesne was shrewd, blessed with street smarts. Should Sebold appear to be overanxious to obtain information from him, should Sebold commit a subtle blunder that would tip his hand to the Old Boer, then this potentially fabulous cornucopia of information would be shut down, and

Sebold's mother, brothers, and sister in Mülheim would suffer quick Gestapo vengeance. All was in readiness at Centerport, but Duquesne, Stein, Lang, and others (who were now being tailed by the Feds) showed no inclination to feed secrets to Sebold.

Then one night Duquesne took Sebold to the Little Casino beer joint and introduced him to a covey of bakers, cooks, and stewards who worked on the North German Lloyd liners. The Old Boer was at his boastful best and explained that these German seafarers had "for some time" been acting as couriers between Hamburg and New York.

The next day Sebold, who had computerlike recall, gave the couriers' names and ships to his FBI contact, and tails were placed on the German crew members.

Toward the last of April, the Old Boer and Sebold were guzzling beer in the Little Casino when a furtive figure slipped up to their table. He was one of Duquesne's gang, Wilhelm Siegler, the head butcher on the SS *America* and a veteran and trusted courier. After glancing around to make certain that hostile ears were not listening, Siegler leaned over and whispered to Duquesne that he had brought news from Hamburg: Sebold was to open radio communication with the Third Reich at precisely 7:00 P.M., Eastern Standard Time, on May 15. Sebold was to use the call letters that had been assigned to his set, CQDXVW-2, and contact Station AOR, a radio transmitter in Hamburg.

Sebold's (that is, FBI Agents Price and Ellsworth's) transmission would be encoded in a key picked from a current bestseller book by Rachel Field, *All This and Heaven, Too.* (Which triggered an FBI quip: "All This Is Heavenly.") The key to the code was in the date a radio message would be sent. The day and month were totaled up and twenty was added on to the sum, indicating the page of Field's book on which the message would be contained. Starting with the first line on that page, the agents manning the Centerport transmitter would work up and down in a complicated series of squares.

The Centerport radio line would be used primarily for short SSD (*sehr sehr dringend*, very very urgent) reports. Longer, less timely reports and bulky shipments of blueprints and the like would continue to be sent to the Third Reich by regular mail, with the couriers on the fast German ocean liners, and with certain stewards on the Pan American clippers flying between Lisbon and New York.

Abwehr spymasters in Germany had envisioned that the secret radio link would be unmasked if a parade of Nazi agents traipsed in and out of the station. So before Sebold had departed Hamburg, Major Ritter told him that five thousand dollars would be deposited in a New York City bank for opening an office in midtown Manhattan where he could meet German agents and collect their material. Sebold formed the phony Diesel Research Company and rented an office in the Knickerbocker Building on 42nd Street.

Sebold had several "silent partners" in his company—FBI agents who created elaborate props to allow the firm to operate more efficiently. A mirror on the wall of Sebold's office reflected the image of anyone looking into the glass—but in the adjoining room this mirror became a window through which G-men could take movies of everything that transpired in the research firm's office. Walls were painted white in order to produce clearer pictures.

Hidden microphones would carry each word spoken to a recording device. There were other deft touches. On Sebold's desk was a clock and behind it a flip-over day-by-day wall calendar, which would reveal on film the precise time and date when Sebold had a visitor. There was only one extra chair in the room, and it was placed near to Sebold's desk so that the visiting spy would always have to sit facing the mirror—and the movie camera.

Now all was in readiness for the cat-and-mouse game between the Federal Bureau of Investigation and the espionage masterminds in the Third Reich.

As the May 15 Centerport target date neared, Fritz Duquesne, curiously, expressed no interest in being present at the launching of the clandestine radio station. J. Edgar Hoover suspected a trick. He concluded that the Old Boer was playing dumb with Sebold, then would slip out to Centerport and pay a surprise call at the station. Hoover had to make a crucial decision; he was not yet ready to spring a trap on Duquesne's gang, but now the FBI chief's hand had been forced. To prevent the radio station ploy from being unmasked, if the Old Boer showed up, he would be arrested. So when May 15 arrived FBI agents disguised as telephone linemen, ditch diggers, and a mail carrier were posted near to the Centerport cottage. But Fritz never appeared.

Inside the cottage, the two G-men waited tensely as 7:00 P.M. approached. The gentle ticking of a small clock seemed oppressive. Three minutes to seven . . . two minutes to seven . . . one minute. Now! One agent began tapping out the call letters CQDXVW-2. Anxiously the two men waited for a response. There was none. Again the call letters were tapped out. Again the wait—in vain. For an hour the G-man kept at it. There was only silence from Hamburg.

Apparently something had gone wrong. Had the cunning Fritz Duquesne discovered Bill Sebold's double dealing? Was that why the Old Boer had not come to Centerport? Agents Ellsworth and Price tried again the next night. The receiver refused to crackle. On the succeeding nights of May 17 and 18 the G-men tried yet again.

On May 18 FBI suspicions were heightened. G-men had had Duquesne's Manhattan apartment near Central Park under surveillance on the crucial nights since May 15. Fritz apparently had spent all four nights in his dwelling and had made no attempt to contact Hamburg. He had been seen going inside the building at about dinnertime each night and had not been spotted leaving.

On this night of May 18, G-men thought he was again in his apartment, for they had seen him enter the building shortly after 5:00 P.M. But at 10:00 P.M. the shadows got a jolt: They spotted Fritz walking toward his apartment building from the direction of Central Park. Did this mean that the Old Boer, as slippery as a greased eel, had sneaked out another exit and had, in some manner, informed Hamburg that the Centerport station was an FBI blind? Was this why Centerport had received only silence?

Meanwhile that same night, the two radio-station G-men continued to tap out signals to Hamburg. Suddenly, at midnight, they were electrified: Their receiver began to crackle; a message was coming through from Hamburg. Uncoded by the G-men, it read:

> Send only two times per week. We are prepared to send
> and receive daily. We are prepared 7:00 A.M., 1:00 P.M. and
> 5:00 P.M.
>
> —AOR.[3]

The two Feds let out whoops of joy, then dispatched a coded
reply:

> Your signal weak. Can you improve it? I will send Tuesdays
> and Thursdays 1:00 and 5:00 P.M. Will listen daily except
> Saturday night and Sunday.
>
> —CQDXVW-2 [4]

Hoover formed a "little brain trust" of his most devious-
minded men to create an ongoing script for Sebold's shortwave
transmissions. These early days would be crucial, for the Abwehr would instruct agents in the United States to check on the
validity of the information Sebold was sending to Hamburg. So
the "scriptwriters" had to include true facts and data along with
a mass of twisted or bogus military secrets. Magnified to en-
hance their significance, the phony secrets were largely out-
dated information or that deemed relatively harmless. Aircraft
that had been declared obsolete by the army could be described
in great—and accurate—detail.[5]

17

A Nazi Pipeline into the State Department

Fritz Duquesne, elated to hear from Bill Sebold that the Centerport radio station was in contact with Hamburg, took the counterspy into the park across from the New York City Hall to learn details of the shortwave operation. The Old Boer felt more comfortable in this pristine setting for he knew he would not be talking into an FBI bug. However, the Feds were indeed on hand: An agent with a telescopic lens was taking movies of the park-bench Treff for evidence in a future prosecution.

Perhaps thirty minutes after the discussion began, Duquesne walked Sebold to the waterfront, where they boarded a ferry for New Jersey. Fritz said he wanted to slip Sebold some information to send over the Centerport radio and also look over a few ships berthed in the Hudson River. Duquesne was determined to one day torch or blow up a major vessel or two in New York harbor. It was fitting that the Old Boer's data should be the first to go to Hamburg by wireless communication, for he was the Godfather of German espionage in the United States.

When the New Jersey ferry was in midstream, Duquesne handed his information to Sebold. It stated:

> Rolls Royce have engine designed to go into the wings like a meat sandwich. I sent blueprints to China. Allies ordered

159

10,000 additional machine guns, motorcycles and sidecars. U.S. Intelligence getting info from Myron Taylor in the Vatican. A priest there is bringing it to him. The S.S. *Champlain* is taking munitions cargo from USA in day or so. She is armed with anti-submarine and anti-aircraft protection.[1]

Before Sebold radioed Duquesne's message, the FBI brain trust for the radio-station operation had to dissect and analyze its contents. Part of the information was accurate, part was slightly in error, and some points were dead wrong. What could be sent along to Hamburg without injuring America's security? That riddle was solved by slightly twisting some of Duquesne's facts, while allowing accurate facts to go through. In the meantime, the correct information (such as the sailing date of the SS *Champlain*) was altered by Washington so that no harm would ensue.

As the FBI had known for weeks now, Fritz Duquesne was one slick customer. He was on the go constantly, knew every trick in the book to throw off or detect tails. On occasion the G-men lost track of him for days at a time when they had to cease shadowing him for fear of unmasking themselves. Some four weeks after the Centerport contact was opened, Duquesne gave the slip to the FBI men and took a "scouting trip" through the Midwest. On his return, he turned over to Sebold to be microfilmed a goldmine of intelligence: precise figures on the production of tanks at the Chrysler plant in Detroit and restricted information from the Firestone Steel Products Company in Akron, along with a wealth of other crucial information from those two war-production corporations.

All of this data was carefully studied by the brain trust, then altered, and the Centerport station passed it on to Hamburg.

As the weeks went by, the Abwehr masterminds in Hamburg and Berlin became ecstatic with the work of Sebold's shortwave station, and soon were sending other Nazi agents to him for the rapid transmission of the information they had collected. "Customers" started drifting in and out of the Knickerbocker Building "research office" to turn over their materials. As each spy sat in the "hot seat," as the adroitly placed chair in the office came to be called, the hidden movie camera rolled and the recording device listened.

Unknowingly, Hitler's spies were convicting themselves. "This is like shooting fish in a barrel!" one FBI man in the adjoining room exulted.[2]

While the Centerport radio station melodrama had been unfolding during the early months of 1940, Dr. Hans Thomsen, the masterspy/diplomat at the German Embassy in Washington, had pulled off a dynamite Intelligence coup: a pipeline into the inner sanctum of the United States State Department. The coup was scored due to the incredibly lax security in the State Department's code room in Washington. Secrets there had long been waiting to be plucked, and the Nazi spy apparatus was eager to do the picking.

State's code room was located in the old State, War and Navy building on Pennsylvania Avenue, and had been headed for twenty-nine years by David A. Salmon. Even when code books had been stolen repeatedly, the code room did not change its most secret means for communicating with embassies overseas. That method had been installed in the late 1930s and was a cryptography system invented 150 years earlier by Thomas Jefferson, the first secretary of state.

Even in 1939, when Admiral W. H. Standley, Ambassador to Russia, cabled home that it was "a matter of gossip" in Europe that State Department codes were insecure, nothing was done to alter Jefferson's antiquated cryptology system.[3]

Less than a year after Standley's warning, on April 30, 1940, Thomsen cabled Berlin: "A reliable and tried confidential agent who is friendly with the director of the [State Department] code room reports as follows after having seen the relevant telegraphic reports." The chargé d'affaires then related verbatim a secret message sent from London by Joseph Kennedy, the U.S. Ambassador to England.[4]

A few days later Thomsen cabled Berlin a message sent to the State Department from Madrid by the U.S. Ambassador to Spain. Its contents revealed that the Spanish foreign minister had been lying to his opposite number in the Third Reich, Joachim von Ribbentrop, when he had insisted that Spain would not receive needed grain (from the United States) in return for Spain remaining neutral.[5]

This deep Nazi penetration of the U.S. State Department proved to be an enormous advantage to Adolf Hitler and Ribbentrop, for it permitted them to plan strategy with full knowledge of what was going on inside enemy and neutral camps.

Dr. Thomsen's "reliable and tried confidential agent" was a paid German spy who had cultivated the friendship of Joseph P. Dugan, technical operating chief of State's code room. Dugan allowed himself to be trapped in an enormous indiscretion due to the haphazard security measures in the code room and his deep-rooted and emotional isolationist views, similar to those held by millions of patriotic Americans.[6]

Dugan often discussed cables reaching the code room with his trusted friend who, he thought, shared his opinions. So when the friend asked Dugan to bring home key cables for him to copy, Dugan dutifully complied. The other man had explained that the information was for "certain [isolationist] friends in Congress" who were "entitled to know what is going on."[7]

There was nothing in the Nazi spy's background or remarks and actions to indicate that he was anything other than a selfless American patriot who was deeply worried that his country was plunging hell-bent down the road toward war. So this devastating code-room security leak continued over seventeen months.

Meanwhile, homegrown Nazi-oriented scandal sheets, some slickly done but most of them on the lunatic fringe, continued to spew out venom at their archenemies, J. Edgar Hoover and the FBI, with occasional broadsides aimed at the "war monger," President Roosevelt. In August 1939 the Nazi rags had gained a new ally, the New York-based *Daily Worker*, American mouthpiece for the Moscow-directed Communist Party line.

At that time, the *Daily Worker* had intensified its salvos against the FBI after Hitler and Ribbentrop had negotiated a Treaty of Friendship with dictator Josef Stalin and the Soviet Union. The Nazi leaders had pulled off a clever coup: The claws and teeth of the Russian bear had been extracted until the fuehrer completed the conquest of Western Europe.[8]

Hardly had the odd couple, Communist leader Stalin and

Hitler, the sworn arch-foe of communism, toasted each other in "friendship" than the *Daily Worker* began screeching: Don't send American boys to die for the ill-gotten British Empire.

Hoover decided to strike back. Speaking before the forty-ninth Continental Congress of the Daughters of the American Revolution in Washington on April 18, 1940, the Director pointed out that "since the FBI is in the first line of national defense against the saboteur, the espionage agent, and the revolutionist, it also is among the first to bear the brunt of attack.

"No method is too foul, no lie too rotten, for these people . . . Overzealous groups are often the victims of . . . the vipers of alien 'isms' whose poisonous fangs are fatal."

Hoover told the cheering, overflow crowd that "these scoundrels are under instructions to permeate our Army and Navy. These praters against the American way of life are in reality a gang of international con men, seeking to steal our wallets."⁹

Four weeks after Hoover lambasted "the vipers of alien 'isms,'" Adolf Hitler entered a huge bunker located on a heavily forested mountaintop south of the cathedral city of Aachen, along the Western Front. It was 3:00 A.M. on May 10, 1940. Code-named *Fesennest* (aerie on the cliffs), the bunker would be the fuehrer's command post for directing Case Yellow, a powerful Blitzkreig into France, Belgium, Luxembourg, and the Netherlands.

At dawn large numbers of *Fallschirmjaeger* (paratroopers) leaped behind French and British lines, and then, paced by swarms of panzers, the vanguard of the two and half million Wehrmacht men along the Western Front surged over the frontiers. Despite a flood of advance warnings that Hitler would strike, the Germans gained total surprise all along the line.

Across the English Channel early that morning, seventy-year-old Neville Chamberlain, a mild-mannered, conscientious man who for two years had been trying to appease Hitler, resigned as British prime minister. A few hours later King George VI summoned sixty-six-year-old, rotund Winston Churchill to Buckingham Palace and asked him to take over the reins of government.¹⁰

Churchill plunged into his duties with customary vigor, but

there was nothing he could do to halt the Allied catastrophe unfolding on the Continent. In only six weeks the German juggernaut forced Belgium, Luxembourg, and the Netherlands to surrender, shattered the larger French army (reputed to have been the world's finest), and trapped remnants of the British Expeditionary Force at the small Channel port of Dunkirk.

On May 27, under a pounding by the Luftwaffe, some 850 vessels of all shapes and sizes began Operation Dynamo, the successful evacuation of 337,131 British soldiers to England. Coming out with the troops were only 25 tanks, 12 artillery pieces, and a handful of machine guns. Left behind along the sands of Dunkirk were 575 tanks, 120,000 vehicles, 2,300 artillery pieces and mortars, 8,000 Bren guns, 90,000 rifles, and 7,000 tons of ammunition.

Great Britain had suffered a humiliating military debacle, one of the worst in her long history. She was virtually defenseless. In Berlin, Hitler called on England to surrender, but the spunky Churchill declined to even reply. So the fuehrer issued orders to prepare Operation Sea Lion, a leap across the English Channel to finish off Great Britain, and for the Luftwaffe to launch a massive blitz of the island, concentrating on sprawling London.

In the meantime, the Nazis planned to conduct another enormous blitz—this one the propaganda variety—in the United States in an effort to induce Churchill to run up the white flag. With the Soviets neutralized by the Treaty of Friendship, Hitler knew that there remained only one nation with the potential manpower and industrial might to throw a monkey wrench in his plans for conquest—the United States of America.

So Dr. Hans Thomsen, the chargé at Washington's German Embassy, was spending every dollar he could lay his hands on to support American isolationists in their efforts to keep the United States out of the war, thereby discouraging the beleaguered England from continuing to resist. The first target of the Nazi propaganda mill would be the quadrennial circus known as the Republican and Democratic presidential nominating conventions, which would be held in midsummer.

Dr. Thomsen let no grass grow under his feet. When Adolf Hitler gave a speech in Berlin on June 13 calling for peace in

Europe, Thomsen arranged to have advance translated copies distributed widely to American newspapers and radio stations. He cabled Ribbentrop that he had personally slipped an advance copy of the "peace" speech to a reporter for the Hearst newspaper chain, and it was published in the *New York Journal-American*.[11]

Scores of U.S. newspapers ran stories on the fuehrer's plea, even though the Nazi warlord's price for "peace" was the capitulation of England and the permanent merging of the conquered European nations into the Greater Third Reich. Thomsen was ecstatic with the flood of favorable publicity and cabled the German Foreign Office that he had printed 100,000 extra copies of the *Journal-American* article and was distributing them to influential leaders and opinion molders across the nation.[12]

On June 14 Thomsen fired off a cable to Berlin: A "well-known Republican congressman who is working closely with the [German] Embassy" had offered, for three thousand dollars, to invite fifty isolationist congressmen to the forthcoming Republican convention "so they can influence" delegates to adopt an isolationist foreign policy platform.[13]

What's more, the chargé told Berlin, "this same Republican congressman" had asked for thirty thousand dollars to help defray the cost of full-page newspaper ads to be headed: "Keep America Out of the War!"[14]

Only a day later Thomsen cabled Berlin about a new scheme "from which I expect great results." He had sought out American reporters and authors to enlist them in the high-powered propaganda offensive and was negotiating a deal through a New York literary agent in which five "well known American authors" had agreed to write books with keep-out-of-the-war themes. This propaganda bonanza would cost only twenty thousand dollars, Thomsen pointed out. A few days later Joachim von Ribbentrop approved the expenditure.[15]

On June 26, three weeks after the British army had pulled out of Dunkirk, Prime Minister Winston Churchill, in his bomb-proof bunker deep beneath the pavement at Storey's Gate in London, received word that Hans Thomsen had sent out feelers regarding a secret meeting with Lord Lothian in Washington. Apparently Thomsen sought to have Lothian, the British ambassador to the United States, appeal to Churchill to come to terms with the fuehrer. The prime minister fired off a cable to Washington: "Lord Lothian should . . . on no account make any reply to the German chargé's message." [16]

In that same month of June 1940, suddenly concerned Americans found themselves faced with the hard facts of international life. Hitler controlled most of Western Europe, the mighty Wehrmacht was poised to leap the English Channel and pounce on a nearly defenseless Great Britain, and the Atlantic Ocean didn't look so broad or reassuring as it had only six months earlier. At that time, in December 1939, an Elmo Roper organization poll had revealed that 67.4 percent of the American people were opposed to taking sides in the violent dispute in Europe. Now, in June, public opinion had flip-flopped. Another Roper poll showed that 67.5 percent of Americans favored giving active help to England. [17]

Yet a third of Americans still thought that the United States should not involve itself in "other nations' quarrels." This minority bloc was an energetic and noisy one, with deep historical roots. A strong isolationist strain had existed in the American makeup since President George Washington had warned his countrymen to "steer clear of permanent alliances with any portion of the foreign world."

Among those in the forefront of the isolationist fight was Congressman Hamilton Fish of Buffalo, New York, who was the leader of the National Committee to Keep America Out of Foreign Wars. Headquarters for that group was in Room 1424—Fish's office—in the Capitol in Washington. Numerous other members of Congress loaned their names to Washington-based organizations, including the Islands for War Debts Committee, War Debts Defense Committee, and the Make Europe Pay War Debts Committee.

Yet another isolationist group, this one based in Chicago and led by a wealthy businessman, Avery Brundage, was the Citizens Keep America Out of the War Committee. Lanky, boyish-looking Charles A. Lindbergh, who had gained enduring fame in 1927 when he became the first person to fly the Atlantic alone, was the keynote speaker at a massive rally produced by Brundage's group at the 100,000-seat Soldiers Field in Chicago.

Seeking to speak even louder and with one voice, fifty delegates from assorted isolationist groups met in Washington to form a single national coalition, the No Foreign Wars Committee. Named to lead the organization was Verne Marshall, publisher of a staunch isolationist newspaper in the Midwest.

Hardly had Marshall's committee opened its headquarters in Washington than William Rhodes Davis, the wheeler-dealer oil baron, came calling. Davis, who had pocketed millions of dollars while playing footsie with Hitler's regime and was carried on the Abwehr roster in Hamburg as Agent C-80, offered to cough up $100,000 to finance a nationwide keep-out-of-the-war advertising blitz.

The No Foreign Wars Committee launched a hectic series of broadcasts over coast-to-coast radio hookups and newspaper ads. Marshall himself shouted that his committee would "fight to the last ditch to foil the interventionists, the rabble rousers, and the deceptionists in their high-financed campaign to start this country shooting."

One of the busiest Nazi agents at this time was Carl Alfred Reuper, a German-born American citizen who had returned to the United States at Christmastime 1939 after having taken the spy course at the Academy in Hamburg. The thirty-seven-year-old Reuper was a skilled mechanic, and he found the ideal job for a German agent: working for Bendix Air Associates in New Jersey on U.S. government classified contracts.

Reuper was a meticulous spy. He had organized his own network, mainly members of the German-American Bund who worked in several vital defense plants in New Jersey and eastern Pennsylvania. They regularly turned over information to Reuper, who was masterminding the operation as though he were chief executive of a holding company that controlled various subsidiaries. Each agent had received from him a precisely worded directive: He was to collect code books, documents, photographs, and blueprints "relative to the national defenses of the United States."[18]

Reuper lived on Palisade Avenue in Hudson Heights, New Jersey, and after returning home from an eight-hour work day at Air Associates, he regularly changed clothes and took a bus across the George Washington Bridge to Manhattan, where he held Treffs with his operatives amid the hustle and bustle of Pennsylvania Station. During one of these Treffs, on June 11, 1940, thirty-three-year-old U.S. Army Private Peter Franz Donay, who was posted at Governor's Island, slipped Reuper a top-secret field manual that the soldier had "borrowed" and had to return.

Reuper took the purloined booklet to Queens, where a go-between rushed it to a commercial photographer, Frank Grote, in the Bronx. Grote reduced each page to tiny microfilms, then took the negatives to a cut-out, the owner of a bookstore on East 85th Street in Yorkville. The filmstrips were placed into a book, which was carefully wrapped in plain brown paper and stored under the counter.

Two days later a man walked into the bookstore. Without the exchange of a word, a young clerk handed the wrapped book to the man. Browsing nearby in the store were two FBI agents, who had had the store under surveillance for several weeks. One of the Feds tailed the caller, who went to the waterfront and boarded the SS *Manhattan*. (Subsequent investigation revealed that the man was a courier posing as the ship librarian.)

Meanwhile in Washington, the Federal Bureau of Investigation had created a Rogue's Gallery of photographs of German-American Bund kingpins and others suspected of spying for the fuehrer. These pictures, hundreds of them, had been taken over the months across America by a "secret weapon"—special cameras concealed in the palms of G-men's hands. The complicated mosaic of Nazi espionage in the United States was beginning to come into focus, but J. Edgar Hoover was not yet ready to cast out his dragnet. When the time was ripe to strike, the FBI chief wanted to make certain that the largest possible number of Nazi "fish" would be hauled in.

Fuehrer Adolf Hitler. *(Author's Collection)*

FBI Director J. Edgar Hoover. *(Author's Collection)*

Karl Schlueter, Nazi chief courier on trans-
Atlantic liners. (New York Post, 1939)

Fritz Wiedemann, Hitler's World War I
captain, was U.S. West Coast Nazi
spymaster. (New York Post, 1939)

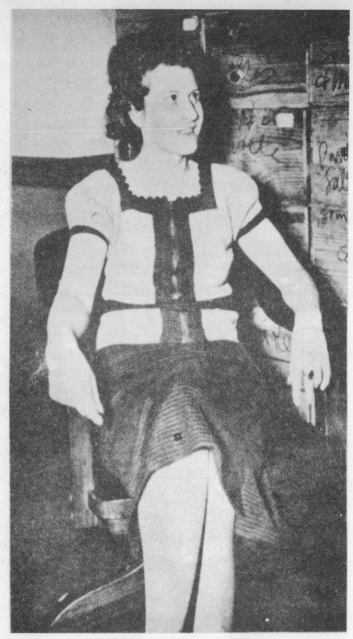

Johanna "Jenni" Hofmann, hairdresser on German
liner and Abwehr courier. (New York Post, *1939*)

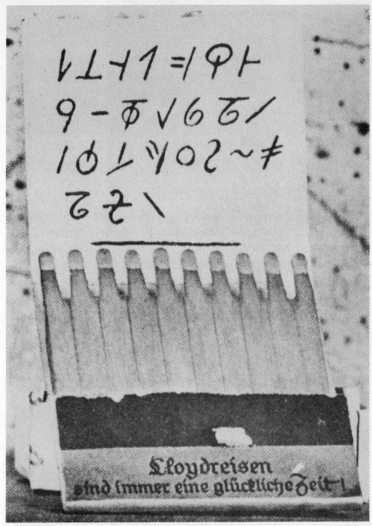

Nazi spies in the United States used the above authentic code. But this is an exhibit. The matchbook is the kind used, but the coded message was written lower down, so that it was concealed by the matches. *(FBI)*

Dr. Ignatz T. Griebl, New York physician
and chief of Nazi spy ring. (New York Post,
1939)

Guenther Rumrich, masterspy, who stole
many U.S. military secrets. Abwehr code
name was "Crown." (New York Post, *1939*)

Kate Moog, the married Dr.
Griebl's wealthy girlfriend.
(New York Post, 1939)

Guenther Rumrich made initial
contact with the Abwehr through
a blind ad in *The New York Times*
under the name Theodor Koerner
(fifth message down). *(FBI)*

Abwehr chief Admiral Wilhelm Canaris masterminded Nazi espionage operations in the United
States. *(Imperial War Museum)*

American oil tycoon
William Rhodes Davis
was Agent C-80 on
Abwehr registry. He
called on President
Roosevelt in the White
House. *(Imperial War
Museum)*

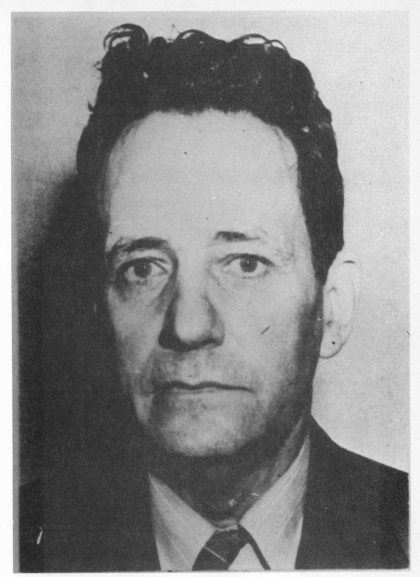

The Old Boer—masterspy Fritz Duquesne—wanted to bomb
President Roosevelt's Hyde Park estate. *(FBI)*

Wilhelmplatz 8/9, Berlin, Nazi propaganda minister Josef Goebbels's nerve center for directing operations in the United States. (*Signal*)

The May 1, 1941 issue of *The Free American*, the official newspaper of the German-American Bund, which took the Nazi Party line from Josef Goebbels's headquarters in Berlin. *(Author's Collection)*

To
George Sylvester Viereck
with all good wishes
from

Theodore Roosevelt

Oct 1st 1913

George Sylvester Viereck, who operated a Nazi propaganda
mill inside the Capitol in Washington, had long cultivated
the friendship of prominent figures. One of these was
Theodore Roosevelt, who had inscribed one of Viereck's
books. *(Courtesy of Ronald von Klaussen)*

Masterspy Kurt Ludwig. *(FBI)*

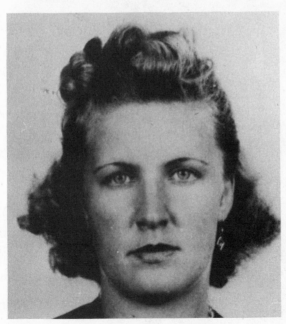

Kurt Ludwig's assistant, teenager Lucy
Boehmler. *(FBI)*

Photo found in Kurt Ludwig's camera shows the entrance to the Cuyahoga River from Lake Erie, a waterway essential to U.S. defense production. *(FBI)*

FBI agents took this photo of a secluded cottage in Centerport, Long Island, which was rented by Nazi spy agent Kurt Ludwig to radio information to Germany. *(FBI)*

Shortwave radio station as set up prior to its purchase by master-spy Kurt Ludwig. *(FBI)*

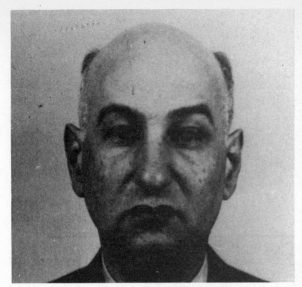

Nazi Major Paul Borchardt, the cagey old
pro. *(FBI)*

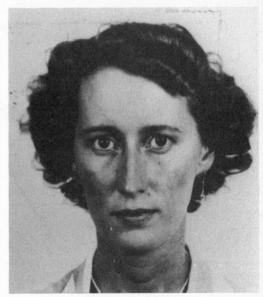

Helen Pauline Mayer, American-born
and zealous Nazi agent. *(FBI)*

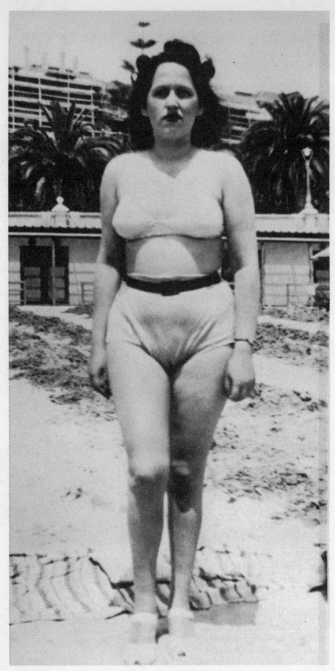

Lilly Barbara Stein used her New York
City home to forward spy reports to the
Third Reich. *(FBI)*

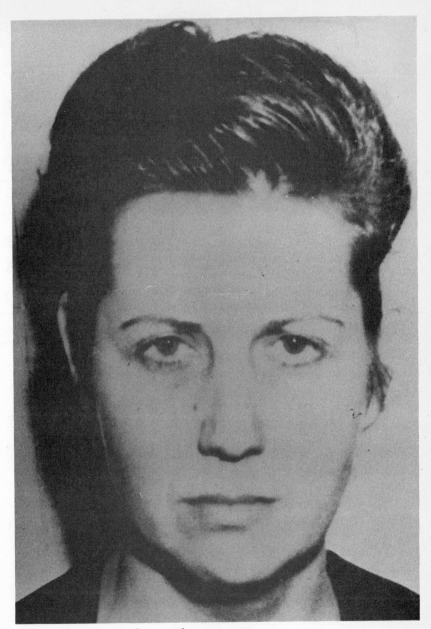

Evelyn Clayton Lewis, housewife agent. *(FBI)*

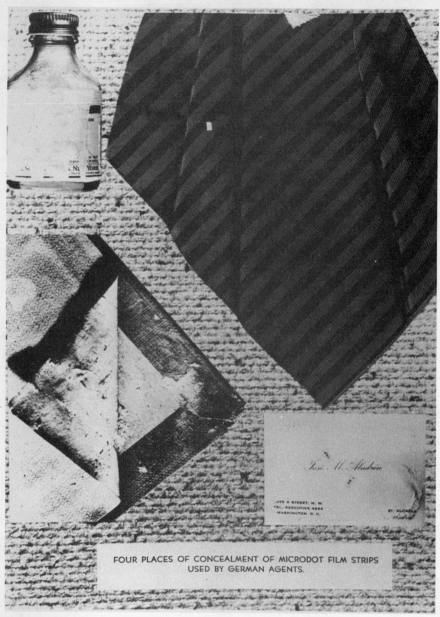

FOUR PLACES OF CONCEALMENT OF MICRODOT FILM STRIPS
USED BY GERMAN AGENTS.

Four places of concealment of microdot film strips used by
German agents in the United States. *(FBI)*

'rederick Duquesne in phony New York City office of FBI counterspy
Iarry Sawyer (real name William Sebold). Sawyer is the other man. The
'BI took these photos covertly through a two-way mirror in the adjoin-
ng office. *(FBI)*

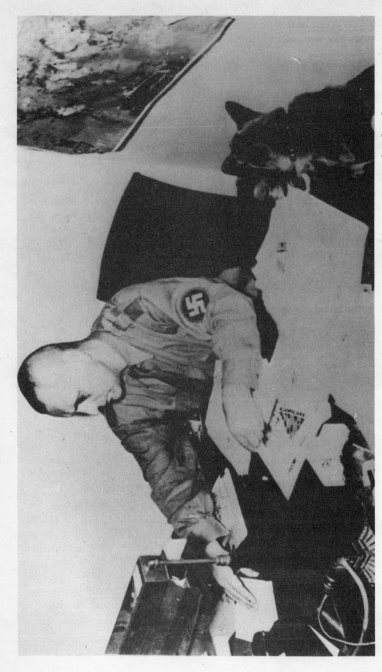

Wealthy Anastase A. Vonsiatsky, wearing Nazi swastika on arm and guarded by a German shepherd, at his Thompson, Connecticut, estate. *(FBI)*

Scene in Thompson, Connecticut, armory of Anastase A. Vonsiatsky. He directed his Nazi spy network from here. Note rifles at right. *(FBI)*

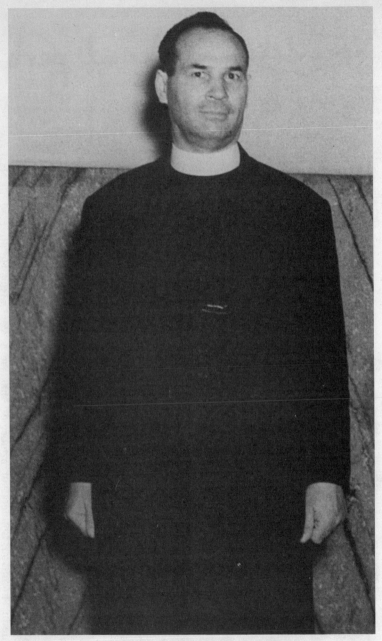

Ace Nazi agent Anastase A. Vonsiatsky in one of his
disguises—a priest's garb. *(FBI)*

Secret photo of Frederick Duquesne taken by
an FBI agent. *(FBI)*

Fritz Duquesne and Harry Sawyer (FBI counterspy
William Sebold) in covert photo. Note FBI has
blacked out Sebold's face. *(FBI)*

Percy E. Foxworth, Special Agent in charge of New York City FBI office. *(FBI)*

FBI Special Agent in Charge,
Thomas J. Donegan, who directed
the search for Operation Patorius
saboteurs. *(FBI)*

Lieutenant Reinhard Hardegen surfaced
his U-boat in New York harbor a month
after America went to war. *(National
Archives)*

A freighter explodes after being torpedoed by U-boat. In 1942, scenes like this occurred almost nightly off the United States eastern coast. Often U-boat skippers had been tipped off by Nazi spies. *(U.S. Coast Guard)*

Two months after Hitler declared war on the United States, the huge luxury liner *Normandie* was destroyed by fire at its New York dock, on February 9, 1942. Most Americans refused to accept the official verdict of carelessness on the part of workers. *(U.S. Navy)*

George John Dasch (left), a one-time New York waiter, and Ernest Peter Berger, a former member of the Michigan National Guard, were the only Nazi spies of Operation Pastorius to escape execution in mid-1942. *(FBI)*

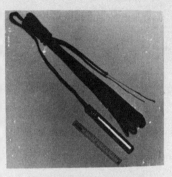

**ELECTRIC BLASTING CAP WITH
COPPER WIRES**

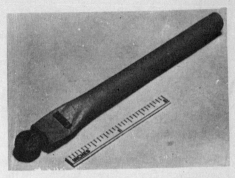

**SAFETY FUSE LIGHTER FOR THE IGNITION
OF STANDARD SAFETY FUSE**

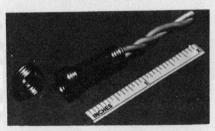

**ELECTRIC MATCH WITH SCREW CAP REMOVED--USED IN
CONJUNCTION WITH TIMING MECHANISM AND BATTERY**

**CAPSULE CONTAINING SULPHURIC ACID ENCASED
IN RUBBER TUBING FOR PROTECTION**

Tools brought ashore by Operation Pastorius saboteurs. *(FBI)*

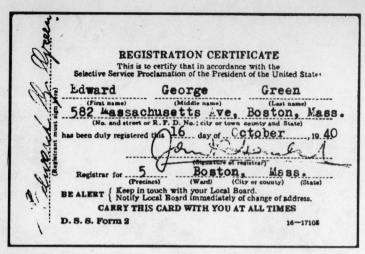

REGISTRATION CERTIFICATE
This is to certify that in accordance with the
Selective Service Proclamation of the President of the United States

Edward   George   Green
(First name)   (Middle name)   (Last name)

582 Massachusetts Ave, Boston, Mass.
(No. and street or R.F.D. No.; city or town county and State)

has been duly registered this 16 day of October , 19 40

(Signature of registrar)

Registrar for   5   Boston,   Mass.
(Precinct)   (Ward)   (City or county)   (State)

BE ALERT { Keep in touch with your Local Board.
Notify Local Board immediately of change of address.

CARRY THIS CARD WITH YOU AT ALL TIMES

D. S. S. Form 2   16—17105

Forged draft card crafted by the Abwehr in the name of
Edward George Green and carried into the United States
by Nazi spy Erich Gimpel. *(FBI)*

Unsung heroes in the war on Hitler's espionage apparatus in America were the FBI
laboratory technicians, such as the one
above. *(FBI)*

18

Harassing the Fuehrer's Crony

In July 1940 Great Britain was a lion at bay. But even if England were overrun, the British were determined to continue the fight against Nazi Germany from overseas bases. A few billion pounds sterling had already been smuggled across the Atlantic to Canada, and preparations had been made to evacuate the royal family and the government. In this desperate climate, Prime Minister Winston Churchill would need a base for the British secret service if England were seized, so he presented his old friend Franklin Roosevelt with an astonishing proposal, the like of which the United States had never known.

Churchill suggested that a foreign power—Great Britain—be permitted to establish in New York City a center for cloak-and-dagger operations in the Western Hemisphere. The President expressed interest, so William Stephenson, a short Canadian millionaire industrialist with a background in covert operations, sneaked into Washington in the guise of a businessman on a commercial trip to sell the President—and FBI chief J. Edgar Hoover—on Churchill's plan.

Following secret discussions in the White House, an agreement was hammered out in what Roosevelt would call "the closest possible marriage between the FBI and British Intelligence." The entire affair was so hush-hush that not even the U.S. State Department was let in on the secret.

Known as "Little Bill," Stephenson was small only in physical stature; he possessed a stout heart, enormous drive, and a keen and devious mind. He quickly set up his command post on the thirty-fifth and thirty-sixth floors of the International Building in Rockefeller Center. In what was supposed to be a British Passport Control Office, Stephenson and his covert operatives would investigate and take counteraction against German undercover operations, including the prevention of sabotage to British shipping. Adopting the name British Security Coordination (BSC), Stephenson's organization mushroomed rapidly to major proportions, and the headquarters staff alone would eventually number more than one thousand persons.

Bill Stephenson (code-named Intrepid) and J. Edgar Hoover hit it off harmoniously from the beginning—much to the astonishment of those who knew the two strong-willed supersleuths. In a delicate situation that could have resulted in incessant bickering, back-stabbing, and fireworks between the FBI and the BSC, Hoover and Stephenson became trusted partners and mutual admirers in the secret war against the Nazi espionage apparatus in the United States.

In mid-1940, with the ominous shadow of war with Hitler's Germany edging ever closer, the U.S. Army and Navy requested the FBI to inspect some two thousand industrial plants, aircraft factories, and ammunition arsenals and to suggest methods for tightening security and preventing sabotage. It was a mammoth task, but Hoover's men plunged into it with customary vigor. In Detroit, Feds were told by a proud company official that management had already launched a unique security program to detect potential troublemakers. A full-time phrenologist had been hired to interview each employee, and he could tell by the shape of a person's head if he was disloyal or dishonest.

"That's what the man said," an FBI agent reported to his home office, "and so help me God they do employ a phrenologist!" [1]

* * *

At the same time that the phrenologist was studying head contours in Detroit, Klaus Mehnert, a young German intellectual, was teaching anthropology at the University of Hawaii in Honolulu. A highly regarded professor on campus, Mehnert was also a clever and productive spy, one deeply imbued with the glories of Teutonic splendor and the ideals of Nazism.

A few years earlier Professor Mehnert had belonged to a group of German plotters, headquartered in Breslau, called the *Osteuropa Gesellschaft* (East Europe Society). Mehnert and his fellow conspirators dreamed of a world dominated by Nazi Germany and felt that Russia was a weak spot against which the first major blow should be struck. But by early 1938 the East Europe Society began to have doubts and concluded that the Soviet Union would be a tough nut to crack. So the focus of this band of zealots shifted in other directions. Mehnert and a few others from the society hooked up with a group of Germans headed by Major General Karl Haushofer, the "inventor" of geopolitics, which assesses the influence of such factors as geography, economics, and demography on the political and foreign policy of a country. Diehard Nazi Mehnert was impressed by what he had learned at the knee of Haushofer, so he became one of the free-lancing geopolitical spies who, financed by Dr. Alfred Rosenberg's Foreign Political Bureau, were scattered throughout the world.

Mehnert was sent to the United States, where he recruited a ring of geopolitical spies on college campuses, including students at the University of California at Berkeley; Miami University at Oxford, Ohio; and the University of Hawaii. His post as a professor in Honolulu provided an excellent camouflage for his true role—spying.

In 1938 Mehnert learned of the vulnerability of Pearl Harbor, America's major naval base in the Pacific, when Admiral Ernest J. King launched a successful mock air strike from the carrier *Saratoga* to conclude major war games called Fleet Problem XIX. King's pilots sneaked through Pearl Harbor's defenses undetected and "bombed" the naval base and nearby airfields.

Mehnert, who had been eavesdropping on the naval exercise, sent to his masters in Berlin an exhaustive report in which he (accurately) detailed woefully weak spots in the Hawaiian Islands' defenses. An astute student of naval tactics, Mehnert suggested that a daring and skillfully executed attack by a foreign power (that is, Japan) could break through these defenses and strike a telling blow against the U.S. Pacific fleet. American forces would then be paralyzed and unable to carry a war westward from Hawaii, Mehnert pointed out.[2]

Since Germany and Japan were still locked in the espionage alliance negotiated by the wily Colonel Nicolai back in 1935, Mehnert's report on glaring American weaknesses in the Pacific was eventually shuttled on to Tokyo. There, unknown to their German allies, Japanese warlords were already drawing up operational plans for war with America.

(After World War II, some top United States Naval Intelligence officers concluded that Mehnert's hand was visible in Japan's grand strategic design for conquest in the Pacific, including the opening sneak attack against the U.S. fleet at Pearl Harbor.)[3]

In late 1940 U.S. Naval Intelligence covered Mehnert's student spy ring and notified the heads of the various universities. Most of the academic leaders shrugged off the warning, but the president of the University of Hawaii launched an investigation into the charge. A few days later Professor Mehnert hightailed it out of the islands and never returned.

At the same time as the respected anthropology professor had vanished mysteriously from the Honolulu campus, Captain Ellis Zacharias was suffering pangs of frustration in his new post of Naval Intelligence chief for the West Coast of the United States. It was the same malady that gripped many American military officers who knew that each day the nation was edging closer to war, yet the citizens and most government leaders were indifferent to their peril.

It was Zacharias who, back in 1935, had unmasked the Washington-based espionage alliance between Japanese navy Captain Tamon Yamaguchi and the German military attaché, an operation centered in the Alban Towers. Yamaguchi's covert house of cards had collapsed and he was called back to Tokyo when the German-Japanese spy operation had received a thorough airing in United States media. (No doubt the media had been tipped off by U.S. Naval Intelligence.)

On his return to Tokyo, Yamaguchi had been promoted to rear admiral and assigned to the Navy Ministry as a principal aide to Admiral Isoroku Yamamoto, chief of the Imperial Fleet. Yamaguchi was given the task of translating the many theories of war against the United States into a single operational plan. On January 1, 1940, the former Washington spymaster reported to Admiral Yamamoto that the Nipponese fleet was ready to attack.[4]

Ever since he was eight years old, Zacharias had yearned to be a sailor. But on October 20, 1920, the Naval Academy graduate reported to an assignment in Naval Intelligence with mixed emotions. Like most of his fellow military pros, Zacharias regarded "Intelligence" with suspicion—he had only a hazy notion of even the meaning of the word. But he applied himself diligently over the years and became recognized as one of the handful of Americans who were experts in the field.

Now, in mid-1940, Captain Zacharias's frustration was fostered not only by America's apathy toward her peril, but also because he knew that the West Coast was thick with Nazi and Japanese spies and their sympathizers and that he had only a handful of Intelligence men to deal with this menace. And Zacharias's domain was staggering in scope, stretching along the coastal states from the Canadian to the Mexican borders.

However, in the face of these enormous obstacles, Zacharias took the offensive from his post in San Diego: He launched a campaign to locate and record the addresses of the five thousand persons in his district who were on the Naval Intelligence loyalty-suspect list. This was the first time a security program of this type had been conducted in the United States. It would prove to be a gargantuan task.

The naval sleuth's spirits were buoyed when Sheriff Eugene W. Biscailuz of Los Angeles County volunteered to throw the entire resources of his department into the cataloging operation. Biscailuz's support was especially crucial for it was in the Los Angeles region that the greatest number of loyalty suspects were congregated. Enthusiastic, dedicated, and capable, Sheriff Biscailuz, a navy reserve officer, told Zacharias: "You give the orders, Captain, and I'll carry them out."

When the immense cataloging job was completed, Captain Zacharias sent the list to ONI headquarters in Washington. With it went an urgent recommendation that each naval district in the United States compile similar lists. The recommendation was approved, and when America went to war in early December 1941, the lists allowed a rapid and simultaneous pickup of enemy agents and sympathizers.

At the same time that Zacharias was compiling his lengthy list, he was deeply worried about the espionage vulnerability of American aircraft plants, over half of which were located along the West Coast. To test his theory, Zacharias dressed two German-speaking officers in civilian clothes and sent them to a major aircraft factory in the San Diego area to test security. The two men got inside merely by strolling past a bored watchman, then wandered all over the plant for nearly two hours without once being halted or questioned. From time to time the disguised navy officers would halt, point to a warplane being assembled or to a crucial piece of machinery, and confer animatedly—in German.

Captain Zacharias was appalled—but not surprised—when his undercover sleuths reported back to him. So he immediately launched a drive to tighten up security in airplane plants, an effort that met with indifference and often hostility when the navy men asked for the cooperation of corporation officials.

Zacharias himself called on Ruben Fleet, head of the Consolidated Aircraft Company in San Diego (where counterspy William Sebold had worked and where a Gestapo mole had been planted). Zacharias told Fleet that Consolidated should beef up the guard force and begin issuing identification tags with facial photographs to all employees. Fleet was unimpressed, pointing out that Consolidated Aircraft had no "spy problem." (At the time Fleet had no inkling that his firm's secrets had been flowing to Berlin and Hamburg for years.)

Fleet was foremost a shrewd businessman trying to keep costs down, so he added: "Besides, Captain, that would be too expensive." Zacharias would not be fended off. "But, Rube," he said with an air of finality, "you are going to have to do it and like it later on, so why not now?"[5]

Fleet pondered that blunt remark, then agreed to cooperate, and in a short time security at Con Air was tightened dramatically.

Captain Zacharias had another iron in the fire in battling espionage on the West Coast: He was keeping a watchful eye on the German consulate in San Francisco and its leader, the suave Fritz Wiedemann, Hitler's crony and World War I company commander and for the past year Nazi espionage chief on the West Coast. No legal action could be taken against Wiedemann, who ostensibly was a diplomat of a country that was officially "friendly" with the United States government. So Zacharias concocted a devious scheme to harass him, to keep him off balance, to direct his attention elsewhere from spying.

Zacharias called in one of his double agents who had important contacts in Berlin and was supposed to be spying for Wiedemann. No doubt with impish delight, the navy officer outlined his scenario, in which the double agent was to play the star's role. Then the man was dispatched to San Francisco to put on the show; he would perform with Barrymore-like stage skill.

The double agent sought out Fritz Wiedemann and, in a conspiratorial tone, disclosed alarming (and phony) news. The man said that he had learned from his contacts in the Third Reich that Wiedemann had fallen into disfavor with the fuehrer and would soon be relieved of his post and brought back to Germany in disgrace.

Customarily unflappable, the spymaster was visibly upset over the news, so much disturbed that he reacted in a manner that exceeded Zacharias's fondest hopes. Wiedemann promptly sent a member of his staff to Berlin, seven thousand miles away, on a wild goose chase to find out from Hitler himself how he had failed. In the meantime, the San Francisco consul general put espionage activities on the back burner.

Fritz Wiedemann's San Francisco outpost was not the only German consulate in the United States that was being operated, in effect, as a branch of German Intelligence. In Boston the debonair diplomat Dr. Herbert Scholz, who had been the toast of Washington society until being transferred to New England in late 1939, had rapidly recruited a stable of agents. One of them was a reserve captain attached to U.S. Army Intelligence who kept Scholz informed on steps being taken to counteract German espionage activities in New England. Scholz also made

contact with a group of hoodlums who claimed to be members
of the Irish Republican Army and who hated the British. Their
professed goal was to blow up British shipping in Boston harbor, and one freighter was sunk in the Charles River under mysterious circumstances.[6]

In Los Angeles, it was an open secret that Consul General
Georg Gyssling was the *Kreisleiter* (Nazi Party district leader)
for California. He had a string of spy posts stretching along hundreds of miles of coastline, and much of the information he
collected from these agents was of particular interest to the Japanese, who soon received the data.

Consul General Karl Kapp in Cleveland was an especially industrious diplomat/spy who penetrated the Cleveland civil defense system, procured voluminous information on plants that
were converting to war production, and even sent home an experimental U.S. army gas mask that had been stolen by one of
his American agents. With the active connivance of a sixty-year-
old Akron, Ohio, attorney who compiled mailing lists, Kapp
sent out tens of thousands of pamphlets whose theme was that
President Roosevelt was "a captive of international Jewry."[7]

Then there was Baron Edgar von Spiegel, New Orleans consul general, a former U-boat skipper and a crude but often effective operative. Von Spiegel's clumsy effort to blackmail an
American newspaper publisher in his region brought about a
noisy State Department investigation—but no other official
action.

In Chicago, Consul General Hans Krause-Wichmann's domain was the Midwest, and about ten Abwehr and SD agents
took orders from him. Krause-Wichmann wrote Berlin that, for
a few dollars per month, an American was supplying him with
the takeoff airfields and dates of departure of warplanes being
flown to England.

German diplomats in the United States had no problem with
sending stolen or acquired intelligence to the Fatherland—it
was sent by couriers in bulging diplomatic pouches. But the
swarm of ordinary Nazi agents operating in America had to
send reports and documents through the regular mails. To dry
up or put a crimp into this espionage conduit between America

and the Third Reich, the British established the Imperial Censorship station at Hamilton, Bermuda. It was staffed by a force that would eventually number twelve hundred handwriting experts, chemists (to detect invisible inks), cryptanalysts (to solve complicated codes), and assorted sleuths. Nerve center for the operation was in the Princess Hotel, a pink colonial structure that was one of the most ornate buildings on the island.

All Pan American Clippers and ocean liners traveling between the Western Hemisphere and Europe were required to halt at Bermuda and deliver their bags of mail to the censorship station. Hundreds of thousands of assorted letters, packages, and postcards flooded the facility each week.

The British were extremely skillful in the art of scrutinizing mail and, with the survival of the Empire at stake, were not the least bit squeamish about opening sacrosanct diplomatic mail of neutral nations. Examiners had developed a technique for removing diplomatic seals and replacing them without any outsider being the wiser. This process was done so adroitly that the opened and resealed diplomatic mail would stand up to subsequent ultraviolet or chemical tests that might be conducted to determine if a particular piece of mail had been tampered with.

Both the Federal Bureau of Investigation and Bill Stephenson's British Security Coordination office in New York City helped recruit specialists for the Bermuda censorship station. Personnel analysts had discovered that women were the most skilled openers of mail and that those with the greatest dexterity had slender, attractive legs. Female job applicants who were interviewed by the FBI and asked to show their lower legs often left the building speculating uneasily about just what would be expected of them at the mysterious censorship outpost.[8]

19

An Abwehr Agent
Penetrates Congress

Each week during the first half of 1940, George Viereck, the world's highest-paid propaganda virtuoso, had been dashing between his plush Manhattan apartment (which was adorned with large portraits of Kaiser Wilhelm and Fuehrer Hitler) and the hallowed halls of Congress in Washington. Despite the capital's notorious sweltering summers, Viereck began commuting twice weekly during June, for he had an urgent mission to prevent a seven million dollar arms bill from passing Congress and to influence the forthcoming Democratic and Republican presidential conventions to adopt keep-out-of-the-war platforms.

In Washington, Viereck's propaganda mill operated in the Capitol suite of Senator Ernest Lundeen, a devout isolationist from Minnesota. Although the senator had contacts in Nazi Germany and made speeches before German-American groups, he apparently knew Viereck as a free-lance journalist (his current "cover") and considered him to be a consummate publicist and speech writer.

Viereck was totally at ease working in the office of a United States senator and made no effort to conceal the fact that he was writing speeches for and allegedly collaborating with Lundeen on a variety of projects.

Viereck dictated speech drafts to Mrs. Phyllis Spielman, a secretary to Lundeen, and he would break off his delivery on occasion to telephone the German Embassy for needed information. A short time later a messenger would arrive with an envelope bearing the return address of Dr. Hans Thomsen, the chargé d'affaires and masterspy at the embassy.[1]

Viereck found one flaw in Senator Lundeen's office suite: Its mailing facilities were inadequate for the hundreds of thousands of reprints of Lundeen's Senate-floor isolationist speeches that the propaganda saboteur wanted to send out. So arrangements were made for Viereck's bulk mailing to be done in Room 1424 of the House Office Building. Room 1424 happened to be the suite of Congressman Hamilton Fish, who had known Viereck for several years.

In Fish's office, the New York legislator introduced Viereck to forty-five-year-old George Hill, a mild-mannered clerk on Fish's staff. Hill, a thin, nervous little man with a trace of a mustache, was told by his boss that Viereck wanted to send out reprints of Senator Lundeen's speech and for Hill to use Fish's frank (that is, free mailing privilege) and the mailing list of the National Committee to Keep America Out of Foreign Wars—whose chairman was Hamilton Fish.[2]

Hill was apprehensive. Use taxpayers' money to send out massive amounts of what might be called politically motivated propaganda? But an order was an order. It was a major logistics task, for there were 125,000 names on the list to receive the keep-out-of-the-war speech that Viereck had written and Senator Lundeen had delivered on the Senate floor. Hill had to hire an extra crew of women to get the job done on time.[3]

When the mailing task was completed, George Viereck covertly slipped two rolled-up fifty-dollar bills into Hill's hand. The propagandist's sly wink told the nervous little clerk: "Well done!"[4]

From that point, unpretentious George Hill, a hapless family man trapped by Dame Fate in a high-stakes game of international poker, would be sucked deeper and deeper into Viereck's high-powered Washington propaganda machine.

Wily Viereck knew that he had stumbled onto a propaganda bonanza in his congressional operation and moved rapidly to exploit it. He flooded George Hill with mailings: reprints of anti-Roosevelt and antiwar editorials, transcripts of radio broadcasts, newspaper and magazine clippings, and anything else with keep-America-neutral themes. Included in the bulk mailings were speeches by isolationist members of Congress and articles that Viereck himself had authored under a phony name, then connived to get published.

Hill contrived to get most of the material to be mailed inserted in the *Congressional Record,* a daily compendium of every word spoken and action taken on the floor. This ploy permitted congressional clerk Hill to get hundreds of thousands of reprints from the Government Printing Office.

At George Hill's direction, U.S. postal trucks were used to haul tons of keep-America-neutral mailings to the Washington post office. Not only was Congressman Fish's franking privilege used, but also those of twenty-four other isolationist members of Congress who were allegedly collaborating in the propaganda project or were Viereck's dupes.[5]

In between creating speeches for Lundeen, Viereck was masterminding a camouflaged propaganda campaign aimed at the Republican convention, which would open in Philadelphia during the last week of June 1940. Even before the GOP delegates reached the convention site, a bitter ideological clash was developing. Fifty Republican congressmen, mainly first-termers, under Karl E. Mundt of South Dakota would stump for an isolationist plank (which, Hans Thomsen told Berlin, had been drafted by Viereck). The plank would be pitted against one proposed by Christopher T. Emmett, Jr., of New York. Promoting the latter proposal was the Committee to Defend America by Aiding the Allies, headed by the widely known William Allen White, editor and publisher of the *Emporia Gazette* in Kansas.

On June 25, the day before the GOP convention was to adopt a platform, a full-page ad appeared in the influential *New York Times.* The ad's headline shouted: "Delegates to the Republican National Convention and to American Mothers, Wage-earners, Farmers and Veterans!" The text of the ad called on America to: "Stop the war machine! Stop the warmongers! Stop the Democratic Party, which is leading us to war!"[6]

The ad was signed by Congressman Fish's National Committee to Keep America Out of Foreign Wars. Viereck took credit for creating the ad, which may or may not have been the truth. Perhaps he at least influenced its wording. But the Republicans declined to adopt the isolationist plank and instead came out with one calling for help to beleaguered Great Britain "by all means short of war." [7]

In the meantime, a brawl had been brewing within the Philadelphia conclave over who would be the GOP's presidential choice. One faction was promoting the dark horse of the century, a tousle-haired, broad-grinning Hoosier from Indiana named Wendell A. Willkie. Some called Willkie "the barefoot boy from Wall Street," for he was the highly paid president of the Commonwealth and Southern Corporation, a large utilities firm, yet he wore rumpled suits, adorned day after day with the same old tie, which gave him the air of a country bumpkin.

Across the Atlantic in the Third Reich, Foreign Minister Joachim von Ribbentrop had avidly been monitoring proceedings at the Republican convention, for Hitler had charged him with masterminding a stratagem to keep the United States neutral. Ribbentrop had been receiving from Hans Thomsen a blow-by-blow account of what was going on at the big Philadelphia pow-wow. Nazi bigwigs hoped Senator Burton K. Wheeler, a patriotic American with staunch isolationist views, would get the GOP presidential nomination.

Most of America was shocked when the convention, on the fifth ballot, nominated the relatively unknown Willkie to be the Republican party's standard-bearer. Feeling the shockwaves from afar was Ribbentrop, who fired off a cable to Thomsen requesting information on Willkie's background and views. Thomsen had bad news to report: Country bumpkin Willkie's selection "is unfortunate for us—he is certainly no isolationist." [8]

Hardly had the Philadelphia hoopla subsided than George Viereck and Hans Thomsen took aim at the upcoming Democratic convention in Chicago. Thomsen cabled to Berlin that Viereck had created a full-page ad appealing to Democrats to keep America out of the war in Europe. On July 15 an ad ran in the *Chicago Tribune*, isolationist publisher Robert R. McCormick's influential newspaper. As with the GOP-targeted ad, this one carried the signature of Congressman Fish's committee. With slight variations, the ad had the same theme as the one aimed at the Republicans: Don't allow the Democratic Party to become "the Party of intervention and war." [9]

Meanwhile, political old pro Franklin Roosevelt was playing

it coy. Faced with a 144-year-old precedent against a president serving a third term, Roosevelt remained mysteriously silent throughout the political jockeying leading up to the Chicago convention, but he "allowed" himself to be "drafted" by his party *in absentia*. While the President played solitaire beside the White House radio, his campaign managers adroitly orchestrated a demonstration that rocked the Chicago convention hall with shouts of "We want Roosevelt!" Whereupon the President decided that he could not "decline to serve my country."

Indiana country bumpkin Willkie and New York sophisticate Roosevelt would slug it out at the polls in November.

On July 15, 1940, even while Democratic leaders were descending on Chicago, Adolf Hitler was being fêted as a conquering hero. That night the Kroll Opera House in Berlin was packed with bemedaled Wehrmacht officers in dress uniforms, their exquisitely gowned and coiffed wives, and assorted Nazi Party faithful. There was a gala spirit in the air, a blend of electricity and Teutonic nostalgia.

Suddenly the majestic old edifice rocked with applause as the fuehrer of the Greater Reich, who had conquered all of Western Europe, save for the neutral nations, in an astonishing fifty-two days, strode to the lectern.

Clad in a simple gray uniform adorned with an Iron Cross, the medal he had been awarded in 1914 for heroism in the bloody battle of Ypres, Hitler told the hushed audience, "I appeal once more to reason and common sense in Great Britain." Then, extending an olive branch across the English Channel, the fuehrer added, "I consider myself in a position to make this appeal, since I am not the vanquished begging for favors, but the victor speaking in the name of reason. I can see no reason why this war must go on."[10]

At the same time that Adolf Hitler was singing his siren song of peace, the FBI in the United States was diligently laboring to hold back the floodtide of German espionage. But in many ways the democracy that was America remained a spy's paradise. There was handy over-the-counter espionage. A trip to the Government Printing Office in Washington could yield confidential information at a nominal price. Many of the U.S. Army's and Navy's training, equipment, and weapons manuals were offered for sale—no questions asked.

Nazi agents were regular callers at the document rooms of the United States Senate and House of Representatives. Since none of the agents wore a tag with the word spy, each was treated just like any loyal citizen. An abundance of information of great value to the espionage masterminds in the Third Reich could be obtained at a cost of a few dollars.

In France, England, and elsewhere, Nazi spies often had to pay thousands of dollars, and risk their lives or freedom, to acquire specifications of new airplanes, but much similar data could be acquired in the United States for the expenditure of a few cents, merely by buying a newspaper or trade magazine.

Often important American technical information could be obtained at the cost of a five-cent postage stamp. One high-grade and productive Nazi agent, forty-eight-year-old Edmund Carl Heine, relied on Uncle Sam's mails—and a gullible citizenry—to generate a flow of classified American industrial data that was highly prized by Hamburg and Berlin.

In mid-July 1940 Heine purchased (for ten cents) an aviation trade magazine and took it to his home at 4447 Baldwin Avenue, Detroit. Poring over the publication, he spotted an advertisement of the Consolidated Aircraft Corporation in San Diego. The ad boasted that it had taken Consolidated only nine months to conceive and fly a new airplane. It did not identify the plane, presumably because such information was restricted by the military.

Heine concocted a scheme to obtain the missing ingredient. On July 22 he wrote a letter to Consolidated Aircraft, using the stationery of the Chrysler Motor Company, for which he had been an executive of late. (He gave his home address for a reply.) The letter said:

> In order to settle a few disputes among a number of friends, would you kindly answer the following question: Was it the B-24 [bomber] that was conceived and made its first flight in nine months?

Only a few days later Norman Davidson, a public relations executive at Consolidated Aircraft, fired back a reply: Indeed it had been the B-24. Clearly Davidson and others at Con Air were quite proud of this exceptional achievement.[11]

Within a few days Heine's information on the new U.S. Army bomber was in the hands of "model" Lilly Stein. Heine had earlier struck up an acquaintance with Lilly, and she was one of his contacts in New York. Lilly in turn passed along the data to William Sebold, who made microfilms of it—after the information had been doctored by the FBI. Sebold then slipped the tiny negatives to one of the Abwehr couriers on the fast German liners still crisscrossing the Atlantic.

Edmund Heine, well bred and a flashy dresser, had worked as an executive for the Ford Motor Company since 1920 in Spain, South America, and Germany. At the latter post, he became friends with Dr. Ferdinand Porsche, an automotive design genius who had developed the Volkswagen (People's Car) and was sort of a free-lance scout for the Abwehr.

In a series of relaxed conversations over cocktails, Porsche convinced the $30,000-per-year (a hefty sum at the time) auto executive to return to the United States, seek a position in Detroit, and collect information "not normally available" about the American aviation and automotive industries. Porsche appealed to Heine's "patriotism."

Heine went through the espionage course at the Academy in Hamburg and was told that he would be given a captain's commission in the Luftwaffe Reserve. Back in Detroit, he took a high-paying job with Chrysler and launched his spying career by placing ads in *Popular Aviation* magazine, stating that he was seeking information on the latest developments in the aircraft industry. A flock of replies came in, some of them providing useful data from knowledgeable sources, and Heine paid each respondent twenty dollars for his information. The Abwehr agent then shuttled the materials on to Hamburg and took full credit for them as products of his own efforts.

Meanwhile, in mid-summer 1940, Abwehr station AOR in Hamburg was bombarding the Centerport shortwave station with demands that Hermann Lang, the inspector at the Norden bombsight plant in Brooklyn, steal pieces of the instrument and bring them to the Fatherland. Lang had gone to the Third Reich in 1938, received a hero's welcome from the Abwehr, and told German scientists everything he could recall about the details of the bombsight. But despite this information and the blueprints that Lang had stolen, the Germans still could not refine a similar Norden bombsight that they had built.

Sebold approached Lang and asked if he could steal some components of the bombsight. A cinch, Lang responded, adding that he could haul off the company president's desk without anyone questioning the action. But, Lang declared, the Nazi government would have to assure him that he would be compensated should his three thousand dollars in securities decline while he was in the Third Reich.

Sebold (that is, FBI agents Price and Ellsworth) radioed Hamburg with Lang's demand. Two days later AOR replied: "Promise Lang anything. Repeat, anything. All we want to do is to get him over here with the pieces, and we'll take care of him after we get a completed bombsight."

It was grim business, but Hoover's men guffawed. They knew how the Gestapo would "take care of" Lang after he was of no further use to the fuehrer.[12]

In early August 1940 George Viereck's mission to sabotage through propaganda America's defense buildup took on an increased urgency. Congress was embroiled in an acrimonious debate over the Selective Service and Training Bill, which called for the first peacetime draft in the nation's history. The measure had been introduced in June by Senator Edward R. Burke and Representative James W. Wadsworth.

As the debate raged, staunch isolationists were nearly apoplectic. "If you pass this bill," Senator Burton Wheeler thundered, "you accord Hitler his greatest and cheapest victory to date." Congressman Martin L. Sweeney, vice chairman of the House Armed Forces Committee, howled that "conscription was a scheme to deliver the United States to the British devils."[13]

However, Viereck knew in mid-August that the bill would pass. At that time a Gallup poll disclosed that 71 percent of

Americans favored a draft. The measure became law on September 16. Having conceded defeat a month earlier, propaganda saboteur Viereck had already been hard at work trying to influence the fall presidential election campaign.

Even though there was hardly an iota of ideological difference in the views of Franklin Roosevelt and Wendell Willkie, the campaign was a shrill and bitter one, fought against a backdrop of the brutal war in Europe and the Luftwaffe blitz that was pounding London. Both candidates saw eye to eye on aid to Britain and on domestic issues.

Slogans hurled back and forth sounded home-grown, pure Americanisms. But behind these strident outcries lurked the hand of German-born George Viereck. Hans Thomsen cabled home the contents of assorted slogans that Viereck said he had dreamed up, and within days the words were falling out of millions of American mouths, their true source unknown. One of the most prevalent was that Roosevelt, the "war monger," would "plow every fourth American boy under." Another popular Viereck-inspired slogan was "American boys are already on the transports."

Roosevelt's political braintrust was deeply worried over evidence that the President had been severely wounded by the isolationist attacks. Letters from Democratic faithful poured into the White House, beseeching the chief executive to "do something about it." Roosevelt, too, had grown concerned. So on October 30, only a week before the election, the President trumpeted in a speech: "I have said this before, but I shall say it again and again and again: your boys are not going to be sent into any foreign wars!" [14]

On election day, November 5, Wendell Willkie received some 22 million votes—the most votes that a Republican candidate had received in the twentieth century. But 5 million more Americans, totaling 27 million, cast their ballots for Franklin Roosevelt.

One week after the election, on November 12, bomb blasts rocked three war-production plants. At Allentown, Pennsylvania, the Trojan Powder Company was blown up, killing sixteen persons and injuring scores of others. At Woodbridge, New Jersey, two buildings of the United Railway and Signals Corporation, which manufactured torpedoes, were leveled by explosions. And at Edinburg, Pennsylvania, the Burton Powder Works was destroyed.

The blasts occurred at ten-minute intervals—at 8:00 A.M., 8:10, and 8:20. Secretary of War Henry L. Stimson suggested that the clockwork precision "might represent Teutonic efficiency." [15]

Despite President Roosevelt's ringing pronouncement that American boys would not be sent into foreign wars, the nation was being dragged steadily into the conflict. The Luftwaffe pounded into rubble the English city of Coventry a week after Roosevelt was reelected, and Winston Churchill informed him that "we are entering upon a somber phase of what must evidently be a protracted and broadening war." [16]

In the meantime, J. Edgar Hoover and his G-men were stepping up their own covert war—this one against the fuehrer's spy invasion.

20

Who Is the Mysterious Joe K?

Hard on the heels of the bitter presidential election campaign, the Federal Bureau of Investigation began picking up reports from covert sources that Fritz Wiedemann, the German consul general in San Francisco and Nazi spymaster on the West Coast, was anxiously trying to get in secret touch with British Intelligence. Following these tips, cautious inquiry by a British diplomat indicated that Wiedemann had grown disillusioned with his World War I corporal. Wiedemann was convinced that the fuehrer was now ignoring the advice of his generals and felt that their professional opinions were far more reliable than was Hitler's intuition.[1]

Even though the German warlord and his mighty Wehrmacht reigned supreme over most of Western Europe, Wiedemann wanted to learn what terms England would demand to bring an end to the war before the fuehrer's dreams of conquest resulted in eventual disaster for the Fatherland. In the wake of Wiedemann's feelers, there had apparently been a flurry of behind-the-scenes activity, for on November 26, 1940, an English nobleman, using a fictitious name, checked into Room 1026 at the fashionable Mark Hopkins Hotel in San Francisco. The visitor, called Sir John, was a widely known international banker, and the Feds knew that he had contacts with British Intelligence in the United States.

Hardly had Sir John unpacked his bags than there was a timid knock on his door. He opened it to admit Her Serene Highness, Princess Stefanie, the European socialite who had consorted with Adolf Hitler and Hermann Goering prior to the outbreak of war and for the past two years had been a confident of Fritz Wiedemann's in California. The British nobleman and the princess talked for two hours and forty-five minutes. Sir John said that he represented a group of his countrymen who felt that satisfactory peace terms could be negotiated between England and Germany "before the United States is drawn into the war." [2]

The pair discussed the possibility of Princess Stefanie going to Berlin to lay a peace proposal before *Der Fuehrer* himself. Her Serene Highness was enthusiastic: Here was the opportunity to resume her rightful position in the international spotlight. Sir John said that he would recommend to "Number Ten Downing Street" (Winston Churchill's address) that Stefanie's peace mission be given unofficial approval by the British government.

After dining together that night, Sir John and the princess were joined in Room 1026 by Fritz Wiedemann. Now the two men did most of the talking, and the proposal to send the princess to Hitler was shoved into the background. But red-haired Stefanie came up with another approach: Why not double-cross Hitler, the master of the double cross? She suggested an alliance between England and Germany, and then "Churchill could fool the fuehrer." Much to her disillusionment, the two men rejected her brainstorm. [3] It was finally concluded that the best means for returning stability to Europe was to covertly seek the Wehrmacht's help, bounce Hitler out of office (or execute him), and put a king back on the throne.

Five weeks later, on January 4, 1941, Walter Nipkin, a German-born American citizen who was a lathe operator at the Air Associates plant in Bendix, New Jersey, was approached by a fellow employee, Carl Reuper, the Nazi spy with the executive management style. After a lengthy recital of the grandeurs of the New Germany, Reuper disclosed that he worked for the Abwehr and his mission was to ferret out U.S. military secrets.

Sensing from Nipkin's silence that the potential recruit was eager to help the cause of Nazism, Reuper glanced around to make certain that no one was watching, then pulled from his pocket several sketches and blueprints. These were the kinds of materials needed by the Fatherland. Would Nipkin show his loyalty by pilfering similar ones?

For the first time Nipkin seemed hesitant. How could he get away with stealing secret blueprints? Easy, Reuper replied. Nipkin would simply slip the documents to him. He would photograph them and have the originals back to Nipkin within an hour. But Nipkin was not yet sold. How much money would he get for that? Reuper flushed in anger. How could Nipkin think of money when the Fatherland was fighting for its life? When the spy prospect insisted that he should receive something for his efforts, Reuper brightened and told him that indeed he would be rewarded—with an autographed picture of *Der Fuehrer*.

Reluctantly, Walter Nipkin agreed to cooperate—for *Der Fuehrer*.

A week later the two men huddled in a secluded nook of Air Associates, and Nipkin, nervous and perspiring, deftly slipped secret drawings to the spymaster. Reuper was delighted. Within ten days copies of the blueprints were on the way to Hamburg.

However, the blueprints would only mislead German aviation engineers, for the drawings bore about as much resemblance to Air Associates secrets as J. Edgar Hoover did to Adolf Hitler. After Reuper had first identified himself as an Abwehr agent, Nipkin had gone to the FBI office in Newark and told his story. The G-men had advised Nipkin to play along with the spymaster, so when Reuper demanded secret blueprints, the FBI accommodated him—with phony drawings.

For five months the mild-mannered native of Mülheim would continue in his masquerade as a Nazi agent and periodically slip Reuper authentic-looking but worthless blueprints and specifications, mainly those of obsolete military aircraft. At no time would Reuper gain an inkling that Nipkin, who loved the Old Germany but cherished his adopted land, was putting the finger on nearly every member of the Nazi's gang.

Meanwhile, in early 1941, sharp-eyed mail scanners at the British Imperial Censorship Bureau in Bermuda had taken note of a series of letters signed "Joe K" that had New York postmarks and were destined for addresses in Spain and Portugal. Joe K's English was stilted, even forced, thereby arousing suspicion that he could be a German spy. But who was the mysterious Joe K?

On January 30 Charles Watkins-Mence, chief of the Bermuda bureau, ordered a watch for more letters from Joe K, and two or three letters were intercepted and studied each week. A team of experts began analyzing his communications to see whether he was using a code. Results were negative. One member of the team, a young woman named Nadya Gardner, became convinced that the letters contained invisible writing, but the customary tests with chemicals that bring out ordinary secret inks revealed nothing.

Undaunted, Gardner continued to experiment. Under Dr. Enrique Dent, recognized as an expert in invisible inks, chemists applied an iodine-vapor test—and secret writing appeared on the blank back of the typed sheets of paper. The persevering staff in the Princess Hotel had struck pay dirt. A letter of April 15, 1941, addressed to Manuel Alonso, Partado 718, Madrid, carried on its back in invisible ink a long list of ships that had docked in and sailed from New York harbor. A letter of April 21, addressed to Miss Isabel Machado Santos in Lisbon, said in invisible ink that the British had stationed about 70,000 men in Iceland, that the SS *Ville De Liege* had been sunk by U-boats (whose skippers could not always wait around to see if a torpedoed vessel went under), and that the U.S. army had released twenty Boeing B-17 bombers to Great Britain.[4]

All of Joe K's letters, the British chemists concluded, had been written in a solution of Pyramidon.

Joe K appeared to be masquerading as a New York exporter, for yet another intercepted letter to Alonso in Madrid read like a routine business communication to a customer. However, no one at Bermuda knew at this time that the Madrid address was a mail drop for letters to be forwarded to SS and Gestapo chief Heinrich Himmler in Berlin. This time chemical tests failed to bring out invisible ink on the back of the sheets.

The typed letter read:

> Your order of No. 5 is rather large—and I with my limited facilities and funds shall never be able to fill

such an immense order completely. But I have already many numbers in stock, and shall ship whatever and whenever I can. I hope you have no objections to part shipment.

The No. 352, 853, 854 and 857 are not so very easy to obtain now . . . Please give me more details about the merchandise to which our customers have any objections. Since they are paying for it, they are entitled to ask for the best. From the paying customers I take any time criticism—and I also should appreciate your suggestions for improving the quality and delivery.[5]

The communication itself seemed innocent enough to the casual observer. But the experts at Bermuda knew the ways of spies and soon recognized that Joe K's letter was double-talk. Translated into its true meaning, Joe K was saying to Reichsfuehrer Himmler:

Your instructions to me in communication No. 5 call for a lot of work and will take time to execute. Remember that I have only a few people working for me, and not too much money. I already have some of the information you want, and shall send it at once. The rest will follow as soon as I can get it . . . The No. 352 [and the other code numbers for items Himmler wanted to learn about] are harder to run down now than they used to be . . . You say that some of my reports are not too detailed, enough, or not clear. Sorry about that. Tell me exactly how they fall short. You are paying me to spy for you, and I want to do the job right. I shall appreciate any instructions that you can give me that will improve my work and make more certain that my reports will fool the [British] censors and get through to you.[6]

Bermuda kept the FBI informed about Joe K's letters. Clearly he was a German agent, and an important one.

Just past eleven o'clock on the night of March 18, 1941, two men were walking briskly together in Manhattan's busy Times

Square. One was a short man with hunched shoulders, a ruddy face, and thick-lensed eyeglasses. Every few steps he would jerk his head to one side or the other and glance sharply about. The other man was a few years older, perhaps fifty-two, and walked ramrod straight, surging onward as though bent on reaching a specific destination as quickly as possible. He was black-haired, dark-skinned, and an old scar slashed across his face. In one hand he clutched a brown briefcase.

At traffic-congested Broadway, the two men started to cross the street against the light. The dark-complected fellow bolted ahead with such determination that he failed to notice a taxicab racing toward him. He leaped from its path just in time only to dart in front of another cab coming from the opposite direction. There was no time for the cabbie to put on the brakes.

Moments later Times Square was converted into a cacophony of shrill police whistles, flashing red lights, and gasps from the crowd that gathered around the body lying in the center of Broadway. For a moment the short man with the thick eyeglasses stood motionless, stunned by the sudden violence. But he rapidly pulled himself together, snatched up his prostrate companion's briefcase, and melted into the crowd. Only later would the FBI learn that this man was the mysterious Joe K.

A New York detective happened by, and he quickly questioned the distraught cabbie. "Some guy grabbed a briefcase the other guy had been carrying and run off," the taxi driver said. An onlooker told the sleuth that "the guy who took the briefcase yelled back in a thick German accent, 'It's a Jew plot!'"

The sleuth's suspicions were aroused. Why would a man snatch up his seriously injured companion's briefcase, leave him lying there to die, and rush off while shouting anti-Semitic oaths?

An ambulance clanged up to the scene and the stricken man was loaded aboard. Theorizing that the man who had snatched up the briefcase would mingle in the crowd long enough to see the hospital name on the vehicle, the detective went along on the ride to St. Vincent's at Seventh Avenue and 11th Street. If anyone were to telephone the hospital concerning the victim, the sleuth wanted to arrange to have the call traced.

At the hospital, the detective's gut feeling that something sinister was afoot in this curious episode was intensified when

attendants found a roll of fifteen hundred dollars in the unconscious man's clothing. A Spanish passport identified the victim
as Don Julio Lopez Lido.

Earlier, Joe K, customarily a cool customer, had grown pan-
icky. Judging from the pool of blood in the street, he knew that
his companion had been injured seriously or was perhaps dead.
But what about the victim's luggage that was in his room at the
Taft Hotel? Suppose the FBI got hold of it? The baggage might
contain evidence that would reveal who Lopez really was. And
there might be clues in Lopez's belongings that would point to
Joe K. Something had to be done—and rapidly.[7]

Even while his companion was still sprawled on Broadway,
Joe K stepped into a phone booth and called the Taft. He told
the clerk on the other end of the line, "Mr. Lopez has been injured in a traffic accident, and he wants you to get the luggage
from his room and hold on to it until someone claims it." When
the clerk began to ask questions, Joe K panicked again and
slammed down the receiver.

The curious call triggered a quick conference among Taft officials, who had already considered Lopez to be an odd duck. He
had registered about a month earlier and had given an address
in Buenos Aires, Argentina. Even though the Taft was a large
hotel, Lopez had been singled out by employees as a target for
harsh epithets. He usually had his meals sent to his room, paid
for them with a fat roll of bills, but gave the room-service waiter
only a nickel tip. Lopez seldom left his room, never had any
visitors, never made or received any telephone calls.

Now the suspicious night manager notified New York police
of the strange telephone call regarding Lopez's luggage, and a
detective soon arrived at the hotel and began poking through
the accident victim's room. The guest's luggage bore the trade-
mark of a Buenos Aires department store, but the bags had no
secret compartments. And his elaborate room bore nothing of
interest. Then the sleuth pulled back the bottom of a picture on
the wall and a roll of plain white typing paper fastened by a
rubber band fell to the floor. Next he discovered ten hidden con-
tainers of the popular headache remedy Pyramidon, and finally
he found a large map of the United States. After unfolding the
map, the sleuth saw that it contained a rash of red-and-blue

crayon marks at points along the eastern seaboard from Boston to Miami.

Convinced that Julio Lopez—or whatever his name might have been—was a spy, the detective rushed all the evidence he had collected from the guest's room to New York police headquarters. There the items were examined by members of a confidential squad whose function was to investigate those engaged in espionage in New York City. They reached a quick conclusion: This was Nazi spy stuff.

The map had been marked by someone who had a thorough knowledge of defense installations along the eastern seaboard, for each red-and-blue mark pointed to an army post, a naval facility, or a major defense plant. A quick check with military authorities revealed that the markings were deadly accurate.

Meanwhile at St. Vincent's Hospital, where Lopez was still unconscious and at death's door two hours after the accident, a telephone call came to the switchboard. Standing by was the detective who had been at the accident scene. Coached in advance by the sleuth, the switchboard woman gave him the sign, and he put a tracer on the call, then picked up an extension phone. The man on the line spoke English with a Spanish accent, and said that he understood that a friend of his named Julio Lopez had been struck by a car in Times Square. There was only one way that this caller could have known that Lopez had been brought to St. Vincent's, the detective knew, and that was if he had been tipped off by the man with the thick eyeglasses.

Playing her role to perfection, the switchboard operator stalled to allow time for the trace to be made. The hospital had no one listed by the name of Julio Lopez, she told the caller. Could he describe his friend? The voice then told in detail what the man looked like. Yes, she now recalled, an unidentified man fitting that description had been brought in to the emergency room. Now a trace of concern slipped into the caller's tone. He wanted to know if hospital attendants found any papers on this victim, anything that would identify him. No, replied the woman.

The switchboard operator strung out the conversation for nearly five minutes. Listening avidly, the detective noted that the "friend" of the injured man never once inquired about his condition. Mainly the caller was trying to find out if any incriminating papers had been found.

A second operator tiptoed up to the detective and held up a scratch pad with the words "Spanish Consulate, 515 Madison Avenue." The trace had been made. The source of the call came as no surprise to the sleuth. Spanish diplomats in New York (and other U.S. cities) long had been suspected of being in bed with Nazi masters of skulduggery.

At 10:45 P.M. on March 19, twenty-four hours after he had been struck in Times Square, Julio Lopez died without regaining consciousness. But his ghost was destined to haunt the Nazi espionage apparatus in the United States.

21

The Ludwig Gang

On the afternoon following the pedestrian accident in Times Square, two out-of-town fabric salesmen were in the same Taft Hotel guest room that had been occupied by the victim, Don Lopez Lido. Fabric samples were strewn about the premises. While awaiting the arrival of retail customers, the salesmen were engaging in a game of pinochle.

Suddenly there was a light tap at the door. One man opened it to see a young woman of exceptional beauty—blond hair, sparkling blue eyes, and a curvaceous figure. She seemed to be surprised and her eyes widened. Quickly she glanced into the room at the scattered fabric samples, then looked up at the numbers on the door.

Flashing a scintillating smile, the young woman replied with a trace of a German accent, "Oh, I guess I've made a mistake."

"Quite all right," replied the salesman, bidding her good-bye and closing the door.

After her departure, the two men began discussing the significance of the blonde's visit. For they were actually New York detectives who had rigged the fabric-salesmen blind and staked out the room to see who might call on Lopez. Police had arranged for newspapers to carry stories that the Times Square victim was unidentified in order to not frighten off Lopez's confederates.

When the blond girl had started for the elevator and pushed the "down" button, she was joined by a third detective who had been concealed in a room across from the "fabric salesmen." The girl paid no attention to the sleuth, and when the elevator reached the ground level the detective signaled to a fourth officer who had been loitering around the lobby for tailing purposes.

Outside the Taft, a detective posing as a street photographer who took pictures of passersby, then tried to sell them orders of the photo, snapped the girl's picture. Her suspicions had not been aroused.

The blonde was tailed to a house in a pleasant neighborhood in Maspeth, Long Island, where discreet inquiries revealed that she was eighteen-year-old Lucy Boehmler, who had recently been a high school student. At Maspeth High School, Lucy's obvious physical attributes, a vivacious personality, and a delightful sense of humor had inevitably drawn wolf whistles from admiring Lotharios.

In the meantime, other detectives went to the Brass Rail, a lounge near the Taft that Lopez had been known to patronize. The sleuths were armed with photographs of the Times Square mishap victim that had been taken in the hospital shortly before he died and with the one of Lucy Boehmler snapped outside the Taft Hotel. Waiters immediately recognized both individuals.

Lopez had often sat at a table in the rear of the Brass Rail and conferred at length with the blond girl and a medium-sized man of about fifty years of age who wore thick eyeglasses. The sleuths were elated. The description of the man with the thick spectacles fit perfectly that of the one who had grabbed the briefcase in Times Square.

Detectives continued to run down their hot leads. The blonde's picture was taken to the Taft, and the elevator operators identified the girl as the same one who had come to the hotel each day and always got off at the same floor—one level above that on which Lopez's room was located. The sleuths theorized that the girl walked down the stairway one flight, so that prying eyes would not connect her visits with the mysterious Lopez.

* * *

While New York detectives were probing mysteries growing out of the Times Square traffic accident, Adolf Hitler's secret invasion of the United States was at its peak. Every German agency that dabbled in espionage had spy rings operational in America, including those of Admiral Wilhelm Canaris's Abwehr, Heinrich Himmler's Gestapo, Reinhard Heydrich's Sicherheitsdienst, Joachim von Ribbentrop's Foreign Ministry, and various offices in the Nazi Party.

Against this background of German intrigue, authorities in the New York police department, realizing from the evidence that the Nazi conspiracy reached far beyond the boundaries of that city, turned over the materials collected from the Taft Hotel room to P. E. Foxworth, the FBI's assistant director who was in charge of the New York office in Foley Square. Foxworth quickly contacted J. Edgar Hoover in Washington, and the big chief ordered an all-out investigation of Julio Lopez's background connections.[1]

G-men were dispatched to the Taft Hotel to comb the Times Square victim's room again. In some manner, the sleuths uncovered a shocking piece of evidence: a detailed report on defenses at Pearl Harbor, Hawaii, and at nearby Hickham Field, a key U.S. Army air base. Written in longhand on several sheets of an ocean liner's stationery, the report concluded with the statement: "This may be of special interest to our yellow friends." (The Japanese.) The report was signed merely "Conrad," obviously a code name. What concerned the Feds was that the report was a copy—no doubt the original was already in Berlin or Hamburg.[2]

Hoover's men checked the report with Military Intelligence in Washington and were told the Pearl Harbor information was incredibly accurate.

Now the FBI was certain that the dead man, whatever his true name, was a big spider in the Nazi web of intrigue.

Federal agents began poring over assorted articles that the New York detective and FBI men had combed out of Lopez's Taft room: receipted hotel bills, steamship ticket stubs, and a folder of matches bearing the name of George's Diner in Ridgewood, Long Island, and a sketched diagram of how to get to there from Manhattan. (Later the FBI would learn that George's Diner was a favorite meeting spot for Nazi agents.)

Through tedious digging, G-men were able to trace Julio Lopez's recent itinerary. About two months before he was killed, the suspect had docked in San Francisco, coming from Japan where he had spent considerable time, apparently working with Nipponese Intelligence. On the way to America, his ocean liner had put in at Honolulu, where, through his own efforts or with the help of spies already operating in Hawaii, he had compiled the Pearl Harbor intelligence report.

On the day after Lucy Boehmler had been identified, a pair of FBI shadows saw her enter a Swedish restaurant on West 57th Street. She took a table in a corner, and the Feds sat down nearby. Soon one G-man nudged the other. "Do you see what I see?" he remarked. Walking toward Lucy was a medium-sized man wearing thick eyeglasses and carrying a brown briefcase. No doubt this was the mysterious figure who had been with the Times Square victim and had snatched up a brown briefcase.

The two sleuths saw Lucy take out a stenographer's pad and for fifteen minutes scribble furiously as her companion talked. Then the pair left the restaurant. One G-man tailed Lucy, but her male companion leaped into a cab and sped away. There was no other taxi on the scene, so the FBI man could not follow.

Meanwhile, within hours of Lopez's death, Hoover notified the British censorship post in Bermuda to be especially watchful for communications regarding the death of the still unidentified Lopez. A few days later Bermuda hit pay dirt. An unsigned, routine typewritten letter destined for a mail drop in Spain contained an invisible-ink message that electrified the FBI. It revealed that Lopez was not even a Spaniard; his true name was Major Ulrich von der Osten, a German army officer who had been known to U.S. military Intelligence since World War I as an old pro in the twilight world of global machinations, and he had been sent to the United States to coordinate spying operations.

The writer, whose stilted style the British censors had quickly recognized as being that of Joe K, went on to tell about von der Osten's death, which he labeled "a Jew plot." However, Joe K assured Heinrich Himmler, everything was well in hand, for he was taking over command of the Nazi espionage operation "where Herr von der Osten left off."

Joe K, or Joe Kessler, as he sometimes signed himself, became the focus of FBI attention, and G-men staked out numerous spots in New York where he might appear. One of these was the German consulate in the Whitehall Building in downtown Manhattan. A few days after von der Osten had died, FBI watchers saw the man with the thick spectacles and the brown briefcase enter the consulate, where he remained for nearly two hours.

When Kessler emerged, his shadows followed him to a rooming house in the 6400 block of Fresh Pond Road, Brooklyn. There the G-men quickly discovered that his real name was Kurt Frederick Ludwig. He had been born in Fremont, Ohio but had been taken to Germany as a child. His wife and three children now lived in Munich.

Ludwig had been a successful businessman there and knew many figures high on the Nazi totem pole, including Gestapo chief Heinrich Himmler. In 1939, shortly after Hitler's panzers had plunged into Poland, Ludwig told Himmler that, even though he was still an American citizen, he was eager to contribute to Germany's war effort. Himmler replied that Ludwig could best serve the Third Reich by spying in the United States.

So after learning about secret codes, invisible inks, radio communication, and other espionage techniques at the Academy in Hamburg, Ludwig, in the guise of a leather goods salesman, arrived in New York in March 1940. His Abwehr orders were to organize his own spy network and report to Germany details on the "size, equipment, location, and morale of American army units; on the routing of convoys between the United States and England; and on aircraft production figures."[3]

An insignificant-looking little man with a nervous manner, Kurt Ludwig took to spying as a duck takes to water. He promptly contacted members of the German-American Bund in New York and northern New Jersey and, with their willing help, rapidly created a smoothly functioning ring consisting of eight high-grade agents along with a swarm of cut-outs, scouts, couriers, informants, and straphangers. Shrewd, industrious, and innovative, Ludwig was soon flooding Hamburg and Berlin with American information, much of it secret or classified.

Ludwig had a powerful car—courtesy of Adolf Hitler's

pocketbook—and he loved to race along the highways at speeds up to eighty miles per hour. Hidden in his automobile was a portable shortwave radio set over which he could send coded signals to clandestine Nazi stations in Brazil or to U-boats off the eastern seaboard of the United States for relay to Germany. However, for fear of detection, the car radio was used sparingly, and then only for urgent matters.

In addition to typed letters in double-talk to convey his information to the Third Reich, Ludwig used an ingenious code, a complicated mixture of ciphers (which are fairly easy for an expert cryptanalyst to break) and a form of German shorthand called Gabelsberger, invented in 1834 and long obsolete and largely forgotten. Ludwig did most of the invisible-ink writing himself, especially for letters sent through the Abwehr blind in Madrid to "Marion," code name for Heinrich Himmler.

Like any "corporation," operating a widespread spy ring had a high overhead, and Ludwig required regular infusions of funds. Often he did not know the source of the money. He would receive a message to be at a certain place at a specific time and meet a stranger, whose appearance would be described. On one occasion, Ludwig was told to go to Childs Restaurant on 34th Street and watch for a man carrying a *New York Times*. Ludwig spotted a man seated at the counter and holding up a *Times*, apparently absorbed in reading its contents. Joe K slid into the adjoining seat, the pair exchanged passwords, and moments later the stranger slipped Ludwig an envelope containing five hundred dollars. Joe K casually finished drinking his coffee, then sauntered out into the street. Typically, he would never again see the Nazi bagman.[4]

Teenaged, full-bosomed Lucy Boehmler had been one of Kurt Ludwig's first recruits. Born in Stuttgart, Germany, she had been brought to America at age five. Although her parents were known to be outspoken Hitler foes, not so the daughter. This seemingly all-American schoolgirl had been active in the German-American Youth society, an offshoot of Fritz Kuhn's German-American Bund.

Ludwig had spotted Lucy at a social function. His eyes had lighted up: In Lucy he sensed not only a potential first-rate spy but an enchanting playmate as well. Bit by bit, Ludwig lured her into his espionage network. She had been fascinated by his spying tales and finally joined him in search of "excitement." Lucy posed as Ludwig's secretary, and the spymaster quickly noted that she possessed a hidden talent that was invaluable in espionage work—a phenomenal memory.

Two of Joe K's most zealous agents were Walter and Helen Mayer. Although American-born, Helen was an even more gung-ho Nazi than was her husband, a German citizen, who seemed to be sort of a fifth wheel in the Mayer household with the strong-willed Helen calling the shots. An attractive woman of about twenty-four years of age, she cut a striking figure in her nattily tailored clothes. Her rosy face was framed by light, wavy hair, and she possessed a vivacious personality.

The Mayers' Brooklyn home was a haunt for Ludwig's spies, and the young couple assisted Joe K in every way that they could. Helen had a key to Ludwig's mailbox in New York's General Post Office, and when the spymaster was away on a scouting trip she would get his mail for him.

One of the Mayers' principal ploys was to invite aircraft-plant employees to their home and then to subtlely pick their brains. One of the assistant foremen at the Grumman Aircraft Corporation, a key target of Ludwig's gang, was Alfred Frick (not his real name), German-born but a naturalized American citizen. Frick was a frequent visitor, and while he was not disloyal to his adopted homeland, he had been a prized dupe of the Mayers.

The Grumman foreman was an aviation buff, loved his work, and enjoyed talking about it. The Mayers saw to it that Frick had plenty of chances to talk. On one occasion Helen asked him if he couldn't "do something" to slow down production at the Grumman plant. Frick was shocked and muttered that such would be impossible. The woman flew into a rage, shouting at Frick that he was "a very bad German" and that she would make certain that the Gestapo "took care" of him.[5]

Another of Ludwig's operatives was René Froelich, born in Germany and a magazine subscription salesman. Black-haired, long-nosed, and with a nervous tic, the thirty-two-year-old Froelich was drafted into the United States Army in early 1941 and stationed at Fort Jay on Governor's Island, where he was assigned as a clerk in the post hospital. Patients from area camps were admitted to the Fort Jay facility, where each day a list of new admissions and discharges was drawn up and placed on the desk of the hospital's commanding officer. One of Froelich's duties was to remove the day-old lists and file them, but instead he passed them on to Ludwig.

Joe K was delighted with the coup. The lists would reveal, for example, that a discharged patient was Sergeant John Smith of the 76th Field Artillery. This knowledge permitted Ludwig to inform Hamburg that the 76th Field Artillery was stationed at Fort Dix, New Jersey. Private Froelich also pilfered restricted army manuals, and he acquired technical publications on U.S. aviation production by ordering them himself on official hospital letterheads.

Meanwhile early in 1941, a thousand miles south of Fort Jay, another of Ludwig's agents, Carl Herman Schroetter, had an ideal "cover"—skipper of a charter boat, *Echo of the Past,* in Miami. The craft was aptly named. Swiss-born Schroetter, who had two sisters living in the Third Reich, had been traveling in Germany when war broke out with England and France. By holding his sisters hostage, the Abwehr recruited the American as a spy and ordered him to return to Miami and become a "sleeper" agent.

Schroetter promptly burrowed into Miami's community life to await his call. He even displayed his civic-mindedness by volunteering for election duty as a registration clerk in Dade County's precinct 34. In early 1940 the Abwehr activated Schroetter and ordered him to report on ship movements along the Florida coast, a function he could perform while piloting *Echo of the Past* on legitimate excursions.

Throughout 1940 and into the spring of 1941, Schroetter mailed off to Ludwig in New York a stream of coded messages, some of them written in invisible ink. One morning a British warship off Miami laid down a smokescreen to mask from a cruising civilian craft the fact that she was engaged in anti-U-boat practice. At the helm of the snooping boat was Carl Schroetter.

Through Ludwig, the Abwehr in Hamburg was demanding information on the growing naval air station outside Miami, but Schroetter failed in efforts to penetrate the station. So he got a job as a night cook at the Greyhound Club, a bar and grill near the air station that was frequented by navy officers and men. Unaware of any spy menace, the servicemen talked freely to the affable chef, and each day Schroetter mailed to Ludwig the information he had gleaned at the club.[6]

Another of Ludwig's foot soldiers was thirty-five-year-old Karl Victor Mueller. Deep furrows in his brow gave him a prematurely old countenance, and he even walked like an elderly man, his body leaning forward and head bobbing with each step. Born in a small Austrian village, Mueller was a naturalized American, but his allegiance was not to his adopted homeland: He yearned to return to Austria. In the meantime, Mueller did all that he could for the Fatherland and often went with Karl Ludwig on visits to defense plants.

Mueller and Joe K functioned smoothly as a team. Each carried a camera on these spying jaunts, and even though both men had thick German accents, guards and attendants at war-production plants and airfields often went out of their way to assist the two Nazi spies in getting the photographs they sought. Mueller and Ludwig took one trip to the U.S. Naval Academy at Annapolis, Maryland, where they snapped away furiously and got scores of excellent pictures of cadets drilling, training facilities, and buildings.

On a trip to Washington, the two men ventured into the White House on a regular guided tour, and Ludwig was delighted to report to Hamburg a vivid personal description of what it was like for a Nazi spy to be sauntering around inside the home of the President of the United States.

One of Ludwig's most fanatical Nazi agents who would do nearly anything asked of him for the Fatherland was Hans Pagel. A short, fair-haired youth with apple cheeks, Pagel looked harmless enough. But his special job was to cover the New York waterfront and report on ship sailings. U-boat commander Admiral Karl Doenitz was eager to find out in which ships Americans were sending supplies and equipment to England. Doenitz would send his submarine wolfpacks to intercept and sink the targeted freighters.

Pagel's close pal and fellow spy was twenty-year-old Frederick Edward Schlosser, who had been a district youth leader in the German-American Bund. Tall and light complected, Schlosser was engaged to Pagel's sister, but he had resisted the older man's incessant pleas to become a spy. Finally Schlosser consented, and he joined Ludwig's stable of agents. Joe K put the towheaded youth to work trekking up and down the New York piers culling shipping information. Soon Schlosser became an enthusiastic agent and even stole a portion of the new antiaircraft gun being manufactured in the plant where he worked.

Most of those in Kurt Ludwig's gang were at best hardworking, dedicated, often clever amateur spies. But one member, fifty-four-year-old Dr. Paul Borchardt, was an old pro in the Fritz Duquesne mold. Known to intimates as "The Professor"—a tribute to his keen, analytical mind—Borchardt was a major in the German army, and in World War I he had served the Kaiser in the Middle East and later taught military geography in Munich. Stocky, stern-faced, bald with a gray fringe, the Professor's role in the Nazi spy conspiracy was veiled in mystery.

Borchardt had come to America in February 1940, under the auspices of a New York City Catholic organization whose function was to bring Catholic refugees out of Hitler's Europe. Somehow the Professor had made his way to England, where he told screeners for the New York committee that he was part Jewish and had served time in the Dachau concentration camp. Indeed he had "served time" at that notorious center—two days, in order to give credence to his refugee masquerade.

Not long after his arrival in New York, Borchardt received a telephone call at his rented flat at 577 Isham Street, in upper Manhattan near the George Washington Bridge. The voice on the other end of the line identified himself as Joe Kessler and made an appointment to come to Borchardt's home. On his arrival Kessler, who was actually Kurt Ludwig, gave the German army officer $250 in cash.

From this point onward, the relationship between the two men would be a curious one. Borchardt knew Ludwig only as Joe Kessler, and Ludwig was puzzled by the fact that Borchardt studiously avoided any contact with other members of Joe K's network. In fact, only one person associated with the ring even knew that the Professor existed. That person was Lucy Boehmler, who had once brought a package from Ludwig to Borchardt at this flat.

Dr. Borchardt, although ostensibly a member of Ludwig's ring, actually was in direct contact with Berlin, and part of his mission seemed to be to spy on Ludwig as well as to assist him in his espionage operations.

One by one, J. Edgar Hoover's men were unmasking members of Ludwig's gang, and, until the time was ripe to strike, the G-men, working in relays, were shadowing the spies night and day.

22

A Boom-and-Bang Treff

The Thompson, Connecticut, neighbors of the wealthy Count Anastase Andreyevich Vonsiatsky-Vonsiatsky had long considered him to be eccentric. Had the count been poor he would have been labeled a nut. Vonsiatsky was leader of an insidious Ukranian underground movement that had thrown a smokescreen over its pro-Nazi allegiance by stressing its anti-Russian viewpoint.

Vonsiatsky-Vonsiatsky (V-V to many), called "The Millionaire" by confederates, was a handsome playboy who had anointed himself into nobility, then married into great wealth. Vonsiatsky had been a teenager in the Ukraine when he fought with the White Russian army against the Soviet Communists. After the White Russians collapsed, Vonsiatsky fled to Paris, where he worked as a chauffeur.

Vonsiatsky's rugged good looks caught the eye of one of the richest women in the United States, Mrs. Marion Buckingham Ream Stephens, heiress to the fortune of Norman B. Ream, a Chicago financier. The penniless chauffeur and Mrs. Stephens, twenty-two years his senior, were married in Paris six months later—after the groom had bestowed upon himself the title count.

Now V-V lived on a fabulous, two-hundred-acre Connecticut estate, and had attracted the attention of both the Thompson townfolks and the FBI. Thompson residents had grown irritated over V-V's penchant for painting swastikas on turtles and turning them loose in the area. Hoover and his men had focused on Vonsiatsky after he had paid bail for the rabble-rousing Fritz Kuhn, the former Ford Motor Company chemist and fuehrer of the German-American Bund. Kuhn had been slapped in the clink for disorderly conduct and public drunkenness.

G-men learned that the count, a tall, lean man in his early forties, often strolled around the little community of Thompson and told people that he would be the leader of a government that would take over after Communist dictator Josef Stalin had been rubbed out. V-V also assured numerous local laboring men that he would take them to Russia with him and appoint them high government officials.

J. Edgar Hoover and his men didn't consider V-V to be a screwball, however. They considered him to be a dangerous, pro-Nazi radical, especially after the sleuths learned from workers on the project that Vonsiatsky had built on a hill within his estate a concrete bunker with walls two feet thick. Machine guns poked out of apertures along each wall, and a turret on top held a machine gun on a swivel.

Behind the count's desk inside the bunker was a large wall map of the world. Swastikas had been painted onto England, France, and other countries in Europe that Hitler's legions had either conquered or were threatening. Large swastikas were also plastered on the United States, although Rising Sun symbols along the West Coast indicated that the count was willing to divvy up California, Oregon, and Washington to the Empire of Japan.

Since 1939 Vonsiatsky had been building a clandestine military force, training its members on his vast estate. Guarded by private detectives and howling bloodhounds, the rolling acreage concealed an arsenal of rifles, machine guns, grenades, and explosives. The count was especially proud of his goon squad of young Ukranian boom-and-bang desperadoes, which he had trained in sabotage and assassination.

Early in December 1940 G-men in Chicago tailed Dr. Otto Willumeit, the strident leader of the German-American Bund in the Windy City, all the way to Thompson. Hoover and his men had for many months been shadowing Willumeit, and they considered him to be the brains behind a Midwest Nazi spy ring.

Behind the closely guarded walls of Vonsiatsky's sprawling grounds, the count and Willumeit conferred for two days, then the Chicago Bund leader returned home. Two days later V-V packed his bags, took his chauffeur-driven limousine to the railroad station, and caught a train to Washington, D.C. There he went directly to the Japanese Embassy, where he spent more than two hours.

After leaving the Nipponese building, V-V rushed to Union Station and bought a ticket to Chicago. The two G-men in the line behind him also purchased tickets to the Windy City on Lake Michigan. Early on the morning after his arrival in Chicago, the count left his hotel and took a cab to a house about five miles away—the home of Otto Willumeit.

From confidential sources, the FBI had learned that Willumeit, a large, square-jawed man with a dueling scar on one cheek, and the count were going to attend a Treff the next day at Chicago's Bismarck Hotel. The secret confab had been called, Hoover's men discovered, by the highly active leader of the German-American Bund in Philadelphia, Wilhelm Kunze (who soon would succeed the defrocked Fritz Kuhn as fuehrer of the national Bund).

Hoover's men had long had Kunze under surveillance, but had been unable to pin anything illegal on him. So when Kunze walked into the Bismarck lobby, idling G-men recognized him immediately. Kunze swaggered up to the registration desk and asked for one of the most expensive rooms in the ornate hotel. Earlier FBI agents had set up listening devices in a guest room and made arrangements for Kunze to be assigned to the room next to theirs.

Hardly had Kunze reached his quarters than the eavesdroppers in the adjoining room heard two other men arrive—Count Vonsiatsky-Vonsiatsky and Dr. Willumeit. The three men greeted each other like long lost brothers. Hoover's men chuckled when the count cautioned to keep their voices down, for "those FBI bastards" might try to snoop on them.

A few minutes later a fourth conspirator arrived—the Reverend Kurt E. Molzahn, a Lutheran minister from Philadelphia and a former German army officer. Molzahn, who had long been neck-deep in Nazi machinations, was Kunze's deputy and had been receiving his marching orders from Berlin through the German consulate in the City of Brotherly Love.

It was not long before the G-men knew that something big was afoot. Kunze (acting on orders from Berlin, it would later develop) had called the secret Treff to activate the count's Ukranian boom-and-bang boys, who had been lying low since 1939 while awaiting orders to start blowing up things.

Now Hoover's eavesdroppers received a short course on sabotage techniques. Speaking in a tone of great excitement, Vonsiatsky told about how simple it would be to sabotage American factories and military installations. A sprinkling of emery dust would knock out a key piece of machinery, the count declared. Word from the Third Reich was that the Nazis were having difficulties with Czechoslovakian workers who used emery dust, he added.

A gun could be destroyed by pouring a little water down the barrel when it was cooling, V-V told his comrades. After the first shot was fired, the barrel would crack. The conspirators speculated over how much damage would result to an aircraft if a tiny explosive charge were inserted in a spark plug at the factory. The device would not activate until an airplane was in flight for a specified period of time.

The Nazis discussed new incendiary pencils, in which the false lead points would be sliced off when the pencil was ready for use, thereby letting oxygen into the narrow chamber containing chemicals. This would ignite an intense fire and leave no trace of an incendiary device. Another gimmick worked on the same principle as the pencils, only the chemicals were injected into potatoes, beets, corn, or turnips.

Kunze related how chemicals could be introduced into twin compartments of an ordinary envelope, then when the envelope was crumpled and tossed into a wastebasket in, say, a powder plant, the saboteur would have time to walk away before the two chemicals mixed and a bright blaze erupted.

Laughter erupted when one of the Nazis told about an ingenious device that the German army was said to have perfected. Small bombs would be placed inside cans that had counterfeit labels of a popular brand of tomatoes used extensively by the United States armed forces. The idea was to slip these deadly cans into regular military stocks of tomatoes. Once the bogus can was punctured, it would explode, killing or maiming those within twenty feet of the blast.

After the meeting broke up and the Nazi conspirators left for their homes, J. Edgar Hoover and his agents were uneasy. Clearly a devious sabotage campaign had been discussed at the Bismarck, but the eavesdroppers had learned no specific details.

Meanwhile, G-men followed Doc Willumeit as he dashed around the Midwest, where he held Treffs with suspected Nazi agents at key defense plants in East St. Louis, Illinois, in Peoria, Illinois, in Pittsburgh, and in other cities.

There followed a series of strange events in the eastern part of the United States. On January 10, 1941, the British freighter *Black Heron*, carrying a cargo of bombers bound for England, burned under mysterious circumstances at her New York harbor pier. Ten days later fires of undetermined origin damaged the Navy Department building in Washington, and within ninety-six hours a building at the Norfolk naval base was destroyed by a blaze.

A month later three fires of undetermined origin broke out in powder plants in the Pennsylvania area, including one at the Franklin Arsenal in Philadelphia, hometown of Wilhelm Kunze and the wayward minister, the Reverend Molzahn. In April a mysterious fire at the navy's Indian Head, Maryland, powder plant caused heavy damage, and in May the Jersey City, New Jersey, waterfront went up in smoke,[1] causing $25 million worth of destruction.

By early 1941 a simmering feud between FBI chief J. Edgar Hoover and Major General Sherman Miles, the army's top Intelligence officer, was coming to a head. Apparently each man felt that the other had been poaching on his own countersubversive game preserve. On February 12 Secretary of War Henry Stimson, the army's civilian boss, railed in his personal diary: "Instead of [Hoover] coming to me with his complaint [against Miles] he had gone directly to the White House and poisoned the mind of the President."[2]

Perhaps part of the Hoover-Miles vendetta was due to the FBI boss's unique status in the federal government. Even though the FBI was under the attorney general (a cabinet-rank post) in the Department of Justice, Hoover functioned at a level comparable with the War and Navy departments. And, neatly bypassing his boss, the attorney general, Hoover had direct access to the big chief, President Roosevelt, who was one of the supersleuth's most ardent boosters.

The day after Secretary Stimson had penned in his diary the blast against Hoover, a deeply perturbed General George C. Marshall, the army chief of staff, rushed to Stimson's office. The low-key Marshall had just received a message from "Pa" Watson, Roosevelt's White House aide, asking who was going to be Miles's successor as army G-2. Marshall hit the ceiling. He felt that Hoover had convinced the President that General Miles should be sacked.

Marshall brought with him a letter that the top G-man had written to Miles and that had reached the White House. The chief of staff called its tone "very childish, petulant . . . [more] like that of a small child, than [of] a responsible officer." [3]

Stimson huddled with Attorney General Robert H. Jackson and Navy Secretary Frank B. Knox in an effort to resolve the Hoover-Miles hassle. Jackson conceded that Hoover was "difficult to deal with" but pointed out that the supersleuth had been doing an outstanding job and had the support of most of the nation. Behind the scenes, bruised egos were massaged, and in May Secretary Stimson wrote in his diary that the Hoover-Miles squabble had been smoothed over and that Miles would remain as the army's G-2. [4]

Despite the bickering at high levels, the covert war against Hitler's spy invasion had been gaining momentum steadily. FBI tails had been put on a few score members of the Fritz Duquesne and Kurt Ludwig rings, and a few hundred suspects across the nation were under periodic surveillance. Among those being shadowed was the blond teenager, Lucy Boehmler, who was clearly playing a key role in Ludwig's network.

A tail followed the girl into a Western Union office at 84 Hudson Street, Manhattan, where he overheard her ask if there were any cables for "Aggiebor," Ludwig's cable designation. Told that there was none, Lucy looked disappointed and departed.

A check of Western Union records revealed that Lucy had picked up numerous cables from Madrid and Lisbon in recent weeks, so the FBI obtained a subpoena and collected copies. With a cable address, Ludwig was operating his spy network with the sophisticated flair to be found in a legitimate business corporation.

Another shadow picked up Lucy as she left the Western Union office and followed her to the main New York post office. He saw the girl don gloves (presumably to prevent her from leaving fingerprints) and open Box 185. Her only mail was two magazines wrapped in brown paper, but the tail could not identify the name of the publications. Post office officials told the G-men that two magazines had arrived that day for distribution, one of them an aviation magazine and the other dealing with steel production. Both magazines were published in New York City, and an inquiry disclosed that a subscriber to each journal was Kurt Ludwig.

Meanwhile, the German army major with the analytical mind, bald-domed Paul Borchardt, had gained a new neighbor in his rooming house in upper Manhattan near the George Washington Bridge. A G-man, posing as a starving artist, had been planted in the room next to Borchardt's, with the connivance of the middle-aged landlady who had grown suspicious of the enigmatic "refugee" from Hitler's New Germany.

When the landlady had entered Borchardt's room to clean she noticed that there were always large numbers of newspaper clippings and maps scattered about. Once the curious woman had asked Borchardt the nature of his occupation, and he replied "geographer," which presumably accounted for the many maps. She also spotted a copy of *Lloyd's Register*, which gives tonnage of all ships, and thought it to be a curious publication for a geographer.

The "artist" could hear Borchardt's typewriter clicking throughout many nights; no doubt the spy was composing detailed reports for Berlin and Hamburg. When Borchardt had infrequent visitors—Ludwig on occasion, Lucy Boehmler another time—the eavesdropping G-man could pick up snatches of conversation through the thin walls.

Even though the "artist" was engaged in grim business, he grinned as Ludwig prepared to depart. The G-man would hear a clicking of heels, followed by two muffled voices calling out, "Heil, Hitler!"

One night early in April 1941, Paul Fehse, an Abwehr agent whose mission was to report on shipping in New York harbor, had some hot news to send to Ast X in Hamburg. Dispatched by the Centerport shortwave station, Fehse's message told of the sailing from New York of the Belgian freighter *Ville d'Ablon*, which was loaded with aircraft engines, copper, and machinery. Fehse had had no trouble in identifying the cargo: He had simply sought out one of the freighter's crew in a waterfront saloon the night before and asked him what the vessel was carrying.

Destined for England, the ship would make a juicy target for U-boats lurking in Atlantic waters off America's eastern seaboard.

The next day Fehse vanished. Spymasters in Berlin and Hamburg were worried; had the FBI unmasked the crucial Centerport station? But within a few days Nazis on both sides of the Atlantic breathed sighs of relief. Fehse, it developed. had been picked up accidentally by law enforcement authorities, but instead of being charged with the serious offense of espionage, he was facing a relatively minor count of failing to comply with the Alien Registration Act. Eagerly the spy pleaded guilty to the lesser charge and was sentenced to a year and a day in the federal penitentiary at Atlanta.

Even though American newspapers had made no mention of Fehse's espionage involvement, Ast X continued to have nagging doubts. It radioed Centerport and asked if Fehse could have betrayed the clandestine shortwave operation on Long Island. The two G-men manning the station quickly assured the Abwehr chiefs that there was no cause for concern, that the fallen spy did not know enough about Centerport to have squealed to the Feds.

At this time, early in 1941, the espionage masterminds in Berlin and Hamburg were feeling smug about operations in the United States and almost seemed to be challenging the FBI. Admiral Wilhelm Canaris was among those who found it hard to believe that J. Edgar Hoover's organization could be so inept. Nazi agents continued to be planted in key defense factories and near to army, navy, and air bases. Berlin's and Hamburg's subtle complacency reached across the Atlantic, and the spy apparatus in the United States was operating with increasing arrogance. Many agents and their spymasters violated the cardinal principles of security, apparently convinced that they were immune to detection and arrest.

Even the boastful Old Boer, Fritz Duquesne, with forty years of cloak-and-dagger machinations tucked under his belt, had shown signs of nonchalance, apparently unaware that the FBI had been shadowing him for fourteen months. Fritz had grown so audacious that when he read an item in *The New York Times* about a new gas mask the army's Chemical Warfare Service had developed, he wrote a letter to the War Department—and signed his true name:

> We are interested in the possible financing of a chemical war mask which may or may not be original. This we do not know. However, we would like to study the subject in order to get a little better understanding of the subject before we commit ourselves.
>
> We understand the government has published a pamphlet on this subject . . . Will you please inform us how we might be able to procure a copy?
>
> We are good citizens and would not allow anything of a confidential nature to get out of our hands.
>
> —F. J. Duquesne [5]

Indeed the Old Boer would not let the pamphlet "get out of our hands"—those being the hands of the Abwehr and Hitler's high command.

Duquesne's suspicious letter was turned over to the army G-2, and a deceptively courteous reply was sent to the self-styled "good citizen." While the War Department could not release the chemical warfare pamphlet, it was explained, the army had no fear that Duquesne was the kind of person who would misuse such restricted information.

Duquesne for several months had been playing house in his ornate apartment on West 74th Street, off Central Park, with a thirtyish woman who had been socially prominent in the Southwest. She went by the name of Mrs. James Dunn, but actually she was Evelyn Clayton Lewis, who had been born in Fayetteville, Arkansas, without a drop of German blood in her veins.

Evelyn Lewis had been a toy designer and sculptress in New York when she first met Fritz Duquesne in 1931. At that time he was working as a writer for a motion-picture magazine, and Evelyn fell in love with him. To her he was a dashing, romantic figure, and he regaled her with colorful tales (some of them true) of his covert exploits for the Kaiser during World War I.[6]

In early 1941, still enchanted by Duquesne's seeming importance and clandestine achievements, Evelyn began living with the masterspy, and he wasted no time in putting her to work for *Der Fuehrer*. Evelyn busily clipped military-related items from newspapers and technical magazines. Like her lover, she was a prolific letter writer, and flooded defense industries with requests for information on new inventions.

One morning late in March G-men tailed Duquesne's mistress to Central Park where they saw her drop a letter into the mailbox. Evelyn returned to her apartment, and her tail quickly got postal officials to open the Central Park box. An envelope had the name of Mrs. James Dunn and her return address. The letter was being sent to the Eastman Kodak Company in Rochester, New York.

An FBI agent was waiting in Eastman's offices when the letter arrived and the firm's officers opened it. "Mrs. Dunn" billed herself as an expert photographer interested in new developments in the industry, and she inquired into what advancements were being made in antifog photography. Eastman, Fritz Duquesne had learned, was developing an antifog camera for the War Department. In order to prevent the Old Boer from becoming suspicious, a courteous but evasive reply was sent to "Mrs. Dunn," who hardly knew where the shutter was on a camera.

This was one of the few rebuffs Evelyn Lewis had received in her letter-writing campaign. Most corporations provided her with all the information she asked for.

*   *   *

At about the same time that Fritz Duquesne's playmate was trying to wheedle military secrets from Eastman Kodak, G-men in Washington and New York received copies of a letter written by Kurt Ludwig and intercepted by the British censorship station in Bermuda. In secret ink brought out by heat treatments, Ludwig told Hamburg that two of his agents, Hans Pagel and Karl Mueller, had been reconnoitering the French liner *Normandie*, which was berthed in the Hudson River. Pagel and Mueller had told him, Ludwig wrote, that the mighty *Normandie* had virtually no security and would be "a cinch to sabotage." [7]

Exceeded in length only by Britain's *Queen Elizabeth* (and then by only a few feet), the 1,029-foot *Normandie* had bolted safely into New York harbor when Hitler had invaded Poland, on September 1, 1939. Since that time, the French ship had languished at Pier 88, a short distance north of 42nd Street. The *Normandie*'s owners were spending a thousand dollars per day in berthing charges, so they kept only a skeleton crew on board to keep her engines from deteriorating. No one seemed concerned about possible sabotage, and there was little worry over fire. Vladimir Yourkevitch, the *Normandie*'s designer, had suggested that the vessel was as nearly fireproof as any ship ever built. [8]

In Germany, Hitler's high command had long had a wary eye on the French vessel. Two weeks before France surrendered, on June 3, 1940, the Abwehr had flashed an order to Nazi spies in the United States through the secret Centerport station: "Observe *Normandie*." [9]

Hitler and his commanders had good reason to be concerned over the *Normandie*'s presence in New York harbor. Should the United States be drawn into the war against the Third Reich, the monstrous French ship could be taken over by the U.S. Navy and quickly converted to a transport that could carry to Europe nearly twelve thousand troops at one time.

PART THREE

Demolition of a Spy Apparatus

23

Eavesdropping on the Siamese Twins

Hardly anyone paid attention to the man in work clothes who was methodically going about his business of inspecting apartment buildings in the Bronx area of New York. In the palm of his hand he carried a "snifter," a tiny meter that could tell if electronic signals were coming from a certain building. For this ordinary-looking city inspector was in fact a sleuth in the Radio Intelligence Division (RID) of the Federal Communications Commission.

In peacetime it was RID's responsibility to police the airways, to use its portable and stationary monitors to detect outlaw transmitters and other violations of federal radio regulations. Early in 1941 the RID detected the illegal radio set in the Bronx and had sent in the "building inspector" to pinpoint its location. But the transmitter, signing itself with the call letters REN, had suddenly gone off the air.

George E. Sterling, chief of the RID, informed the FBI of the outlaw station. Convinced that this clandestine set was a Nazi operation, J. Edgar Hoover ordered his New York office to track it down, so agents began canvassing stores selling parts that might be used for constructing a shortwave radio station.

The G-men quickly hit pay dirt. At a shop in downtown Manhattan, a salesman recalled having sold radio parts to a man who had drawn the clerk's suspicions. The reason he recalled this particular transaction, the salesman explained, was that the customer was highly nervous and kept looking back over his shoulder toward the front door. It occurred to the clerk that this furtive individual might be planning to use this equipment for some sinister purpose.

At the request of the G-men, the clerk thumbed through records and came up with the customer's name—Joseph Klein. He gave his address as a rooming house on East 126th Street.

Hoover's men questioned residents in that area and found that Joseph August Klein, a German-American who scratched out a livelihood as a part-time commercial photographer, had been the subject of considerable neighborhood gossip: He lived with two other men, a Mr. Hill and a Mr. Frederick—and a large German shepherd dog.

As the sleuths continued to probe into Klein's activities, other revealing facts surfaced. He was a longtime radio ham, and his two roommates had close ties to Nazi Germany. Mr. Frederick was an alias of thirty-eight-year-old Felix Jahnke, who had been an officer in the German army and became an American citizen in 1930. Mr. Hill was pegged as Alex Wheeler-Hill, a forty-year-old native of Russia, who had come to the United States in 1923, was naturalized, and worked for a decade as a motorman for the Third Avenue El.

Jahnke had been called to the Third Reich in 1939 to be trained as a radio operator by the signal corps of the German army, then returned to the United States as a "sleeper," awaiting a specific assignment from Hamburg. At about the same time a restless Wheeler-Hill had given up what he considered to be his humdrum life as a railroad motorman and went to Germany, where he joined a Nazi organization. He was soon sent to the Academy in Hamburg and trained in receiving and sending coded radio messages.

Wheeler-Hill proved to be a plodding student. He had trouble with codes and couldn't grasp the intricacies of operating a shortwave radio. But in January 1940 Wheeler-Hill's Abwehr masters sent him back to New York, where he was to team up with the bright Felix Jahnke, who had taken easily to radio operations.

Despite his lack of aptitude for the job, Wheeler-Hill was determined to succeed. Hardly had he set foot in New York than he joined a class in radio communications at the West Side YMCA in Manhattan.

Wheeler-Hill and Jahnke had been ordered by the Abwehr to construct their own shortwave station with parts purchased locally, and it was their job to radio to the Third Reich military information collected by the network of the energetic Carl Reuper, the masterspy who worked at the Air Associates plant in Bendix, New Jersey. The Jahnke–Wheeler-Hill radio center (call letters REN) was code-named Operation Jimmy.

There was a good reason why the RID eavesdroppers had lost touch periodically with outlaw station REN. Jahnke and Wheeler-Hill had been having trouble finding a location that would provide clear broadcasting, so they had moved their portable set to another site before reassembling it a third time in a rooming house on East 126th Street, the address Joseph Klein had given to the radio-store clerk.

Apparently that base was also unsatisfactory for broadcasting, for FBI agents who had staked out the rooming house observed Jahnke and Wheeler-Hill laboriously lugging the dismantled radio set to the top floor of a rooming house on Caldwell Avenue. The two Nazis were apparently satisfied with results obtained in their new *Meldekopf* (communications center).

However, the FCC listeners and the FBI were frustrated. Through electronic monitors, they were recording each message sent to Hamburg from the sixth-floor site on Caldwell Avenue, but the communications did not make sense because the Feds lacked the title of the book on which the Jahnke–Wheeler-Hill special code was based. Through the FBI's trump card, William Sebold, Hoover's men knew the basic principles of the Abwehr's code, that transmissions were based on popular novels of the time. Sebold's (Centerport's) messages were encoded in Rachel Field's current best-seller, *All This and Heaven, Too.*

So by deduction, the G-men concluded that the Jahnke–Wheeler-Hill code was also pegged to a book. But how could that key volume be identified? There was great urgency in the search to uncover the book's title, for the FBI agents could only presume that a flood of sensitive military information was being beamed to Hamburg by the Caldwell Avenue shortwave set.

FBI attention focused on a Yorkville bookstore that was known to be frequented by Nazi espionage suspects. G-men observed Paul Alfred Scholz, owner of the store, remove a volume from a shelf, wrap it in brown paper, and hand it over to a customer—Felix Jahnke. The sleuths felt that this book could be the key to unlocking the Jahnke–Wheeler-Hill code, but they had been unable to see the book's title.

Hoover's men learned that the targeted store had a policy of stamping its name on the flyleaf of each of its books. But the sleuths were prohibited by law from sneaking into the Caldwell Avenue flat when its tenants were absent to hunt for the book without first obtaining a search warrant. Such an action would tip the FBI's hand.

However, Congress had passed no law that kept cleaning women from snooping in an apartment in which they were working, so the G-men prevailed upon a housekeeper to look over the books in the Nazis' flat. A few days later the woman reported that there were several books on the premises, but only one of them had the Yorkville store's name stamped on the flyleaf.

That book, *Halfway to Horror*, indeed proved to be the key to solving the Jahnke–Wheeler-Hill code. Now Operation Jimmy's messages to Ast X made sense—and their contents stunned the FBI. They disclosed that events were about to take place in the United States, happenings that would involve prominent Americans in high places, that could place the nation in great peril.[1]

To mask his illegal activities, Alex Wheeler-Hill had a "cover," a job as a deliveryman for a soft-drink firm that had a distribution warehouse in Greenwich Village. He was allowed to take his truck home at night, and the vehicle itself served as a blind. On each side of the truck was emblazoned the soft-drink firm's name and below that was a catchy slogan. So the spy could park the vehicle near most sensitive locales without arousing undue suspicions. For what spy would operate in a truck rendered so conspicuous by large wording plastered on both sides?

Almost nightly the Siamese twins, Jahnke and Wheeler-Hill, drove about New York. On one occasion FBI tails followed the two Nazis to the Brooklyn waterfront, where Jahnke climbed out of the truck and walked, unchallenged, to a large stack of

crates—munitions bound for England. Jahnke beamed a flashlight on the crates and copied down the stenciled lettering,
which gave the contents of each box and its destination. Then
he strolled over to the dark freighter berthed beside the crates
and obtained her name.

Now the two spies needed only the freighter's sailing date, so
they went to a waterfront saloon that was a haunt for merchant
seamen, where they struck up a conversation with two crew
members of the munitions freighter and learned its date of departure. Less than twenty-four hours later, Operation Jimmy
was beaming to Ast X in Hamburg complete details of the
freighter's sailing, her cargo, and destination. But the FCC electronic eavesdropper was also privy to the same message, so the
freighter's departure date would be changed and her course altered, which no doubt would leave U-boat wolfpacks in the Atlantic frustrated and their skippers conjecturing.

In the spring of 1941 the New York waterfront, Brooklyn, and
the port cities of New Jersey were hotbeds of Nazi intrigue.
Dingy saloons and flophouses catering to merchant seamen
from all over the world were honeycombed with German agents
and sympathizers. Naval Intelligence was aware of these spots
and, as best it could, despite limited manpower, was keeping an
eye on them.

One of the most notorious of these places was the Highway
Tavern in New Jersey. Another was the Old Hamburg in Manhattan, and yet another was Schmidt's Bar in Bayonne, New Jersey.
A bartender at Schmidt's was a Nazi agent, and he regularly
plied seamen with drinks on the house, then listened avidly as
their tongues loosened and they swapped tales of their adventures at sea.[2]

A favorite ploy of Nazi waterfront agents and informants was
to take down the names of American merchant seamen and
their home addresses. Then after the dupe had gone to sea, his
wife would receive a telephone call from a friendly individual
who would ask: "Is Joe there? Has he gotten back yet?" The un-
suspecting wife would believe that this was a friend of her
spouse, and she would tell the caller everything she knew about
her husband's movements.[3]

Nazi agents and sympathizers were thick in New York harbor branches of the Salvation Army and the Seaman's Missions. Hoboken, New Jersey, had a German Seaman's Mission. It was clean, well lighted, and provided wholesome meals. However, many German merchant sailors were irritated by its pastor, the Reverend Hermann Brückner, who constantly spoke out against the evils of Nazism.

None of the German seamen knew that the Reverend Brückner was actually a clever Abwehr agent. His function was not only to pick up shipping information but also to discourage foreign merchant sailors from working on vessels taking war materials to beleaguered England. Brückner would send his evangelists into taverns and flophouses to urge the sinners—many of whom were drunk—to repent. One of the evangelists, who went by the name of Richard Warnecke, was particularly zealous in redeeming the souls of seamen who had fled from their Nazi-occupied countries—Belgium, the Netherlands, France, Greece, Yugoslavia, and Norway.

After praying over those targeted to have their souls saved, Warnecke would get quite solicitous regarding their physical redemption as well. "Why risk your lives at sea when you can return to your homeland and get a good-paying, safe job?" the evangelist would ask. "Even though your country is occupied, when the war is over you will be alive and free."

Sailors from Nazi-occupied countries were told that Warnecke had a method for shipping them home from South America and that their tickets would be paid for. "After all," the fatherly Warnecke purred, "we German missionaries wish you well, and only want you to be safe in your homeland with your families and loved ones."[4]

Hesitant seamen were told that it was all strictly legal, since they were not American citizens. However, Warnecke felt compelled to warn them that should they remain in America, they were likely to be drafted. As a clinching incentive, Warnecke explained that Pastor Brückner, a charitable human being, would provide them with free bed and board at his Hoboken mission and pay them three dollars a day until they shipped out for South America and home.

Warnecke's evangelistic net hauled in a good-sized catch of dupes. Only later would they learn how cunningly they had been conned. When the men reached Spain or Italy, they were promptly collared and forced to work on German or Italian merchant vessels. If a shanghaied sailor balked, a threat to loved ones in his Nazi-occupied homeland was sufficient to bring him into line. Untold numbers of Warnecke's "converts" were destined to die when their ships were sunk by Allied guns, bombs, or torpedoes.[5]

Meanwhile in early April 1941, J. Edgar Hoover and his associates were convinced that they were tangling covertly with at least four separate and well-organized Nazi spy rings—those headed by Fritz Duquesne, Kurt Ludwig, Carl Reuper, and the German chargé d'affaires in Washington, Dr. Hans Thomsen. In addition the G-men had to contend with Count Vonsiatsky-Vonsiatsky's Ukranian boom-and-bang desperadoes, "Scar-Face Otto" Willmeit's gang in the Midwest, and the suave Captain Fritz Wiedemann's underground machinations on the West Coast.

The FBI chief was now confronted with a major decision: How much longer could he, in the interest of bagging the largest number of Hitler's agents, continue to allow the German networks to send secret or restricted information to Hamburg and Berlin before the G-men struck? This was the agonizing question that would haunt Hoover relentlessly.

Not all the Nazi spies in the United States belonged to networks. One of the most productive of the solo operatives was Paul Scheffer, a burly bruiser who was the Abwehr's ace political agent. Scheffer had long been the editor of a major daily newspaper in Berlin and since late 1939 had been masquerading in New York as correspondent for *Das Reich*, Dr. Josef Goebbels's slick weekly propaganda magazine.

A jovial, extroverted type with impeccable manners, Scheffer's reputation as an illustrious journalist known in many parts of the world gained him entrée to some of Manhattan's wealthiest and most prestigious private clubs. There he rubbed elbows with the elite and subtly extracted from them a flow of juicy political tidbits, including the sexual peccadillos of Washington bigwigs. As a ploy to mask his true loyalties, the Nazi spy titillated club members with whispered, off-color jokes about Adolf Hitler, then joined in the guffaws.

Scheffer's secret analytical reports on the U.S. political scene were read avidly in Hamburg and Berlin; even Wilhelm Canaris insisted on seeing them. But the journalist's "fans" were not limited to Nazi honchos in the Third Reich—staffers at the British censorship station in Bermuda as well as FBI agents in Washington and New York also were poring over Scheffer's political analyses.

The German correspondent's propensity for melodramatic covert actions resulted in his being unmasked. Although he lived at 227 East 57th Street, Manhattan, his heavy volume of mail was sent to an unoccupied brownstone townhouse on East 51st Street. Each day the political spy would take a cab to the brownstone, leap out and snatch his mail from the box, then dash back to the taxi and race away.

Neighbors had long noticed this curious scenario, but it was the suspicions of a mail carrier on East 51st Street that had drawn the FBI's attention to the *Das Reich* correspondent. Why, the postal carrier had conjectured, would the elusive figure named Paul Scheffer receive mail at the old brownstone when it was obvious that no one lived there? And who had been picking up the mail there each day after the carrier had made his rounds?

The mailman had told superiors of his misgivings, and they passed the information along to the FBI, who in turn had notified Bermuda to put Scheffer's letters on the watch list.[6]

Another zealous Nazi free-lancer was Carl Heine, the long-time Ford Motor Company executive who had turned his back on a hefty $30,000 annual salary from the Detroit manufacturer to labor in the espionage vineyards of Adolf Hitler. Early in 1941 Heine moved his base of operations from Detroit to New York City, where he took up residence in the stylish Governor Clinton Hotel under the alias Mr. Blackwell.

The industrious Heine, who by now had learned all the evasive tactics used by professional spies to shake tails, was being shadowed by G-men, who occasionally lost him. But they did tail Heine to the Glenn Martin aircraft factory near Baltimore, where the German agent flashed his bogus credentials as a Ford official and was taken on a guided tour of the plant.

From Baltimore, Heine drove to nearby Washington, where he met secretly with a captain in the U.S. Army Air Corps. FBI men checked into the captain's background and discovered, much to their astonishment, that he had been an officer in the German army—a fact not revealed in the captain's U.S. Army file.

Next Hoover's agents tailed Heine to Bridgeport, Connecticut, where he contacted the owner of Thorell's Aircraft Photo Service, a legitimate and ethical firm specializing in airplane photographs. Posing again as a Ford executive, the glib Heine talked the proprietor into agreeing to mail him a set of photographs that would reveal new technical devices on army fighters and bombers.

Two G-men called on the Thorell Aircraft Photo Service proprietor. The bewildered man was shaken over the fact that he had nearly become an accomplice of a Nazi spy. Working with the FBI and air corps officers, he created a set of doctored airplane photographs—which revealed no secrets—and mailed them to Heine at the Governor Clinton.

A day after Heine received the photographs, G-men staked out in an adjoining room overheard through listening devices a gleeful conversation between Heine and two Forschers who had come to collect the airplane photos and carry them back to the Third Reich.

"Just take these [pictures] as they are," Heine told his visitors.

"You mean you're not going to have them microfilmed?" a courier asked in a surprised tone.

"Hell, no!" Heine replied. "I don't trust that bastard Sebold!" [7]

In March 1941 William Sebold, at his bugged "research office" in the Knickerbocker Building, was contacted by Wilhelm Siegler, chief butcher on the United States liner *America*, and Franz Stigler, head baker on the same ship. Both German-born American citizens were Abwehr couriers. In excited tones, they told

Sebold that they wanted him to go with them to Hoboken to hold a Treff with an "important" person.

The Treff was held in the men's toilet of the Lackawanna Railroad station. The "important" person turned out to be one René Mezenen, a steward on a Pan-American Clipper that had just splashed down off Washington, Long Island. An emaciated, furtive man, the French-born Mezenen glanced nervously around to make certain that hostile eyes were not watching, then pulled out a tiny microfilm from his sock. He handed the film to Bill Sebold and said in an urgent tone, "Get this to Fritz [Duquesne] immediately; they are in a hurry for the information." "They" were the Hamburg spymasters.

Within the hour Sebold turned over the microfilm to his covert FBI contact, and a short time later G-men in Foley Square were studying an enlarged version of its message. It was clear that the Abwehr, probably acting at the request of Hitler's military high command, had altered its approach in the United States. Technical data no longer interested Ast X, the message said. What was wanted now was strictly military information. There followed a lengthy "shopping list," most of it concerning the growing U.S. air forces—their strengths, data on flying and ground crews, instruction manuals, flying schools and their locations.

This information might be difficult to come by, Hamburg conceded. Therefore, it was suggested, Duquesne and his mob might have to find "friends" in the U.S. air forces to provide the secret data.

After reproducing the microfilm's message, the G-men returned the film to Sebold who handed it over to Fritz Duquesne. Armed with knowledge of the future thrust of the Old Boer's spy ring, the FBI began taking covert counteractions to minimize chances of air force secrets being pilfered.

A few days after Heine sent off to Germany his worthless airplane photographs, Fritz Duquesne showed up at Bill Sebold's bugged office in the Knickerbocker Building. The Old Boer was in a grumpy mood and groused that his mistress and accomplice, Evelyn Lewis, had accused him (no doubt with merit) of seeing another woman on the sly.

"We'd be in a hell of a mess, Fritz," Sebold said, "if your gal ever turned on you and squealed to the FBI."

Duquesne mulled over that observation. Then he looked up at Sebold and exclaimed, "We'd be in a hell of a bigger mess if *you* went to the FBI!"

Sebold projected outrage at such a suggestion—just as the G-men had coached him to do should he be charged with per- fidy by Nazi gang members.

After a few moments of silence, the Old Boer added: "If I ever found out that you weren't on the level, Sebold, I'd kill you with my own hands! That would make five dead in one fam- ily—you, your mother, two brothers and a sister!" [8]

24

A 4,000-Mile Espionage Safari

Seated at his desk in the Oval Office, President Franklin Roosevelt was peering through pince-nez at the document before him. He looked up at his press secretary and confidant, Stephen Early, and remarked, "This is really a fast piece of work for Washington."[1]

Then with a stroke of his pen Roosevelt signed into law the Lend-Lease bill that he had ramrodded through Congress in record time. It was 3:51 P.M. on March 11, 1941.

Lend-Lease was an ingenious method to supply tanks, airplanes, vehicles, weapons, and munitions to beleaguered England in return for only nominal payments.

Britons joyously flew American flags in the streets of London. Winston Churchill hailed America's foresight and courage. American isolationists howled that Lend-Lease was the opening salvo in the United States' involvement in the shooting war. Adolf Hitler screamed defiantly that Lend-Lease or no, "England will fall."[2]

Lend-Lease created a flap in the lairs of the spymasters in Berlin and Hamburg. The Sleeping Giant that was America was starting to build up her own defenses, and army camps, naval bases, and military airfields were sprouting like dandelions after a spring rainstorm. The Abwehr and Hitler's high command were demanding detailed reports on this rapid American

232

military expansion, so masterspy Kurt Ludwig prepared to take a "scouting trip" along the eastern seaboard, an espionage safari of four thousand miles that would hit nearly every armed forces facility between New York and the tip of Florida.

Ludwig would travel under the guise of a leather-goods salesman, and he would take along the blond beauty Lucy Boehmler, who was thrilled to be a part of such an exciting caper. The girl would pose variously as Ludwig's secretary or "kid sister" and add plausibility to his masquerade. And he knew that when the vivacious teenager turned on her feminine guile, unwary soldiers and sailors would tell her everything she wanted to know.

Getting inside a military base had always been a simple matter, for Ludwig knew the right answers to gain admittance— especially when guards were distracted by gawking at the curvaceous Lucy, who would be standing by and smiling provocatively.

Always the routine would be the same. Once inside a military base, the two Nazi spies would cruise around, and Ludwig would halt periodically to snap photographs. Lucy would saunter up to passing soldiers, engage in flirtations, and ply them with "harmless" questions. After the pair was outside the gate, Lucy would scribble notes furiously into a stenographer's pad of everything they had heard and seen.

In mid-April 1941 Ludwig picked up his teenage accomplice at her Long Island home and, with two FBI agents trailing at a discreet distance, sped through the Holland Tunnel under the Hudson River into New Jersey and on southward. That night the spies registered at a Frederick, Maryland, hotel as Joseph Kessler and Lena Boehm, his secretary, both of San Francisco.

Early in the morning Ludwig and Lucy headed for Camp George G. Meade, Maryland, where they went through their customary scenario. Then it was on to the U.S. Army Proving Grounds (where weapons and munitions were tested) at Aberdeen, Maryland.

Next the spies beat it for the Chemical Warfare Center at Edgewood Arsenal, Maryland. In a saloon outside the main gate that night, they joined six soldiers at a table, and with the convivial Ludwig footing the bill for round after round of beer, the loose-tongued servicemen regaled Lucy with tales about the tests being conducted inside the secret Chemical Warfare Center.

A fresh set of tails took over in the morning, and for forty-eight hours they followed the spies as they reconnoitered Fort Belvoir, Fort Meyer, Langley Field, and the Newport News and Norfolk naval bases, all in Virginia; and the Marine Corps' Camp Pendleton in North Carolina.

Then the espionage safari plunged on into South Carolina, where the German agents looked over Fort Jackson and cased a defense plant outside Charleston. Observing through high-powered binoculars, the G-men saw Lucy halt a young worker as he left the plant's main gate and talk to him for twenty minutes. Later one FBI agent quizzed the employee and found that the girl had used a clever ploy. She had told him that her older brother was ill in New York and that his doctor had suggested that he move to a warmer climate. Would her brother be able to get a job at this plant?

Certainly, the young man had responded. The plant had recently received a large number of military contracts and was putting on new employees in wholesale lots. He then had spilled everything he knew about the plant's operation—the number of workers, the types of work being done, production facts and figures, the destination of finished goods.

Shortly after sunrise the Nazi spies raced on into Georgia, where they hit Camp Stewart, Camp Wheeler, and Fort Benning. At the latter post they noticed that few soldiers were to be seen. So the blonde sauntered up to a sentry, flashed her provocative smile, and with a hurt expression said, "I wanted to see some soldiers. Where have they all gone?"

Wilting under her guile, the soldier blurted out, "They're in Tennessee on some big maneuvers." [3]

Now the espionage junket continued on into Florida, to the Opa Locka Naval Base outside Miami, to Camp Blanding, and to naval installations in the Keys. At the Naval Air Station at Pensacola, where aviation cadets were trained, Ludwig was challenged for the first time. When the masterspy got out of his car to snap pictures, he was collared by two stern navy security men, who promptly bounced him off the base—much to the delight of the watching G-men.

On the homeward lap, the spies drove into Alabama, buzzing like bees around defense plants at Mobile, Montgomery, and

Birmingham, and hitting Fort McClellan, Selma Air Base, and Riley Field.

Back at her home in Maspeth, Long Island, Lucy burned the midnight oil for a week while transcribing the shorthand notes with which she had filled fourteen stenographer's pads. Concealed in the shadows down the street, two FBI men had been watching her house, and they rightly deduced that the late-night lights in her room meant that she was writing up exhaustive reports on the 4,000-mile espionage jaunt for Ludwig to send to Germany.

Consequently, the FBI alerted the Bermuda censorship station to be on the lookout for a rash of mailings from Joe K. These anticipated letters, addressed to Abwehr mail drops in Spain and Portugal, were intercepted, given the heat treatment, and Ludwig's messages, written in invisible ink on the back of the sheets, were brought out. The most damaging disclosures were deftly deleted without a trace of having been tampered with, then Joe K's letters were allowed to continue on to Berlin and Hamburg.

Now industrious Lucy Boehmler, through her own initiative, began assembling a card index file that would eventually include nearly every military installation in the United States. The compilation would list the significant facts about each place—principal officers, number of personnel, service branch of units, home states of National Guard outfits, equipment, vehicles, kinds of training (armored, amphibious, artillery, infantry), morale—everything.[4]

Not long after Ludwig and Lucy returned home, a man whom Bill Sebold didn't know called on him in the Knickerbocker Building. The visitor identified himself as Leo Waalen, a Yorkville house painter, and he pulled out a number of credentials to satisfy Sebold that he was "one of the boys."

Waalen said that he had been "scouting" the shipyards of industrial tycoon Andrew J. Higgins in New Orleans and that he had a detailed report on his findings to be sent to Ast X over the Centerport shortwave station. Poring over Waalen's report, Sebold hid his shock over the fact that this clearly unsophisticated Nazi spy could obtain such vital navy secrets merely by prowling around shipyards unchallenged and talking to loose-tongued workers. Waalen had written, in part:

> Report of trial run of Motor Torpedo Boat [PT boat] [70 feet], built by A. J. Higgins, New Orleans. Captain for trial run Lieutenant Earl Caldwell, U.S. Navy.
>
> No armament aboard whatsoever . . . Three 1,500 horse-power Packard motors. Boats plywood but of sturdy construction . . . High octane gas used in trial runs, about 280 gals. per hour . . . PT boats will be equipped with four torpedo tubes which can fire simultaneously . . . Torpedos are supposed to be fired four to five miles from the enemy, while the PT boats are still hardly visible.[5]

Meanwhile in New York, peripatetic Kurt Ludwig regularly prowled the waterfront to report to Hamburg on the berthed luxury liner *Normandie*. A G-man who had been tailing the Nazi spy wrote in a report:

> On June 18 [1941] he walked down Twelfth Avenue from 59th Street. He was watching the piers. When he came to the *Normandie's* pier he stopped for some time. He seemed to be examining carefully. Then he walked on, looking back. At 42nd Street he took the Weehawken ferry (across the Hudson), went to the upper deck and kept watching the *Normandie*.[6]

After reaching Weehawken, the FBI agent added, Ludwig sat on a park bench and for nearly twenty minutes scribbled furiously in a little black book.

Far from the New York waterfront, Adolf Hitler once again shocked the world. At dawn on June 22, 1941, he launched Operation Barbarossa, a surprise smash by three million men of the Wehrmacht against the Russian border along a two thousand-mile front. The Soviets were taken by surprise, and their defenses collapsed like houses of cards in a typhoon.[7]

In London, Winston Churchill was elated. No longer did Great Britain stand alone against the mighty Wehrmacht. Even though the rotund prime minister hated and distrusted the Russian Communists, he remarked to his private secretary: "If Hitler invaded hell I would make at least a favorable reference to the Devil in the House of Commons!" [8]

Late on the afternoon of June 25, three days after German legions had plunged into Russia, Fritz Duquesne called on the FBI double agent Bill Sebold in the Knickerbocker Building. In shirtsleeves, Sebold shook hands with the Nazi masterspy. While the FBI camera hidden in the adjoining office rolled, Duquesne leaned over, took off a shoe, and removed from his sock a white envelope, which he handed to Sebold. Inside the envelope was information that the Old Boer had collected while covering the vast maneuvers of the United States Army in Tennessee.

While the FBI bugs recorded every word, Duquesne told how he had poked around at will within the maneuvers area, snapping pictures of troops, equipment, vehicles, tanks, and weapons without once being challenged. His haul included photos of a new "baby tank," a secret antitank device and the new Garand semiautomatic rifle, reputed to be the world's best.[9]

Duquesne also handed over a collection of other photographs. Sebold would send them to Hamburg and Berlin—after the FBI had studied and doctored them. One photo was of a new PT boat. "I got the speedboat picture right from [a mole in] the Navy Department in Washington," Fritz boasted.

Typically, Duquesne was in an expansive mood. He bragged of the American military secrets he had stolen over the years and warned Sebold not to carry secret papers on his person unless absolutely necessary. "Those FBI bastards are a bunch of *dümkopfs*," Fritz explained, "but they might pick you up by accident." [10]

While Sebold listened impassively, Fritz talked about guns and bombs and pantomimed aiming a Garand rifle, gesturing all the while like a veteran of the old Hollywood silent films. Watching through the mirror, G-men thought Duquesne made a lousy thespian.

Suddenly Fritz told Sebold, "I want you to get me some dynamite caps and a slow-burning fuse." He explained that he had been reconnoitering the General Electric plant at Schenectady, New York, and that he could "blow the joint up" with a slow-burning fuse. Duquesne also proposed planting a bomb at Hyde Park, President Roosevelt's estate on the banks of the Hudson north of New York City.[11]

Taking a candy bar that Sebold had just unwrapped, Duquesne pointed out that "if this piece of candy was broken in two, and some combustible phosphorous were placed inside, it would make a very effective incendiary bomb." However, an even more destructive device could be rigged by chewing Chiclets (gum) thoroughly, then folding the gum around a phosphorous compound, the Old Boer explained. These tiny incendiary bombs could be scattered on docks and in ships and factories "through a hole in the pocket of your coat while you're merely walking along." Fritz chuckled and added, "These Chiclet bombs could be planted even while you're talking to the boss." He was quite proud of his Chiclet-bomb invention, saying that he had "used it with great success in the past."

His lengthy espionage and sabotage recital concluded, Duquesne returned to his ornate apartment off Central Park and found his mistress, Evelyn Lewis, gripped by a case of nervous tension. Somehow, the glamour and excitement of espionage work had vanished, and her life had become fraught with hand-wringing worry. She often peered into the street from behind curtains to see whether her apartment was being watched. She was suspicious of electricians who called at the building and of window washers. In a frightened tone, she told Duquesne that people were looking into their apartment from windows across the street.

Two days after Fritz Duquesne had visited Sebold's "research office," the FBI swooped down on and arrested a covey of German agents operating in Brooklyn and reporting on shipping. Newspapers labeled them the "Harbor Spy Gang." Kurt Ludwig's ring got the jitters. Ludwig, René Froelich, the traitorous Fort Jay soldier, and Major Paul Borchardt knew some of the men arrested.

Ludwig was especially shaken, for he had had a close call only a day earlier. He had made an appointment to hold a Treff with Paul Alfred Scholz, the Yorkville bookstore operator. Just as Ludwig neared the front door of Scholz's store, two men entered ahead of him and began browsing through the shelves.

A sixth sense flashed a red warning light before Ludwig's eyes, so instead of seeking out Scholz he walked to the back of the store and pretended to examine books. Then he saw the two men who had entered the store ahead of him—now clearly FBI agents—close in on Scholz and haul him away.

Suddenly Ludwig felt an overpowering urge to vanish, to get out of bustling New York City and away from the FBI. For more than a year the one-time Munich businessman had carried out his espionage mission with cocksure confidence, convinced that he was too smart to be caught. But for a few weeks prior to his close shave in the Yorkville bookshop, the masterspy had been haunted by the fear that he was being shadowed.

His fretful mood was reflected in a letter to Berlin: "I am having to hump myself to keep ahead of the competition." (Nazi spies called the FBI "the competition" or "the competitors.") [12]

Early in June one of Hoover's men tailed Ludwig to the Battery, in lower Manhattan, where he met René Froelich, the Fort Jay hospital clerk. Froelich alighted from the Governor's Island ferry and handed Ludwig a package of restricted materials that he had stolen at his army post.

The G-man shadowed the two Nazi spies all over Manhattan. He saw them go into a German movie house on 96th Street that was showing Hitler's propaganda film, *Victory in the West*, a documentary of the Blitzkreig that had overrun most of Europe in late 1939 and 1940. When Ludwig and Froelich emerged, the tail followed them until they parted at midnight, when the soldier took the ferry back to Governor's Island.

With each passing day Ludwig was growing more nervous. He wrote Hamburg: "It is so hot in New York I think I'll go to the mountains for a rest." Indeed it was "hot" for the Nazis in New York—and Hoover's men were stoking the furnace. [13]

Everyone in the German espionage apparatus in the United States was keeping posted as best he or she could on developments in the Harbor Spy Gang affair. Bits and pieces gleaned from newspapers led Ludwig to conclude—accurately—that the Brooklyn spies were chirping like canaries to federal authorities. Furious, Kurt Ludwig fired off a letter to Gestapo chief

Heinrich Himmler in Berlin. Addressed to the customary Himmler mail drop in Madrid, the letter was intercepted by the Bermuda censorship station and given the heat treatment.

Ludwig identified for Himmler the "rats" who were making "unpleasant statements" to the FBI, and he hoped that the Gestapo might "take reprisals against their families." [14]

25

"The Greatest Spy Roundup"

Curious events were unfolding in the Yorkville German colony. For years Richard Eichenlaub and his plump wife had placidly drawn beer and served *Wiener Schnitzel* to customers at the Little Casino bar at 206 East 85th Street. Among the cafés and shops that crowded the sidewalks of Yorkville, the Little Casino was barely noticeable to the casual pedestrian. So the bar had been an ideal hangout for members of Fritz Duquesne's Nazi spy ring—and in the past year it had been a haunt for FBI agents in disguise. Suddenly, on the morning of Saturday, June 29, 1941, Eichlenlaub disappeared.

Elsewhere in New York City and in neighboring towns, other men and women, many of whom had been Eichenlaub's customers, also vanished. Seventy-two hours later J. Edgar Hoover, who could barely conceal his deep satisfaction, told the world that thirty-three spies had been swept up in an FBI dragnet.

The coordinated sweep had been "the greatest spy roundup in U.S. history," Hoover declared. "This is one of the most active and vicious gangs we have ever had to deal with."[1]

Hoover's dramatic announcement shocked most Americans. The spies' sinister game, the FBI chief said, was "snitching important national defense secrets and transmitting them to a foreign power." Even the most naive Americans knew the identity of that "foreign power."

241

At the conclusion of the FBI's spectacular weekend, most members of Fritz Duquesne's and Carl Reuper's rings were in jail—including both masterminds themselves. Among those peeking through bars were Hermann Lang, the Norden inspector who had connived with Abwehr Major Nickolaus Ritter to steal the supersecret Norden bombsight; Everett Roeder, an engineer at the strategic Sperry plant on Long Island, who had been an accomplice in the bombsight theft; Joseph Klein and Alex Wheeler-Hill, two of the three Operation Jimmy boys; mop-haired "model," Lilly Stein; and Duquesne's mistress, Evelyn Lewis.

All thirty-three persons snared in the FBI dragnet were charged with conspiracy to violate United States espionage laws.

In Washington, the German chargé d'affaires, Dr. Hans Thomsen, was stunned by the sledgehammer blow against the Nazi spy apparatus. Until he could collect his wits and sort out the pieces of the debacle, Thomsen hid out from Joachim von Ribbentrop, his boss in the Third Reich.

However, the chargé could not duck the issue indefinitely. On July 4 he received an urgent cable in which the clearly agitated foreign minister demanded an immediate, detailed report. Thomsen's one-page response confirmed that thirty-three German agents had been jailed, that the FBI had struck after a two-year surveillance (a fact gleaned from U.S. newspapers), and that nine of those caught had already confessed to spying for the Third Reich.

In Berlin, the demolition of the spy networks created an enormous flap. At Abwehr headquarters, Admiral Canaris was grimly poring over a list of Nazi agents swept up by the FBI. One significant name was missing. "Where is Tramp?" the admiral demanded of Colonel Hans Piekenbrock, the Abwehr officer who was responsible for espionage operations in North America. "What happened to Tramp?" Tramp was the Abwehr code name for its ace operative, William Sebold, who had presumably been manning the secret Centerport shortwave radio station.

Colonel Piekenbrock admitted that he did not have the answer. For the next several days he and Canaris waited anxiously for some word from Tramp. If Sebold was still at liberty, they concluded, he would soon be contacting Ast X from Centerport with a complete rundown on the espionage disaster.

Tramp would never call again—Centerport station CQDXVW-2 had gone out of business. But Bill Sebold would surface again soon, and in a most dramatic fashion.

Following the radio station's shutdown, J. Edgar Hoover—gleefully, no doubt—turned over to the United States Treasury a check in the amount of eighteen thousand dollars, representing the "profit" the FBI had realized from the funds Adolf Hitler's surrogates had given Sebold to purchase the Centerport house and the radio equipment.

Relations between the United States and Germany, in the meantime, had grown more tense. President Roosevelt had taken to the airwaves to tell millions of Americans that "the United States will not wait until [Hitler] invades to strike back. We in America will decide for ourselves whether and when and where our American interests are attacked or our security threatened."[2]

Hard on the heels of the FBI's massive spy roundup, President Roosevelt struck another telling blow against Nazi skulduggery in the United States. He ordered German consuls general to close down their consulates (which had been little more than Abwehr branches) and to board the first ship for the Third Reich. The President's note was couched in diplomatic language: The Nazi consuls general had been "engaging in activities wholly outside the scope of their legitimate duties."

Within hours Joachim von Ribbentrop fired off urgent cables to his consulates in the United States: All "compromising papers" were to be destroyed. At 17 Battery Place in Manhattan, Consul General Rudolf Borchers and his subordinates assembled large stacks of documents, tied them into bundles, and summoned Walter Morrissey, the chief janitor, to lug the bales to the basement and burn them.

Morrissey was an Irish-American in his early fifties who hated the Germans in the consulate; for nearly a year he had been an FBI mole. Before carting the bundles to the basement, he set the furnace draft in such a way that when the bundles were pitched inside and the door closed the fire would die out almost at once.

Apparently young consul Siegfried Lurtz did not want to soil his hands or his expensive suit, so neither he nor a clerk moved a finger to help as Morrissey wrestled the bales into the basement. Then the two Germans watched until the custodian had hurled all the papers into the furnace and closed its door. Satisfied that the documents were burning brightly, Lurtz and his clerk went back upstairs, and Morrissey quickly retrieved the bundles. Although singed, the papers were largely intact, and the next morning G-men in Foley Square were examining them.

Walter Morrissey had scored a bull's-eye. Among the papers was found a roster of Nazi agents, informants, and sympathizers in the New York City region. Siegfried Lurtz, customarily a model of Teutonic efficiency, had botched monumentally what should have been a routine paper-burning task.

Three days after the FBI dragnet had been cast into the espionage waters, the Bermuda censorship station intercepted a letter that Joe K (Ludwig) had mailed to his friend "Marion" (Heinrich Himmler):

> I know three of those who have been arrested . . . they are stupid, cowardly and lazy, just like Americans.[3]

Meanwhile that summer of 1941, a bitter controversy was raging across the United States over the extension of the September 16, 1940, Selective Service Act. That bill had modified the one-year term of military service by the phrase "except that whenever the Congress has declared that the national interest is imperiled, such 12-month period may be extended by the President to such time as may be necessary in the interest of national defense."

Extending the draft generated heated congressional debate. Senator Arthur H. Vandenberg of Michigan exclaimed, "My opinion is that the situation today . . . looks infinitely safer."[4]

"If Hitler conquers Russia," Senator Josh Lee of Oklahoma countered, "seasoned troops can be withdrawn from the eastern front and [invade] the British Isles . . . If Hitler conquers Russia, he will be within shouting distance of Alaska."[5]

Extension of the draft won by a squeaker in the House—203 yeas, 202 nays, and 27 not voting. Congress came within a whisker of emasculating the nation's armed forces only three months before America would be bombed into war at Pearl Harbor.

Late in July 1941 Kurt Ludwig felt that the "heat" was too oppressive in New York City, so he holed up at Lutherville, a resort in the beautiful Pocono Mountains of Pennsylvania. But within a week the masterspy could sense the net closing in. Suddenly the Poconos were not nearly far enough away from New York City. In fact, the entire United States had become an unhealthy place, so he decided the time was ripe to return to Germany—and the sooner the better.

Ludwig contacted his Miami ring member, charter-boat skipper Carl Schroetter, and asked him to obtain a small craft in which the masterspy could slip across the Caribbean Sea to sanctuary in Cuba. Impossible, Schroetter replied, the heat was on in Florida too, and Schroetter was convinced that he himself was being shadowed.[6]

Desperate, Ludwig decided to drive to the Pacific Coast where he would catch a ship to Japan and go from there to the Third Reich. So early in August, under cover of darkness, he sneaked into New York City to take care of a few urgent matters, then climbed into his high-powered automobile and headed westward alone—or so he thought. Two FBI agents were on his tail.

Two days later the tails found themselves in Fremont, Ohio, which they knew to be the spy's birthplace. At the county seat in Sandusky, Ludwig obtained a copy of his birth certificate. Now it was clear to Hoover's men: Ludwig, who was still an American citizen by virtue of his birthplace, was preparing to flee the country and would need his birth certificate.

Even though Ludwig was heading for the Third Reich, he continued to spy, casing Camp Erie and Fort Clinton in Ohio and Selfridge Field outside Detroit. Unable to get through the gate at Wright Field, where experimental bombers were being tested, Ludwig drove onto a little-used road at the end of a runway, pretended to be fixing a flat tire, then photographed each new bomber as it took off a short distance over his head.[7]

Then it was on westward. The FBI agents, working in relays,

could have nabbed the fleeing Abwehr spy at any time, but, hoping that he would drop clues leading to unknown members of his ring, they continued to nip discreetly at his heels.

Past Chicago, Ludwig seemed to suspect he was being tailed. In an effort to unmask or shake off the tails, Ludwig would slow down to a crawl, then roar off at high rates of speed. Reaching Nebraska, he felt like a hunted animal. His money had nearly run out, so he telephoned Lucy Boehmler back on Long Island and, through double-talk, declared, "The 'competition' is very bad!" The G-men were prohibited by law from tapping telephones, but there had been nothing to keep a switchboard operator from eavesdropping, then telling the Feds what she had heard.

Ludwig pleaded for money. Lucy wired him a measly twenty dollars.[8]

In Nebraska, Ludwig stopped at an express office and mailed a package to an address in New York City. Hoover's men closed in and claimed the bundle. It contained pilfered U.S. documents that Ludwig had apparently planned to carry back to Germany.

The twenty-first day of August was stifling hot. Nearly exhausted, Ludwig reached Yellowstone National Park and rented a cabin for the night near Mammoth Hot Springs. After dark, watching G-men saw the spy slip out of his cabin and go to his car, carry an armful of papers into the cabin, then return for two more loads. Minutes later wisps of smoke curled upward from the chimney: Ludwig was burning the papers in a small stove with which each cabin was furnished.

Shortly after dawn Ludwig sped out of Yellowstone, with a new G-man in a different car racing after him. Two of Hoover's men had entered the cabin and examined the residue in the stove. Most of the papers had been burned to black powder, but numerous fragments, although badly charred, were gingerly placed in a score of small, cotton-lined boxes and shipped to Washington.

At the FBI laboratory, technicians took infrared photographs of each tiny fragment of charred paper, bringing out secret-ink handwriting. When the photographs were greatly enlarged, they revealed that the papers contained an abundance of U.S. military information.

Meanwhile, the latest tail caught up with the spy at Butte, Montana, where Ludwig entered an express agency and shipped a portable typewriter and a suitcase to an address in Dumont, New Jersey. Then the Abwehr agent parked his car in a commercial garage, sneaked out a side door, and dashed to catch a bus that was pulling out for the West Coast.

Hoover's sleuth spotted Ludwig boarding the bus and telephoned ahead. Then the G-man took possession of the spy's automobile and found the built-in shortwave radio with which messages were dispatched to U-boats off the eastern seaboard for relay to Hamburg and Berlin.[9]

A day later a Greyhound bus pulled into the hamlet of Cle Elum, Washington. A neatly dressed man wearing a straw hat climbed aboard and walked slowly down the aisle, peering at each male passenger. He halted next to a long-nosed, blond man, whipped out a badge, and called out, "FBI!" Kurt Ludwig turned pale and was led off to jail.

Four days later G-men intercepted Ludwig's luggage in a New Jersey express office. Inside the suitcase were fifty military maps and the accoutrements of the espionage profession: a camera, photographs of defense installations, and items for writing in secret ink—a few bottles of Pyramidon headache tablets, a packet of stained toothpicks, and an eyecup. Clearly Ludwig had not wanted to be caught with this incriminating evidence in his possession.

Meanwhile, G-men searched Ludwig. A pocket yielded a little black notebook crammed with curious-looking, hand-written do-dads, a mixture of a numerical code and the ancient Gabelsberger shorthand. The black book was whisked to Washington, where FBI experts cracked the code. Disclosed were the names and addresses of the masterspy's gang and listings for contacts in Shanghai, Portugal, Argentina, and Spain.

Arraigned on espionage charges before a federal magistrate in Spokane, Washington, the one-time Munich businessman was held in bail of $50,000, which he could not meet, and he was locked up in the county jail in Spokane.

Now, with the spymaster behind bars, J. Edgar Hoover flashed word for his agents to swoop down on Ludwig's ring. Simultaneously, without dramatics or fanfare, Lucy Boehmler, Hans Pagel, Karl Mueller, Helen Mayer, and Private René Froelich were collared. The mystery-shrouded intellectual, Major Paul Borchardt, would be given more rope to see where it might lead.

Adolf Hitler's espionage apparatus in the United States had been struck yet another devastating blow.

When Kurt Ludwig had informed Hamburg that the "heat" in New York was stifling prior to his flight to the West Coast, strange things began to happen. Old pro Borchardt, while ostensibly a member of Ludwig's ring, apparently was taking his orders directly from an unknown source in Berlin. Now Borchardt received a message from his mysterious superior in the Third Reich, warning him to "take care of your health and stop running around with young girls like Josefa [Joe, or Ludwig]." Translated into plain talk: "Ludwig is hot as hell—keep away from him!"

The old pro replied confidently in double-talk:

> As for my girlfriend Josefa, I have slowly but certainly drawn myself away from her. I told her openly that nothing could be said of marriage . . . She understood quite well, gave me her new address [in the Poconos], and disappeared.[10]

Indeed Borchardt had tried to disassociate himself from the suddenly "hot" Ludwig. While Ludwig was holed up in the Poconos, the Professor had told his landlady, "If Mr. Kessler [Ludwig] calls at my apartment or telephones, please tell him that I am not in."[11]

When word of Ludwig's arrest on the West Coast hit the newspapers, the Professor showed his landlady a newspaper clipping of an automobile accident and a man's picture next to it. She noted that Borchardt had deleted the victim's name from below the picture. "Too bad about poor Mr. Kessler," Borchardt remarked sadly. "He's been killed in this car accident."

What kind of game was her tenant playing? The landlady had seen "Mr. Kessler" several times when he came to visit Borchardt—and the man in the newspaper clipping was not "Mr. Kessler." Only later would she learn that her roomer had anticipated that she might be called as a witness at Ludwig's trial, and he hoped to confuse her as to Ludwig's facial appearance in order to prevent her from positively identifying him.

Kurt Ludwig had been behind bars in Spokane for more than a week, and he concluded that his Nazi overlords had no intention of bailing him out. Recovering from his initial shock over being arrested, the masterspy's nimble mind had been working in high gear. Now he called over Deputy Sheriff Ray Killian, who had been sworn in as a temporary U.S. marshal to keep an eye on the federal prisoner until he could be taken East to stand trial.

Ludwig, an amiable fellow, told Killian that if the United States government valued him at fifty thousand dollars (the amount of his bail), then certainly the Hitler regime would consider him to be worth an equal sum. Killian made no response. Encouraged, Ludwig asked: "How would you like to earn that amount of money?"

The guard did not reject the proposal outright, so the spy outlined his plan. All Killian would have to do would be to unlock the cell door and the two men, captive and captor, could sneak away together, to South America, perhaps. There, Ludwig promised, Killian would receive his reward from the German government.

The jailer said he would "think it over" and promptly notified the FBI of the bribe offer. Play along with the prisoner and see what develops, the Feds instructed Killian. A day later the marshal slipped up to Ludwig's cell, glanced furtively up and down the corridor, and whispered that he had thought the proposal over and that "things can be arranged." Ludwig grinned broadly.

But the deal was not yet sealed. What guarantee would he have, Killian inquired, that he would actually get the fifty thousand dollars in South America? How did he know that Ludwig could raise the money? Was there someone in the United States who could make a "down payment" as a show of good faith?

The spy pondered the question. Why, yes, there was. Killian could telephone a certain number in New York City and tell the man who answered that Joe K wanted two hundred dollars.

Less than an hour later the FBI identified the owner of that telephone number: Paul Borchardt, Abwehr code-name Oakland.

Forty-eight hours later Ludwig, guarded by two U.S. marshals, was on an airplane bound for New York. At the same time the FBI struck again, arresting Borchardt and four other members of Ludwig's ring.

Hardly had the jail doors slammed shut behind some forty-five Hitler agents scooped up in FBI sweeps than spymasters in Hamburg and Berlin began plotting to rebuild the demolished espionage apparatus.

26

"Tricycle" Clashes with the Big Chief

On the afternoon of August 24, 1941, thirty-one-year-old Dusko Popov, a wealthy Yugoslavian businessman, was a passenger aboard a Pan-American Clipper that splashed to a landing on Long Island Sound. Popov was met by G-men, who confiscated his toothbrush, comb, spare shoes, and other items, all of which were sent to the FBI laboratory in Washington for meticulous examination. For the Yugoslav was a double agent, ostensibly working for both sides—and J. Edgar Hoover didn't trust double agents. "How do you know whose side these birds are really on?" the supersleuth had barked to associates.

At the outbreak of war in Europe, Popov had been in Belgrade. There he was contacted by an Abwehr officer who suggested that the extensive Popov family holdings in Europe might be "protected" by the Hitler regime if Dusko would become a German spy. Grasping the implied threat of confiscation, Popov agreed to serve the fuehrer. However, he sought out a British intelligence officer in Belgrade, revealed his Abwehr connection, and volunteered to work for England. Popov was told to go through the motions of spying for the Nazis.

After being trained in Germany, Popov—code-named Ivan by the Abwehr—was sent to England, arriving in London on December 20, 1940, during the Luftwaffe's savage blitz. Under the guise of a businessman buying goods for Yugoslavia, Popov's

mission was to ferret out information on British defenses and
troop strength.

Popov underwent intensive grilling by the British secret service and made a "most favorable impression."[1] Then he was
taken under the wing of the XX-Committee, a clandestine group
that Winston Churchill had created early in the war to conceive
and implement devious stratagems for confusing and misleading Adolf Hitler and his high command. Controlled by a bright,
energetic Seaforth Highlander, thirty-year-old Major Thomas A.
"Tar" Robertson, the XX-Committee (so-called because the Ro-
man numerals XX also stood for the double-cross) mainly used
captured and "turned" German spies to send false information
to the Third Reich.

Rechristened "Tricycle" by the British, Popov's reports to the
Abwehr were created by the clever men and women of the Dou-
ble-X Committee and consisted of a witch's brew of "secret"
British data: harmless truths, half-truths based on information
the Germans were known to have had, and outright lies in matters that the Abwehr could not verify independently.

During the first half of 1941, Tricycle flooded Berlin with this
high-grade intelligence (or so it seemed to the Abwehr), explaining that it came from "contacts high up in British officialdom." So by mid-year Popov had established himself as
Hitler's ace operative in Great Britain, one who had the total
trust of the spymasters in the Third Reich. But when J. Edgar
Hoover dropped his blockbuster and virtually wiped out the
Nazi espionage apparatus in the United States, and with America edging closer to involvement in the shooting war, the Abwehr decided that Popov could better serve the Third Reich by
helping to rebuild the dismantled Nazi network.

Popov was ordered to travel first to Lisbon, where he drove to
a secluded house on the outskirts for a Treff with Ludovico von
Karsthoff, a tall, heavyset man with black hair and a jovial dis-
position. An Austrian by birth, Karsthoff was chief of the Abwehr in Lisbon. His real name was Major Erik von Auenrode.

Over cocktails, Karsthoff gave Popov his marching orders.
They were in the form of a lengthy questionnaire to guide Popov
while in the United States. About one-third of the document
dealt with installations at Pearl Harbor, Hawaii.

Twenty-four hours later Popov told British operatives in

Lisbon of the questionnaire, and J. Edgar Hoover was notified that Tricycle was coming to the United States with "highly significant intelligence" from the German camp to hand over. Hoover received the news with a notable lack of enthusiasm, but assigned a G-man to be Tricycle's contact in New York.

Less than two weeks after Popov reached America, he aroused the straitlaced Hoover's ire by settling into a luxurious lifestyle, ensconcing himself in the twenty-second-floor penthouse of a fashionable Park Avenue building. Tricycle's FBI contact remarked wryly, "I don't think Mr. Hoover will like all this . . . all this plush layout." [2]

Popov merely shrugged. Adolf Hitler was footing the bill. Tricycle had brought along sixty thousand dollars in Abwehr money to bankroll the creation of a new spy network, but he was using the funds to support his high living.

Hoover hit the ceiling when he learned that Popov was carousing nightly in such plush watering holes as El Morocco, "21," and the Stork Club with the sultry French cinema siren, Simone Simon, who was making a movie in the United States.

"I'm running the world's cleanest police organization," the FBI chief railed to aides. "So we don't need this bogus spy running wild in Manhattan."

Tricycle too had grown angry. He wanted to call on Hoover in Washington, but his FBI contact told him, "Sit tight and instructions will be given to you in New York." Popov's fury heightened when he discovered a bug hidden in his penthouse study and then found two more in his living room and bedroom.

Hoover had good cause to suspect Tricycle's credibility. A G-man had tailed the double agent and found that a known Abwehr operative in Manhattan had slipped eight thousand dollars to Popov, a covert transaction that the Yugoslavian had not reported to his FBI contact. [3]

The FBI chief and his associates had been suspicious of the validity of Popov's Abwehr questionnaire right from the beginning. To them, the document seemed to be too pat, too precise. Was it a devious Abwehr ploy in which Popov was to slip the questionnaire to the FBI in order to send the sleuths chasing down blind alleys?

Whatever may have been Popov's true intentions, he did provide the FBI with a monumental piece of intelligence—the secret of the ingenious German microdot, the riddle that had baffled the G-men since January 1940. The microdot revelation would prove to be a bonanza, for it would permit the FBI to intercept hundreds of miniature messages and get a daily insight into the activities of Nazi operatives in the United States.[4]

Nearly a month after Popov had reached America, a telephone caller told him to come at once to an office in a certain building in Manhattan. After walking into the office, he encountered a grim-faced J. Edgar Hoover sitting behind a desk and "looking like a sledgehammer in search of an anvil."[5]

"Sit down, Popov!" Hoover barked. A shouting match promptly erupted. Tricycle yelled that he had come to America to organize a Nazi spy ring and that he would put it under the FBI's control. "I can catch spies without your or anybody else's help!" Hoover roared. He accused Popov of being "like all double agents. You're begging for information to sell to your German friends so you can make a lot of money and be a playboy!"[6]

Tricycle got up and stomped off toward the door. "Good riddance!" the FBI chief shouted after him.[7]

It had long been Director Hoover's habit to send tidbits of espionage information to President Roosevelt. So he forwarded to the White House photographs demonstrating the microdot technique, in which full-sized, typewritten pages were reduced to a fly speck, then would be magnified two hundred times to its original size. Hoover also passed along an edited version of Tricycle's questionnaire, omitting the Pearl Harbor portions.[8]

However, the FBI, working with Naval Intelligence, used the information in the questionnaire to concoct plausible lies designed to convince the Japanese warlords that Pearl Harbor was much better defended than was actually the case. These bogus rumors were filtered through Nipponese naval officers who were in the United States ostensibly to take English-language lessons.[9]

Not long after Popov's shouting match with Hoover, the double agent became concerned. It had been five weeks since he had taken off from Lisbon, he was blowing the Abwehr's $60,000 kitty as though money was going out of style, and he had not sent one iota of intelligence to Berlin. Hoover refused to provide him with even phony data. What could he do to maintain his credibility with Berlin?

Tricycle went to the New York Times building on 43rd Street and thumbed through issues for the past six weeks. He collected a large batch of clippings: stories on troop training, production, military construction, and the like. Bringing his imagination into play, Popov conjured up an array of authoritative sources to whom these "highly important findings" could be attributed. Back at his sumptuous penthouse, Popov labored for many hours writing invisible-ink reports based on the "inside" intelligence he had obtained from back issues of *The New York Times*.[10]

During the early days of September 1941, Hoover was poring over an astonishing document that his agents had uncovered entitled *Memorandum of Instruction to Saboteurs*. In a brazen display of contempt for the FBI, the spymasters in the Third Reich had distributed the document widely to its agents in the United States.

Couched in precise military language, the *Memorandum of Instruction* was a sabotage battle plan. It outlined assorted techniques for blowing up or severely crippling the U.S. railroad system. A small dynamite charge in a locomotive's boiler could immobilize an entire train, the memo explained. Tactically, a series of carefully timed explosives at key points along rights of way could paralyze railroad traffic throughout a region.

Within days FBI men uncovered another aid to saboteurs—an Abwehr-compiled *Index of American Industry*. The document had been created with painstaking thoroughness, and Hoover noted that it was more detailed in many respects than were any legitimate similar compilations to be found in the United States.

G-men had sniffed out the existence of the *Index of American Industry* due to the "indiscretion" of an industrialist from a country sympathetic to the cause of Hitler's Germany. At a cocktail party in New York, the foreigner had struck up a conversation with a guest and, in an unguarded moment, boasted that he could get confidential data on any United States defense plant "within twenty-four hours." The other guest was fascinated but politely doubted the claim. So he named a certain key defense plant and challenged the industrialist to produce a detailed report on it. The boaster had no way of knowing that his newfound friend was a G-man.

Twenty-four hours later, as promised, the foreigner showed the undercover Fed an exhaustive report on the plant. It listed by name scores of key management and production employees and notations opposite each name of his or her "loyalties and international sympathies." [11]

In the meantime, George Viereck, the world's highest-paid propagandist, was having his troubles. Dispensing Nazi propaganda was a perfectly legal way for a U.S. citizen to make money—provided he told the federal government everything he was doing and who was paying him to do it. However, a New York City grand jury concluded that Viereck had suffered a convenient loss of memory when he had registered as an agent of a foreign power and indicted him on five counts.

The propaganda saboteur pleaded innocent on all counts and was released on $25,000 bail. Speaking to reporters outside the courtroom, Viereck said that his indictment was "only an incident in a perfidious plot to smother any opposition to arbitrary forces constantly at work to destroy the America we know and love." [12]

On September 3, 1941, tension was thick enough to cut with a knife in a vast, high-ceilinged room in the Federal Courthouse in Brooklyn. The nineteen accused members of the Fritz Duquesne and Carl Reuper spy rings sat solemnly before Judge Mortimer W. Byers, a jurist widely respected for his impartiality and calm decorum on the bench. It was the opening of the largest—and most electrifying—espionage trial in U.S. history.

Fourteen defendants had already pleaded guilty, and they had chirped like canaries to U.S. Attorney Harold M. Kennedy, who appeared in court weighted down with incriminating evidence to be hurled against those who had chosen to go to bat with the government.

Families of the Nazi Nineteen had hired lawyers to defend them. Also hovering over proceedings was a high-priced New York attorney who had been retained by Dr. Hans Thomsen, the chargé at the German Embassy in Washington. This lawyer's function was, in effect, to represent the Abwehr, for his hefty fee was being paid by Admiral Canaris with funds filtered through Ribbentrop's Foreign Ministry.

At the very beginning of the trial, U.S. Attorney Kennedy dropped a bombshell. Pointing an accusing finger at the stoical Hermann Lang, Kennedy declared that "the secret of the Norden bombsight, this country's most jealously guarded air defense weapon, had been in the hands of the German government since 1938, and that man is the man who stole it!" [13]

There were gasps in the audience.

Meanwhile in Berlin, Wilhelm Canaris, who had been monitoring the trial through reports from Nazi agents in New York and Washington, remained puzzled concerning the whereabouts of Tramp (William Sebold). Sebold had vanished mysteriously two months earlier when the Centerport shortwave station had suddenly gone off the air. Efforts by Abwehr agents to track him down had been fruitless.

At noon on September 8, shockwaves struck Canaris's headquarters. An urgent cable had been received from Dr. Thomsen: "According to a V-Man [part-time agent], arrests were made possible through the collaboration of an engineer named Seebold who is said to be an agent of the American secret service."

Twenty-four hours later "Seebold" would surface—in a Brooklyn courtroom. Prosecutor Kennedy told the jury the entire story of the Centerport radio station, how it had been a scheme of the Nazi spymasters in Hamburg to provide for the prompt transmission of American defense secrets.

"But the plan boomeranged," Kennedy continued, "because William G. Sebold betrayed the operation to agents of the FBI on his return from Germany early in 1940." [14]

Minutes later the prosecutor, with a dramatic flourish, introduced the government's star witness, and for two days Bill Sebold gave testimony that revealed much of the covert Nazi operations in the United States, naming scores of people, places, and dates. He told in detail how the Abwehr's spy school in Hamburg operated and disclosed its two principal functionaries, Dr. Rankin (Major Nickolaus Ritter) and Heinrich Sorau (Captain Hermann Sandel).

In the prisoners' dock, Fritz Duquesne glared constantly at the man on the witness stand. That night the Old Boer told a cellmate (and an FBI bug) that he only prayed he would live long enough to strangle Sebold with his bare hands.

The following day Fritz and the other defendants sat stoically as the prosecution began throwing on a screen selected portions of the tens of thousands of feet of film that the FBI's hidden camera had taken in Sebold's "research office" in the Knickerbocker Building. Without doubt, the Old Boer was the star of the cinema with his constant gesticulating. The audience snickered when Duquesne pantomimed on the screen how to aim a rifle.

The FBI's case had been watertight, the evidence devastating. Several weeks after the trial had begun, the jury retired to deliberate. All of the defendants were found guilty on assorted counts. Duquesne and Lang were given sentences of eighteen years; Carl Reuper, sixteen years. Everett Roeder, the Sperry Gyroscope employee, was given sixteen years; Paul Scholz, the bookstore owner, sixteen years; and the reluctant would-be Mata Hari, Lilly Stein, ten years. Tried on a lesser charge of failure to register as an agent of a foreign power, Evelyn Lewis, Duquesne's mistress, was sentenced to a year and a day.

The fate of one defendant, Julius Georg Bergmann, alias Georg Busch, would be cloaked in mystery. Bergmann was the self-styled master saboteur who had suddenly appeared at the German Embassy in Washington in the spring of 1940 to demand money from Hans Thomsen. During the long Brooklyn trial, Bergmann had simply vanished.[15]

While the American public was focusing on the Nazi spy trial, President Roosevelt and eight high government leaders were growing alarmed over a looming peril from another direction— the Pacific. Code-named Ultras, the tiny group had been reading daily the top-secret communications between the Japanese government in Tokyo and Ambassador Kichisaburo Nomura in Washington.

Roosevelt's pipeline into the inner sanctums in Tokyo resulted from U.S. Signal Corps cryptanalysts having cracked "Purple," Nippon's super-secret diplomatic code. Since January 23, 1941, this high-grade intelligence—code-named "Magic"—had been flowing over the desks of the nine Ultras.

Japan and the United States had been on a collision course since mid-1941 when Tokyo announced plans for creating a Greater East-Asia Co-Prosperity Sphere. The military clique that had seized control of the Japanese government was preparing to go to war to drive America from the Pacific.

Grimly, the Ultras monitored Magic as the danger in the Pacific drew ever closer. November 4, Tokyo to Ambassador Nomura in Washington: "Relations between Japan and the U.S. have reached the edge." November 22: "We will wait until November 29. After that, things are automatically going to happen."

Tokyo to the Japanese consul general in Honolulu: "With regard to warships and aircraft carriers, report on those at anchor, tied up at wharves, buoys and docks." Four days later, on December 3, Tokyo to Honolulu consul general: "Let [us] know day by day if there are any observation balloons above Pearl Harbor." And on December 5, the agent-in-charge of the FBI office in Hawaii warned the Pearl naval base that the Japanese consulate was burning its confidential papers. (The FBI had only nine agents in Hawaii, and the agency was not directly responsible for counterespionage in the islands.)

It was 7:58 A.M. on Sunday, December 7, 1941. Rays from a brilliant sun, rising majestically over Mount Tantalus, began drenching Pearl Harbor, where seventy combat ships and twenty-four auxiliaries of the U.S. Pacific Fleet were roosting drowsily. Suddenly there was heard the roar of powerful airplane engines, then all hell broke loose. Pearl was turned into an inferno of exploding bombs and thick clouds of oily black smoke. In one hour and fifty minutes, eight battleships, three cruisers, three destroyers, and six auxiliary vessels were sunk or badly damaged, 188 planes were destroyed (nearly all of them on the ground), and 2,400 American servicemen were killed.

A dozing America had suffered a devastating catastrophe.

27

A Mysterious Disaster in Mid-Manhattan

Twenty-four hours after the last Japanese bomber had roared away from Pearl Harbor, President Roosevelt painfully climbed the podium in the House of Representatives on the arm of his son, marine Captain James Roosevelt. Crippled by polio at age thirty-nine, the President wore a fifteen-pound brace on each leg.

Before the hushed joint session of Congress, Roosevelt began speaking: "Yesterday, December 7, 1941—a date which will live in infamy—the United States was suddenly and deliberately attacked by the naval and air forces of the Empire of Japan . . . there is no blinking at the fact that our people, our territory and our interests are in grave danger . . . the American people in their righteous might will win through to absolute victory!"

It had been a ringing appeal for Congress to declare war on Japan. Only one vote kept the verdict from being unanimous. Sixty-one-year-old Republican Representative Jeannette Rankin of Montana, the first woman elected to Congress, voted "present."

Immediately following Roosevelt's speech, Hans Thomsen, at the German Embassy on Massachusetts Avenue, began firing off cables to Joachim von Ribbentrop in Berlin. Thomsen detected a ray of light in the President's address: "The fact that he [Roosevelt] did not mention Germany with one word shows that he will try to avoid sharpening [the conflict] in the Atlantic." That night Thomsen dispatched another upbeat message: "From the standpoint of the American military it would be logical to avoid everything that could lead to a two-front war." An hour later a third signal: "War with Japan means transferring all U.S. energy to its own rearmament, a corresponding shrinking of Lend-Lease help [to England] and a shifting of all activity to the Pacific." [1]

On the following day, December 9, Thomsen received an urgent order from Ribbentrop: "Burn your secret codes and confidential papers immediately." The masterspy was stunned. What was the meaning of this puzzling order? Thomsen had no way of knowing of the deadly cat-and-mouse game that had been unfolding behind the scenes in Berlin and in Washington.

When Roosevelt had been preparing to address Congress on December 8, after consultations with Secretary of State Cordell Hull and other key advisors, there had been pressure on the President to include Germany and Italy in his call for a declaration of war. But Roosevelt had decided to wait to see if the often headstrong Adolf Hitler might instead declare war on the United States first. Such an action by the fuehrer would solidify American factions behind the war, as Roosevelt saw it, for it would establish the Third Reich as the "aggressor" against the United States.

The President's view that Hitler might declare war first had been based on a Magic intercept of a message sent by Japanese Ambassador Hiroshi Oshima from Berlin to Tokyo on November 29. In it Oshima stated that Ribbentrop had assured the Japanese that the Third Reich would join Japan if she became "engaged" in a war with America. In the aftermath of the Pearl Harbor sneak attack, Roosevelt felt that pressure was being exerted on Hitler to honor his pledge.

The Nazi warlord indeed was eager to beat America to the punch in declaring war. As Roosevelt had theorized, Hitler had by now generated a full head of steam in his hatred for America—and for the President. For months he had been ranting about Roosevelt's attacks upon him and Nazism, and he was furious over what he considered to be the warlike acts of the U.S. Navy against U-boats in the Atlantic.

Hitler was so fearful that the United States might declare war on Germany first that, on December 10, Ribbentrop cabled Thomsen not to "commit some indiscretion" that might tip off the U.S. State Department to what the fuehrer planned to do the next day—declare war on America. "We wish to avoid under all circumstances," Ribbentrop declared, "that the Government there beats us to such a step."[2]

When Hitler called the Reichstag (Parliament) into session to rubber-stamp his declaration of war against the United States on December 11, he thundered to the cheering deputies, "We will always strike first! We will always deal the first blow!"

Hitler spent most of his address hurling personal insults at Roosevelt, who, the fuehrer bellowed, had provoked the war in order to cover up the failure of the New Deal (Roosevelt's domestic program for economic recovery). "This man alone, backed by the millionaires and the Jews, is responsible for the Second World War!" Hitler thundered.[3]

A spellbinding orator, the Nazi warlord whipped his audience into a frenzy. When he began to announce that he was going to war against America, the Reichstag deputies leaped to their feet and drowned out his words in the bedlam.

Later that same day Hitler's crony, the bombastic Italian dictator Benito Mussolini, joined in declaring war on the United States.

America was stunned by suddenly being dragged into a global war. For many months her citizens had shrugged off warnings by J. Edgar Hoover that a "definite spy menace" was threatening the United States. Even the spectacular disclosures of Nazi skulduggery at the recent Brooklyn trial of the Fritz Duquesne gang had been quickly forgotten.

Now the general public had become consumed by the specter of a spy, saboteur, or subversive hiding behind every bush, all of the sinister figures boring into America's vital core like a worm inside an apple.

In this national climate of spy-mania, many local law enforcement officers took matters into their own hands. In Norfolk, Virginia, site of a major naval base, the chief of police rounded up and jailed all fourteen Japanese aliens living in the city, whether or not they were on the FBI's subversives list. The public safety director of Newark, New Jersey, ordered police to board trains and arrest "all suspicious Orientals" and "other possible subversives," leaving it up to the individual policeman to determine who "looked suspicious" and who did not.[4]

North Carolina's governor ordered state police cars to be painted black (presumably to make them inconspicuous at night) and instructed his officers to make arrests without warrants, otherwise they could not act "even if they saw an offender preparing to blow a bridge." Oregon's governor proclaimed a state of emergency, although he explained he didn't know what kind of emergency he was heralding.[5]

In Galveston, Texas, a civilian guard thought a blinking light in a house was flashing signals to unseen enemy ships offshore, so he fired a rifle round into the building. Farmers armed with shotguns posted themselves at each end of the Missouri town of Rolla and carefully inspected each passing vehicle, halting those that "looked suspicious."[6]

Various local governments organized armed civilian bands to thwart potential saboteurs, and the vigilantes stood watch over likely targets: bridges, railroad trestles, water reservoirs, docks, tunnels, dams, and public buildings. Most of these modern-day Minute Men were armed with a motley collection of weapons: antiquated pistols, shotguns, hunting rifles, even knives. Few had had military training. A woman driving across the San Francisco Bay bridge failed to hear a challenge by a band of armed civilians, one of whom shot at and seriously wounded her. On Lake Michigan, sentries shot and killed a duck hunter and wounded his companion.[7]

In Denison, Texas, the mayor and city council convened in emergency session and were debating buying a machine gun for the police department. An excited man dashed into the chamber and called out that New York City was being bombed. So the mayor proposed that, instead of one machine gun, the city buy *two*.

With the outbreak of war, hundreds of FBI men, together with military Intelligence agents and local law enforcement officers, fanned out across the nation and methodically picked up several thousand persons who were on subversives lists (by mid-

July 9,405 loyalty suspects would be taken into custody). Piled on top of that task, Hoover's men joined in tracking down the sources of thousands of rumors about enemy spies and saboteurs that flooded FBI field offices.

Under this enormous wartime burden, FBI manpower was stretched to the breaking point. On December 7, 1941, there were 2,602 agents, and Hoover rapidly obtained approval to beef up his force. Candidates had to be graduates of the FBI National Academy at Quantico, Virginia, a Hoover innovation for training local law officers, and meet other rigid qualifications. But the requirement that G-men must have legal degrees was waived. During the next two war years, the number of agents would skyrocket to 5,072.

A month after the United States went to war, Edmund Scott, a reporter for the New York daily newspaper *PM*, masquerading as a longshoreman, got a job with a crew hired to lug furniture aboard the *Normandie* at Pier 88 on the Hudson River. Taken over by the U.S. Navy and rechristened the *Lafayette*, the huge French vessel was being converted into a sorely needed troop transport, and some fifteen hundred civilian workers were swarming locustlike all over her.[8]

There was great urgency to the conversion task. It was to be finished by February 28, 1942, at which time Captain Robert C. Comand, the *Normandie*'s skipper, was to sail her from New York to Boston. She would be loaded with more than ten thousand troops—almost an entire division—plus assorted weapons and equipment, before proceeding into the Atlantic under sealed orders.

Scott had been assigned to investigate reports that the New York waterfront was wide open to sabotage. The *Normandie* was guarded casually by a private firm, Scott found, and anyone who had fifty dollars for a union initiation fee could become a stevedore and board the vessel. Alone and unmolested, the disguised newspaper reporter prowled all over the *Normandie*, and was struck by how easy it would be to set fire to the ship. A pocketful of incendiary pencils, Scott visualized, could be used with devastating effect. So could a few small, strategically placed explosive devices.

Eight hours after "longshoreman" Scott had boarded the *Normandie*, he knew her destination, when she would leave New York, how many guns she would mount, and the thickness of armor being put over portholes—information gained from loose-tongued workmen who were in no way spy conscious.

When Scott filed his blockbuster story with *PM* editors, even these hard-bitten old pros were appalled. Calling the story a "blueprint for sabotage," one that would advise the Nazis how simple it would be to wreak havoc with vessels in New York harbor, the editors held up publication of the exposé. But they did report Scott's adventure to Captain Charles H. Zearfoss, the U.S. Maritime Commission's antisabotage chief, who denied the findings (*PM* would say) and ordered: "Get your reporter off there before he gets shot!" [9]

At 2:34 on the afternoon of February 9, less than three weeks before the *Normandie* was to sail for Europe, shouts of *"Fire!"* rang out on the ship. Men rushed frantically to put out the blaze, but it was a windy day and they could not get the fire under control. Flames began whipping rapidly through corridors, and within an hour the ship was a blazing inferno.

As the conflagration spread, civilian workers, crew members, navy and coast guard men—some three thousand in all—began clambering over the sides of the *Normandie* and sliding down ropes to the pier, or else dashing to safety down gangplanks. New York City firefighters swore that the heat was the most intense that they had known. [10]

Perhaps thirty thousand New Yorkers choked Twelfth Avenue to watch. Among them was a small, graying man with a heavy accent and agony etched into his face—Vladimir Yourkevitch, who had designed the *Normandie*. Policemen, suspicious of his accent, refused to let the naval architect through their lines. However, Yourkevitch would have been powerless to save his creation. At 2:32 A.M. the doomed ship, listing heavily from tons of water poured into her by fireboats, rolled over onto her side and, like a beached whale, lay in the Hudson's gray ice.

At a time when every ship was crucially needed, the United States had lost its largest transport vessel. One man was dead. Thirty-six-year-old Frank Trentascosta fractured his skull when he fell down a ladder. Some 250 others suffered cuts, bruises, burns, or temporary eye or lung irritations. [11]

Now several investigating groups tried to pinpoint the blame for this monumental disaster along a Manhattan waterfront known to be teeming with Nazi operatives and their sympathizers. The FBI and U.S. Attorney Frank S. Hogan grilled more than a hundred witnesses, and a navy court of inquiry was established under Rear Admiral Lamar R. Leahy (Retired). Two months later a congressional Naval Affairs subcommittee, which had been set up to probe the *Normandie* debacle, concluded that "the cause and consequences of the fire are directly attributable to carelessness [by civilian workers] and lack of supervision."

However, millions of Americans refused to buy that verdict— especially after *PM* belatedly published reporter Scott's startling story. They were convinced that they knew the identity of the real culprits—Nazi saboteurs.[12]

In early 1942 U.S. Attorney General Francis X. Biddle and FBI chief J. Edgar Hoover began to lower the boom on the Nazi propaganda saboteurs who, in peacetime America, had enjoyed relative impunity. One of the first to be hauled into court was the famed aviatrix Laura Ingalls, who had prepared for her fire-eating America First speeches by studying Nazi propaganda materials. On February 24 Ingalls was sentenced to a prison term of from eight months to two years for failure to register as a Nazi agent.

It was brought out during the trial that Ingalls had written a letter to the female president of a "peace" group in which she said, "I want to invite you to visit me in my chalet at Bergtesgaden after the war." (Bergtesgaden was the Bavarian Alps site of Adolf Hitler's retreat.)[13]

Testimony disclosed that Ingalls had been getting a $300 monthly payoff from Baron Ulrich von Gienanth, reputed Gestapo chief in the United States whose "cover" had been Second Secretary at the German Embassy in Washington, but she told the sentencing judge: "My motives were born of a burning patriotism and a high idealism . . . I am a truer patriot than those who have convicted me."[14]

Three weeks later George Sylvester Viereck, who had gotten rich tooting a Nazi trumpet in his adopted homeland, was facing a different kind of music. Many times the bespectacled, thick-lipped Viereck had told confederates that there was "no infallible safeguard" against clever propaganda. But on March 13 he discovered that there indeed was a safeguard—a cell in a federal prison. A jury found that operating a Nazi propaganda mill in the U.S. Capitol was not a legitimate activity for an American "author and journalist." Viereck was sentenced to serve two to six years.

At about the same time that Viereck was being tried, a jury in another Washington courtroom returned a guilty verdict against frail, introverted George Hill, secretary to New York congress-man Ham Fish, who had been doing Viereck's bidding in the operation of the Nazi Capitol Hill propaganda mill. Hill, a pitiful figure who had been sucked deeper and deeper into Nazi machinations, was given a term of two to six years.

Nearly eleven months after the Nazi spymaster Ulrich von der Osten had been killed by a taxi in New York's Times Square, nine members of Kurt Ludwig's spy ring were brought to trial in a federal court in New York presided over by Judge Henry W. Goddard. Two gang members had pleaded guilty: Carl Schroetter, skipper of the Miami charter fishing boat, and the blond beauty Lucy Boehmler, now nineteen years of age.

The first spy trial held in the United States since the nation went to war opened on February 3, 1942. Mathias F. Correa, the able young U.S. Attorney, and his associates would present a huge collection of devastating evidence: three hundred exhibits and in excess of two thousand pages of interrogations.

One of the most crucial exhibits was the copy of von der Osten's detailed report on Pearl Harbor's defenses, a document that had been found in his Taft Hotel room after his death. Another exhibit that stunned the court was the report that Ludwig had sent to Hamburg back in April 1941. (It had been intercepted by the Bermuda censors.) In that letter Ludwig had told Ast X that the *Normandie* was virtually unguarded and could be easily sabotaged. At almost the time this report was presented to the court, the *Normandie* was burning fiercely a short distance away.

Only Kurt Ludwig, who was dubbed the "Spy Ring Mastermind" by New York newspapers, failed to take the stand in his defense. No doubt he knew that his wife and children in Munich would be handed over to the Gestapo should he talk.

After five weeks of listening to the incriminating evidence, the jury returned a guilty verdict against all of Ludwig's gang.

In consideration of her voluntary cooperation with the government, Lucy Boehmler received the lightest sentence—five years in prison. Schroetter, although he had pleaded guilty, had refused to testify against his confederates, and he received double Lucy's term. (A few days after he entered the federal prison in Atlanta, Schroetter, whose relatives were, in effect, being held hostage in the Third Reich, committed suicide in his cell by hanging himself with a sheet.)

Helen Mayer, the Brooklyn housewife whose specialty had been extracting defense secrets from unwary aircraft plant dupes, Karl Mueller, and Hans Pagel all were sentenced to fifteen years. Twenty-year-old Frederick Schlosser, who had been badgered into spying by his sister's fiancé, received twelve years. Old pro Paul Borchardt, the traitorous soldier René Froelich, and Kurt Ludwig were given the maximum penalties allowed by the law—twenty years.

Conviction of Ludwig's network put a severe dent in the Nazi espionage apparatus in the United States. But there were plenty of other German agents to take up the slack.

28

Taps for "the Millionaire's" Gang

Hans Peter Krug, a young Luftwaffe bomber pilot, was not at all happy with accommodations at his prisoner-of-war camp in Ontario, Canada. As he chafed over the dreary humdrum of everyday life behind barbed wire, Krug's mind flashed back more than a year to the time another Luftwaffe pilot, *Oberleutnant* Franz von Werra, had gained world fame by escaping from Canada and eventually making his way back to the Third Reich. Now, in 1942, Krug was plotting to follow in Werra's footsteps.

On the bitterly cold day of January 24, 1941, Baron von Werra had leaped from an open window of a moving train that was carrying a few hundred German prisoners through Ontario to a camp on Lake Superior. He worked his way southward for twenty-five miles to the broad, frozen St. Lawrence River, where he found a rowboat along the bank and paddled across to Ogdensburg, New York.

There Werra felt a flash of exultation. No doubt the government of neutral America would provide him with the means to get back to Germany. Instead the U.S. Immigration Service charged him with illegal entry and turned him over to the Odgensburg police, who pitched him into a cold, drafty jail.

Undaunted by his plight, Werra called in American reporters and news photographers and conducted a unique press conference from his cell. He regaled the newsmen with fanciful tales of his exploits in the European air war, giving the impression, as one cynical journalist would write, that "he apparently had single-handedly shot down the entire British air force."

The zany press conference bore the desired fruit: The fact that Werra was behind bars in Ogdensburg was plastered on front pages across America. Consequently, a member of the German consulate in New York came running, put up a $5,000 cash bond, and spirited away the escapee to New York City.

There *Oberleutnant* von Werra became an instant celebrity, one who was wined and dined royally by the Big Apple's society elite at such plush watering holes as the Diamond Horseshoe, El Morocco, Sardi's, and "21." Late in March Werra's celebrity bubble burst: The German consulate advised him that the U.S. government was preparing to turn him over to Canadian authorities on a criminal warrant—for stealing the $25 rowboat in which he had crossed the St. Lawrence.

So Werra, wearing civilian clothes, sneaked aboard a train at Grand Central Station and rode it to the Mexican border at El Paso. Disguised as a Mexican laborer, the pilot slipped over the border, and the German Embassy in Mexico City arranged passage to the Third Reich for him. In Berlin, the beaming *Oberleutnant* Franz von Werra received a conquering hero's welcome. Adolf Hitler awarded him the Knight's Cross, Field Marshal Hermann Goering promoted him to *hauptman* (captain) and gave him command of a crack fighter squadron.[1]

Now, a year later, in March 1942, *Leutnant* Hans Peter Krug was determined to emulate Baron von Werra's daring feat and become the second German POW to escape from Canada and reach the Third Reich. With the aid of comrades a dummy was rigged from newspapers and straw and carried to the predawn roll call. The dummy was crude, but it masked Krug's absence long enough for him to get a good running start after slipping out of the POW enclosure. He made his way to Windsor, Ontario, and crossed the Detroit River into the United States.

Krug had with him when he reached Detroit the name of Margaretta Johanna Bertlemann and a street address. German prisoners in the Canadian camp had found this information written on a slip of paper and concealed in a pair of socks sent in a gift package.

Krug located the Bertlemann home, knocked on the door, and

asked for a drink of water. Once inside, he identified himself and displayed the epaulets he had cut from his Luftwaffe uniform.

Mrs. Bertlemann accepted the identification, gave breakfast to the famished German, and told him she knew a man who could assist him in his flight. He was Max Stephan, a naturalized U.S. citizen who owned a Detroit restaurant that had been a gathering place for members of the German-American Bund.

Stephan gave *Leutnant* Krug shelter and money, coached the escapee on how he should act to avoid suspicion, and bought him a bus ticket to Chicago. Then the restaurant operator outlined an escape plan: Krug was to proceed by stages toward the Mexican border, slip over into Mexico, and then catch a ship back to the Third Reich.

Krug's escape plan unfolded as scheduled, and when he reached San Antonio, Texas, he registered in a dingy hotel as Jean Ette. A few hours later two FBI agents and a pair of San Antonio policemen pounced on the German bomber pilot and arrested him. The hotel clerk had recognized the escapee from an FBI wanted notice.[2]

As a result of Krug's apprehension, Max Stephan was taken into custody. The Detroit man was convicted of treason—the first American to be found guilty of that crime since 1794—and sentenced to death. (President Roosevelt would commute Stephan's sentence to life imprisonment.)

Meanwhile in the early weeks of 1942, Count Anastase Vonsiatsky-Vonsiatsky, the wealthy adventurer and leader of a Ukranian underground movement in the United States, was being shadowed around the clock by G-men. Early in February the count climbed into his chauffeur-driven limousine at his vast Connecticut estate and sped to Camden, New Jersey, where he entered the home of Wilhelm Kunze. By now Kunze had taken over from the discredited drunk and woman chaser Fritz Kuhn as Bundesfuehrer of the German-American Bund.

A few hours later Vonsiatsky and Kunze were joined by the Lutheran reverend Kurt Molzahn, the Nazi firebrand who lived across the river in Philadelphia. The tails were able to catch glimpses (through binoculars) of an animated conversation between the three Nazis, who were bending over what apparently was a map of the United States. The FBI concluded that Something Big was brewing.

Early the next morning the count—known as "the Millionaire" to confederates—caught a train for Chicago. In the adjoining compartment were a pair of G-men, who trailed him to the home of "Scarface Otto" Willumeit, the doctor who ran his Midwest espionage network from a Chicago saloon, the *Haus Vaterland* (Fatherland House). Soon Wilhelm Kunze arrived at Willumeit's home, and an hour later Dr. Wolfgang Ebell, a naturalized American who enjoyed a thriving medical practice in El Paso, Texas, joined the conspirators.

When the Treff broke up, the participants scattered. Two G-men trailed Dr. Ebell to El Paso, where Kunze appeared a few days later. When the two conspirators crossed the Rio Grande into Mexico, the FBI men asked Mexican police to take over surveillance. Ebell and Kunze drove to a fishing village five miles south of Vera Cruz, where they registered at a dumpy hotel, then walked to the waterfront. There the Nazi agents held conversations with native fishermen and handed something (apparently bribes) to a few of them.

Meanwhile, Count Vonsiatsky was dashing around the eastern United States like a man possessed, traveling in a luxurious style befitting one of his great wealth. His pattern was always the same, FBI tails knew. After arriving at a shipyard or defense plant, Vonsiatsky would make a telephone call from a pay phone outside, wait in his limousine, and a few minutes later a worker from inside the facility would walk up to the automobile. The chauffeur would get out and stroll around the vicinity while the count and the employee (one of Vonsiatsky's moles) would hold a Treff.

For several weeks G-men trailed "the Millionaire" on his espionage tour. Helped by prior information from FBI contacts, they were able to identify some thirty-five suspected Vonsiatsky moles in defense plants and shipyards.

When the count finally returned to his Connecticut estate, he continued to collect a large volume of defense information. A number of his agents were seen bringing packages to him, and still others mailed reports to him. (The FBI had long had a "cover" on Vonsiatsky's mail, meaning that post office authorities were recording names and addresses of senders.)

One morning the Philadelphia clergyman, Kurt Molzahn, arrived at the Vonsiatsky estate and left a few hours later lugging a large suitcase. FBI shadows were convinced that the suitcase held the U.S. defense secrets that the count had collected during his lengthy safari, a trek that had taken him all the way to the southern tip of Florida and as far west as Cleveland, Toledo, and Detroit. Molzahn took the suitcase to Chicago, where he left it with Dr. Willumeit, who took it to Dr. Ebell in El Paso.

Next day Ebell, together with the seemingly always present Wilhelm Kunze, drove across the Mexican border, going directly to the fishing village south of Vera Cruz. (Mexican police had again taken up surveillance.) There the two Nazis turned over Vonsiatsky's suitcase to a pair of native fishermen, whom they had earlier bribed.

The FBI now felt that the Mexican accomplices would rendezvous, under cover of darkness, with a U-boat offshore and turn over the count's suitcase to the skipper. But Hoover and his men were not concerned. Due to an elaborate counterespionage system that had been in operation for more than two years, FBI contacts in each plant visited by Vonsiatsky had concocted phony data that was cleverly allowed to get into the hands of the count's moles. So it would be these bogus defense secrets that would find their way to the spymasters in the Third Reich.

Meanwhile J. Edgar Hoover in Washington had been keeping in close touch with the Vonsiatsky ring's surveillance, but the supersleuth was not yet ready to close in—he wanted to make doubly certain that the FBI's case would be watertight.

Then the Reverend Molzahn pulled a blunder. In a code that the FBI had long since cracked, he sent a report to Berlin by way of a mail drop in Lisbon. The letter was intercepted by the Bermuda censors, and its contents pulled the noose tighter around the necks of the Vonsiatsky conspirators.

Now Hoover flashed word to strike, and, in a series of swift movements, his men picked up five of the net's ringleaders. They appeared before federal judge J. Joseph Smith in Hartford, Connecticut, and all of the ring, except for the wayward Lutheran minister, pleaded guilty. Molzahn, whose careless action had driven the final nail in the coffin of Vonsiatsky's gang, was tried, found guilty, and given a ten-year sentence. (Later, under circumstances that would remain a mystery, the Reverend Molzahn would be pardoned.)

Curiously, perhaps, the gang's mastermind and driving force, Anastase Vonsiatsky-Vonsiatsky, received the lightest sentence—five years.[3] (Possibly he had covertly sold out his confederates and cooperated with federal prosecutors.) The Chicago physician, Scarface Otto Willumeit, also got five years. Dr. Wolfgang Ebell was sentenced to seven years, and Bundesfuehrer Wilhelm Kunze was nailed with the stiffest term, fifteen years.

While the FBI had inexorably been tightening the screws on the Vonsiatsky gang, the Abwehr in the Third Reich was concocting an elaborate plot to severely cripple America's industrial might. Code-named Operation Pastorius, the stratagem would be one of the boldest and largest single sabotage missions ever undertaken.[4]

Masterminding the scheme was pudgy, bull-necked Lieutenant Walter Kappe, who had first come to the FBI's attention in the 1930s when he had beat the propaganda drums for Nazifront groups in Chicago and New York. Returning to the Third Reich in 1937, Kappe had been given an Abwehr commission and specialized in American affairs.

In late 1941 Lieutenant Kappe had begun recruiting English-speaking Germans in the Third Reich. They would be trained as saboteurs, fully equipped with modern accoutrements of destruction, taken to the United States by submarine, and told to blow up key industrial and transportation targets already pinpointed.

Once the sabotage network was established, Kappe himself would slip into the United States to take charge of the operation. His headquarters would be in Chicago, a city he knew thoroughly, and he would maintain contact with his widespread bands of saboteurs through coded advertisements in the *Chicago Tribune*.

Hitler's high command in Berlin was hounding Admiral Canaris to get the sabotage operation launched, and the Abwehr chief in turn was putting the heat on Lieutenant Kappe. So on

April 10, 1942, Kappe gathered his first eight agents at Quentz Lake, a heavily wooded estate on the outskirts of Berlin. All were German-born but had lived in the United States for extended periods before returning to the Third Reich. Two of them were American citizens. They were to receive hefty monthly salaries and promised high-paying jobs in Germany after Hitler had won the war.

The Pastorius saboteurs were:

Ernest Peter Berger, who had worked as a machinist in Detroit and Milwaukee and had been a member of the Michigan National Guard.

George John Dasch, alias George Davis, alias George Day, who at age thirty-nine was the oldest of the group, had been a waiter in New York and had served in the U.S. Army Air Corps.

Herbert Hans Haupt, who had worked for an optical firm in Chicago and, at twenty-two years, was the youngest of the saboteurs.

Heinrich Heinck, alias Henry Kanor, who had been employed as a waiter in New York City.

Edward Kerling, alias Edward Kelly, who had been with a New Jersey oil corporation and a butler.

Hermann Neubauer, alias Herman Nicholas, who had been a cook in Chicago and Hartford hotels.

Richard Quirin, alias Robert Quintas, who had worked in the United States as a mechanic.

Werner Thiel, alias John Thomas, who had been employed in Detroit automobile plants.

On the Berlin estate, the saboteurs were put through a rigorous routine of physical training and close-in combat; classroom lectures on secret writing, incendiaries, explosives, fuses, and timing devices; grenade-pitching and rifle-shooting. They carried out stealthy mock sabotage operations, including one to blow up the Berlin railroad yards.

Each man was required to memorize scores of targets in America. They rehearsed phony life stories over and over, backgrounds that were documented with bogus birth certificates, draft deferment cards, automobile driver's licenses, and Social Security cards.

On May 23, their examinations and trial runs concluded, the eight men were divided into two teams and given their boom-and-bang assignments in the United States. Team No. 1 would be led by the "old man," George Dasch, and include Berger, Heinck, and Quirin. It was to destroy hydroelectric plants at Niagara Falls, New York; blow up Aluminum Company of America factories in East St. Louis, Illinois, Alcoa, Tennessee, and Massena, New York; blast locks in the Ohio River between Louisville, Kentucky, and Pittsburgh, Pennsylvania; and wreck a Cryolite plant in Philadelphia.

Team No. 2 would be under the command of Edward Kerling, and his companions would be Haupt, Neubauer, and Thiel. It was to cripple the Pennsylvania Railroad by blowing up its station at Newark, New Jersey, and Horseshoe Bend near Altoona, Pennsylvania; disrupt facilities of the Chesapeake and Ohio Railroad; send New York City's Hell Gate railroad bridge crashing into the East River; destroy the canal and lock complexes at St. Louis, Missouri, and Cincinnati, Ohio; and demolish the water-supply system in greater New York City, concentrating on suburban Westchester County.

The Nazi saboteurs were to make no effort to conceal the fact that they were on a violent rampage in the United States. They were to constantly seek opportunities to blow up public buildings in order to promote panic. If any saboteur gave indications of weakening in resolve or jeopardizing the boom-and-bang mission, the others were to "kill him without compunction." [5]

Early on the morning of May 26, the two Pastorius teams were at the Kriegsmarine submarine base at Lorient, France. There Lieutenant Walter Kappe doled out $50,000 to each of the leaders, as a general fund and to pay bribes and accomplices, plus another $20,000 to be divided among the men as needed. In addition, each man was given a money belt containing $4,000 and a wallet stuffed with $400 in small bills. Altogether, the Abwehr was spending a minor fortune of $175,200 in a desperate gamble to knock out or severely cripple America's industrial might.

On the night of May 26 Kerling and his men climbed aboard U-201. Packed into the submarine were ingenious sabotage devices: dynamite bombs disguised as lumps of coal and wooden blocks; special timing gadgets; TNT carefully packed in excelsior; rolls of electric cable; a wide array of fuses; and incendiary bombs that looked identical to pencils and fountain pens.[6]

Just past 8:00 P.M. Kerling's undersea raider departed. Two nights later U-202, the *Innsbruck*, carrying George Dasch and his team, slipped out to sea and headed for a pinpoint landfall three thousand miles across the Atlantic.

29

They Came to Blow Up America

Just past eight o'clock on the night of June 12, 1942, the submarine *Innsbruck* reached United States coastal waters off Long Island, 105 miles east of New York City. The U-202 submerged and lay on the bottom in about 100 feet of water, where it waited for the right time for the four Pastorius saboteurs to sneak ashore. As midnight approached, the *Innsbruck* surfaced and, propelled by its nearly silent electric motors, edged closer to the dark and silent beach.

Huddled on the slippery deck, George Dasch and his teammates praised Providence for the thick, swirling fog that would mask from hostile eyes their arrival on shore. Visibility was limited to only fifteen or twenty feet. Each saboteur was wearing the uniform of a German marine, so that in case of being captured on landing they would be treated as prisoners of war.

Boxes of explosives, two shovels, a duffel bag full of clothes, and Dasch's gladstone bag with tens of thousands of dollars sewed into its lining were loaded onto a rubber raft. Lieutenant Walter Kappe's pupils climbed in, and two U-202 crewmen began paddling silently to shore. Should hostile parties be encountered on the beach, Dasch and his men had been given strict orders to overpower them and lug the bodies to the raft. In the event the saboteurs could not subdue those confronted ashore, the two sailors had been given submachine guns and would begin shooting. "You bring the bodies back," the U-202 skipper had told the raft paddlers, "and we'll feed them to the fish when we get back out to sea!"[1]

After the raft nudged onto the sandy beach, the four saboteurs scrambled out, and Dasch whispered to his men to start carrying the boxes of explosives from the waterline to higher ground. Minutes later Dasch glanced over his shoulder and felt a surge of alarm. Coming toward him through the murky fog was the muted glow of a flashlight. Carrying the torch was twenty-one-year-old Coast Guardsman John Cullen, who fifteen minutes earlier had set out from the Amagansett Coast Guard station, half a mile away, to make a routine beach patrol. He was unarmed.

Cullen, close enough to faintly see unloading operations at the raft, called out, "What's going on here?" Dasch rushed up to the sailor and explained that he and his friends were fishermen and that they had become lost in the fog. Now Dasch was again stricken by concern. Unseen in the fog, his teammates were talking—in German.

Cullen too had grown alarmed and momentarily stood glued to the spot. Dasch grabbed the sailor's arm and snapped, "You got a mother and father, haven't you? Wouldn't you like to see them again?" Then the saboteur thrust a wad of currency into the startled Cullen's hand. "Take this and have a good time," Dasch said. "Forget what you've seen here."[2]

Seaman Second Class Cullen sensed that he had stumbled onto some sinister venture that was far beyond his ability to cope. Step by step he backed off, then whirled and raced off for the Coast Guard station. Dasch and his men quickly shed their German marine uniforms and, in a hastily dug hole, buried four waterproof cases packed with explosives, timing devices, and detonators. They planned to retrieve this arsenal later and conceal it in New York's Catskill mountains.

Back at the Amagansett Coast Guard station, the excited John Cullen aroused four of his mates and rapidly told them of his encounter on the fog-shrouded beach. The others were skeptical: No doubt Cullen was pulling a trick to relieve the lonely monotony. Then Cullen showed them the wadded bills—$265 worth—that Dasch had thrust into his hand. Now fully awake, the four Coast Guardsmen armed themselves and, along with

Cullen, rushed to the beach where the saboteurs had been detected.

Daylight had arrived. The Coast Guardsmen found footprints and followed them into the dunes, where they uncovered the buried cache of explosives and the German uniforms. In the foggy darkness, the saboteurs had apparently been too nervous to smooth over their tracks and the burial site.

At the same time the telltale cache was being uncovered, George Dasch and his mates were trudging across fields to the tracks of the Long Island Railroad. They followed the tracks to the Amagansett station, where commuters caught the early-morning train for New York City. While the others sat on the platform, Dasch approached the ticket agent, Ira Baker, and bought four tickets. "You're out early this morning," Baker said pleasantly. "Yes," Dasch replied. "We've been fishing."[3]

Dasch bought newspapers and handed one to each man, telling them to keep their mouths shut and to stick their noses in the papers just like the other commuters gathering on the platform. The four saboteurs boarded the 6:57. When they reached New York, the team split in two. Dasch and Berger checked into the Governor Clinton Hotel on West 31st Street, across from Pennsylvania Station, while Quirin and Heinck registered at the Martinique.

Hardly had Dasch and Berger reached their hotel room than Dasch said that he planned to notify the FBI of Operation Pastorius. "If you don't agree, I'm going to kill you—right here and now!" Dasch exclaimed. Berger assured the team leader that he was in agreement.[4]

Shortly after 8:00 P.M. on the following night agent Dean F. McWhorter answered the FBI office telephone in Foley Square. A voice with a German accent told him that he had just landed in a Nazi submarine and had important information. "I'll be in Washington within the week to deliver it personally to J. Edgar Hoover," the telephone voice said.

FBI offices had been deluged with crackpot calls since Pearl Harbor, but McWhorter asked, "What is your information?" There was a click and the line went dead. The G-man shrugged. Another screwball call. But he made a note of it for the record.

Within the hour the mysterious call taken by McWhorter suddenly leaped into monumental significance. Special Agent in

Charge T. J. Donegan of the same FBI office received a telephone call asking him to rush to the office of Coast Guard Captain J. S. Bayliss. There the FBI heard details of the Amagansett affair and examined the cache of explosives found at the site by the Coast Guard.

In the meantime, more than a thousand miles to the south, U-201, carrying Pastorius's Team No. 2 under Edward Kerling, surfaced off Ponte Verdra Beach, twenty-five miles southeast of Jacksonville, Florida, in the early-morning darkness of June 17. Kerling, Haupt, Thiel, and Neubauer were paddled ashore by two sailors armed with submachine guns. Quickly the saboteurs buried their explosives and German marine uniforms, and walked to U.S. Highway 1 where they caught a Greyhound bus for Jacksonville.

Early the next morning Haupt and Neubauer were on a train bound for Chicago, and Kerling and Thiel were en route to Cincinnati.

Kerling was no stranger to the FBI, which knew that he had been active in New Jersey's German-American Bund since 1939. At that time he and six confederates had been spotted by the Coast Guard loitering in a yawl off Long Island, presumably to rendezvous with a U-boat, as the yawl had been crammed with food and other provisions.

George Dasch, meanwhile, had taken a train to Washington, where he telephoned FBI headquarters at 10:05 A.M. on June 19. "I'm the man who called your New York office last Sunday," Dasch told an agent. "My name is George John Dasch. I am in Room 351 at the Mayflower Hotel." [5]

Within minutes two G-men arrived at Room 351 and listened in amazement as the former New York waiter poured out his incredible story of the Nazi saboteurs who had come to blow up America. For two days Dasch spilled the beans to Hoover's men. Every two hours a fresh stenographer arrived at Room 351 to record his story.

Dasch told of Abwehr Lieutenant Walter Kappe and the Operation Pastorius sabotage school outside Berlin, revealed the United States industrial and transportation targets of Team No. 1 and Team No. 2, described each of the other seven saboteurs in detail, and gave the names and addresses of their likely contacts in America.

Rapidly the FBI closed in. A pair of G-men stealthily opened the unlocked door of Ernest Berger at the Governor Clinton in New York and surprised the Nazi, who was clad only in his underwear. Less than two hours later, Heinrich Heinck and Richard Quirin strolled into the lobby of the Martinique Hotel after enjoying an afternoon at the movies and were pounced on by waiting G-men.

A thousand miles to the west Herbert Haupt, the youngest of the saboteurs, walked into the Chicago office of the FBI, bent on outsmarting any G-men who might be tailing him by appearing to be open and aboveboard. Haupt's parents lived in Chicago, and they had told him that FBI agents had been inquiring about his whereabouts with regard to his draft status.

"There's been a misunderstanding," Haupt explained. "I went to Mexico [actually he had been in Germany] to avoid being forced into marriage, and that caused trouble with my draft board. But," he added, "all that's been straightened out now." [6]

The G-men assured Haupt that they were no longer interested in his Selective Service case. And indeed they were not—they had known who he was from the minute he walked into the field office, and now Hoover's men were far more concerned with his role as a Nazi saboteur.

When Haupt sauntered out of the FBI office, two tails shadowed him in an effort to ensnare any accomplices. The one-time Chicago optical worker felt smugly secure. He had no way of knowing that the FBI men already had his picture, taken months earlier by tiny cameras held in the palms of G-men shadowing German-American Bund activists.

Edward Kerling's face was also well known to the FBI, thanks to the palm-held cameras. On June 22 Kerling came east from Cincinnati to see his wife, who lived in New York City. Her flat had been staked out, and the next night FBI agents closed in and arrested Kerling and Werner Thiel, who had accompanied the Team No. 2 leader.

Five days later Herbert Haupt was taken into custody at his parents' home in Chicago, and Haupt led G-men to Hermann Neubauer.

Fourteen days after the Operation Pastorius saboteurs had landed outside Amagansett, all eight had been nabbed by the FBI. J. Edgar Hoover immediately informed President Roosevelt, who instructed the supersleuth to make the blockbuster news public at once in order to discourage the Nazi espionage masterminds in the Third Reich from launching more sabotage expeditions to the United States.

Five days later, on July 2, Roosevelt appointed a military tribunal to hear the case of the eight saboteurs. It was the first such commission to be convened in the United States since the assassination of Abraham Lincoln in 1865. Army colonel Kenneth Royall, a distinguished trial attorney in civilian life, was appointed defense counsel for the accused men.[7]

During the secret trial, the eight defendants swore that it had never been their intention to commit sabotage and that they had volunteered for Operation Pastorius as a ploy for getting safely out of Germany and back to their loved ones in the United States. Each of Lieutenant Kappe's pupils took the stand and tried to outdo one another in bitterly denouncing Adolf Hitler and the Nazi regime.

All the defendants were found guilty, and on August 8 they stood before the tribunal of military officers. George Dasch was sentenced to thirty years in prison, Ernest Berger received a life term, and the others were to be executed in the electric chair. President Roosevelt approved the sentences that morning, and at noon the six saboteurs were electrocuted and buried in unmarked graves on a government plot in Washington.

While the dark invaders of Operation Pastorius were being rounded up and tried, the New York City waterfront continued to be a hotbed of Nazi intrigue. Long gone were the German agents masquerading as evangelists and assorted soul savers of merchant seamen; these undercover operatives had vanished as soon as Hitler had declared war on the United States. One of those filling the void was Marie Hedwig Koedel, the twenty-six-year-old foster daughter of the slick Nazi agent, Simon Koedel, the one-time "sleeper" who lived on Riverside Drive.

Koedel was the nondescript movie-house projectionist who had often told friends that he would be "willing to die" for the Fatherland. Carried on the Abwehr registry in Berlin as A.2011, Koedel had produced such a mass of high-grade intelligence that, in May 1941, he had been promoted from captain to the rank of Abwehr major.

Marie Koedel covered her waterfront "beat" almost daily. She would saunter into a dingy saloon, cast a few flirtatious glances, and soon one or more merchant seamen would join her. Loose-tongued from booze and wanting to impress the willowy brunette, the seamen told her about departure dates, convoy routes, ships' armaments, cargoes, and other maritime secrets.

Based on Marie's information and his own connivances, Simon Koedel kept detailed shipping reports flowing to the Third Reich, from where the data were relayed to U-boat wolfpacks in the Atlantic. Outwardly a Caspar Milquetoast type, Koedel compiled and sent to the U-boat command one especially devastating document entitled "Report on the Conduct of Enemy Ships in Convoy at Sea in the Atlantic, Based on Conversations with British Seamen."

Also casing the New York waterfront was fifty-six-year-old Ernest Frederick Lehmitz, who had an ingenious "cover"—a volunteer Civil Defense air-raid warden. In fact, good old Ernie Lehmitz was regarded by his neighbors on Staten Island as a kind-hearted gentleman and a super patriot. Ernie really took his air-raid warden's job seriously, they would say, for he would bawl people out for not masking lights. And Lehmitz tenderly nurtured the neighborhood's largest backyard "victory garden" in response to the government's request that citizens raise their own vegetables.[8]

Tall, lean, and stoop-shouldered, Lehmitz had first come to the United States in 1908 as a clerk in the German consulate in New York. During World War I he had served as a spy for the Kaiser but later became a naturalized American citizen. While visiting the Fatherland in 1939, Lehmitz had been recruited by the Abwehr, and after training as a coastwatcher at the Academy in Hamburg, he came back to the United States on the liner *Siboney* in March 1941.

Ernest Lehmitz bore no resemblance to the stereotype of a spy dashing about with a bomb in one hand and a stolen blueprint in the other. There was no glamour in his life, no beautiful women accomplices. He wore ill-fitting suits, old-fashioned rubbers on his feet, and his most daring vice was a glass of beer at a tavern on his way home from work. And he talked constantly about the chicken farm he hoped to buy one day.

Lehmitz made little money from his perilous work: a paltry fifty dollars per week from the Abwehr. So, in order to make ends meet, his Hungarian-born wife brought in extra money by letting rooms. That dovetailed neatly with her husband's covert endeavor, for her favorite roomers were young sailors and merchant seamen, whom she mothered and from whom she learned the sailing dates of ships.

The air-raid warden became a handyman in a waterfront saloon frequented by merchant seamen, and he sent his New York harbor reports to Hamburg through a mail drop in Lisbon, signing his letters "Fred Sloane" or "Fred Lewis." On the night of February 20, 1942, a censor in Hamilton, Bermuda, plucked from the avalanche of newly arrived mail a typewritten, seemingly innocent letter being sent to an address in Lisbon. That particular address had been on the censorship station's watch list, for it was known to be an Abwehr blind. Given the heat treatment, the letter brought out the invisible-ink writing:

> Eleven ships leaving for Russia including steamer with airplane motors and 28 long-range guns. One steamer has deck-load airplanes, below deck airplane motors. Boeing and Douglas airplane parts on steamer with Curtiss-Wright airplanes, and small munitions, searchlights and telegraphic material.[9]

The letter was signed "Fred Sloane." Within ten days the alert Bermuda censors fished out a second letter from "Sloane," then a third. Copies were rushed to the FBI in New York City, and an investigation was launched to locate him. The only clue to his identity was a brief mention that he was an air-raid warden—but there were 98,276 air-raid wardens in greater New York.

While Nazi agents were prowling the New York waterfront, Waldemar Othmer, a German-born naturalized American working as an electrician and Electrolux vacuum cleaner salesman, was sending Hamburg reports on the huge naval base at Norfolk and on the marines' training center at Camp Pendleton, North Carolina. A blue-eyed, blond, personable young man, Othmer had been the fuehrer of the German-American Bund at Trenton, New Jersey, in the late 1930s and, in 1937, during a visit to the Fatherland, had volunteered to spy for Adolf Hitler. In 1939 the bespectacled Othmer, who had a wife and young son, was activated by the Abwehr and ordered to serve his espionage apprenticeship at the Brooklyn navy yard. Later he was sent to Norfolk where he reconnoitered the naval base from his vantage point as a plumber's helper. Then it was on to Camp Pendleton, where he got a job as an electrician.

Othmer's zone of responsibility stretched from Chesapeake Bay to the south, and he kept the Abwehr informed on British and U.S. warships and merchant vessels being repaired at Norfolk and at other ports. One of his reports gave details of a dramatic increase in range of a pair of fifteen-inch coastal guns capable of firing up to twenty shells per minute at a range of twelve thousand yards.[10]

No doubt the shipping secrets culled by Nazi harbor spies such as Simon and Marie Koedel, Ernest Lehmitz and his wife, Waldemar Othmer, and others buried deep in the fabric of American life contributed enormously to the success of German U-boats that were inflicting a monumental debacle along the eastern seaboard, one that was threatening to knock the United States out of the war in Europe.

30

History's First Nuclear Spy

Grossadmiral Karl Doenitz, commander of Germany's powerful U-boat fleet, was in a euphoric mood when he called on Adolf Hitler at the Reich Chancellory in Berlin on June 19, 1942. "*Mein fuehrer,*" the fifty-year-old admiral exulted, "I wish to inform you of the astonishing success of Operation *Paukenschlag!*" When Doenitz had completed his recital, Hitler rubbed his hands in glee.

Five months earlier, on January 12, Doenitz had launched *Paukenschlag* (Roll of the Drums), which was designed to blockade America's Atlantic ports and cut her crucial shipping lanes to Europe, especially those extending from New York. Doenitz had selected twelve ace U-boat skippers to stalk the American eastern seaboard, and during the first half of 1942 they had sunk so many vessels in coastal waters that the loss was equivalent to Nazi saboteurs blowing up eight or ten of America's largest war plants.

Admiral Doenitz had been tactically directing *Paukenschlag* from the U-boat base in Lorient, France. As reports flowed in from harbor spies and coastwatchers in the United States and from the Kriegsmarine's B-Dienst (an electronic monitoring network), the U-boat chief, like a chessmaster adroitly moving pawns, shifted his underwater wolves into position to intercept ships steaming out of America's Atlantic ports.

One of the audacious skippers chosen for *Paukenschlag* was handsome, blond *Leutnant* Reinhard Hardegen who, just before midnight on the first day of *Paukenschlag,* had boldly surfaced his U-123 off the port of New York. Through high-powered, infrared binoculars, Hardegen and Second Officer Horst von Schroeter could discern couples blissfully dancing the night away on the roof garden atop the Astor Hotel in Times Square.[1]

Hardegen and his crewmen were mesmerized by the dazzling sight before them. Even though the United States had been at war for more than a month, Manhattan was aglow with thousands of lights that twinkled through the night like fireflies. "It's unbelievable!" Hardegen exclaimed.[2]

During daylight hours on January 13, the U-123 nestled silently on the bottom in one hundred feet of water off Wimble Shoal, a few miles south of New York City. The resolute skipper was straining at the leash. Throughout the day his radioman reported incessant sounds of ships overhead. "*Gott!*" Hardegen exploded. "Can you imagine what we could do with twelve U-boats in here [New York harbor]?"[3]

Aware that America's coastal defenses were virtually nonexistent, wolfpacks marauding along the eastern seaboard grew steadily more brazen, often not bothering to submerge after an attack. Off the mighty naval base at Norfolk on March 13, a freighter was sunk and the U-boat remained on the surface for four hours, shining a yellow light in its conning tower.

Meanwhile, during a three-week period beginning March 1, a mysterious malady struck eight freighters sailing from Philadelphia, Boston, and New York and bound for hard-pressed Russian forces. Loaded heavily with tanks, trucks, airplane parts, munitions, and war supplies, each vessel had sailed separately. A few days out to sea each foundered and was unable to reach its destination.

Heavy seas caused improperly secured deck cargo to shift. Guns, tanks, and trucks broke loose, careened over the deck, plunged into the ocean. Crippled by the shifting loads, each ship was forced to slow, then turn back for its home port. A few never made it. A sitting duck, the SS *Collmar* was torpedoed and sunk, with the loss of seven crewmen, as it limped back toward home.

The National Maritime Union smelled Nazi skulduggery in U.S. ports and launched an investigation. It was found that, in several instances, cotter pins were not in place on the shackles holding the deck cargoes. Joseph Curran, president of the Maritime Union, testified before a House committee in Washington on March 26, 1942, that shifting cargoes had hardly ever been a problem in the past, even in the heaviest seas.

"We, as seamen, for many years, have been sailing ships that carried deck loads, sometimes as high as you could get it, and we never lost any of that cargo," Curran declared. "We never had a problem with deck loads [in peacetime]." [4]

By June Admiral Doenitz's eager U-boat skippers became so smug that they began sinking ships in broad daylight. Thousands of bathers at Coney Island, New York; Virginia Beach, Virginia; Atlantic City, New Jersey; and Miami, Florida watched in horror as oil tankers were torpedoed, causing the vessels to explode in balls of fire and thick black smoke. Surviving crewmen, most horribly burned, mutilated, and covered with oil, struggled ashore.

Three months had passed since the launching of Operation *Paukenschlag* along what U-boat crewmen called the "American Front" before the U.S. Navy announced that German submarines were being guided by lights and electric signs in cities along the coast. Miami and its suburbs alone provided some ten miles of garish illumination against which the U-boats could see the silhouettes of north- and southbound vessels hugging the coastline to avoid the opposing current of the Gulf Stream.

When Washington ruled that the eastern seaboard lights would have to be extinguished, howls of protest erupted from Atlantic City to the tip of Florida: Such an action would "ruin the tourist season." It would be two more months before the last light blinked out.

Three thousand seven hundred miles from America's East Coast, Nazi propaganda minister Josef Goebbels took to Radio Berlin on June 18 and trumpeted: "German heroism conquers even the widest oceans!" [5]

For once there had been no need for Goebbels to sugarcoat a

war report for the consumption of Germany's armed forces and the *herrenvolk*. On June 19 the U.S. Army chief of staff, General George Marshall, wrote gloomily to the chief of naval operations, Admiral Ernest J. King: "The losses to submarines off our Atlantic seaboard now threatens our entire war effort . . . I am fearful that another month or two of this will so cripple our means of transport that we will be unable to bring sufficient men and planes to bear against the [German and Italian] enemy . . ."[6]

It was a shocking evaluation of the war situation by America's top-ranking soldier. Marshall was saying that the redoubtable U-boat skippers were threatening to pen up America's armed forces, weapons, munitions, and supplies within her own borders.

While the U-boats were marauding off America's eastern seaboard, on July 2, 1942, a New York grand jury indicted twenty-six German-American Bund leaders on charges of conspiracy to evade the Selective Service Act. An FBI Blitzkreig quickly hauled in the Bund honchos, including Bundesfuehrer Wilhelm Kunze; Gustav Elmer, Bund treasurer; August Klapprot, New Jersey Bund fuehrer; and Herman Max Schwinn, West Coast fuehrer.

J. Edgar Hoover told the press: "Our goal is to put the Bund out of business."[7]

Three weeks later, on July 23, a Washington grand jury indicted twenty-seven men and a woman for sedition, charging that they had carried on "a systematic campaign of personal vilification . . . of public officials" in order to convince "citizens and the military . . . that such public officials are traitorous, corrupt, dishonest, incompetent and mentally unbalanced."

The grand jury also charged that the twenty-eight persons had conspired "to publish and convey to . . . the people and the military [false information] . . . for the purpose of obstructing, and intending to impede and defeat, the preparation of our national defenses against aggression and invasion and the national war effort."[8]

Among the thirty publications cited by the Washington grand

jury as part of the conspiracy were the official Nazi newsletter
World Service and the Bund's *Duetscher Weckruf und Boebach-
ter,* along with pro-Nazi sheets in Noblesville, Indiana; Wichita,
Kansas; San Bernardino, California; Muncie, Indiana; Wash-
ington D.C.; San Diego, California; New York City; and Omaha,
Nebraska.

Meanwhile, President Roosevelt and Prime Minister Churchill
had agreed to launch Operation Torch, an invasion of French
northwest Africa. It would be an all-American operation, with
three task forces storming ashore at Algiers, Oran, and Casablanca late in the fall of 1942.

Chief planner for Torch was tall, gangling, forty-six-year-old
Major General Mark W. Clark, called the "American Eagle" by
Churchill after the general's sharp nose and equally sharp
mind. At planning headquarters in London's Norfolk House,
Clark and his staff were confronted by a monumental problem
that threatened to disrupt Torch, possibly even cause its can-
cellation. Supplies—mountains of them—that were to be
shipped from the United States were mysteriously failing to arrive in England, Torch's principal staging base.

U-boat wolfpacks stalking the Atlantic were continuing to
sink ships daily, but entire shiploads of crucially needed guns,
munitions, spare parts, and other war matériel were simply
vanishing, lost in a logistical maze in the United States or side-
tracked in New York harbor by unknown parties. One freighter
loaded with combat equipment for the 1st Infantry Division
sailed from New York three times and had to return to port each
time when its cargo suddenly shifted and the ship was in danger of capsizing.[9]

Only two months before the November 8, 1942, D-Day for
Torch, General Clark learned that one of his assault divisions in
England had not received all of its assigned weapons. Frantic
investigation disclosed that the weapons were still sitting on
New York docks because someone had altered the markings on
the crates.[10]

*   *   *

Even while American forces under General Dwight D. Eisenhower were landing successfully in North Africa, U.S. and German scientists were engaged in a high-stakes race to develop a revolutionary atom bomb. The victor would win World War II and could gain absolute control of the globe. America's hush-hush project was being carried out under the cover name Manhattan Engineering District and was so supersecret that only a handful of government and military leaders and a few scientists knew the massive development program's true objective. Even Congress was unaware of Manhattan's existence, for the project was being financed by $2 million from a special presidential emergency fund.

World scientists had had an inkling of the atom since 400 B.C. when the Greek philosopher Democritus theorized that if matter were divided into finer and finer pieces, it would eventually reach a point where it could no longer be divided. This smallest bit of matter was called an atom, from a Greek word meaning "not cuttable." In 1938, 2,338 years later, German chemists Fritz Strassmen and Otto Hahn studied the effect of neutron bombardment on uranium atoms, and in January 1939 Austrian physicists Otto R. Fritsch and Lise Meitner explained this reaction as the splitting of a heavy atom into two medium-size atoms. They called this process fission. These Nazi scientists were on a course toward development of the most powerful weapon that mankind had known.

Some of the physicists who had fled from the Third Reich to the United States in the 1930s recognized the military possibilities of atomic energy. One of these Jewish refugees, world-renowned Albert Einstein, was so haunted by the specter of an atom bomb in Adolf Hitler's hands that he wrote a letter to President Roosevelt in the summer of 1939, explaining the nature of the problem and the urgent need for the federal government to become involved. Consequently, using his secret emergency funds, an alarmed Roosevelt set up the Uranium Project to study the possibility of unleashing atomic energy, and in early 1940 the scientists received their first funds for research.

On December 2, 1942, Dr. James B. Conant, president of Harvard University, received a telephone call from his friend, Dr. Arthur Holly Compton, who had shared the 1927 Nobel physics prize for one of his discoveries. Both scientists had been and were active in the Uranium Project.

"Jim," Compton said to Conant, "the Italian navigator has just landed in the New World." After pausing briefly, he then added, "The earth was not as large as he had estimated."

"Were the natives friendly?" Conant asked.

"Yes, everyone landed safe and happy." [11]

What sounded like a nonsensical conversation was actually impromptu double-talk, a ruse to guard against prying hostile ears. Compton was advising his colleague that physicist Enrico Fermi, "the Italian navigator," had scored an unexpectedly early success in an experiment that resulted in history's first controlled atomic chain reaction. It had taken place in an improvised laboratory under the spectator stands at Stagg Field, a college football stadium in Chicago.

Compton's remark about the earth not being as large as had been estimated meant that the size of the atomic pile was smaller than had originally been thought necessary. Conant's question was in reference to possible unforeseen problems with the experiment.

Never in American history had security been so tight as it was around the Manhattan Project (as the atom-bomb development came to be known). Everybody and everything had code names. Brigadier General Leslie R. Groves, who was in charge of the project, was called "Relief." Dr. Compton was A. H. Comas or A. Holly, and Enrico Fermi became Henry Farmer. Stagg Field was known as the Chicago Metallurgical Laboratory; the gaseous diffusion plant at Oak Ridge, Tennessee, was K-25; a facility at Los Alamos, New Mexico, was Site X; and the scientist in charge of the atom-splitting operation at Stagg Field had the title Coordinator of Rapid Rupture. [12]

American leaders were hoping that the tight security net would keep the Manhattan Project a secret from Nazi Germany. So they were jolted early in 1943 when the FBI uncovered a chilling microdot message being sent from Ast X to Nazi agents in the United States:

> There is reason to believe that the scientific works for the utilization of atomic energy are being driven forward into a

certain direction in the United States. Continuous information about the tests made on this subject are required and particularly the [answers to these questions]:

1. What process is used in the United States for transporting heavy uranium?
2. What tests are being made with uranium? (Universities, industrial laboratories, etc.)
3. Which other raw materials are being used in these tests?
    Entrust only the best experts with this.[13]

Names and addresses of several American scientists involved in atomic research followed.

For more than two years military leaders and scientists in the Third Reich had suspected that America was trying to develop an atom bomb. The Germans' first clue had come on November 12, 1940, when an Abwehr spy in America, Alfred Hohlhaus, reported to Ast X that a number of helium plants were expanding in order to increase production of the gas. A longtime resident of the United States with a high-salaried job as an industrial chemist, Holhaus had used his professional connections to be taken on escorted tours of helium plants across the nation.

The German-born Hohlhaus pointed out to the Abwehr that since helium production had been ample to meet normal needs in the United States, the expansion must be related to some other purpose—the harnessing of atomic energy for military purposes, perhaps.

Back in the Third Reich, Colonel Josef "Bippo" Schmidt, chief of Luftwaffe Intelligence, watched for evidence to support Hohlhaus's theory, and telltale clues began to mount up. On January 19, 1942, Schmidt sent a report to the Wehrmacht high command. "As far as it is known," he wrote, "work in the field of nuclear physics is already so far advanced [in the United States] that, if the war were prolonged, it could become of considerable significance." Schmidt added, "It is therefore desirable to acquire through the Abwehr additional information about American plans and of the progress being made in the United States in the field of nuclear research."[14]

Now the heat was put on Admiral Canaris to ferret out the

secrets of America's nuclear experiments, and a search was launched for a qualified spy, preferably a physicist. Chosen for the crucial mission was fifty-one-year-old Walter Koehler, a native of Gouda, the Netherlands, who had been a spy for the Kaiser in World War I. Koehler was not the ideal candidate, for he was a jeweler by profession. But he had had engineering training and possessed a working knowledge of technical matters.[15]

Koehler had lived in New York for several years as an Abwehr "sleeper" before being recalled to the Third Reich in mid-June 1941. Ast X promised him substantial sums of money to ferret out nuclear secrets in the United States, and the grasping Koehler could never resist the lure of the greenbacks. Besides, he had concocted a scheme to double-cross his Nazi masters: Once he arrived back in New York he—and Adolf Hitler's money—would promptly vanish.

At the Academy in Hamburg, Koehler was given a crash course in nuclear physics and provided with a new "cover" and phony American credentials. Ast X officers were appalled by Koehler's seeming lack of enthusiasm for his mission, but time was short, the task was urgent, and he was the best the Abwehr could do at the time. However, Koehler had a few plus factors: He was no newcomer to the espionage game, he knew the United States well, and his harmless appearance—he was a chubby, shy man who squinted through thick-lensed glasses— would not draw undue attention toward him.

It was not until July 1942 that Walter Koehler, probably history's first nuclear spy, and his wife left Hamburg for Madrid on the first leg of the trip back to the United States. They would be posing as anti-Nazi, devoutly Catholic refugees on the run from the Gestapo. Crammed into Koehler's pockets and sewn into the linings of his luggage were the initial valuables he had been given by the Abwehr: $16,230 in cash, travelers' checks, and gold coins. On reaching Madrid, Koehler and his wife took a number of evasive actions to shake off possible tails, then headed for the American consulate.

31

Helping to Confuse Hitler on D-Day

Madrid had long been a hotbed of international intrigue, so the vice consul at the American consulate eyed Walter Koehler with deep suspicion while the Dutchman poured out his fantastic story of being an Abwehr agent whose mission was to dig out nuclear secrets in the United States. Koehler explained that he had orders to establish a clandestine radio station in America and send back reports by wireless.

The American was unimpressed. So Koehler dug into a suitcase and pulled out the accoutrements of espionage that he had been given by the Abwehr—a special Leica camera, call signs, security checks, chemicals for making secret ink, a personal cipher, a Dutch prayer book on which his code would be based, and instructions for operating a shortwave radio station. Finally, Koehler revealed the Abwehr's $16,230 in cash, travelers' checks, and gold coins.

Koehler stressed that he had accepted the espionage job only to escape the clutches of the Nazis, and if permitted to enter the United States he would serve as an American agent while pretending to work for Ast X in Hamburg. A call was put in to Washington, and Koehler's record was found in FBI files—a German spy in two world wars. J. Edgar Hoover still distrusted double agents but decided to take a calculated risk that might produce big dividends. "Send him along," the FBI radioed.[1]

In August 1942 Koehler and his German wife sailed from Lisbon aboard a Portuguese vessel, and on arrival in America the couple was taken in tow by an FBI reception committee. Ensconced in a comfortable Manhattan hotel, the Koehlers were furnished with a generous weekly allowance—with the Abwehr money the FBI had confiscated. However, unknown to the G-men, Mrs. Koehler had smuggled in ten thousand dollars that had been sewn into her girdle.[2]

Hoover's men immediately went to work setting up a clandestine shortwave station for Koehler in a large, rambling old house on a secluded estate on Long Island. Police dogs guarded the premises. The scenario was almost identical to the one organized for William Sebold at Centerport in the spring of 1940.

This would be an especially tricky operation, one in which even a minor blunder could destroy the entire scheme. The FBI knew that the Abwehr had an officer who could identify the radio-sending style of anyone with whom he had once worked —and he knew Koehler's technique intimately. The FBI laboratory made phonograph records of Koehler's radio-sending, and two G-men practiced almost incessantly until they could imitate his touch of the Morse key. A third special agent, a linguist, studied the nuances of Koehler's language peculiarities, those of a Dutchman using German.

Koehler was not present at 8:00 o'clock on the cold, gray morning of February 7, 1943, when the G-men manning the shortwave station flashed the double agent's first message to Hamburg: "Am now ready to operate. Necessary to be careful, but feel I am safe. Will listen for you at nineteen hundred [7:00 P.M.]."

Five days passed and no reply came. No doubt Ast X was closely studying "Koehler's" style for telltale flaws. Then the Long Island radio crackled and a message came in from Hamburg: "Uncle is highly pleased. He declares his appreciation and well wishes." Uncle was the Abwehr's big chief, Admiral Wilhelm Canaris.

The FBI men operating the station on an around-the-clock basis grinned widely. They too were "highly pleased."

From that point on, the Germans were fed military and industrial information (cleared with the armed forces), much of which was true—and trivial or misleading. As had been the case with the Sebold masquerade, the FBI brain trust concocted a steady stream of doctored intelligence to beam across the Atlantic. It was crucial not to pretend that Koehler knew too much, for the Germans were well aware that a lone operative would have but limited information. So in order to increase the flow of phony data, the brain trust gave birth to a pair of sub-agents for Koehler. Both phantoms were shipyard workers, one in the Brooklyn Navy Yard and the other in Philadelphia.

As the weeks and months rolled past, Walter Koehler's stature rose steadily with his Abwehr spymasters. But conspicuous by its absence was the intelligence that Koehler had been sent to ferret out—data on American nuclear developments.

In order to subtly provoke Ast X into revealing the identity of other Nazi spies who might be operating in America, the G-men at the shortwave station had Koehler regularly plead with Hamburg for more money, claiming that he was nearly broke and unable to continue spying. Since Koehler was one of the few *Grossagenten* (super spies) in the United States who was not behind bars, Abwehr officers tried frantically to placate him.

Ast X offered to deposit two thousand dollars in a Swiss bank account and arrange for the money to be cabled to a New York bank. But the FBI was hoping to lure a Nazi agent or two out from under cover to pay Koehler in person, so G-men turned down the offer, claiming (for Koehler) that cabling money was too risky. Finally the Abwehr radioed that it was sending a Dutch business tycoon to the United States; one of his missions would be to deliver Koehler $6,000 worth of jewelry.

J. Edgar Hoover and his men were faced with a dilemma. If they arrested the bagman after his arrival in New York, the Abwehr might become suspicious that Koehler had double-crossed Hitler and conclude that the Long Island shortwave station was in fact an FBI ploy. But if the G-men permitted the Dutchman to make personal contact with Koehler to turn over the jewelry, Koehler, whom the FBI still did not trust, might tip off the man that he was working for the Americans.

Now the scenario took a curious twist. On reaching Madrid, the Dutchman, who identified himself as Hubert Blyleven (not his real name), called at the American consulate and offered to serve the Allies. But could the jewelry bagman be trusted?

J. Edgar Hoover wasn't certain, but he told the Madrid legation to send Blyleven along. Meanwhile, the FBI set up a ruse to ostensibly allow the Dutchman to turn over the jewelry without actually being in personal contact with Koehler, whom the G-men wanted to keep under cover.[3]

Ast X had radioed Koehler instructions for making contact with Blyleven for the jewelry payoff. Koehler was to telephone the bagman at his hotel, identify himself as "Mr. Kliemann," and arrange to meet for the exchange. So when Blyleven arrived in Manhattan, a G-man telephoned instead of Koehler and said, "This is Mr. Kliemann. Have you anything for me?"

Indeed he had, Blyleven responded. Hoover's sleuth arranged for a meeting with the Dutchman in the lobby of a mid-Manhattan hotel, and on exchange of the password "Kliemann" Blyleven was to hand over the jewelry. The G-man had deliberately designated a hotel lobby that was customarily packed with people, a necessary ingredient to the ruse.[4]

When Blyleven walked into the lobby with the jewelry package under one arm, he was engulfed by the large number of persons milling about. How could he single out Koehler? Moments later someone approached him from behind, whispered "Kliemann" into his ear, grabbed the jewelry bundle, and vanished into the crowd. "Kliemann"—who was actually an FBI operative—had moved so swiftly that Blyleven never saw who had snatched the package. But the Dutchman could report to Hamburg that he had personally delivered the jewelry to Koehler.[5]

Meanwhile, other FBI agents in New York were continuing with the maddening chore of trying to identify the ace Nazi harbor spy, mild-mannered, grandfatherly Ernest Lehmitz, whose shipping reports had resulted in the U-boat sinkings of untold numbers of Allied freighters and the deaths of scores of crewmen and injuries to hundreds of others. Since February 1942 the Bermuda censorship post had been intercepting Lehmitz's shipping reports, which were being sent to Hamburg through an Abwehr mail drop in Lisbon.

On April 13, 1943, Bermuda detected the thirteenth letter

signed by Fred Sloane or Fred Lewis. It contained an innocent reference to the "wonderful week I had spent on the beach at Estoril."

Estoril! The name rang a bell with the G-men: This could be the break they had been seeking. Estoril, the sleuths knew, was a popular resort outside Lisbon—and a clearing house for Nazi spies. So, armed with copies of Fred Lewis's signature, a team of FBI agents descended upon the U.S. Customs office in New York and began comparing Lewis's handwriting with those on many thousands of baggage declarations by those who had entered the United States from Portugal since 1941.

It was a gargantuan task. Day after day, night after night, for many weeks, the bleary-eyed G-men waded through the mountain of baggage declarations. Just after 9:00 P.M. on June 9, 1943, a weary special agent picked up the 5,192nd form that had been inspected. Suddenly he felt a surge of exultation. He grabbed his magnifying glass, intensely compared the Fred Lewis signature with that of one Ernest F. Lehmitz on the bottom of the baggage declaration, and let out a loud warhoop. The handwriting matched perfectly.

At the FBI laboratory in Washington, both signatures were greatly enlarged and photographed, and handwriting experts confirmed that the same man had signed both documents. An order was flashed to the New York FBI office: Put Ernest F. Lehmitz, 123 Oxford Place, Staten Island, under immediate surveillance.

Just before 7:00 A.M. the next morning the suspect sauntered from his home and was tailed to the waterfront saloon where he worked and in which merchant seamen were constantly talking about sailing dates and cargoes. For more than two weeks G-men clad in seamen's clothing hung around the saloon, watching Lehmitz's every action. Other FBI sleuths, posing as insurance salesmen, meter readers, and deliverymen, were picking up incriminating evidence through discreet inquiries from Lehmitz's neighbors on Oxford Place.

On June 27 Lehmitz was arrested. Taken to Foley Square, he was shown copies of many of his letters to Hamburg that had been intercepted at Bermuda and the mass of other evidence against him collected by G-men in his neighborhood and at the waterfront saloon. Lehmitz admitted all and signed a confession. In it he implicated one of his subagents, middle-aged Erwin Harry DeSpretter.

In September 1943 Lehmitz and DeSpretter were tried for wartime espionage in Federal Court in Brooklyn. Each was found guilty and sentenced to a term of thirty years in prison. Lehmitz's Hungarian-born wife, seated at the rear of the courtroom, burst into tears on hearing the sentence. She was fearful, she told friends, that the notoriety surrounding her husband's conviction would frighten off roomers at her house on Oxford Place.

Even while Hoover's sleuths were laboriously tracking down Ernest Lehmitz, another Nazi spy was operating from Sheepshead Bay in Brooklyn, facing Staten Island. Burton Samuel Huffberg (not his real name), a tall, handsome, well-built member of the U.S. Navy, had made good money as an employee of the Ford plant in Detroit before being drafted. But he had been approached by an Abwehr mole in the Ford facility and offered even more money for merely pilfering drawings of war equipment. Huffberg had accepted eagerly.

It was but a short time before Huffberg learned that he had become a member of a Nazi spy ring that had been operating with considerable success in Detroit since the middle of 1942. The brains and motivating force behind the Detroit network was Grace Buchanan-Dineen, a glamorous beauty and a native of Canada. Grace was well bred and a graduate of both exclusive Vassar College in Poughkeepsie, New York, and the espionage Academy in Hamburg.[6]

When Huffberg entered the navy in early 1943, he continued to spy for the Detroit Mata Hari by merely changing his role from industrial spying to harbor spying. Assigned to duty at Sheepshead Bay, in June 1943 the twenty-seven-year-old sailor began sending New York harbor shipping intelligence to his boss in Detroit.

Meanwhile, the FBI had uncovered information that pointed to an organized spy ring in the Motor City, and agents were infiltrated into the Ford plant. It was found that Grace Buchanan-Dineen's gang had been offering—and in some cases, paying—big money to obtain secret blueprints of tanks and airplane engines.

In late 1943 the FBI swooped down on Buchanan-Dineen and several members of her ring, including Burton Huffberg. Aware that she faced execution for wartime espionage, the Vassar socialite sang like a canary, telling the FBI everything she knew about the Nazi spy apparatus in America.

Grace Buchanan-Dineen came to trial in Detroit in March 1944, pleaded guilty, and received a sentence of twelve years in prison. A short time later Burton Huffberg, appearing in court in his navy uniform, was tried. He too faced the electric chair. Hardly had the trial opened than Huffberg began going through a series of strange gyrations. On the witness stand he admitted that he had sent shipping reports to Detroit, but swore he did not remember why he had done so or to whom he had mailed them. Prosecutors' questions received nonsensical replies.

Psychiatrists were ordered to examine Huffberg. After weeks of observing the defendant, they concluded that he was "mentally unbalanced," and the case against him was dismissed.[7]

At this time in the Third Reich, the Sicherheitsdienst (SD), Intelligence branch of Reichsfuehrer Heinrich Himmler's elite Schutzstaffel (SS), had grown suspicious of a small group of socially well-placed Germans who gathered for tea and conversation once each month at the sumptuous home of a wealthy, elderly widow, Frau Hanna Solf. So the SD connived to wrangle an invitation for one of its agents—Dr. Joachim Reckzeh, a Swiss of impeccable manners and grooming.

Frau Solf was delighted with the new addition to the group, for Dr. Reckzeh was a delightful and personable man. But then she was unaware that her charming guest was reporting to the SD the "traitorous" (by Nazi standards) remarks that he had heard at the tea. Otto Kiep, once the consul general in New York, had bitterly castigated Adolf Hitler, and within hours Kiep was arrested.

Kiep's arrest set off a chain reaction within the Abwehr around the world. Kiep, through Canaris, had arranged to have a number of young Germans with British and American connections posted overseas, so that he could maintain communication channels with Intelligence in Washington and London. Fearing that they would be arrested, Kiep's Abwehr protégés in Lisbon, Istanbul, Casablanca, and Stockholm quickly defected to the Allies.[8]

Hitler was furious when, on February 20, 1944, the SD reported the defections. But no doubt Reichsfuehrer Himmler was secretly delighted. The conniving one-time chicken farmer was already one of the three most powerful leaders in the Third Reich, for he commanded his own private army, the SS, and was in control of the Gestapo. But he hungered for even more potency and had long plotted to bring the Abwehr under his wing. Now was his chance to strike.

Himmler gained an audience with the fuehrer and pointed out that the Third Reich's perilous situation demanded that all German Intelligence agencies be brought under the direct control of one man, someone who was a dedicated Nazi Party member. That man, Himmler implied, was Heinrich Himmler. Hitler briefly mulled over the proposal, then agreed.

Himmler, however, had to proceed with extreme caution for he knew or suspected that Canaris had compiled a damaging dossier on him. So Himmler arranged for the Reich's top-ranking officers, Field Marshal Wilhelm Keitel and General Alfred Jodl, to perform the head-chopping operation—gently.

Keitel and Jodl called on Canaris at Abwehr headquarters, praised him for his long service to the Third Reich, decorated him with the *Deutches Kreuz ein Gelt* (German Cross of Gold), then invited him to take a leave of absence. Wilhelm Canaris, who for a decade had been masterminding Hitler's secret invasion of the United States, had been booted out of office.[9]

Himmler moved immediately to consolidate his new power. He convened a conference at Salzburg, and forty-one-year-old Ernst Kaltenbrunnger, a husky, one-time municipal chief of police who had succeeded the assassinated Reinhard Heydrich as head of the SD, was named chief of the new combined Intelligence Service. Directing the day-to-day operations of the agency would be thirty-four-year-old SS general Walter Schellenberg, a shrewd, energetic disciple of Nazism since his student days at the University of Bonn.

* * *

With the arrival of spring 1944, much of the civilized world was tensely awaiting the outcome of a looming battle that could decide World War II and set the future course of history. It was an open secret: The Allies were massing almost their entire industrial might and manpower in Great Britain to launch a gigantic assault across the English Channel against German-occupied Europe. The Allied operation's code name was Overlord.[10]

Since the Pas de Calais region only twenty miles across the Channel from Britain's White Cliffs of Dover was such a logical locale for a military landing, the Allies set in motion a mammoth and intricate deception stratagem code-named Operation Fortitude to convince Adolf Hitler and his high command that that would indeed be the invasion site.

The centerpiece of Fortitude was Quicksilver, the fabrication of an entire United States Army group that was to appear to consist of a million men. The phantom force, known as the First United States Army Group (FUSAG), would be stationed in southeastern England, across from the Pas de Calais. FUSAG's mission was to keep the powerful German Fifteenth Army in place at the Pas de Calais on D-Day, while Allied troops stormed ashore in Normandy, 160 miles to the west.

At the same time, nearly all of Germany's Intelligence resources were concentrating on one crucial question: Where would the Allies strike from their British springboard? Early in 1944 Ast X began bombarding double agent Walter Koehler with demands for information on troop units embarking for England from New York. The FBI was delighted to cooperate with the requests, and the Long Island station fed Hamburg plenty of preinvasion information. Some of the messages sent in Koehler's name were accurate, for the FBI considered it inevitable that the Germans would be able eventually to identify the real American units in Great Britain. But much of the information was about departing units that did not exist; it was hoped that the German high command would conclude the units were destined for the fictitious First United States Army Group.

It had become apparent that Ast X trusted Koehler. At Easter the Abwehr radioed him their warmest greetings, and the G-men at the shortwave station responded in kind, concluding their message with "Heil, Hitler!" With his bona fides securely established in Hamburg, Koehler (under the supervision of his

FBI brain trust) began mailing Hamburg periodic reports written in invisible ink. Ast X was elated to learn from one of these letters that Koehler had obtained a job as night manager at the Henry Hudson Hotel, on West 57th Street in New York City. (He had never set foot inside the hotel.) This was an especially advantageous position, he explained, for the United States Army used the hotel to lodge officers bound for overseas.[11]

In Koehler's name, the FBI would send 121 messages to Hamburg, data that helped influence German Intelligence to create a faulty *Feindbild* (a picture of the enemy) in England. By early 1944 tens of thousands of real GIs were pouring into Britain's ports—and so were large numbers of phantom soldiers for the phony FUSAG.

Spearheaded by American and British paratroopers, Allied amphibious forces struck at Normandy shortly after dawn on June 6, 1944. The Allies' intricate, worldwide deception campaign (in which the FBI played a minor yet significant role through the Koehler masquerade) resulted in the Germans being taken totally by surprise. So convinced was the Wehrmacht high command that the phantom FUSAG would make a second—and main—landing at the Pas de Calais that the Fifteenth Army, whose rapid intervention in Normandy could possibly have driven the invaders into the sea, remained in place and idle for six weeks.

(After the war, American officers examined Walter Koehler's Abwehr file in Hamburg. It was found that Ast X had received a total of 231 radio messages from Koehler, not just the 121 dispatches sent in his name by the G-men at the Long Island shortwave station. Many of the messages Koehler had managed to send were in code other than the one based on the Dutch prayer book that the FBI had been using. Evidence would indicate that the devious Koehler had furtively made contact with another Nazi agent, who had also been sending Koehler's information to Ast X. Koehler had succeeded in double-crossing both sides. He was not only a double agent, but a triple agent.)

On the heels of the massive Allied invasion of northern France, the *Schwarze Kapelle* (Black Orchestra), a clandestine group of high-ranking German military and government leaders who had long plotted to eliminate Adolf Hitler, prepared to take an explosive action. They were more convinced than ever that the fuehrer was taking Germany hell-bent down the road toward total destruction.

32

Operation Magpie— A Desperate Venture

At approximately 12:40 P.M. on July 20, 1944, a tall, handsome German nobleman, Lieutenant Colonel Klaus von Stauffenberg, strode into the map room at the fuehrer's battle headquarters, *Wolfsschanze* (Wolves' Lair), a sprawling complex of buildings and underground bunkers set among gloomy woods outside Rastenburg, East Prussia. Count von Stauffenberg wore a black patch over one eye, for the previous year he had lost an eye, an arm, part of one hand, and a piece of scalp while fighting in Tunisia. There was nothing about Stauffenberg's demeanor to betray that he had flown in from Berlin on a desperate mission: to kill Adolf Hitler. Despite his devout religious beliefs, the count had volunteered to be the "hit man" for the Schwarze Kapelle.

Minutes later Hitler entered the room for his daily military briefing and stood at the conference table along with some ten generals and colonels. While General Adolf Huesing was outlining the situation on the Russian front, Stauffenberg slipped over to the corner of the table at Hitler's right and placed his briefcase, containing a time bomb, on the floor near to the fuehrer.

"I will leave this here for a moment," Stauffenberg whispered to Colonel Heinz Brandt. "I have to make a telephone call." [1]

Moments later Brandt found that the briefcase was in his way, so he reached down and moved it to rest against the heavy, thick support of the table on the side farthest from Hitler. Meanwhile, Stauffenberg took up a position near a bunker a hundred yards from the wooden hut holding the map room.

Suddenly a thunderous blast rocked Wolfsschanze. Hitler's conference table was shattered, the roof caved in, the windows were blown out. The explosion killed two generals and the official stenographer, seriously wounded one general and one colonel, and inflicted lesser injuries on four more generals. Stauffenberg's target, Hitler, was not killed; the heavy upright support had deflected the blast away from him. But his right arm was paralyzed (temporarily), his hair was set on fire, both of his eardrums were affected, there was a nasty cut across his face, and his back and buttocks were peppered with wood splinters. One of his trouser legs was blown off. However, Hitler reacted calmly and was led away from the ruins by Field Marshal Keitel.[2]

A revolution that the Schwarze Kapelle had plotted to launch following Hitler's death was nipped in the bud. Heinrich Himmler and his SS troops in Berlin were again in full control within twenty-four hours. In the weeks ahead a manhunt of unprecedented scope raged throughout the Third Reich, and hundreds of those involved in the bomb plot—or those merely suspected of complicity—were arrested and tried, and scores were shot or hanged. Among the conspirators who were executed was Count von Stauffenberg, the Schwarze Kapelle hit man.

Shortly after noon on July 23, three days after the ill-fated Wolfsschanze blast, young SS general Walter Schellenberg, chief of the SD, rang the doorbell at the home of Admiral Canaris at Schlachtensee, a pristine lake resort outside Berlin. The white-haired former overlord of the *Fuchsbau* (Fox's Lair), as Abwehr headquarters had been called, had been living alone with two servants since Himmler had connived to get him booted from his post five months earlier.

For ten years the shadowy Canaris had led a schizophrenic life. On one hand, he had played a crucial role in helping Hitler toward his goal of world conquest, and on the other, the admiral had been the motivating force in the Schwarze Kapelle, whose goal was the elimination of the fuehrer.

Now when Canaris opened his door and saw the caller, he said quietly, "Somehow I felt that it would be you." [3]

Schellenberg had been sent by SS Obergruppenfuehrer Heinrich Mueller, the chief of a special commission set up by Himmler to investigate the Schwarze Kapelle and the twentieth of July bomb plot. Canaris was to be placed under "protective custody," for evidence against him at the time was sketchy.

However, General Schellenberg offered Canaris the opportunity to commit suicide, but the admiral said, "No, my dear Schellenberg, I won't kill myself." [4]

At dawn on October 23, 1944, three months after the Hitler assassination effort had fizzled, the elderly projectionist in a movie theater at peaceful Harpers Ferry, West Virginia, was deep in slumber at his rooming house. Suddenly he was awakened by a sharp rap on the door, and he opened it to be confronted by two strangers. One man flashed a badge and said, "FBI."

Simon Emil Koedel (Abwehr registry number A.2011), who held a major's commission in the German army, was arrested and charged with "conspiracy to commit espionage."

Neighbors were stunned to learn that this soft-spoken, meek theater employee had been one of the slickest Nazi spies in the United States. Koedel had come to Harpers Ferry a few months earlier after fleeing from his home in Manhattan because he sensed that the FBI net was closing in on him.

A few days later the masterspy's foster daughter, Marie Hedwig Koedel, was picked up. For many months she had served the fuehrer well by extracting shipping information from merchant seamen at New York waterfront saloons.

Tried in federal court in Brooklyn, Simon Koedel was sentenced to fifteen years in prison. Marie, whose spying had no doubt resulted in the deaths of many merchant seamen, received a term of seven and a half years. [5]

* * *

At first light on the bitterly cold morning of November 29, 1944, a U-boat skippered by Lieutenant Hans Hilbig was threading its way through shoals and islets into Frenchman Bay, a body of deep water protruding ten miles into the rugged coast of Maine. On board were two spies, Erich Gimpel and William Curtis Colepaugh, a renegade American. The two men were embarked on *Unternehmen Elster* (Operation Magpie), a last-gasp espionage mission to the United States concocted in desperation by German Intelligence.

Colepaugh, twenty-six years of age, was born and reared in Niantic, Connecticut, on Long Island Sound, and had been a member of the United States Navy Reserve before going to the Third Reich to embrace Nazism in 1941. Six feet two inches tall, Colepaugh was a reed-thin 150 pounds. Gimpel, who had been born in Merseburg, a small town ninety miles southwest of Berlin, was an inch shorter than his companion but weighed 177 pounds.[6]

Both men had met for the first time and been trained at *A-Schule West* (Agent School West), located on a secluded estate named Park Zorgvliet, between The Hague and suburban Scheveningen in the Netherlands. Commandant of the A-Schule was an SS major. Many of the instructors had accompanied the swashbuckling German commando, SS Lieutenant Colonel Otto "Scarface" Skorzeny, when he had electrified the world a year earlier by snatching deposed Italian dictator Benito Mussolini from his prison atop a towering Alps mountain.

Operation Magpie was a curious mission. It had been conceived by the pompous foreign minister, Joachim von Ribbentrop, to analyze the effect of Nazi propaganda on the fall 1944 presidential election, in which Franklin Roosevelt would be seeking an unprecedented fourth term against Republican challenger Thomas E. Dewey, governor of New York. Specifically, Ribbentrop wanted firsthand information on the impact of propaganda broadcasts beamed from the Third Reich to the United States.

However, in a later briefing two SS colonels expanded the scope of Operation Magpie. What was needed, Gimpel and Colepaugh were told, was technical information on airplanes, rocket developments, and ship construction. They were to achieve this by exploiting America's democracy and gleaning information from newspapers, magazines, technical journals, radio, and books. It was important, the SS colonels stressed, that this intelligence reach Germany quickly, through radio transmission.[7]

With preparations completed, Colepaugh and Gimpel each were given a Colt pistol, a tiny compass, a Leica camera, a Krahl wristwatch, a bottle of secret ink, and powder for developing invisible-ink messages from the Third Reich. Instructions for building a radio and transmitting to Germany had been reduced to microdot form. (German Intelligence had no inkling that the FBI already knew about the ingenious microdots.)[8]

Upon arriving at the Baltic port of Kiel where they were to board Lieutenant Hilbig's U-1230, the two spies were furnished phony papers. Gimpel's papers identified him as Edward George Green, born in Bridgeport, Connecticut. They consisted of a birth certificate, a Selective Service registration card showing him registered at Local Board 18 in Boston, and a Massachusetts driver's license. Colepaugh's false documents were virtually the same and were made out in the name of William Charles Caldwell, born in New Haven, Connecticut.[9]

Now, at 11:00 P.M. on November 29, 1944, Gimpel and Colepaugh climbed from Hilbig's submarine into a rubber raft off bleak Crabtree Point, Maine, and were paddled ashore by two sailors. Along with their espionage accoutrements, the spies carried in a briefcase sixty thousand dollars in American money. A blinding snowstorm was raging as Gimpel and Colepaugh stumbled onto land, but neither spy had thought to bring along a topcoat or hat.

The Nazi agents bent their heads to the howling wind and trudged inland until they reached a dirt road. Hardly had they begun walking along it than they were caught in the headlights of a car driven slowly by eighteen-year-old Harvard M. Hodgkins, a high-school senior who was returning to his nearby home. Hodgkins, whose father Dana was a deputy sheriff of Hancock County, thought it strange that two strangers would be traipsing along a back road at midnight in a blizzard and wearing only light clothing.[10]

Gimpel and Colepaugh continued through snowy woods for about five miles until they reached U.S. Highway 1 where they flagged down a passing taxi. The driver agreed to take them the thirty-two miles to Bangor, Maine, for six dollars. At the Bangor station, the spies caught a train to Portland, Maine, and from there took another train to Boston.

Meanwhile, Deputy Sheriff Hodgkins had returned from a hunting trip and was told by his son of the two lightly dressed strangers in the blizzard. The elder Hodgkins promptly notified the FBI field office in Boston, and agents were rushed to Crabtree Point to launch an investigation.

After spending a night in Boston, Gimpel and Colepaugh entrained for New York on the morning of December 1. Upon arrival at Grand Central Station, they checked a suitcase holding their spying accoutrements, then taxied across town to Pennsylvania Station, where they put their cash-filled briefcase in a locker. Then they checked into the Kenmore Hall Hotel at 145 East 23rd Street.

They urgently needed to find an apartment to serve as a short-wave radio studio, and on December 8 they rented a place on the top floor of a townhouse at 39 Beekman Place. "Caldwell" and "Green"—they were using their aliases—left the town-house early each morning and returned late in the evening, as though they were legitimate businessmen. On the same day that they had moved into their apartment, the spies bought a sec-ondhand commercial radio broadcast receiver at a store at 124 East 44th Street, and a few days later they purchased other ra-dio components in Greenwich Village in lower Manhattan.[11]

These radio components were carried into the Beekman Place townhouse a package or two at a time to avoid suspicion. The spies hoped to have the radio assembled and in contact with Germany in less than a month. Meanwhile, they had re-trieved the briefcase with the money.

Now Gimpel's and Colepaugh's enthusiasm for spying began to waver. Forgotten was their mission of digging up technical information. Instead they began wining and dining in plush restaurants and taking in the latest Broadway stage shows. They were sprinkling Hitler's money around Manhattan as though it were going out of style. Colepaugh, especially, was on a money-spending binge. When not picking up girls, he was buying ex-pensive suits at a Roger Kent store.

On the night of December 21, Colepaugh waited outside a Robert Reed store in Rockefeller Center while Gimpel was buying a topcoat and a suit to replace his German-made "American" clothing. When Gimpel came out, his companion had vanished. Colepaugh had taken the subway to the plush St. Moritz Hotel on Central Park and registered as "Mr. and Mrs. William Caldwell." (Before the night was over, he expected to pick up a young woman.)

Loaded with part of the Abwehr's money, Colepaugh spent two nights at the swank St. Moritz. Then he went to see an old buddy, Edmund F. Mulcahy, who lived on 111th Street, Richmond Hill, a part of the borough of Queens. Colepaugh told his friend that he was a Nazi spy and, with Colepaugh's approval, Mulcahy called the FBI.[12]

Taken to Foley Square, Colepaugh was eager to talk. He told G-men what Gimpel looked like, that his alias was Edward Green, and that he often bought newspapers at a stand in Times Square. Gimpel had a peculiar habit, his defected comrade pointed out, of keeping dollar bills in his breast pocket.

At once a manhunt was launched by the FBI, not only in New York but across the nation.

Times Square was cold and windswept on the night of December 30, when, just before 9:00 P.M., two G-men staking out the newsstand saw a tall man resembling Gimpel's description approaching. He went to the newspaper rack, picked out two publications, and reached into the breast pocket of his coat to pull out a dollar bill in payment. The sleuths nodded to each other, then closed in on the suspect.

After the G-men flashed their badges, Gimpel tried to bully his way out of the arrest. "What's this all about?" he sputtered indignantly.[13]

The German protested that he was a law-abiding citizen and claimed that his name was Edward Green, but the G-men found $10,574 in cash in his pockets. A search of Gimpel's hotel room turned up $44,100 in cash, ninety-nine small diamonds wrapped in tissue paper (furnished by the Abwehr to be used as bribes), a Leica camera, two loaded Colt pistols, blank Selective Service registration forms, and three bottles of secret ink.

Colepaugh and Gimpel were charged with espionage and tried by a military court at Governor's Island. They were found guilty and on February 14, 1945, were sentenced to be executed. (President Roosevelt died less than two months after the verdict, and his successor, Harry S Truman, commuted the sentences to life imprisonment.)

While the Operation Magpie melodrama had been unfolding, America's homefront Christmas gaiety was shattered by shocking battlefield news from the rugged, snow-blanketed Ardennes Forest in Belgium.

33

The Abwehr Goes Out of Business

At dawn on December 16, 1944, tens of thousands of Hitler's shock troops and hundreds of low-slung panzers, paced by bands of German commandos driving captured American vehicles and wearing GI uniforms taken from prisoners, burst through thinly held American lines in the Ardennes and eventually plunged sixty miles into Belgium. The huge offensive was the fuehrer's final roll of the dice for victory in the West—and it would come within a whisker of success.

From Supreme Commander Eisenhower down to the private on outpost duty in an icy Ardennes foxhole, the Americans had been taken by total surprise as the result of a masterful German deception campaign. Savagery reigned—no quarter asked, none given—in what came to be known as the Battle of the Bulge.

Mass confusion—sometimes panic—gripped the Allies at all levels. An alarming report declared that German paratroopers would be dropped on London and Paris during the Christmas season to spread terror and chaos. Another report swore that a group of German commandos, "blood-thirsty killers" wearing American uniforms and led by the notorious (to the Allies) SS colonel Otto Skorzeny, was heading hell-bent for Paris to murder General Eisenhower.[1]

Across the Atlantic in Washington, Harry Hopkins, a confidant of President Roosevelt's, breathlessly informed FBI chief J. Edgar Hoover of an amazing Nazi plot to murder Roosevelt. Hopkins said his information came from confidential Intelligence sources in London. At this time there were nearly 425,000 German prisoners of war in the United States, and some 75 of them were escaping each month. (Most of the escapees had been caught.) According to Hopkins's source, the attempt to kill Roosevelt would be made while German POWs created enormous confusion by a mass escape from American prison camps.[2]

President Roosevelt scoffed at the idea that Nazis might storm the White House, or infiltrate it, to murder him. But Mike Riley, the veteran chief of the White House Secret Service detail, refused to take the threat lightly. He beefed up security around the President and kept it extremely tight until mid-January 1945, when a defeated German army limped back out of Belgium and to the Siegfried Line along the German border.[3]

At the same time that the Roosevelt murder plot report had surfaced, the FBI and Naval Intelligence were probing another possible Nazi threat to the United States. Erich Gimpel and William Colepaugh had told G-men that before leaving Hamburg, the Abwehr had told them that a flotilla of U-boats would follow them to America. These submarines, the two spies swore they had been told, were "outfitted with special rocket-firing devices" that would enable the skippers to bombard New York and Washington from beyond the horizon.

Other evidence was uncovered that indicated these U-boat "special devices" could launch Hitler's *Vergeltungswaffe* (vengeance weapons) against America's East Coast. These devilish weapons had long been known to the Allies as buzzbombs, and since June 1944 they had been raining down on London and other locales in England, causing widespread destruction and thousands of casualties. Called the V-1 by the Germans, the buzzbomb was a pilotless aircraft with speeds up to 440 miles per hour, far faster than any Allied fighter plane could fly. A timing device would cause the engine to shut off over a target, and the buzzbomb would plunge earthward and explode with the impact of a 4,000-pound blockbuster.

In the wake of the two spies' startling disclosure, Naval Intelligence groped for clues to confirm or deny the fearful report. Along the eastern seaboard, a net of high-frequency direction finders—electronic sleuths from which no U-boat could remain concealed—disclosed that German radio traffic had rapidly increased in the North Atlantic. Although the evidence was inconclusive, Naval Intelligence took this development as an indication that U-boats, after a long lull, had returned to their one-time happy hunting grounds and were preparing a sneak buzzbomb attack on New York and Washington.

So, on the gray morning of January 8, 1945, a flock of reporters, pencils and notepads at the ready, hovered around Admiral Jonas Ingram, commander of the Eastern Sea Frontier, in his wardroom aboard a warship in New York harbor. The scribes had come for what Ingram's public-relations staff had promised would be a "historic press conference."

Ingram, a heavyset, flat-nosed old salt who had gained national recognition as football coach at the Naval Academy, was one of the navy's colorful characters—and most outspoken. Seated behind a long table, Ingram said, "Gentlemen, I have reason to assume that the Nazis are getting ready to launch a strategic attack on New York and Washington by robot bombs."[4]

There was a gasp of astonishment from the reporters.

"I am here to tell you that [robot bomb] attacks are not only possible, but probable as well, and that the East Coast is likely to be buzzbombed within the next thirty or sixty days."[5]

Ingram eyed his listeners, then added grimly: "But we're ready for them. The thing to do is not to get excited about it. [The buzzbombs] might knock out a high building or two, might create a fire hazard, and most certainly would cause casualties. But [the buzzbombs] cannot seriously affect the progress of the war."

The hard-nosed Ingram added that "it may be only ten or twelve buzzbombs, but they may come before we can stop them."

"At any rate," the admiral concluded, "I'm springing the cat from the bag to let the Huns know that we are ready for them!"[6]

Admiral Ingram's blunt warning was splashed over newspapers across the nation. A blaring headline in *The New York Times* screamed

ROBOT BOMB ATTACKS HERE HELD POSSIBLE

But after sixty days had passed, citizens, particularly those in New York and Washington, began to breathe easier. The expected buzzbomb attacks had failed to materialize.

Apparently the Americans had been victimized by a gigantic hoax perpetrated by Adolf Hitler, whose Third Reich was teetering on the brink of utter defeat. The fuehrer, no doubt, wanted to enjoy one final horse-laugh on the hated Americans.

Meanwhile in the crumbling Third Reich, Admiral Wilhelm Canaris was being held under protective custody at the Sicherheitspolizei school at Fuerstenberg. But in early 1945 the former Abwehr chief was brought to Gestapo headquarters in the Prinzalbrechstrasse in Berlin, where he was shoehorned into a jail cell with Schwarze Kapelle conspirators. SS Obergruppenfuehrer Heinrich Mueller, chief investigator of the July 20 bomb plot and the Schwarze Kapelle, insisted on personally grilling Canaris.

The cerebral little admiral was far too clever for Mueller, and the interrogation hit a dead end. Then Canaris pulled a major blunder. Confident that a fellow conspirator, Major Werner Schrader, had destroyed them as ordered, Canaris admitted that he had kept diaries. But Schrader had not destroyed the incriminating Canaris diaries; he had committed suicide without burning any of the Schwarze Kapelle's documents that had been placed in his hands for safekeeping.

Mueller sent investigators to Wehrmacht headquarters in Zossen, a Berlin suburb, and inside a large safe they found a mass of documents, including the entire history of the Schwarze Kapelle conspiracy. Fifty-two of the files contained important military information collected by German agents abroad; most of the data had been doctored before being passed along to the Wehrmacht high command.[7]

On the night of April 8, 1945, Wilhelm Canaris was given a kangaroo trial by a "court" and was charged with high treason and conspiracy to murder Adolf Hitler. Found guilty, Canaris asked to be sent to the Russian front to fight as a *Feldgrau* (field gray, the average German soldier). The request was denied, and the admiral was ordered to be hanged immediately. A short time later Gestapo goons savagely beat Canaris, breaking his nose and leaving him a bloody pulp. Alone in his cell and using Morse code, Canaris tapped out on a pipe with a spoon a final message. It was picked up by Lieutenant Colonel H. M. Lunding, former chief of the Danish secret service, who was in an adjoining cell. The enigmatic Canaris, whose entire life had been wrapped in mystery, said over the pipe:

> I die for my country and with a clear conscience . . . I was only doing my duty to my country when I endeavored to oppose Hitler . . . They've broken my nose . . . I die this morning . . . Farewell.[8]

Just before dawn on April 9—twenty-eight days before the end of the war in Europe—Colonel Lunding peeked through a hole in his cell door and saw Canaris being dragged naked down the corridor. Minutes later the admiral was dangling from a meat hook with a piano wire around his neck. It took thirty minutes of excruciating agony for the man who had masterminded Hitler's secret invasion of the United States to die.

On April 26, 1945, with the Third Reich virtually cut in half by Allied forces converging from the west and east, G-men at the Long Island shortwave station beamed the final "Walter Koehler" intelligence report to the Overseas Message Center in the Hamburg suburb of Wohldorf. Located in a huge bunker, the once-bustling facility was operating on emergency generators, for Hamburg had been pounded into rubble and British forces had surrounded the city.

A young Abwehr lieutenant, now the senior watch officer at the Overseas Message Center, sent a reply to Koehler, Germany's last *Grossagenten* in the United States:

> Conditions compel us to suspend communications. But please continue to stand by on schedule once a week. Do not despair. We will look out for you and protect your interests as usual.

Later that day, April 27, orders were received for the Overseas Message Center and its contents to be destroyed. Dynamite charges were set, the Abwehr men dashed away, and minutes later an enormous blast rocked the bunker, collapsing the roof and sending pieces of concrete cascading into the air.

The Abwehr had gone out of business.

Three days later, on April 30, 1945, Russian spearheads were only two blocks away from the bunker at the Reich Chancellory where Adolf Hitler was directing the final defense of Berlin. The fuehrer stuck the muzzle of a Luger pistol into his mouth and pulled the trigger. With that his Third Reich, which he had boasted would last for a thousand years, passed into history.

Espionage Agents Convicted in the United States, 1937–1945*

	Nationality	Nativity	Sentence
John Farnsworth	American	American	4–12 yrs.
Johanna (Jenni) Hofmann	German	German	4 yrs.
Otto Hermann Voss	German	German	6 yrs.
Erich Glaser	German	German	2 yrs.
Guenther Gustav Rumrich	American	American	2 yrs.
Hafis Salich	American	Russian	4 yrs.
Mikhail Nicholas Gorin	Russian	Russian	6 yrs.
Karl Allen Drumond	American	American	2 yrs.
Frederick Joubert Duquesne	American	So. African	18 yrs.
Alfred E. Brochoff	American	German	5 yrs.
Heinrich Clausing	American	German	8 yrs.
Conradin Otto Dold	American	German	10 yrs.
Rudolf Ebeling	American	German	5 yrs.
Heinrich Carl Eilers	American	German	5 yrs.
Paul Fehse	American	German	15 yrs.
Joseph Klein	German	German	5 yrs.

*Data furnished the author by the FBI.

Hartwig Richard Kleiss	American	German	8 yrs.
Hermann W. Lang	American	German	18 yrs.
Rene E. Mezenen	American	French	8 yrs.
Carl Reuper	American	German	16 yrs.
Everett Minster Roeder	American	American	16 yrs.
Paul Alfred Scholz	German	German	16 yrs.
Erwin Wilhelm Siegler	American	German	10 yrs.
Oscar Richard Stabler	American	German	5 yrs.
Lilly Barbara Stein	Austrian	Austrian	10 yrs.
Franz Joseph Stigler	American	German	16 yrs.
Erich Strunk	American	German	10 yrs.
Leo Waalen	German	German	12 yrs.
Adolph H. Walishewsky	American	German	5 yrs.
Else Weustenfeld	American	German	5 yrs.
Axel Wheeler-Hill	American	Russian	15 yrs.
Bertram Wolfgang Zenzinger	So. African	German	8 yrs.
Omer John Oliver	American	American	10 yrs.
Kurt Frederick Ludwig	American	American	20 yrs.
Lucy Rita Boehmler	German	German	5 yrs.
René C. Froelich	American	German	20 yrs.
Helen Pauline Mayer	American	American	15 yrs.
Karl Victor Mueller	American	Austrian	15 yrs.
Hans Helmut Pagel	German	German	15 yrs.
Frederick E. Schlosser	American	American	12 yrs.
Carl Herman Schroetter	American	German	10 yrs.
Paul T. Borchardt	German	German	20 yrs.
Herman T. Green	American	American	3 yrs.
Jacob Deaton	American	American	$50
William Arthur Schuler	American	American	6 yrs.
Hans Helmut Gros	German	American	4 yrs.
Ralph Eugene Boulton	American	American	2 yrs. (probation)
Max Stephan	American	German	Death (commuted)

George John Dasch	American	German	30 yrs.
Ernest Peter Berger	American	German	Life
Herbert Hans Haupt	German	German	Executed
Heinrich Heinck	German	German	Executed
Edward Kerling	German	German	Executed
Hermann Neubauer	German	German	Executed
Richard Quirin	German	German	Executed
Werner Thiel	German	German	Executed
John Edward Pazkowski	American	American	2 yrs. (probation)
Anastase A. Vonsiatsky	American	Russian	5 yrs.
Wolfgang Ebell	American	French	7 yrs.
Kurt Emil Molzahn	American	German	10 yrs. (pardon)
Gerhard Wilhelm Kunze	American	American	15 yrs.
Otto Albert Willumeit	American	French	5 yrs.
Richard Friedrich Fruendt	American	German	15 yrs.
Peter Franz Donay	German	German	15 yrs.
Richard E. Weber	American	German	15 yrs.
Herbert K. Bahr	American	German	30 yrs.
George Gilbert Alton	American	American	2 yrs. (suspended)
Bernard Julius Kuehn	German	German	50 yrs.
William B. Wiese	American	American	10 mos.
George Frederick Bost	American	American	4 yrs.
Paul Herman Grohs	American	German	15 yrs.
Franz Heinrich Grote	American	German	15 yrs.
Paul Luther Black	American	American	1 yr. (probation)
John Roy Horton	American	American	5 yrs. (probation)
John da Silva Purvis	Portuguese	Portuguese	10 yrs.
Frederich Schroeder	American	German	8 yrs.
Karl Kranz	American	German	8 yrs.
Hans Koenig	American	German	8 yrs.

Grace Buchanan-Dineen	Canadian	Canadian	12 yrs.
Theresa Belwens	German	German	20 yrs.
Walter Abt	American	German	10 yrs.
Karl Leonhardt	American	German	10 yrs.
Erma Leonhardt	German	German	5 yrs.
Ernest Fritz Lehmitz	German	German	30 yrs.
Erwin Harry De Spoetter	German	Uruguayan	30 yrs.
Joseph Benedict Lieblein	American	American	2 yrs.
Harry Jack Herrendan	American	American	3 yrs.
Waldemar Othmer	American	German	20 yrs.
Marie Hedwig Koedel	American	American	7½ yrs.
Simon Emil Koedel	American	German	15 yrs.
Wilhelm Albrecht von Rautter	American	German	29 yrs.
Erich Gimpel	German	German	Life
William Curtis Colepaugh	American	American	Life
Gramin M. von Moltke	German	German	4 yrs.
Laurent H. J. Brak	American	Dutch	9 yrs.
Adolf Johann Striepe	German	German	7½ yrs.
Roberto L. Vallecilla	Colombian	Colombian	10 yrs.
Emilio Hernandes	Spanish	Spanish	10 yrs.
Fred W. Thomas	American	American	15 yrs.
Washington Glendale Spiegelberg	American	American	2 yrs.

Notes and Sources

Part One

Chapter 1

1. Major Hugo Sperrle later rose to field marshal in the Luftwaffe and directed the 1940 London blitz.
2. Max Lowenthal, *The Federal Bureau of Investigation* (New York: Sloane, 1950), p. 276.
3. Ladislas Farago, *The Game of the Foxes* (New York: McKay, 1971), p. 26.
4. Leon Turrou, *The Nazi Spy Conspiracy in America* (Freeport, NY: Books for Libraries Press, 1969), p. 38.
5. Details (including quotes) about Wilhelm Lonkowski's years as a spy in the United States were pieced together by FBI interrogations of those involved in his ring.

Chapter 2

1. Leon Turrou, *The Nazi Spy Conspiracy in America* (Freeport, NY: Books for Libraries Press, 1969), pp. 135–136.
2. In 1938 the FBI pieced together the Griebl-Lonkowski connection through interrogations of Dr. Ignatz Griebl.
3. FBI interrogation reports, 1938.

4. Nazi Conspiracy of Aggression (NCA), Nuremberg trial documents, vol. 7, p. 333, National Archives.
5. Ibid., vol. 6, p. 1018.
6. Peter Fleming, *Invasion 1940* (New York: Simon & Schuster, 1957), p. 194.
7. Ladislas Farago, *The Game of the Foxes* (New York: McKay, 1971), p. 27.
8. Turrou, *The Nazi Spy Conspiracy*, pp. 140–141.
9. Senta de Wanger's involvement in Nazi spy activities was uncovered much later through FBI investigations.
10. Turrou, *The Nazi Spy Conspiracy*, p. 141.

Chapter 3

1. Leon Turrou, *The Nazi Spy Conspiracy in America* (Freeport, NY: Books for Libraries Press, 1969), p. 150.
2. Ellis M. Zacharias, *Secret Missions* (New York: Putnam, 1946), p. 150.
3. Turrou, *The Nazi Spy Conspiracy*, p. 153.
4. Ibid., p. 154.
5. Ibid.
6. Zacharias, *Secret Missions*, p. 152.
7. Ladislas Farago, *The Game of the Foxes* (New York: McKay, 1971), p. 31.
8. Zacharias, *Secret Missions*, p. 152.
9. Ibid., p. 153.
10. Ulrich Hausmann was forced to flee the United States a short time later when his activities were unmasked. He was given a job in the Air Ministry in Berlin.
11. Edwin T. Layton, *And I Was There* (New York: Morrow, 1985), p. 79.

Chapter 4

1. Details of Dr. Ignatz Griebl's and Kate Moog's 1937 visit to Germany came from FBI interrogations of the pair.
2. Quotes in this chapter were those recalled by Dr. Griebl and Kate Moog in FBI interrogations.
3. Griebl identified Admiral Wilhelm Canaris to the FBI as "Colonel Busch." Conceivably Canaris may have donned a colonel's uniform for the meeting in order to confuse

Griebl. However, through Griebl's description, the FBI would conclude that "Colonel Busch" had been the Abwehr chief.

4. Leon Turrou, *The Nazi Spy Conspiracy in America* (Freeport, NY: Books for Libraries Press, 1969), p. 9.
5. Ibid.
6. Ladislas Farago, *The Game of the Foxes* (New York: McKay, 1971), p. 36.
7. Ibid
8. The flood of reports on U.S. missile experiments that Gustav Guellich sent to Germany no doubt greatly aided German scientists in rapidly perfecting the V-2 missiles, which would be showered on London and elsewhere in England in 1944 and 1945.

Chapter 5

1. *Time* magazine, October 9, 1937.
2. Burke Wilkinson, ed., *Cry Spy!* (Englewood Cliffs, NJ: Bradbury, 1969), p. 68.
3. Ladislas Farago, *The Game of the Foxes* (New York: McKay, 1971), p. 43.
4. Postwar interview by historian Farago with Nickolaus Ritter.
5. Additional details of the Norden bombsight theft were learned by reporters Charles Wighton and Guenter Peis in postwar interviews with Major General Erwin von Lahousen, who was Admiral Canaris's right-hand man.
6. Farago, *The Game of the Foxes*, p. 44.
7. David Kahn, *Hitler's Spies* (New York: Macmillan, 1975), p. 329.
8. Wilkinson, *Cry Spy!*, p. 71.
9. Ibid., p. 73.
10. Ibid.

Chapter 6

1. Eleanor Böhme was in no way involved in Nazi spying.
2. Leon Turrou, *The Nazi Spy Conspiracy in America* (Freeport, NY: Books for Libraries Press, 1969), pp. 191–193.
3. Details of efforts by Böning and Rossberg to obtain the al-

leged Panama Canal defense plans were uncovered by the FBI in interrogations of the principals.

4. Ditto the role of Rudolf Bittenberg.
5. Schlenckenbag may or may not have been the true name of the Hamburg Gestapo chief. Karl Herrmann told the FBI that he knew the man by that name.
6. FBI Agent Leon Turrou uncovered details of the Manville-Strassmann "plot" through painstaking investigation.

Chapter 7

1. Café Hindenburg was named after the German World War I hero, Field Marshal Paul von Hindenburg, who later became president of postwar Germany.
2. The luxury liner *Gniesenau* is not to be confused with a later German warship of the same name.
3. After her arrest by the FBI, Jenni Hofmann gave details on how she had been recruited into spying.
4. Michael Sayers and Albert E. Kahn, *Sabotage!* (New York: Harper, 1942), p. 15.
5. Ibid., p. 18.
6. *New York Times*, April 6, 1936.
7. Guenther Rumrich gave his business address because he apparently did not want the Nazis to know that he lived in the Bronx, a predominately Jewish area.
8. Rumrich's activities as a Nazi masterspy were obtained from him by the FBI after his arrest.
9. Leon Turrou, *The Nazi Spy Conspiracy in America* (Freeport, NY: Books for Libraries Press, 1969), p. 58.

Chapter 8

1. America's abhorrence of "spying on neighbors" denied the FBI the right to open mail of suspects under carefully controlled conditions.
2. Mrs. Jennie Wallace Jordan was given a four-year prison term.
3. Leon Turrou, *The Nazi Spy Conspiracy in America* (Freeport, NY: Books for Libraries Press, 1969), pp. 46–47.
4. Details of Guenther Rumrich's passport-blank caper are in FBI interrogation reports.

Chapter 9

1. *New York Times*, Feb. 17, 1938.
2. Ladislas Farago, *The Game of the Foxes* (New York: McKay, 1971), p. 32.
3. Leon Turrou, *The Nazi Spy Conspiracy in America* (Freeport, NY: Books for Libraries Press, 1969), p. 64.
4. Ibid.
5. Unmasked, Karl Schlueter was assigned to battleship duty.

Chapter 10

1. Leon Turrou, *The Nazi Spy Conspiracy in America* (Freeport, NY: Books for Libraries Press, 1969), p. 130.
2. FBI interrogation of Karl Herrmann.
3. FBI interrogation of Fritz Rossberg.
4. Leon Turrou, *The Nazi Spy Conspiracy in America*, p. 227.
5. Ibid, p. 235.
6. When Dieckhoff returned home after Roosevelt and Hitler recalled ambassadors, he concocted propaganda schemes for use in the United States.

Chapter 11

1. Leon G. Turrou, *The Nazi Spy Conspiracy in America* (Freeport, NY: Books for Libraries Press, 1969), p. 264.
2. Marshall Cavendish, *Illustrated History of World War II*, vol. 1 (New York: Cavendish, 1969), p. 4.
3. John Roy Carlson, *The Plotters* (Chicago: Regnery, 1943), p. 113.
4. John Roy Carlson, *Undercover: My Four Years in the Nazi Underworld of America* (Chicago: Regnery, 1943), p. 417.
5. Ibid., p. 418.
6. Ibid.
7. Ezra Bowen, ed., *This Fabulous Century, 1930–1940* (New York: Time/Life Books, 1969), p. 39.
8. *New York Times*, December 3, 1938.
9. *Time*, December 7, 1938.
10. While the trial was in progress, FBI agent Leon Turrou, who had been putting in twelve-hour days cracking the

case, resigned from the Bureau upon the advice of his doctor.

11. Ladislas Farago, *The Game of the Foxes* (New York: McKay, 1971), p. 66.

Part Two

Chapter 12

1. Michael Sayers and Albert E. Kahn, *Sabotage!* (New York: Harper, 1942), p. 12.
2. Don Whitehead, *The FBI Story* (New York: Random House, 1956), p. 233.
3. Ibid., p. 232.
4. The FBI later learned details of the General Hermann Goering "peace" scheme from Princess Stefanie.
5. The FBI has not revealed its "source" for keeping track of the daily activities of Fritz Wiedemann and Princess Stefanie. Wiretaps would be a likely method.
6. In mid-1942 the Chemical Marketing Company was seized by the U.S. Treasury Department's Foreign Property Control Division.
7. Dr. Ferdinand Kertess's activities were later revealed in public hearings by a congressional committee. In 1941 Dr. Friedrich Auhagen was sentenced to two and a half years in prison for failure to register as an agent of a foreign power.
8. *American Mercury*, December 1944, p. 41.
9. Ibid., p. 42.
10. Stanley E. Hilton, *Hitler's Secret War in South America* (Baton Rouge: Louisiana State University Press, 1981), p. 18.
11. Ibid., p. 17.
12. *American Mercury*, December 1944, p. 43.

Chapter 13

1. *Signal*, German Armed Forces Magazine, June 1939.
2. Michael Sayers and Albert E. Kahn, *Sabotage!* (New York: Harper, 1942), p. 154.

3. Ibid., p. 155.
4. *Harper's*, July 1942, p. 9.
5. SD Chief Reinhard Tristan Eugen Heydrich was assassinated by two Czechosolovakian underground fighters in Prague on May 27, 1942.
6. After Germany and the United States went to war, the SD packed Merry Fahrney off to Argentina. There she spent the rest of the war spying for Germany, according to the FBI.
7. Ladislas Farago, *The Game of the Foxes* (New York: McKay, 1971), p. 356.
8. Berle took copious notes of the Roosevelt-Davis talks. His original notes are in the Yale University library.
9. Beatrice B. Berle and Travis Jacobs, eds., *Navigating the Rapids* (New York: Harcourt Brace Jovanovich, 1973), p. 173.
10. Ladislas Farago, *The Game of the Foxes*, p. 356.

Chapter 14

1. Max Lowenthal, *The Federal Bureau of Investigation* (New York: Sloane, 1950), p. 425.
2. Ibid., p. 426.
3. Ezra Bowen, ed., *This Fabulous Century, 1930–1940* (New York: Time/Life Books, 1969), p. 112.
4. Ibid., p. 113.
5. As hotbeds of intrigue, only the Nazi embassies in Romania and Argentina rivaled Washington's.
6. Ladislas Farago, *The Game of the Foxes* (New York: McKay, 1971), pp. 472–473.
7. Michael Sayers and Albert E. Kahn, *Sabotage!* (New York: Harper, 1942), p. 214.
8. Reader's Digest Assn., *Secrets and Spies* (Pleasantville, NY: Reader's Digest, 1964), p. 175.
9. David Kahn, *Hitler's Spies* (New York: Macmillan, 1975), p. 334.
10. William L. Shirer, *The Rise and Fall of the Third Reich* (New York: Simon & Schuster, 1960), p. 684.
11. Ibid.

12. Documents on German Foreign Police, 1918–1945, Thomsen messages, DGFP, Series D.
13. Farago, *The Game of the Foxes*, p. 437.

Chapter 15

1. Michael Sayers and Albert E. Kahn, *Sabotage!* (New York: McKay, 1971), p. 24.
2. Reader's Digest Assn., *Secrets and Spies* (Pleasantville, NY: Reader's Digest, 1964), p. 76.
3. Alan Hynd, *Passport to Treason* (New York: McBride, 1943), p. 30.
4. Sayers and Kahn, *Sabotage!*, p. 77.
5. Hynd, *Password to Treason*, p. 18.
6. Ibid., p. 21.
7. Ibid., p. 22.
8. FBI interview of William G. Sebold, 1940.
9. FBI records.

Chapter 16

1. FBI interviews with William G. Sebold, 1940.
2. Alan Hynd, *Passport to Treason* (New York: McBride, 1943), p. 47. *Normandie* and the British *Queen Elizabeth* and *Queen Mary* were the world's largest ocean liners.
3. Hynd, *Passport to Treason*, p. 55.
4. Ibid.
5. Don Whitehead, *The FBI Story* (New York: Random House, 1956), p. 166.

Chapter 17

1. FBI records.
2. Don Whitehead, *The FBI Story* (New York: Random House, 1956), p. 169.
3. Henry J. Taylor, *Men and Power* (New York: Mead Dodd, 1946), pp. 49–50.
4. Thomsen messages, DGFP, IX, p. 975, National Archives.
5. David Kahn, *The Codebreakers* (New York: Macmillan), 1978, p. 494.

6. Ladislas Farago, *The Game of the Foxes* (New York: McKay, 1971), p. 472.
7. Ibid., p. 473.
8. Russian "historians" have claimed Josef Stalin had not been fooled by Adolf Hitler's Treaty of Friendship but had signed the document to buy time to build up his armies.
9. FBI press release, April 18, 1940.
10. *Times* of London, May 13, 1940. Winston Churchill address in House of Commons.
11. The New York newspaper apparently published the speech because it was "reporting the news," not due to Nazi sympathies.
12. DGFP, IX, pp. 558–559, National Archives.
13. William L. Shirer, *The Rise and Fall of the Third Reich* (New York: Simon & Schuster, 1960), p. 748.
14. Thomsen identified the congressman as Thorkelson of Montana.
15. Shirer, *Rise and Fall of the Third Reich*, p. 749.
16. Winston Churchill, *Their Finest Hour*, pp. 259–260.
17. *Washington Post*, July 2, 1940.
18. Farago, *The Game of the Foxes*, p. 312.

Chapter 18

1. Don Whitehead, *The FBI Story* (New York: Random House, 1956), p. 212.
2. Professor Klaus Mehnert also predicted in his intelligence reports that thousands of Japanese-Americans in Hawaii would stage an uprising if Japan struck. No uprising would occur.
3. Ellis M. Zacharias, *Secret Missions* (New York: Putnam, 1946), p. 193.
4. Admiral Yamamoto had been opposed to war with the United States, although he planned the Pearl Harbor attack. Yamamoto was killed on April 18, 1943, when his aircraft was shot down by Marine Corps fighter planes based on Guadalcanal after "Magic" intercepts revealed the admiral's flight route to the Americans.
5. Zacharias, *Secret Missions*, p. 219.
6. In mid-October 1940 the U.S. Army Reserve captain

tipped off Dr. Scholz that Scholz was about to be charged publicly with espionage. Scholz grabbed the first boat for Germany.

7. In 1941 the lawyer was convicted of failing to register as an agent of a foreign power (Germany), was fined $1,000 and given a two-year suspended sentence.

8. Stanley E. Hilton, *Hitler's Secret War in South America* (Baton Rouge: Louisiana State University Press, 1981), p. 200.

Chapter 19

1. Testimony by Mrs. Phyllis Spielman at 1942 trial of propagandist George Viereck in Washington, D.C.
2. Testimony of George Hill at 1942 trial of George Viereck in Washington, D.C.
3. Ibid.
4. Ibid.
5. Ibid.
6. *New York Times*, June 25, 1940.
7. *Washington Post*, June 27, 1940.
8. Dr. Hans Thomsen messages, DGFP, IX, pp. 976–981, National Archives.
9. *Chicago Tribune*, July 15, 1940.
10. Alan Bullock, *Hitler—A Study in Tyranny* (New York: Harper & Row, 1963), p. 592.
11. Ladislas Farago, *The Game of the Foxes* (New York: McKay, 1971), p. 312.
12. Alan Hynd, *Passport to Treason* (New York: McBride, 1943), p. 91.
13. Ezra Bowen, ed., *This Fabulous Century, 1940–1950* (New York: Time/Life Books, 1969), p. 23.
14. *St. Louis Post-Dispatch*, November 18, 1940.
15. *Time*, November 18, 1940.
16. Winston Churchill, *The Second World War*, vol. 2 (Boston: Houghton-Mifflin, 1948), p. 493.

Chapter 20

1. Don Whitehead, *The FBI Story* (New York: Random House, 1956), p. 234.

2. The FBI learned details of the Mark Hopkins Hotel discussions from an unidentified confidential source.
3. Princess Stefanie would be taken into custody after the United States entered the war and held until its conclusion.
4. David Kahn, *The Codebreakers* (New York: Macmillan, 1978), p. 514.
5. *Harper's*, June 1942, p. 10.
6. Ibid.
7. For no apparent reason, the Taft Hotel in Manhattan had been a favorite lodging place for Nazi spies, going back to 1934.

Chapter 21

1. *Harper's*, June 1942, p. 7.
2. Testimony at Ludwig espionage trial, February 1942, New York City.
3. Ibid.
4. *Harper's*, June 1942, p. 10.
5. Ibid., p. 12.
6. Edwin P. Hoyt, *U-Boats Offshore* (New York: Stein & Day, 1978), pp. 70–71.

Chapter 22

1. Until his death, FBI chief J. Edgar Hoover maintained that not a single case of enemy sabotage occurred in the United States just before and during the war. However, U.S. Intelligence agencies do not agree with that viewpoint.
2. Henry L. Stimson diary, February 12, 1941.
3. Gordon W. Prange, *Pearl Harbor* (New York: McGraw-Hill, 1986), p. 306.
4. Ibid.
5. FBI records.
6. *Harper's*, December 1944, p. 93.
7. Alan Hynd, *Passport to Treason* (New York: McBride, 1943), p. 131.
8. A. A. Hoehling, *Homefront, USA* (New York: Crowell, 1966), p. 17.

9. Michael Sayers and Albert E. Kahn, *Sabotage!* (New York: Harper, 1942), p. 101.

Part Three

Chapter 23

1. The FBI has never released the "shocking information" that would place the nation in peril and involve "prominent Americans."
2. Edwin P. Hoyt, *U-Boats Offshore* (New York: Stein & Day, 1978), pp. 72–73.
3. Ibid.
4. Arch Whitehouse, *Subs and Submariners* (Garden City, NY: Doubleday, 1964), p. 143.
5. Richard Warnecke was no doubt an alias. He suddenly vanished when Germany and the United States went to war.
6. Ladislas Farago, *The Game of the Foxes* (New York: McKay, 1971), pp. 300–301.
7. Alan Hynd, *Passport to Treason* (New York: McBride, 1943), p. 178.
8. Ibid.

Chapter 24

1. Ezra Bowen, ed., *This Fabulous Century, 1940–1950* (New York: Time/Life Books, 1969), p. 25.
2. *Washington Post*, March 13, 1941.
3. *Harper's*, December 1944, p. 93.
4. Later, U.S. military officers were astonished over the thoroughness of teenager Lucy Boehmler's file of information on U.S. defense facilities.
5. FBI files.
6. Michael Sayers and Albert E. Kahn, *Sabotage!* (New York: Harper, 1942), p. 101.
7. For several weeks Winston Churchill had known that Hitler was preparing to attack his Friendship Treaty partner, Russia. Churchill had gained the knowledge through England's supersecret Ultra decoding apparatus. Suspi-

cious of a trick, Stalin brushed off the British leader's
warning.

8. Winston Churchill, *The Second World War*, vol. 3 (Boston:
   Houghton-Mifflin, 1949), p. 331.
9. FBI transcript of electronic surveillance of William G.
   Sebold's "research office."
10. *Time*, September 29, 1941, p. 14.
11. Evidence presented at 1941 trial of Fritz Duquesne's spy
    ring.
12. *Harper's*, June 1942, p. 12.
13. Ibid.
14. Evidence presented at 1942 trial of Kurt Ludwig's spy ring.

Chapter 25

1. *St. Louis Post-Dispatch*, July 2, 1941.
2. *Time*, June 9, 1941, p. 17.
3. FBI files.
4. *Congressional Record*, vol. 87, pt. 6, August 1, 1941, p.
   6571.
5. Ibid., August 4, 1941, p. 6682.
6. Edwin P. Hoyt, *U-Boats Offshore* (New York: Stein & Day,
   1978), p. 75.
7. *Harper's*, June 1942, p. 14.
8. Testimony at 1942 trial of Kurt Ludwig spy ring.
9. Ibid.
10. *Harper's*, June 1942, p. 20.
11. Testimony by Paul Borchardt's landlady at 1942 trial of
    Kurt Ludwig's spy network.

Chapter 26

1. John C. Masterman, *The Double-Cross System* (New
   Haven, CT: Yale University Press, 1972), p. 56.
2. Dusko Popov, *Spy/Counterspy* (New York: Grossett & Dunlap, 1974), p. 163.
3. Edwin T. Layton, *And I Was There* (New York: Morrow,
   1985), p. 105.
4. After the war, J. Edgar Hoover wrote that FBI technicians
   had discovered the secret to the microdot mystery, a viewpoint at odds with that of Dusko Popov.

5. Popov, *Spy/Counterspy*, p. 168.

6. Anthony Cave Brown, *Bodyguard of Lies* (New York: Harper & Row, 1975), p. 67.

7. Popov, *Spy/Counterspy*, p. 171.

8. John F. Bratzel and Leslie B. Rout, Jr., "Pearl Harbor: Micro-dots and J. Edgar Hoover," *American Historical Review*, December 1982, pp. 1346–1347.

9. "Hoover Shared Spy Disclosures on Pearl Harbor," *Pittsburg Post-Gazette*, April 1, 1972.

10. *Reader's Digest*, April 1946, p. 4.

11. During the war period, 1939–1945, the FBI investigated 19,649 suspected sabotage cases.

12. *Time*, October 27, 1941.

13. *New York Times*, September 4, 1941.

14. Ibid., September 10, 1941.

15. The FBI has remained silent over the fate of Julius Georg Bergmann.

Chapter 27

1. Documents on German Foreign Policy Series, U.S. State Department, National Archives.

2. William L. Shirer, *The Rise and Fall of the Third Reich* (New York: Simon & Schuster, 1960), p. 896.

3. Ibid., p. 897.

4. *New York Times*, December 8, 1941.

5. Lee Kennett, *For the Duration* (New York: Scribner's, 1985), p. 68.

6. *Rolla (MO) Daily News*, December 15, 1941.

7. Kennett, *For the Duration*, p. 69.

8. *Time*, February 23, 1942, p. 17.

9. Ibid.

10. John Maxtone-Graham, *The Only Way to Cross* (New York: Collier, 1972), p. 378.

11. A. A. Hoehling, *Home Front, USA* (New York: Crowell, 1966), p. 27.

12. In 1946 an accused German murderer confessed to U.S. military police officers that he had set fire to the *Normandie*. However, his claim was discounted.

13. John Roy Carlson, *The Plotters* (Chicago: Regnery, 1943), p. 409.

14. Ibid.

Chapter 28

1. Don Whitehead, *The FBI Story* (New York: Random House, 1956), p. 239.
2. Ibid., p. 240.
3. Later the FBI said that Count Vonsiatsky's wealthy wife was not involved in her husband's machinations.
4. The sabotage operation was named for Franz Pastorius, one of the pioneer German immigrants to the United States.
5. George J. Dasch, *Eight Spies Against America* (New York: McBride, 1949), p. 37.
6. Ibid., p. 39.

Chapter 29

1. George J. Dasch, *Eight Spies Against America* (New York: McBride, 1949), p. 96.
2. Later Dasch had a different version of his encounter with the Coast Guardsman. He said he had gotten close to the sailor to illuminate his own face with a flashlight beam so that the sailor could later testify that Dasch had gone out of his way to keep him from being harmed.
3. Don Whitehead, *The FBI Story* (New York: Random House, 1956), p. 203.
4. FBI interrogation of George Dasch, June 1942.
5. FBI memorandum, June 19, 1942.
6. Whitehead, *The FBI Story*, pp. 204–205.
7. Colonel Royall became a postwar secretary of the army.
8. Reader's Digest Assn., *Secrets and Spies* (Pleasantville, NY: Reader's Digest, 1964), pp. 190–191.
9. Arch Whitehouse, *Espionage and Counterespionage* (Garden City, NY: Doubleday, 1964), pp. 149–150.
10. Ladislas Farago, *The Game of the Foxes* (New York: McKay, 1971), pp. 502–505.

Chapter 30

1. U-boat skipper Reinhard Hardegen's report to his home base in France was possibly done with tongue in cheek. Even with powerful infrared binoculars, his claim of seeing dancers atop the Astor Hotel is open to conjecture.

2. Jean Noll, *The Admiral's Wolfpack* (Garden City, NY: Doubleday, 1974), p. 138.

3. Ladislas Farago, *The Tenth Fleet* (New York: Obolensky, 1962), p. 46.

4. Joseph Curran testified before the House Committee on the Merchant Marine and Fisheries, March 25, 1942.

5. Anthony Cave Brown, *Bodyguard of Lies* (New York: Harper & Row, 1975), p. 282.

6. William B. Breuer, *Operation Torch* (New York: St. Martin's, 1986), p. 9.

7. *Time*, July 14, 1942.

8. John Roy Carlson, *The Plotters* (Chicago: Regnery, 1943), p. 252.

9. General Mark W. Clark, *Calculated Risk* (New York: Harper & Brothers, 1951), p. 172.

10. General Mark W. Clark to author in 1983 before the general's death in early 1984.

11. David Kahn, *The Codebreakers* (New York: Macmillan, 1978), p. 547.

12. Ibid., p. 545.

13. *Reader's Digest*, March 1946, pp. 3–4.

14. Ladislas Farago, *The Game of the Foxes* (New York: McKay, 1971), p. 647.

15. Walter Koehler may or may not have been the nuclear spy's real name. That was how he had been listed in the Abwehr's registry.

Chapter 31

1. Reader's Digest Assn., *Secrets and Spies* (Pleasantville, NY: Reader's Digest, 1964), p. 233.

2. Anthony Cave Brown, *Bodyguard of Lies* (New York: Harper & Row, 1975), p. 537.

3. After the war J. Edgar Hoover wrote that the Dutch jewelry bagman sincerely cooperated with the FBI.

4. Reader's Digest, *Secrets and Spies*, p. 285.
5. *American Magazine*, May 1946, p. 9.
6. Arch Whitehouse, *Espionage and Counterespionage* (Garden City, NY: Doubleday, 1964), pp. 150–153.
7. Many Americans felt that the sailor had "beaten the rap" by faking mental illness.
8. Anthony Cave Brown, *Bodyguard of Lies* (New York: Harper & Row, 1975), pp. 506–507.
9. Ibid.
10. Winston Churchill has been given credit for christening the operation Overlord.
11. Brown, *Bodyguard of Lies*, p. 538.

Chapter 32

1. John Wheeler-Bennett, *Nemesis of Power* (New York: Macmillan, 1964), pp. 640–641.
2. Anthony Cave Brown, *Bodyguard of Lies* (New York: Harper & Row, 1975), p. 839.
3. Walter Schellenberg, *The Labyrinth* (New York: Harper, 1956), p. 410.
4. Ibid., p. 412.
5. *New York Times*, October 24, 1944.
6. Ibid., January 2, 1945.
7. David Kahn, *Hitler's Spies* (New York: Macmillan, 1975), p. 13.
8. *New York Herald Tribune*, January 2, 1945.
9. Don Whitehead, *The FBI Story* (New York: Random House, 1956), p. 206.
10. *New York Herald Tribune*, January 3, 1945.
11. *New York Times*, February 8, 1945.
12. Whitehead, *The FBI Story*, p. 206.
13. FBI report on interrogation of Erich Gimpel, January 2, 1945.

Chapter 33

1. Whatever may have been Colonel Skorzeny's orders, he never tried to reach Paris. In fact, he never got beyond the German front lines during the Battle of the Bulge.

2. Don Whitehead, *The FBI Story* (New York: Random House, 1956), p. 241.
3. During these tense days of extremely tight White House security, President Roosevelt regularly asked his longtime secretary, Grace Tulley, "Well, have Mike Riley's [Secret Service] boys frisked you yet today?"
4. *New York Herald Tribune*, January 9, 1945.
5. Ibid.
6. Ibid.
7. Karl Bartz, *The Downfall of the German Secret Service* (London: Kimber, 1956), p. 163.
8. Ian Colvin, *Masterspy* (London: Weidenfeld & Nicolson, 1953), p. 248.

Bibliography

Books

Abshagen, Karl Heinz. *Canaris*. London: Hutchinson, 1956.

Adams, Henry H. *Harry Hopkins*. New York: Putnam, 1977.

Bartz, Karl. *The Downfall of the German Secret Service*. London: Kimber, 1956.

Bauer, Eddy. *Encyclopedia of World War II*. New York: Cavendish, 1970.

Beard, Charles A. *President Roosevelt and the Coming of the War*. New Haven: Yale University Press, 1947.

Berle, Beatrice B., and Jacobs, Travis, eds. *Navigating the Rapids*. New York: Harcourt Brace Jovanovich, 1973.

Blackstock, Paul W. *Agents of Deceit, Fraud, Forgeries and Political Intrigue*. Chicago: Regnery, 1966.

Bowen, Ezra, ed. *This Fabulous Century, 1930–1940*. New York: Time/Life Books, 1969.

———. *This Fabulous Century, 1940–1950*. New York: Time/Life Books, 1969.

Breuer, William B. *Operation Torch*. New York: St. Martin's, 1986.

Brown, Anthony Cave. *Bodyguard of Lies*. New York: Harper & Row, 1975.

Brownlow, Donald G. *The Accused*. New York: Vantage, 1968.

Bullock, Alan. *Hitler—A Study in Tyranny.* New York: Harper & Row, 1963.

Burns, James M. *Roosevelt: The Soldier of Freedom.* New York: Harcourt Brace Jovanovich, 1970.

Cameron, Norman, and Stevens, R. H. *Hitler's Table Talk.* London: Weidenfeld & Nicolson, 1973.

Carlson, John Roy. *The Plotters.* Chicago: Regnery, 1943.

———. *Undercover: My Four Years in the Nazi Underworld of America.* Chicago: Regnery, 1943.

Carse, Robert. *Dunkirk 1940.* Englewood Cliffs, N.J.: Prentice-Hall, 1970.

Cavendish, Marshall. *Illustrated History of World War II.* New York: Cavendish, 1969.

Churchill, Winston S. *The Second World War,* vols. 1–6. Boston: Houghton-Mifflin, 1948–1953.

———. *Their Finest Hour. The Second World War,* vol. 2

Clark, General Mark W. *Calculated Risk.* New York: Harper & Brothers, 1951.

Cole, Wayne S. *Charles A. Lindbergh and the Battle Against American Intervention in World War II.* New York: Harcourt Brace Jovanovich, 1974.

Colvin, Ian. *Chief of Intelligence.* London: Gollancz, 1951.

———. *Masterspy.* London: Weidenfield & Nicolson, 1953.

Corson, William R. *The Armies of Ignorance: The Rise of the American Intelligence Empire.* New York: Dial Press, 1977.

Dasch, George J. *Eight Spies Against America.* New York: McBride, 1949.

Deacon, Richard. *History of the British Secret Service.* New York: Taplinger, 1969.

Doenitz, Grossadmiral Karl. *Memoirs.* Cleveland: World Press, 1959.

Dulles, Allen W. *Great True Spy Stories.* New York: Harper & Row, 1968.

Eisenhower, General Dwight D. *Crusade in Europe.* New York: Doubleday, 1948.

Farago, Ladislas. *The Tenth Fleet.* New York: Obolensky, 1962.

———. *The Game of the Foxes.* New York: McKay, 1971.

Fleming, Peter. *Invasion 1940.* New York: Simon & Schuster, 1957.

Frank, Wolfgang. *The Sea Wolves.* New York: Rinehart, 1955.

Gaevernitz, Gero V. *They Almost Killed Hitler.* New York: Macmillan, 1947.

Gimpel, Erich, with Will Berthold. *Spy for Germany.* London: Robert Hall, 1957.

Goebbels, Paul Josef. *The Goebbels Diaries.* Garden City, New York: Doubleday, 1948.

Hilton, Stanley E. *Hitler's Secret War in South America.* Baton Rouge: Louisiana State University Press, 1981.

Hitler, Adolf. *Hitler's Secret Conversations.* New York: Farrar, Straus & Young, 1953.

Hoeling, A. A. *Home Front, USA.* New York: Crowell, 1966.

Hoyt, Edwin P. *U-Boats Offshore.* New York: Stein & Day, 1978.

Hull, Cordell. *The Memoirs of Cordell Hull.* New York: Macmillan, 1948.

Hyde, H. Montgomery. *The Story of the British Intelligence Center in New York During World War II.* New York: Farrar Straus, 1962.

Hynd, Alan. *Passport to Treason.* New York: McBride, 1943.

Ingersoll, Ralph. *Top Secret.* New York: Harcourt, Brace, 1946.

Kahn, David. *Hitler's Spies.* New York: Macmillan, 1975.

———. *The Codebreakers.* New York: Macmillan, 1978.

Kennett, Lee. *For the Duration.* New York: Scribner's, 1985.

Layton, Edwin T. *And I Was There.* New York: Morrow, 1985.

Leverkuehn, Paul. *Abwehr: German Military Intelligence.* London: Weidenfeld & Nicolson, 1954.

Lewin, Ronald. *Ultra Goes to War.* New York: McGraw-Hill, 1978.

Lindbergh, Charles A. *The Wartime Journals of Charles A. Lindbergh.* New York: Harcourt Brace Jovanovich, 1974.

Lowenthal, Max. *The Federal Bureau of Investigation.* New York: Sloane, 1950.

Macintyre, Donald. *The Battle of the Atlantic.* New York: Macmillan, 1961.

Manvell, Roger, and Fraenkel, Heinrich. *The Canaris Conspiracy.* New York: McKay, 1969.

Masterman, John C. *The Double-Cross System.* New Haven, CT: Yale University Press, 1972.

Maxtone-Graham, John. *The Only Way to Cross.* New York: Collier, 1972.

Morison, Etling E. *Turmoil and Tradition: A Study of the Life and Times of Henry L. Stimson.* Boston: Houghton Mifflin, 1960.

Morison, Samuel E. *The Battle of the Atlantic.* Boston: Little, Brown, 1947.

Noll, Jean. *The Admiral's Wolf Pack.* Garden City, NY: Doubleday, 1974.

Papen, Franz von. *Memoirs.* London: Andre Deutsch, 1952.

Pogue, Forest C. *George C. Marshall: Ordeal and Hope, 1939–1942.* New York: Viking, 1973.

Popov, Dusko. *Spy/Counterspy.* New York: Grossett & Dunlap, 1974.

Prange, Gordon W. *Pearl Harbor.* New York: McGraw-Hill, 1986.

Rachlis, Eugene. *They Came to Kill.* New York: Random House, 1961.

Reader's Digest Association. *Secrets and Spies.* Pleasantville, NY: Reader's Digest, 1964.

Reiss, Curt. *Total Espionage.* New York: Putnam, 1941.

Ribbentrop, Joachim von. *The Ribbentrop Memoirs.* London: Weidenfeld & Nicolson, 1954.

Rothfels, Hans. *The German Opposition to Hitler.* New York: Regnery, 1948.

Sayers, Michael, and Kahn, Albert E. *Sabotage!* New York: Harper, 1942.

Schellenberg, Walter. *The Labyrinth.* New York: Harper, 1956.

Shirer, William L. *The Rise and Fall of the Third Reich.* New York: Simon & Schuster, 1960.

Singer, Kurt. *Spies and Traitors of World War II.* Englewood Cliff, NJ: Prentice-Hall, 1945.

Standley, William H., and Ageton, Arthur A. *Admiral Ambassador to Russia.* Chicago: Regnery, 1952.

Stimson, Henry L., and Bundy, McGeorge. *On Active Service in Peace and War.* New York: Harper, 1947.

Taylor, Henry J. *Men and Power.* New York: Dodd Mead, 1946.

Turrou, Leon G. *The Nazi Spy Conspiracy in America.* Freeport, NY: Books for Libraries Press, 1969.

Waters, John M. *Bloody Winter.* Princeton, NJ: D. Van Nostrand, 1967.

Watson, Mark S. *United States Army in World War II, Prewar Plans and Preparations.* Washington, D.C.: History Division, Department of the Army, 1950.

Wheeler-Bennett, John. *Nemesis of Power.* New York: Macmillan, 1964.

Whitehead, Don. *The FBI Story.* New York: Random House, 1956.

Whitehouse, Arch. *Espionage and Counterespionage.* Garden City, NY: Doubleday, 1964.

———. *Subs and Submariners.* Garden City, NY: Doubleday, 1964.

Wilkinson, Burke, ed. *Cry Spy!* Englewood Cliffs, NJ: Bradbury, 1969.

Zacharias, Ellis M. *Secret Missions.* New York: Putnam, 1946.

Magazines

The American, American Heritage, American Historical Review, American Legion, American Mercury, Blue Book, Collier's, Harper's, Liberty, Life, Newsweek, Official Detective Stories, Reader's Digest, Saturday Evening Post, Signal, Time.

Newspapers

Chicago Tribune, Indianapolis Star, Milwaukee Sentinel, New York Daily Mirror, New York Herald Tribune, New York Times, Pittsburgh Post-Gazette, Raleigh News and Observer, Rolla (MO) Daily News, St. Louis Globe-Democrat, St. Louis Post-Dispatch, St. Louis Star-Times, Washington Post, Stars and Stripes (European edition).

Miscellaneous Documents

FBI interrogation reports, data on convictions for espionage (1937–1945), and assorted documents relating to World War II–Era espionage and sedition.

"German Espionage and Sabotage Against the United States," U.S. Office of Naval Intelligence Review, January 1946.

"Impressions and Experiences of the Military and Air Attaches at the German Embassy in Washington D.C. During the Years 1933–1941," General Friedrich von Boetticher, National Archives.

"German Foreign Policy, 1918–1945," U.S. Department of State.

"Special Interrogation Mission to Germany," U.S. Department of State, 1945.

Index